Transnational
Spanish Studies

Transnational Modern Languages

Transnational Modern Languages promotes a model of Modern Languages not as the inquiry into separate national traditions, but as the study of languages, cultures and their interactions. The series aims to demonstrate the value – practical and commercial, as well as academic and cultural – of modern language study when conceived as transnational cultural enquiry.

The texts in the series are specifically targeted at a student audience. They address how work on the transnational and the transcultural broadens the confines of Modern Languages; opens an extensive range of objects of research to analysis; deploys a complex set of methodologies; and can be accomplished through the exposition of clearly articulated examples.

The series is anchored by *Transnational Modern Languages: A Handbook*, ed. Jenny Burns (Warwick) and Derek Duncan (St. Andrews), which sets out the theoretical and conceptual scope of the series, the type of research on which it is based and the kinds of questions that it asks. Following on from the *Handbook*, the series includes a text for the study of the following Modern Languages:

Transnational French Studies, ed. Charles Forsdick (Liverpool) and Claire Launchbury (Leeds)

Transnational German Studies, ed. Rebecca Braun (Lancaster) and Ben Schofield (KCL)

Transnational Spanish Studies, ed. Catherine Davies (IMLR, London) and Rory O'Bryen (Cambridge)

Transnational Italian Studies, ed. Charles Burdett (Durham), Loredana Polezzi (Cardiff) and Marco Santello (Leeds)

Transnational Portuguese Studies, ed. Hilary Owen (Manchester/Oxford) and Claire Williams (Oxford)

Transnational Russian Studies, ed. Andy Byford (Durham), Connor Doak (Bristol) and Stephen Hutchings (Manchester)

Transnational Spanish Studies

edited by
Catherine Davies and Rory O'Bryen

LIVERPOOL UNIVERSITY PRESS

First published 2020 by
Liverpool University Press
4 Cambridge Street
Liverpool
L69 7ZU

Copyright © 2020 Liverpool University Press

The right of Catherine Davies and Rory O'Bryen to be identified as the editors of this work has been asserted by them in accordance with the Copyright, Designs and Patents Act 1988.

All rights reserved. No part of this book may be reproduced, stored in a retrieval system, or transmitted, in any form or by any means, electronic, mechanical, photocopying, recording, or otherwise, without the prior written permission of the publisher.

British Library Cataloguing-in-Publication data
A British Library CIP record is available

ISBN 978-1-78962-135-8 (HB)
ISBN 978-1-78962-136-5 (PB)

Typeset by Carnegie Book Production, Lancaster
Printed in the UK by CPI Group (UK) Ltd, Croydon CR0 4YY

Contents

List of Illustrations ix

List of Contributors xi

Introduction 1
    Catherine Davies and Rory O'Bryen

Section 1: Language

1. Transnational Dimensions in the History of Spanish 43
    Christopher J. Pountain

2. Arabic in the Iberian Peninsula 59
    L. P. Harvey

3. The First Chapter in Ibero-Romance Literatures: The *ḫarja-s* (kharjas) 73
    James T. Monroe

4. Indigenous People of the Andes through Language 89
    Rosaleen Howard

Section 2: Temporalities

5. The Names of Spain and Peru: Notes on the Global Scope of the Hispanic 107
    Mark Thurner

6. Time, Empire and the Transnational in the Early Modern
   Spanish World   127
   Alexander Samson

7. Modern, Modernity, Modernism and the Transnational;
   Or, Goodbye to All That?   145
   Andrew Ginger

8. Flamenco as Palimpsest: Reading through Hybridity   161
   Samuel Llano

Section 3: Spatialities

9. Where is Latin America?: Imaginary Geographies and Cultures
   of Production and Consumption   181
   Philip Swanson

10. Digital Culture and Post-regional Latin Americanism   195
    Claire Taylor and Thea Pitman

11. From 'Imagined' to 'Inoperative' Communities:
    The Un-working of National and Latin American Identities in
    Contemporary Fiction   213
    Emily Baker

12. Post-Soviet (Re)collections: From Artefact to Artifice in the
    Wake of the 'Special Period' in Cuba   227
    Elzbieta Sklodowska

13. Amphibious Visualities: Transnational Archipelagos of Recent
    Latin American Cinema   243
    Francisco-J. Hernández Adrián

Section 4: Subjectivities

14. The Transnational Space of Women's Writing in
    Nineteenth-century Spain   265
    Henriette Partzsch

15. Envisioning African-descent Confraternities in Early
    Nineteenth-century Lima, Peru   283
    Helen Melling

16. Dominican *Trans*: Frank Báez's Global Poetics 305
 Conrad James

17. *'Signos y cicatrices comunes'*: Queerness, Disability and Pedro
 Lemebel's Poetics and Politics of Embodiment 319
 Benjamin Quarshie

Index 339

List of Illustrations

Chapter 6

Figure 1.   *Nova reperta* or *New Inventions of Modern Times*   129

Figure 2.   Emblem 11 *Ex pulsu noscitur*; Emblem 57 *Uni reddatur*   131

Figure 3.   Strasbourg Astronomical Clock, first erected 1352–54   134

Figure 4.   Eight Deer and Four Jaguar   142

Chapter 10

Figure 1.   *Turista Fronterizo*   201

Figure 2.   Geography of Being   202

Chapter 12

Figure 1.   Photograph of Reina María Rodríguez   231

Chapter 13

Figure 1.   Cerebro educates Daniel, *El vuelco del cangrejo*   248

Figure 2.   A luxuriously sensual beachscape, *Post Tenebras Lux*   251

Figure 3.   At the heart of the film, a gigantic ceiba tree, *Jeffrey*   253

Figure 4.   She shows him the island, *Keyla*   257

Chapter 15

Figure 1. *Hermandad de una cofradía portando la cera de la procesión.* Léonce Angrand, 1837. Courtesy of the Bibliothèque Nationale de France — 292

Figure 2. *Negros y frailes llevando las andas de Nuestra Señora de los Incurables.* Léonce Angrand, 1837. Courtesy of the Bibliothèque Nationale de France — 293

Figure 3. *Procesión.* Francisco Javier Cortés, ca. 1827–1838. Acuarela y témpera sobre papel 24 x 19.10 cm. Courtesy of the Museo de Arte de Lima Donación Juan Carlos Verme. Fotografía: Daniel Giannoni. Archi, Archivo Digital de Arte Peruano — 295

Figure 4. *Danzando al son de los diablos.* Francisco 'Pancho' Fierro, undated (Cisneros Sánchez: 1975: 5) — 297

Figure 5. *Sigue el son de los diablos* (1830). Francisco 'Pancho' Fierro, undated. Courtesy of the Pinacoteca Municipal 'Ignacio Merino' de la Municipalidad de Lima — 298

Figure 6. *El son de los diablos.* Francisco 'Pancho' Fierro, undated. Courtesy of the Pinacoteca Municipal 'Ignacio Merino' de la Municipalidad de Lima — 299

Figure 7. *The Interior of an Inn.* Francisco 'Pancho' Fierro, ca. 1832–1841. Courtesy of the Yale University Art Gallery, Donation of the Bingham Family — 300

Figure 8. *Duelo por el difunto.* Francisco 'Pancho' Fierro. Courtesy of the Pinacoteca Municipal 'Ignacio Merino' de la Municipalidad de Lima — 303

List of Contributors

Emily Baker is Lecturer in Comparative Literature and Latin American Studies at University College London (UCL). Previously she held posts as Lecturer in Spanish at Robinson College, Cambridge; and at Birkbeck, University of London. Emily has published in the areas of Latin American and comparative literature, cultural history and film studies. Her interests include the representation of historical events in contemporary fiction, the politics of identity, the relationship between ethics and aesthetics, and environmental futures.

Catherine Davies is Professor of Hispanic and Latin American Studies and former Director of the Institute of Modern Languages Research, School of Advanced Study, University of London. Her publications include *Latin American Women's Writing. Feminist Readings in Theory and Crisis* (ed. with Anny Brooksbank Jones, 1996); *A Place in the Sun? Women's Writing in Twentieth-century Cuba* (1997); *South American Independence: Gender, Politics, Text* (with C. Brewster and H. Owen, 2006); 'Literature by Women in the Spanish Antilles: 1800–1950', in *The Cambridge History of Latin American Women's Literature* (2015). She is editor of *Journal of Romance Studies*.

Andrew Ginger is Head of the School of Languages, Cultures, Art History & Music and Chair of Spanish at the University of Birmingham. He has written widely on the modern Hispanic world, ranging across the history of thought, literature and the visual arts, often taking a comparative approach. He is the author of *Political Revolution and Literary Experiment in the Spanish Romantic Period* (1999); *Antonio Ros de Olano's Experiments in Post-Romantic Prose* (2000); *Painting and the Turn to Cultural Modernity in Spain* (2007) and *Liberalismo y romanticismo: La reconstrucción del sujeto histórico* (2012).

Leonard Patrick Harvey was Emeritus Professor of Spanish, University of London. He held lectureships in Spanish at the University of Oxford, was Head of Spanish at Queen Mary College University of London (1963–1973) and Cervantes Professor of Spanish at King's College London (1983–1990). His numerous publications include *Islamic Spain 1250 to 1500* (1990) and *Muslims in Spain 1500–1614* (2005). Sadly, Professor Harvey died in 2019 after completing the chapter for this book.

Francisco-J. Hernández Adrián is Associate Professor of Hispanic and Visual Culture Studies at Durham University. He has published in edited collections and in *Cultural Dynamics, The Global South, Hispanic Research Journal, Journal of Romance Studies, Studies in 20th & 21st Century Literature* and *Third Text*. He is the author of *On Tropical Grounds: Insularity and the Avant-Garde in the Caribbean and the Canary Islands* (2021) and co-editor of *The Film Archipelago: Islands in Latin American Cinema* (2021). He is an associate editor of *Cultural Dynamics*, a consultant editor of *The Open Arts Journal* and serves on the advisory board of *Karib: Nordic Journal for Caribbean Studies*.

Rosaleen Howard is Chair of Hispanic Studies at Newcastle University. She is a sociolinguist and anthropological linguist specialising on the Andean-Amazonian countries of Ecuador, Peru and Bolivia. Her interests include Quechua language, language policy, language ideologies and language rights for indigenous people. Her publications include: *Por los linderos de la lengua. Ideologías lingüísticas en los Andes* (2007) and *Kawsay Vida. A Multimedia Quechua Course for Beginners and Beyond* (2014). Many of her recent publications arise from an Arts and Humanities Research Council (AHRC)-funded project about translation and interpreting between the indigenous languages of Peru and Spanish.

Conrad Michael James is Associate Professor of World Cultures and Literatures at the University of Houston, Texas. His research explores what Caribbean and Afro-Hispanic sites of creativity reveal about race thinking, the politics of movement, diaspora transformations and the emergence of new world philosophies. He has published widely on Cuban women's writing. He is author of *Filial Crisis and Erotic Politics in Black Cuban Literature: Daughters, Sons and Lovers* (2019) and editor of *Writing the Afro-Hispanic: Essays on Africa and Africans in the Spanish Caribbean* (2012).

Samuel Llano is Senior Lecturer in Spanish Cultural Studies at the University of Manchester. He specialises in urban and transnational studies, and the study of sound cultures and music. He is author of *Discordant Notes: Marginality and Social Control in Madrid* (2018) and *Whose Spain: Negotiating 'Spanish Music' in Paris, 1908–1929* (2012), which won the Robert M. Stevenson Award of the American Musicological Society. His current project explores the building of an auditory order in colonial Morocco (1912–1956) to sustain Spanish and French occupation. His is preparing a book tentatively titled *The Empire of the Ear: Building an Auditory Order in Colonial Morocco, 1912–1956*.

Helen Melling is a Mellon Postdoctoral Fellow at the University of Pennsylvania. She specialises in late colonial and nineteenth-century Peruvian visual culture. Her research explores Afro-Peruvian identity vis-à-vis national republican identity through visual representations of Black subjects from the 1750s to the 1890s. She is preparing a book entitled 'Hidden in Plain Sight: Visualizing Black Subjects in Late Colonial and 19th-Century Peru'. She is a contributor to 'The Image of the Black in Latin America and the Caribbean'.

James T. Monroe was raised in Chile. He studied with Américo Castro at the University of Houston, Texas. After receiving his BA, he studied Arabic at the University of Toulouse and Spanish literature at Harvard, while continuing his Arabic studies under Sir Hamilton Gibb's tutelage. He taught at the University of California, San Diego, transferred to the Berkeley campus, and taught Arabic and Comparative Literature until his retirement. He has written books, monographs and articles on Hispano-Arabic literature, including *Al-Maqāmāt al-Luzūmīyah by Abū-l-Ṭāhir Muḥammad ibn Yūsuf al-Tamīmī al-Saraqusṭī ibn al-Aštarkūwī (d. 538/1143), Translated with a Preliminary Study* (2002) and *The Mischievous Muse: Extant Poetry and Prose by Ibn Quzmān of Cordoba (d. AH 555/AD 1190)* (2017), 2 vols.

Rory O'Bryen is Senior University Lecturer in Latin American Literature and Culture at the University of Cambridge. His research focuses on contemporary Latin American literature and nineteenth- and twentieth-century Colombian culture and history. He is the author of *Literature, Testimony and Cinema in Contemporary Colombian Culture: Spectres of 'La Violencia'* (2008), co-editor of *Latin American Popular Culture: Politics, Media, Affect* (2013) and *Latin American Cultural Studies: A Reader* (2017) and editor of *Journal of Latin American Cultural Studies*. His current work studies Colombia's Magdalena River from 1850 as a conduit for making sense of the fragile interplay between nation-formation and global political and economic processes.

Henriette Partzsch is Senior Lecturer in Hispanic Studies at the University of Glasgow. Her research has focused on the transnational connectedness of

Spanish culture during the long nineteenth century, with special attention to the Press, in particular fashion magazines, and women's participation in the literary system. Recent publications include *Redes de comunicación: Estudios sobre la prensa en el mundo hispanohablante* (2016, co-edited with Yvette Bürki) and the chapter 'How to be a cultural entrepreneur', in *Spain in the Nineteenth Century: New Essays on Experiences of Culture and Society* (2018).

Thea Pitman is Professor of Latin American Studies at the University of Leeds. Her research interests lie in the field of contemporary Latin American cultural production, especially online, and more broadly digital, works, as well as the appropriation of new media technologies by indigenous communities. She has published the anthology *Latin American Cyberliterature and Cyberculture* (2007) and *Latin American Identity in Online Cultural Production* (2013), both with Claire Taylor, and numerous articles and pieces of short-form scholarship. Her current research focuses on indigenous new media arts in the Americas.

Chris Pountain is Emeritus Professor of Spanish Linguistics at Queen Mary University of London. He is the author of *A History of the Spanish Language through Texts* (2001) and *Exploring the Spanish Language* (2003), a wide range of articles on Spanish and Romance linguistics and a number of Spanish language reference works and pedagogical materials. His current research interests lie in the influence of Latin on the languages of Western Europe and linguistic register in the history of Spanish. He is a Co-Investigator in the Open World Research Initiative (OWRI) Research Project Language Acts and Worldmaking.

Benjamin Quarshie is an AHRC-funded PhD candidate in Latin American Cultural Studies at the Department of Spanish and Portuguese and the Centre of Latin American Studies, University of Cambridge. His research explores the ways in which national and transnational ideas about race are manifested in and navigated through Afro-descendent cultural expression, with a focus on popular music, dance and literature in Colombia. He also teaches undergraduate courses on Latin American literature and cinema.

Alexander Samson is a Reader in Early Modern Studies at University College London. His research interests include the early colonial history of the Americas, Anglo-Spanish intercultural interactions and early modern English and Spanish drama. His publications include *Mary and Philip: The Marriage of Tudor England and Habsburg Spain* (2020) and he runs the Golden Age and Renaissance

Research Seminar as well as directing UCL's Centre for Early Modern Exchanges and the Centre for Editing Lives and Letters.

Elzbieta Sklodowska is a Randolph Family Professor of Spanish at Washington University in Saint Louis. She has published widely on contemporary Spanish American literatures and cultures, including: *Testimonio hispanoamericano: historia, teoría, poética*; *La parodia en la nueva novela hispanoamericana (1960–85)* (1993); *Todo ojos, todo oídos: control e insubordinación en la novela hispanoamericana (1895–1935)* (1997); *Espectros y espejismos: Haití en el imaginario cubano* (2009), and *Invento, luego resisto: El Período Especial en Cuba como experiencia y metáfora (1990–2015)* (2016). She is currently working on a project on Cuban women writers and artists.

Philip Swanson is Hughes Professor of Spanish at the University of Sheffield. He has published extensively on Latin American fiction, including books on the New Novel, José Donoso and Gabriel García Márquez, as well as on many other aspects of Hispanic and Hispanic American literature and culture. A former President of the Association of Hispanists of Great Britain and Ireland, Swanson is a member of many editorial boards and professional advisory bodies. He has taught in several universities in Europe and the USA. Recent publications include *The Cambridge Companion to Gabriel García Márquez* (2010) and the edited volume *Landmarks in Modern Latin American Fiction* (2014).

Claire Taylor is Gilmour Chair of Spanish and Professor of Hispanic Studies at the University of Liverpool. She specialises in Latin American culture, with a particular interest in the literary and cultural genres developed online by Latin(o) Americans. She has published numerous articles and book chapters on these topics, is co-author of the recent volume *Latin American Identity in Online Cultural Production* (2012), and author of *Place and Politics in Latin America Digital Culture* (2014). She is currently working on an AHRC-funded project on memory, victims and representation of the Colombian conflict.

Mark Thurner is Professor at the Institute of Latin American Studies at the School of Advanced Study, University of London. His current research and writing traces the critical place of the Indias and the Americas in the global history of historical knowledge. He directs the Leverhulme Trust-funded international research network Latin America and the Global History of Knowledge (LAGLOBAL) project. His books include *El nombre del abismo: meditaciones sobre la historia de la historia* (2012), *History's Peru: The Poetics* of *Colonial and Postcolonial Historiography* (2011), *Republicanos Andinos* (2006) and *After Spanish Rule: Postcolonial Predicaments of the Americas* (2003). He is the recipient of numerous prestigious grants and fellowships.

Introduction

Catherine Davies and Rory O'Bryen

About This Book

The focus of this book is the Spanish language and Spanish-language culture (spoken, written, visual and material) outside the framework of the nation-state. In other words, there should be no neat conflation of Spanish solely with Spain or any other nation-state. The nation-state is a nineteenth-century invention and postdates other state formations, such as Empire, and other concepts of 'nation', such as an extended family unit or clan derived from Latin *'nationem'* (meaning birth, origin, breed or stock). Nations and states long predate the nation-state, and it is in this broader sense that 'transnational' is used in this book. Transnational approaches are nothing new; they are the norm in classical, medieval and early modern studies: the Silk Road connecting China to southern Europe dates from the second century BCE. Nevertheless, the label and concept of transnational lend coherence to what initially may seem a very disparate area of study and allow for scholarly recovery of the past from a new, shared perspective that aims to make connections across time and space.

Precisely for this reason, the title of the book is not 'Transnational Hispanic Studies'. 'Hispanic' means 'pertaining to Spain or its people', which is problematic on two counts: the Spanish language is not limited to Spain, and Spanish is only one of Spain's official languages. 'Hispanic Studies', however, was (and still is) an institutionally recognised discipline, the core subject of which was the languages and literatures of (Roman) 'Hispania', today's Iberian Peninsula (Portugal and Spain), and the former Spanish and Portuguese Empires. The modern nation-states we refer to as Spain and Portugal were not considered as such until the nineteenth century;

previously they were kingdoms forming parts of larger empires, sometimes ruled by the same monarch (between 1580 and 1640). Portuguese, however, is a global language and the complex global, colonial and postcolonial cultures of the Lusophone world cannot be contained under the rubrics 'Hispanic' or 'Iberian'. A separate volume in this Transnational series is therefore dedicated to the vast and dynamic area of Portuguese/Lusophone studies.

Furthermore, the Eurocentric label 'Hispanic' can hardly account for the many languages and cultures of the Americas, least of all – despite its name – 'Latin' America. The term 'Latin America' was coined in the nineteenth century to take account of the small French presence in South and Central America (Haiti, Guyana). Spanish America (*Hispanoamérica*) more properly denotes the 19 countries in South and Central America and the Caribbean where the majority or (co-)official language is Spanish, distinctive from Portuguese-speaking Brazil. But the imperial connotations of 'Spanish America', if thought to refer to Spain, are still strong (the equivalent of referring to the USA and Canada as English America). Spanish is not the only language spoken in 'Spanish' America by any means. In Paraguay Guarani has long been a co-official language. Quechua and Aymara are also recognised as co-official languages in the Andean region. In fact, the 2009 Bolivian Constitution recognises 32 living indigenous languages. The challenge then is how to refer to the multifarious discipline studying the geographical and historical areas where the Spanish language has been influential and has co-existed with, threatened or even eradicated other languages and cultures. The terms 'Hispanic', 'Latin American', 'Iberian' and 'Spanish American' have all been challenged by scholars, but what might be seen as a problematic disciplinary fuzziness indicates instead an acute awareness of the inadequacy of current labels and an acknowledgement of the need to question in-grained traditional assumptions. Hispanic/Spanish/Iberian and Spanish/Latin American studies are excitingly rich, complex and diverse and will not be contained within one disciplinary label. 'Transnational' is not perfect either, but in its broader sense goes some way towards capturing a sense of coherence and common purpose across vast areas through time.

This Introduction is divided into two parts. The first part is a brief transnational history of the development of the Spanish language, inseparable from the political, social and cultural histories to which it is attached. The second part outlines some of the recent debates in transnational studies relevant to the Spanish-language world. As with the other books in this series, the chapters are divided into four sections that focus on language and transnational temporalities, spatialities and subjectivities. Each author presents a particular view of what 'transnational Spanish' might entail, providing a case study relating to their own interests and written in their own style. The bibliography on all these subjects is copious and may be followed through in general further reading, as indicated below, and in the works cited in the separate chapters.

In the last 20 years numerous introductory 'Companions' have been published to assist students in their first approximation to the Spanish-language world. These include the broad-based *The Companion to Hispanic Studies*, ed. by Catherine Davies (London: Arnold, 2002) and *The Companion to Latin American Studies*, ed. by Philip Swanson (London and New York: Routledge, 2003). All these 'Companions' are transnational in focus while some discuss transnational approaches explicitly, for example, the chapter entitled 'Transnational Frameworks' (by Gerard Dapena, Marvin D'Lugo and Alberto Elena) in *A Companion to Spanish Cinema*, ed. by Jo Labanyi and Tatjana Pavlovic (Malden, MA and Oxford: Blackwell, 2012), pp. 15–49. Cinema is an especially rich field for the study of transnational practices and methodologies.[1]

Like the accompanying volumes in the Transnational Modern Languages series, *Transnational Spanish Studies* aims to recast the disciplinary framework of Modern Languages, arguing that it should be seen as an expert mode of enquiry whose founding research question is how languages and cultures operate and interact across diverse axes of connection.[2] *Transnational Spanish Studies* should therefore be read in conjunction with the *Transnational Modern Languages Handbook*, which will be made available on-line. The *Handbook* clarifies key words and concepts, many of which are still shifting and under discussion. It thus complements insights and understandings of the 'transnational' as suggested by the authors in this book. As has been noted, too often contemporary discourses on the

---

[1] For further reading see: *A Companion to Spanish-American Literature*, ed. by Stephen M. Hart (Woodbridge, Suffolk: Tamesis, 1999); *A Companion to Latin American Film*, ed. by Stephen M. Hart (Woodbridge, Suffolk: Tamesis, 2004); *A Companion to Latin American Literature and Culture*, ed. by Sara Castro-Klaren (Malden, MA and Oxford: Blackwell, 2008); *A Companion to Latin American History*, ed. by Thomas Holloway (Malden, MA and Oxford: Blackwell, 2010); *Decolonial Approaches to Latin American Literatures and Cultures*, ed. by Juan G. Ramos and Tara Daly (New York: Palgrave Macmillan, 2016); *A Companion to Latin America Cinema*, ed. by Maria M. Delgado, Stephen M. Hart and Randal Johnson (Malden, MA and Oxford: John Wiley, 2017), and *The Routledge Companion to Latin American Cinema*, ed. by Marvin D'Lugo, Ana M. López and Laura Podalsky (London and New York: Routledge, 2017).

[2] *Transnational Modern Languages Handbook*, ed. by Jennifer Burns and Derek Duncan (Liverpool: Liverpool University Press, 2019).

global, transcultural, postcolonial and decolonial fail to take account of the specificity of the Spanish and Latin American experience and the associated insights emerging from the global south. Sadly, too many researchers outside Modern Languages lack the necessary language skills to do so. This book aims to help remedy this situation and to encourage Modern Languages students and scholars to set the agenda in future transnational research. By taking a transnational approach we can decolonise and denationalise the curriculum.

Part One

As stated, the focus of this book is the language commonly referred to as Spanish or *castellano* (Castilian), a language that is the cumulative outcome of millions of people communicating by the spoken and written word across vast mutating territories for almost two thousand years. This focus will serve as a means to explore the expansive spread and hybridisation over time of the heterogeneous Hispanophone world. The fashionable term 'transnational' falls short of describing the long-term, cross-cultural interaction of Spanish language practice and its continuing development today, particularly when used as a transhistorical descriptor of the language's unification of Hispanophone territories. Spanish has been shaped by the clash of cultures, languages and religions within and between great empires – the Roman, the Islamic and the Hispano-Catholic – each with imperial expansionist policies leading to wars, huge territorial gains and population movements.[3]

A language recognisably Spanish predates the formation of the modern nation-state Spain by more than 400 years. More accurate for the purposes of this volume are the terms 'supranational'[4] or 'trans-imperial' to refer to the sustained, everyday encounters between peoples of different languages and cultures communicating with one another in peaceful or conflictive circumstances over many generations. Needless to say, language is here understood not merely as a system of communication but primarily as a means of interpreting the world according to the distinctive cultural assumptions and values both shared and disputed by a language-community. A common language creates allegiances and identities but may also mask radical

---

[3] An empire is a sovereign state that includes many nations and/or peoples ruled by one monarch or emperor. The empire seeks to impose its values and beliefs on the territories it rules. Imperial language policies are designed to reinforce imperial control, to unite diverse peoples speaking different languages under one central authority.

[4] Having the power to transcend national boundaries and governments.

diversity and inequalities. Above all, language is an instrument of power and a means of enforcing or resisting political and religious supremacy. The Spanish language has co-existed with, threatened and even eradicated other languages. As J. M. Y. Simpson reminds us, whether a language is a minority one or a majority one 'has nothing to do with the language but everything to do with the situation in which it finds itself'.[5]

Transnational is a term first used in a language context. German philologist Georg Curtius referred to transnational language families in the 1860s; in 1868 he correctly noted 'every language is fundamentally transnational'.[6] Since the 1980s it has been used to refer to global finance and powerful multinational corporations operating across the borders of nation-states,[7] and increasingly since the 1990s in migration studies to describe populations that move and settle across borders yet maintain strong ties with their home communities. Long-distance human migration across political boundaries and spheres of influence is as old as humanity itself and is often in the form of forced displacement caused by war, poverty, invasion and persecution. People move and when they settle, they bring with them their languages and cultures. Migrations have contributed to language change with significant consequences for the communities of origin (which may lose their young men yet benefit from remittances) and destination (transformed by the newcomers), and for the migrants themselves (often constituting an ethnolinguistic minority).[8] There is nothing new in this.[9] What is new about today's 'new transnationalism', however, is the facility and speed of communication between relocated migrants and their home communities.

G. E. Fouron and N. Glick-Schiller define transnational migration as 'the process of movement and settlement across international borders in which individuals maintain or build multiple networks of connection to

---

[5] J. M. Y. Simpson et al, *Minority Languages Today* (Edinburgh: Edinburgh University Press, 1981), p. 236.

[6] Pierre-Yves Saunier, 'Transnational', in *The Palgrave Dictionary of Transnational History*, ed. by Akira Iriye and Pierre-Yves Saunier (Basingstoke: Palgrave Macmillan, 2009), pp. 1047–1055.

[7] See Constance Devereaux and Martin Griffin, 'International, global, transnational: Just a matter of words?', *Eurozine*, 11 October 2006.

[8] Paul Kerswill, 'Migration and language', in *Sociolinguistics/Soziolinguistik. An International Handbook of the Science of Language and Society*, ed. by Klaus Mattheier, Ulrich Ammon and Peter Trudgill, 2nd edn, vol. 3 (Berlin: de Gruyter, 2006). Citeseerx.ist.psu.edu

[9] A. Portes, L. E. Guarnizo and P. Landolt, 'The study of transnationalism: Pitfalls and promise of an emergent research field', *Ethnic and Racial Studies*, 22.2 (1999), 217–237.

their country of origin while at the same time settling into a new country'.[10] Historically, long-distance communication between literate individuals was possible only by means of the written word, letters sent across land and sea by various forms of transportation – especially after the introduction of the modern postal services in the eighteenth and nineteenth centuries (packet boat, train, telegraph, telegram, airmail and so on). Communication via the spoken word was possible face to face with individuals (recent arrivals, travellers, seamen) or, more recently, via the telephone. Even modern means of communication, dependent on technological innovation and local infrastructure, involved delays and were inaccessible to most people. A telephone call could only be made where there was a telephone, and a call was expensive. In the twenty-first-century network society, however, verbal and visual long-distance communication between migrants and their communities of origin is not only widely available but typically instantaneous, albeit not universally so.[11] New on-line communication channels (smart phones, social media) make it possible for migrants to interact simultaneously in two places. International money transfers support these transnational circuits. Transnational immigrants (transmigrants) are able to 'forge and sustain multi-stranded social relations that link together their societies of origin and settlement [...] [building] social fields that cross geographic, cultural and political borders'.[12] They do so using visuals and, above all, language.

The Transnational 'Turn' in (Latin) American Studies

Many influential texts shaping the field of transnational migrant studies focus on the United States and, in particular, the influx since the 1970s of Spanish-speaking American and Caribbean populations.[13] This is hardly surprising. The impact of these communities in the United States is immense

---

[10] G. E. Fouron and N. Glick-Schiller, 'The generation of identity: Redefining the second generation within a transnational social field', in *Migration, Transnationalization & Race in a Changing New York*, ed. by H. Cordero-Guzman, R. C. Smith and R. Grosfoguel (Philadelphia, PA: Temple University Press, 2001), pp. 58–86, p. 60.

[11] *The Guardian* reports urban 'internet deserts' in major global cities like São Paulo: <https://www.theguardian.com/cities/2019/jan/11/a-game-of-patience-and-persistence-life-in-sao-paulo-internet-deserts>.

[12] Linda Basch, Nina Glick-Schiller and Cristina Szanton Blanc, *Nations Unbound: Transnational Projects, Postcolonial Predicaments and Deterritorialized Nation-States* (Basel: Gordon and Breach, 1994), p. 7.

[13] Juan Poblete, 'The transnational turn', in *New Approaches to Latin American Studies: Culture and Power*, ed. by Juan Poblete (London and New York: Routledge, 2017), pp. 32–49, p. 34.

with migrant numbers soaring from less than one million in 1960 to almost 19 million in 2010.[14] According to Ruben G. Rumbaut, in 2019 there were more than 60 million Spanish speakers in the USA, 64 million if Puerto Rico is included. This makes the USA the second largest Spanish-speaking country in the world after Mexico.[15] The networks and spaces created by Latino diasporas (mainly from Mexico, Central America, Cuba and the Dominican Republic) are not only transnational and transcultural (relating to more than one culture) but also translingual, a term coined in the context of Global Englishes to describe practices in which users switch between languages in their speech and writing to communicate effectively.[16] In translingual communities, users negotiate between available languages in dynamic and creative ways. Communication takes place across languages in a single speech or writing act, unlike within multilingual communities where users choose between one language or another. This type of translanguaging is often associated with bilinguals who access features of two or more 'standard' languages to maximise communication.

A new hybrid language, formed from English and Spanish, referred to disparagingly as Spanglish, has emerged in the USA featuring different dialects according to migrants' place of origin and settlement. Speakers switch between English and Spanish (codeswitching) according to their requirements (see Pountain, Chapter 1). Written forms are captured in literary texts of dual-identity authors such as the Mexican-American Gloria Anzaldúa, Dominican-American Junot Diaz and Cuban-American Gustavo Pérez Firmat, the latter of whose memoir is tellingly entitled *Life on the Hyphen: The Cuban American Way*.[17] The study of the languages used currently by Latinos (Latin Americans in the US), Chicanos (Mexican-Americans), Nuyoricans (Puerto Ricans in New York) and Dominican Americans, pertains wholly to transnational studies as outlined above (see James, Chapter 16). Spanglish is currently a grassroots language; it has not been imposed by authority, has no official status, has not yet been standardised and is far from laying the

---

[14] Marta Tienda and Susana Sanchez, 'Latin American immigration to the United States', *Daedalus*, 142.3 (2013), 48–64. The authors distinguish between three sources of immigrants: legal permanent residents, refugees and asylees, and unauthorised migrants granted legal status.

[15] See 'The Hispanic legacy in American history', special issue of *History Now*, 53 (Winter 2019), 1. Also, C. Gibson, *El Norte. The Epic and Forgotten Story of Hispanic North America* (New York: Grove Atlantic, 2019).

[16] Suresh Canagarajah, *Translingual Practice: Global Englishes and Cosmopolitan Relations* (London and New York: Routledge, 2012).

[17] Gustavo Pérez Firmat, *Life on the Hyphen: The Cuban American Way* (Austin: Texas University Press, 1994).

basis for any kind of new nation-state. Nevertheless, it is an effective tool for consolidating Hispano-American identities in a global, hegemonically Anglo-American society (see Swanson, Chapter 9). This is a recent example of how Spanish language practice crosses nation-state borders. The major obstacle to studying pre-twentieth-century everyday conversation is the lack of recorded speech, although written representations of speech and song are available (see Harvey, Chapter 2 and Monroe, Chapter 3 for early examples). Despite this difficulty, this book aims to reach beyond the narrow confines of the 'transnational' as defined in recent migration studies and extend its chronological and geographical framework from present-day USA. Historians, many of whom have adopted the term since the 1990s, are well aware of the potential opportunities but also drawbacks of transnational approaches. Transnationalism used loosely and anachronistically can de-historicize nations and nation-states, making them appear 'natural', and underplay the power of nationalism and national identities.[18] The following historical overview of the Hispanophone world aims to avoid presentism and argues, following Curtius, that the Spanish language is and always has been 'transnational' and for this reason should not be identified wholly or solely within the framework of any one nation or nation-state.[19]

---

[18] 'Transnational history' is concerned with cross-national processes and influences. It focuses on the movements of people, cultures, ideas, institutions and technologies across political boundaries (state, nation, empire), mainly from the nineteenth century on. The aim is to 'put national developments in context and to explain the nation in terms of its cross-national influences'. See Ian Tyrell, 'What is transnational history' (2007), <https://Iantyrrell.wordpress.com/what-is-transnational-history>, accessed 14 January 2019. Historians refer to the 'spatial' and 'international' turn in history; 'the international turn has revived interest in conceptions of space by attending to arenas that were larger than nations, unconfined by political boundaries of states, and connected by transnational linkages and circulations', see David Armitage, 'The international turn in intellectual history', in *Rethinking Modern European Intellectual History*, ed. by Darrin M. McMahon and Samuel Moyn (Oxford: Oxford University Press, 2014), pp. 232–252, p. 239. Examples relevant to this book include *Nationalism and Transnationalism in Spain and Latin America, 1808–1923*, ed. by Paul Garner and Angel Smith (Cardiff: University of Wales Press, 2017) and *America Imagined: Explaining the United States in Nineteenth-Century Europe and Latin America*, ed. by Axel Körner, Nicola Miller and Adam Smith (Basingstoke: Palgrave Macmilllan, 2012). For an excellent overview see Simon Macdonald, 'Transnational history: A review of past and present scholarship' (2012), <https://www.ucl.ac.uk/centre-transnational-history/sites/centre-transnational-history/files/simon_macdonald_tns_review.pdf>, accessed 5 January 2019.

[19] Jeroen Duindam challenges transnationalism's tendency to focus on the modern and contemporary periods, that is, after the nineteenth-century invention of the nation-state. See Jeroen Duindam, 'Early modern Europe: Beyond strictures of

Studying Spanish language practice from its origins until today entails a transnational perspective and a transnational approach.[20]

The Trans-imperial Development of Spanish Language Culture: The Long View

1. *Latin*. The Empire that created the conditions for the development of Spanish was the multi-ethnic, multi-lingual Roman Empire, the endurance and extension of which, encompassing all the territories around the Mediterranean Sea, from Britain to Egypt, was of momentous consequence for European culture, thought, law and government. The Romans invaded the Iberian Peninsula in 206 BCE and Emperor Augustus incorporated it into the western Roman Empire in 19 BCE. The province was named Hispania and subdivided into three regions corresponding loosely to today's Andalusia, Portugal and the rest of Spain. Roman civilisation lasted approximately 700 years, until Hispania was overrun by the Germanic peoples (the Goths/Visigoths) in the fifth century. The foundation of today's Spanish is one variety (Castilian) of the conversational Latin (vernacular or Vulgar Latin) spoken in the Peninsula in the northern region of Cantabria. Peoples from across the Empire moved to and settled in Hispania and whole new towns were founded, such as Caesaraugusta (Zaragoza) and Lucus Augusti (Lugo). Christianity became Hispania's official religion, declared as such across the Empire by Constantin in 323. Power passed from the Roman Empire to Visigoth kingdoms between the fifth and the eighth centuries, but the population was already Romanised and Christian, speaking dialects of Latin. Spanish (like Portuguese, French, Italian) is a Romance (or neo-Latin) language evolving from spoken Latin after the collapse of the Roman Empire.

In 'transnational' terms, this long-term process was driven by migrant populations (mainly men) from across the Empire, speaking varieties of conversational Latin, governed from Rome and later Constantinople by imperial institutions and laws. They settled in the Peninsula, displacing pre-Roman languages (such as Celtic, but not Basque), cultures and religions, thereby creating the foundation for shared identities and allegiances that would endure over many generations. Over time, freed from imperial control and immobilised by a crumbling infrastructure, the everyday practices of local

---

modernization and national historiography', *European Historical Quarterly*, 40.4 (2010), 606–623.

[20] The bibliography on the topics discussed in the following section is huge and dates mainly from the beginning of the twentieth century. Indications of further reading are given in the notes.

communities gave rise to cultural and linguistic differentiation. Indeed, the various 'nations' of the present-day Peninsula were formed during the Roman/Christian millennium that began in 206 BCE. The Romance languages that developed alongside Castilian, notably the languages we refer to today as Portuguese, Catalan, Galician, Asturian and Valencian, still underpin strong regional and national identities. Portugal became an independent kingdom in the twelfth century and is now a sovereign nation-state. Catalan, Galician and Basque are officially recognised languages and nations in today's pluri-nation state, Spain. Some three-quarters of the current Spanish vocabulary is derived from Latin.[21]

2. *Arabic*. The foundational Roman/Christian millennium came to a sudden end in 711 when Hispania was overrun by the conquering armies of Islam and renamed al-Andalus. The *jihadists*, commanded by the Berber Tariq ibn Ziyad, crossed the straits of Gibraltar (the rock bearing his name) reaching the Pyrenees five years later. Islam was thus established on the Iberian Peninsula and remained a force to contend with for the next 900 years. In the words of Efraim Karsh, 'Few events have transformed the course of human history more swiftly and profoundly than the expansion of early Islam and its conquest of much of the ancient world.'[22] Within five years the Iberian Peninsula (Hispania) was removed from Western European Christendom and incorporated into the multi-ethnic transnational Umayyad Caliphate, which extended from today's Turkmenistan and Azerbaijan, to Arabia and North Africa, with its capital in Damascus. It was the world's most extensive empire at the time, covering more than five million square miles (13 million square kilometres). Hispania was the only Western European (Roman/Christian) territory to be integrated into the first Caliphate;[23] from then on religious faith and ethno-religious purity became a predominant factor in the Peninsula's history.[24]

The Syrian Umayyad dynasty lost the Caliphate to the Abbasids, whose new capital was Baghdad, but one Umayyad survivor, Abd al Rahman,

---

[21] Simon Keay, *Roman Spain* (Berkeley: University of California Press, 1988); Rafael Lapesa, *Historia de la Lengua Española*, 3rd edn (Madrid: Escelicer, 1955), pp. 39–77.

[22] Efraim Karsh, *Islamic Imperialism. A History* (New Haven and London: Yale University Press, 2006), p. 21.

[23] Apart from Sicily and Malta and part of southern Italy.

[24] Among the many studies of medieval Iberia see Richard Hitchcock, *Muslim Spain Reconsidered. From 711 to 1502* (Edinburgh: Edinburgh University Press, 2014) and *Mozarabs in Medieval and Early Modern Spain. Identities and Influences* (Aldershot: Ashgate, 2008); Hugh Kennedy, *Muslim Spain and Portugal. A Political History of al-Andalus* (Harlow, London and New York: Longman, 1996).

escaped to al-Andalus and established the Caliphate of Cordoba (929–1031). Over time, the Christian kingdoms of the north (Asturias, Leon, Navarre, Galicia, Portugal, Castile, Aragon) consolidated their forces and stage by stage pushed back the frontiers of Islamic Iberia.[25] This *Reconquista* lasted hundreds of years and was equated with the eastern crusades.[26] By the twelfth century the Peninsula was divided roughly in two halves, the fault line between Christendom and Islam running through its centre from roughly Lisbon in the west to Tortosa in the east. The political configuration of al-Andalus and its geopolitical allegiances shifted in response to local and imperial rivalries and Christian pressure from the north. The Caliphate of Cordoba gave way to some 30 *taifas*, small Islamic (mainly Berber) principalities (the *taifas* of Toledo, Zaragoza, Badajoz, etc.) that often invited Christian armies to fight on their behalf. But after the fall of Toledo (captured by Alfonso VI of Leon in 1085) and Lisbon (captured by crusaders in 1147) the *taifas* sought military assistance from their more militant co-religionaries in North Africa. Between the eleventh and thirteenth centuries al-Andalus was incorporated into the Moroccan-Berber Caliphates of the Almoravids and the Almohads. The final Muslim stronghold, the Kingdom of Granada, established in 1230 by the Nasrid dynasty, extended across today's Andalusia (Granada, Malaga, Almeria) and was forced to pay tribute to the Crown of Castile. In 1492, the last Nasrid emirate, Muhammad XII, relinquished Granada to Castile and fled to Morocco. Thus ended almost 800 years of Islamic rule in Iberia. Many Muslims remained in the land of their birth, but were forced to convert, and by 1614 were finally expelled. As Harvey explains, from 1500 on 'there began in earnest the process whereby Spain's Muslims were to be eliminated from Spanish society'.[27] In that same year, some 250,000 Jews, whose descendants had lived in Hispania and al-Andalus since Roman times, were forced to convert or forced into exile (between 40,000 to 100,000 were exiled).

---

[25] The Eastern orthodox schism dates from 1054 and was due to disputes over doctrine and the authority of the Pope.

[26] Thomas F. Madden, *A Concise History of the Crusades* (Lanham, MD, Boulder, CO, New York, Oxford: Rowman and Littlefield, 1999), p. 123. The Christian kingdoms actively participated in the second crusade (1146–1148) and won a decisive victory over the Muslims at the battle of Las Navas de Tortosa (Battle of Al-Uqab) in 1212. For a strong refutation of the 'Conquest–Reconquest' narrative (used to consolidate the Franco regime in twentieth-century Spain) see Alejandro García Sanjuán, *La conquista islámica de la península ibérica y la tergiversación del pasado* (Barcelona: Marcial Pons, 2013).

[27] L. P. Harvey, *Muslims in Spain, 1500–1614* (Chicago and London: University of Chicago Press, 2005), p. vii.

The cultural, scholarly and scientific achievements of al-Andalus are legendary and are continuing to attract a wealth of scholarship.[28] Recent attention has been given to the lives of ordinary people, their everyday social relations and hybrid identities in a culturally complex, translingual society. Although the Christians and Jews were subjected to Islamic authority, the distinctions between the three religions of al-Andalus (Islam, Judaism, Christianity) and their spoken languages were gradually blurred.[29] Romance was spoken by the rural classes and Arabic by the middle and upper classes, regardless of faith. Arabic, spoken and written, was common among Christians as it was required for certain professions. Muslim men might marry Christian women but their children (whose mother-tongue was Romance) had to be brought up as Arabic-speaking Muslims to recite the Qu'ran. By the eleventh century many Christians had acculturated to an Islamic way of life in clothes, food and furniture, giving rise to a new hybridized Mozarabic identity (from the Arabic *must'arab* – would-be-Arab) (Catlos, pp. 104–105). Some indication of the multiple translingual identities formed in al-Andalus and later may be gauged from the newly coined terms: Mozarab (Christians who assimilate Islamic culture); Mozarabic (or Andalusi, the Romance dialects spoken in al-Andalus often written using Arabic or Hebrew script); *mudéjar* (Arabic *al-mudajjan*), a Muslim living under Christian rule (for example in Navarre); *morisco* (Arabic *moriskiyyun*), a Muslim living under Christian rule forced to convert to Christianity, and their descendants; *converso* (a convert to Christianity, usually from Judaism, and their descendants); *ladino* (literary Judeo-Spanish); *aljamiado* (a sixteenth-century literary language in which Romance is written in Andalusi Arabic script); and *muladi* (Arabic *muwallad*), a child of a non-Muslim mother. Harvey prefers the term crypto-Muslim to refer to Muslims subjected to the militant Catholicism and crusader mentality of Christian monarchs during the sixteenth century. These bilingual *moriscos*, or New Christians, had legally converted but practised Islam secretly and were therefore subject to the Inquisition, founded in 1478 (see *Muslims in Spain*, pp. 2–3 for problems with the word *morisco*).[30]

---

[28] Notably in astronomy, astrology, algebra, medicine, agriculture, architecture, ceramics and philosophy.

[29] Brian A. Catlos, *Kingdoms of Faith. A New History of Islamic Spain* (London: Hurst and Company, 2018), pp. 104–105.

[30] See also L. P. Harvey, *Islamic Spain 1250 to 1500* (Chicago and London: University of Chicago Press, 1990); Richard Hitchcock, *Mozarabs in Medieval and Early Modern Spain: Identities and Influences* (Aldershot: Ashgate, 2008); and S. J. Pearce, 'The problem of terminology in Medieval Iberian Studies', *Modern Language Notes*, 134 (2019), 463–474.

In al-Andalus classical Arabic replaced Latin as the written language, while Romance was relegated to everyday use among the poor. By the tenth century classical Latin had almost disappeared other than among clerics. Literature flourished (mainly in Arabic and Hebrew).[31] The phonology of spoken Arabic shifted towards the more softly spoken Romance sounds and Arabic greetings and blessings became part of common speech. The greatest contribution of Arabic to Romance/*castellano* was a large vocabulary, many words identifying new concepts and objects. Arabic, after Latin, is the most important source of words in Spanish (4000 words, roughly 8 per cent) (*Historia de la Lengua Española*, p. 95).[32] The words pertain to distinctive semantic fields: war (*alférez, jinete*); agriculture, flowers (*aljibe, aceituna, azúcar, algodón, azucena, azahar, mejorana*); crafts (*tarea, alfarero, taza, jarra, marfil*); trade and measures (*arancel, aduana, almacén, zoco*); buildings (*arrabal, zaguán, alcoba, azotea, albañil, alcantarilla*); furniture, food (*almohada, alfombra, albóndiga, almíbar*); pastimes (*ajedrez, jaque mate* [check mate, as in chess], *azar*); mathematics (*algoritmo, sifr>cifra, álgebra, zero*); medicine (*alcohol, jarabe*); astronomy (*cenit, nadir, auge*); colour (*azul, añil, carmesí*); exclamations (*ojalá*); government (*alcalde, alguacil*), and place names: Algarve (the west), Alcalá (castle), Calatayud (Ayub's castle), Medina (town), *wadi* (river) as in Guadalajara (river of stones), Guadalquivir (big river or *río grande*) (Lapesa, pp. 95–103). Unlike Latin, neither Arabic nor Andalusi survived in the monoconfessional Iberian Peninsula due to the forced removal of the large *morisco* population who spoke it.

However, this was not the end of Islam or Arabic in Spain. Four hundred years after the *morisco* expulsions Islam has made a remarkable comeback due to mass immigration and increasing numbers of Spanish converts. The Muslim population in 2018 was approximately two million, up from 100,000 in 1990.[33] The huge Islamic Cultural Centre, inspired by the Alhambra, in

---

[31] *The Literature of Al-Andalus*, ed. by Rosa Menocal, Raymond P. Scheindin and Michael Sells (Cambridge: Cambridge University Press, 2000). On language use see Yasime Beale-Rivaya, 'The written record as witness. Language shift from Arabic to Romance in the documents of the Mozarabs of Toledo in the twelfth and thirteenth centuries', *La Corónica*, 40.2 (2012), 2–50, and María Angeles Gallego, 'The languages of medieval Iberia and their religious dimension', *Medieval Encounters*, 9.1 (2003), 107–139. The 'Golden Age' of Jewish learning and Hebrew letters in al-Andalus was during the time of the *taifa* kingdoms; see José Martínez Delgado, 'Secularization through Arabicization: The revival of the Hebrew language in al-Andalus', *Simon Dubnow Institute Yearbook*, 12 (2013), 299–317.

[32] Other examples: *atalaya, acequia, alumbre, azogue, alhóndiga, fanega, laúd, alborozo*, Guadiana (river Anna).

[33] According to the Instituto Nacional de Estadística there are some 618,000

Granada, was opened in Madrid in 1992. Since then thousands of mosques (*mezquitas*) and prayer centres have been established across Spain, including in Granada and Cordoba, many funded by Saudi Arabia in order, some claim, to promote the Wahhabi version of Islam.[34] Sadly, one root motive for the Madrid terrorist attacks of 2004 was revenge for the loss of Andalusia (*Islamic Imperialism*, p. 231).

3. *Castellano*. In the fifteenth century, alongside the emirate of Granada, the Iberian Peninsula was divided into Christian kingdom-states ruled by dynasties originating in the north: to the west Portugal (independent since 1139), in the centre Castile-Leon (united in 1217, including Asturias since 924, and later Galicia), in the east the Crown of Aragon (including Catalonia and Valencia, the Balearic islands, Sicily, Corsica, Sardinia, Malta and the kingdom of Naples) and Navarre in the Basque region. In each, a broad spectrum of dialects of Romance were spoken and in the written form had evolved into early versions of the Romance languages we recognise today. Castilian, Catalan and Galician-Portuguese already had major literary works to their credit. During the *Reconquista* the kingdoms acquired lands previously ruled by Islam whose Arabic, Mozarabic and Hebrew-speaking populations were incorporated into their own. At times, the peoples of different religions, languages and ethnicities lived together more or less harmoniously in much-celebrated (and much-challenged) *convivencia*.[35] The language of the cultured elite was still classical Latin, especially in the Church, but Latin was increasingly rivalled by the vernaculars. In thirteenth-century Castile-Leon *castellano* was recognised as official for legal documents and royal diplomas, and Jewish and Arabic-speaking translators at the famous School of Translators in Toledo translated classical Arabic works not only into Latin but also *castellano*. In the reign of Alfonso X the Wise (1252–1284) *castellano* became the target written language rather than Latin. The libraries seceded to the Christians by the Arabs encapsulated all world knowledge of the period. These Arabic texts (such as the writings of Averroes and Avicenna)

---

speakers of Arabic in Spain today (twice as many as Basque speakers). See Ine.es-jaxi-tabl accessed August 2019. Arabic is the majority language in Ceuta and Melilla, the Spanish 'autonomous cities' of north Africa.

[34] Soeren Kern, 'Spain goes on mosque-building spree: Churches forced to close', Gatestone Institute, 30 December 2010; Isambard Wilkinson, 'After 500 years Granada's Muslims get their mosque', *The Telegraph*, 8 July 2003.

[35] See Maya Soifer, 'Beyond *convivencia*: Critical reflections on the historiography of interfaith relations in Christian Spain', *Journal of Medieval Studies*, 1.1 (2009), 19–35 and Anna Akasoy '*Convivencia* and its discontents: Interfaith life in al-Andalus', *International Journal of Middle East Studies*, 42.3 (2010), 489–499.

proved to be foundational for European thought and science. Many were Arabic translations of Ancient Greek and Hebrew philosophers and scientists, Aristotle, Ptolemy, Archimedes, Euclid, Maimonides and Hippocrates, whose original works were lost. Castile's bi- and tri-lingual population and access to Arabic texts made it the most important centre of learning in Europe, thus strengthening the authority and status of *castellano*.[36]

4. *Spanish*. By the time Isabel I came to the throne in 1474 the kingdom of Castile was prosperous, encompassing the larger part of the Iberian Peninsula.[37] Castile's hegemony was strengthened by its judicious alliance with the Crown of Aragon, cemented in the marriage between Isabel and Ferdinand II of Aragon in 1469, the Catholic Monarchs (both descended from John of Castile). This alliance proved sufficiently powerful to conquer Granada (1492) and benefit from its lands, peoples and immense wealth. From their point of view, after a crusade of almost 800 years, Christian Hispania had been restored, compensating in some way for the fall of the Byzantine Empire and capture of Constantinople by the Islamic Ottomans forty years earlier. To expand their dominions even further, the Catholic Monarchs had to look west. Emir Muhammad handed over the keys of Granada in January 1492; nine months later Christopher Columbus, the Genoese navigator hired by the Catholic Monarchs to find a western passage to India, landed in the Bahamas. By the end of the year he had taken possession of Hispaniola (Insula Hispana or La Isla Española) for the Crown of Castile.[38] Columbus died believing he had reached India, and named the islands the Indies (las indias), leading to confusion about the East and West Indies, Indians in India and the indigenous peoples of America, ever since. This was how *castellano*, the language of the dual Monarchy (*monarquía hispánica*) reached the Americas. It is no coincidence that the first grammar of the *lengua castellana*, written by Antonio de Nebrija, dedicated to Isabel, was published in August of 1492 as an instrument of empire (see Perriam, Chapter 1; Thurner, Chapter 5).

As this brief survey demonstrates, *castellano* (referred to as *hespañol* or *español* from the sixteenth century), was never the only language spoken

---

[36] The kingdom of Portugal remained independent from Castile-Aragon and the Galego-Portuguese vernacular of Galicia in the north-west of the Peninsula developed into the Portuguese language with its own written texts and literary canon. In 1580 Philip II of Spain was crowned Philip I of Portugal (the Iberian Union), but although ruled by the same monarch until 1640 the two kingdoms were governed as separate entities. Portugal was a monarchy until 1910 and then a Republic.

[37] Isabel de Castilla's full title was Queen of Castile, Queen Consort of Aragon, Valencia, Mallorca, Naples, Sicily and Sardinia and Countess Consort of Barcelona.

[38] Today the island is divided into two states: Haiti and the Dominican Republic.

and written in Hispania/España. The state that conferred its power was not 'Spain' but the Crown of Castile and Aragon. Despite enormous efforts to impose *castellano* as the exclusive language of the lands controlled by the *monarquía hispánica* throughout the modern period, from the sixteenth to the nineteenth centuries and later, *castellano* cannot be identified with one people, one nation or one nation-state. Whether as a kingdom in its own right or as part of the vast empires of the Austrian Hapsburgs (in the sixteenth and seventeenth centuries) and French Bourbons (from the eighteenth century), whether (barring brief interludes) governed by absolutist or constitutional monarchs, Hispania/España/Spain has always been translingual, transcultural and multi-ethnic, in which *castellano*/Spanish has coexisted, happily or unhappily, with other languages including Arabic and Hebrew. Other Hispanic languages are recognised today by the pluri-national state Spain as co-official (Catalan-Valencian, Galician, Basque or Euskera) or simply 'recognised' (Asturian, Leonese and Aragonese).[39] The country we call Spain is inherently transnational and translingual and studies of Spanish language cultures necessarily elicit a transnational perspective.

5. *Quechua, Guarani, Aymara, Mapuche and others.* Following Columbus's transoceanic voyages, throughout the 1500s lands hitherto unknown to Christendom were discovered and conquered on an unprecedented scale. Inter-imperial rivalry extended to the oceans. With the Treaty of Tordesillas (1494), the Pope apportioned the New World (as then known) to the *monarquía hispánica* (to the west) and the *Império Portugues* (to the east) divided by a meridian equidistant between the Caribbean and the Cape Verde Islands. The line ran through eastern present-day Brazil where the colonising language was Portuguese. California was claimed for Spain in 1542.

This was a clash of Empires (Hapsburgs versus Aztec and Inca), driven by European technological innovation, territorial ambition and crusading zeal. The conquistadors were fiercely opposed by the indigenous peoples, themselves migrants from Siberia and Asia who had settled on the continent many thousands of years previously. But the Europeans brought with them advanced military technology as well as diseases such as smallpox that wiped out huge swathes of the native population. Hernán Cortés (born in Medellín, Extremadura) conquered the Aztec Empire of city-states, capturing Mexico-Tenochtitlan in 1521. The subjugation of Mayan Yucatan was completed in

---

[39] According to the Instituto Nacional de Estadística, in 2016 98.9 per cent of the population of Spain spoke *castellano* (mother tongue and non-mother tongue), 17.5 per cent Catalan, 6.2 per cent Galician, 5.8 per cent Valencian, and 3 per cent Basque or Euskera. In other words, almost one-third of the population is bilingual.

the seventeenth century. Francisco Pizarro (born in Trujillo, Castile) defeated the Inca Empire, capturing and killing Emperor Atahualpa in 1542. In today's Colombia, the Muisca people were overwhelmed in the early 1540s. The Basque Juan de Garay founded the settlement of Buenos Aires in 1580. Each of the native peoples had their own religions, practices, cultures, social organization, and languages (more than 400, including Nahuatl, Maya, Quechua, Aymara and Guaraní, some with writing systems based on glyphs). Many new words extended the *castellano* vocabulary: *cacique, bohío, maíz, batata, tabaco, caníbal, enaguas* (from the Caribbean area); *cacao, chocolate, hule, jícara* from Nahuatl; and *condor, pampa, alpaca* from Quechua. Castilian, imposed from above, was the language of authority, governance and law, and Christianity (Roman Catholicism) the only permitted religion. The 'indies' were divided into Vice-royalties with Viceroys appointed to rule on behalf of the monarch: the Vice-royalties of New Spain (most of today's USA, Mexico, Central America and the Philippines) founded in 1535; Peru (most of South America excepting Brazil) in 1542; New Granada (today's Colombia, Ecuador, Panama and Venezuela) in 1717 and River Plate (Argentina, Uruguay, Paraguay, Bolivia) in 1776.[40] From 1524 the Vice-royalties were governed by the Council of the Indies, eventually located in Madrid. The interaction between Spanish and the indigenous languages of the Americas, from the sixteenth century until today, constitutes a vast arena of translingual practice (see Howard, Chapter 4) marked by oppression, resistance and survival.[41] With the New World discoveries, *castellano*/Spanish went global.

6. *Spanish goes global.* The Catholic Monarchs' daughter, Juana, married Philip of the Hapsburg House of Austria, son of Maximilian I, the Holy Roman Emperor. Their grandson, born in Ghent, was crowned Charles I of Spain in 1516 and Charles V, Holy Roman Emperor soon after. Charles's son, Philip II, born in Valladolid and buried in El Escorial, was King of Spain (1556–1598), King of Naples, Sicily, Duke of Milan, Lord of the Netherlands and for a time King of Portugal; he was also King of England and Ireland when married to Mary I. His son, Philip III (1578–1621), born in Madrid,

---

[40] The term 'America' was coined in 1507 by Martin Waldseemuller whose world map named the newly discovered lands 'America' after the Italian explorer Americo Vespucci (1454–1512), a subject of the Crown of Castile. Following voyages in 1502 and 1503 Vespucci proved that the Indies were not a part of Asia but a 'New World'.
[41] See Anna Maria Escobar, 'Spanish in contact with Quechua', and Clare Mar-Molinero and Darren Paffey, 'Linguistic imperialism: Who owns global Spanish?', in *The Handbook of Hispanic Sociolinguistics*, ed. by Manuel Díaz-Campos (Oxford: Wiley-Blackwell, 2011), pp. 323–352, pp. 747–764.

inherited most of these titles as did Philip IV (1605–1665) and Charles II (1661–1700). The Hapsburg absolutist *Monarquía universal española* (also known as the Hispanic Monarchy, the Monarchy of the Austrias and the Catholic Monarchy) lasted almost two hundred years. It was an imperial, transoceanic state, controlling vast territories that extended some 1.5 million square miles across Europe, the New World, the East Indies, North Africa and at times the Portuguese Empire. This was the original 'empire on which the sun never sets' (see Thurner, Chapter 5).[42] Its population was multi-ethnic, multicultural, multilingual (more than 20 major languages), and pluri-national. David Armitage suggests that empires project 'various kinds of universalism in order to suspend differences without striving for unification' ('The international turn', p. 239). In the Hispanic Monarchy the subjects of the Crown were held together by the Spanish language and above all the Catholic Church, militant Catholicism – transnational, intolerant and intent on eradicating all other religions whether they be Islam in the east, Protestantism in the north,[43] Judaism, or the religions of the New World. In Iberoamerica the Catholic Church was successful; the most recent Pope, Francis I, is from Argentina.[44]

At the centre of the vast Empire, Castile was powerful and its port, Seville, held the exclusive right to trade with the Indies. *Castellano*, therefore, flourished across Europe and the Americas. Although the other Hispanic kingdoms retained their identities and laws, their languages (notably Catalan), rapidly declined. Even authors born outside Castile wrote in what was now known as Spanish. This was the Spanish 'Golden Age' marked by the publication of Miguel de Cervantes's *Don Quixote* in 1605 and 1615.

Enlarging the mix of peoples and languages was the importation of African slaves. The Portuguese began purchasing slaves from West Africa in the fifteenth century; the first voyage in what was to become the infamous Atlantic slave trade was in 1526 to supply labour to the Portuguese (Brazil) plantations. The slaves, mainly from West and Central Africa, were acquired from powerful sub-Sahara kingdoms.[45] Some 12.5 million slaves were transported to the Americas over

---

[42] See *Historia de España, Siglos XVI y XVII*, ed. by Ricardo García Cárcel (Cátedra: Madrid, 2003).

[43] Martin Luther published his 95 Theses in 1517; the Protestant Reformation lasted until 1648, resulting in a schism in Western Christianity. Meanwhile, the Ottoman-Hapsburg wars were waged between the sixteenth and eighteenth centuries in Eastern and Central Europe.

[44] See Ivan Vallier, 'The Roman Catholic Church: A transnational actor', *International Organization*, special issue 'Transnational Relations and World Politics', 25.3 (1971), 479–502.

[45] Herman L. Bennett, *African Kings and Black Slaves. Sovereignty and Dispossession*

the next 300 years by mainly Portuguese, British, French and Spanish traders; about 10.5 million survived the traumatic crossing. Columbus brought a small number of *negros* to Hispaniola in 1502, as did Pánfilo de Narváez in his disastrous 1527 expedition to La Florida narrated by Álvar Núñez Cabeza de Vaca in the *Comentarios* of 1555 (later *Naufragios*).[46] The Spanish trade began in earnest in the sixteenth century. It peaked in the nineteenth century, mainly due to the British abolition of slavery in the West Indies in 1833 and the subsequent relocation of sugar production to Cuba, where until 1886 slavery was still permitted (although not the trade). Cuba traded slaves with the United States unofficially until 1865 and with Brazil where slavery was not abolished until 1888. In Cuba the language of the Yoruba peoples (present-day Nigeria and Benin), and its liturgical version, Lucumi (used in Santeria), survives today largely due to the black co-fraternities established on the island in the nineteenth century (see Melling, Chapter 15). And in Africa, Spanish is an official language in Equatorial Guinea. The translingual practice of people speaking African languages forced to move to a region where *castellano* was the majority language, as well as Galician, French and English, is an important area of research.

With such mixed populations, the Hapsburg Empire was a complex translingual space. Europeans transacted business in Spain and the Americas on a daily basis. Spanish immigration to the Americas totalled some half a million in the sixteenth and seventeenth centuries, mainly from Andalusia, Castile and Extremadura (joined in the eighteenth century by Basques, Galicians and Catalans).[47] The majority of migrants were in commerce, state administration and the Church. The highly educated missionaries of the Catholic orders (Franciscans, Dominicans and Jesuits) studied the languages and cultures of the indigenous peoples assiduously, pioneering linguistic and ethnographic research, translations and transliteration. Pedro de Gante (of Flemish descent) translated Nahuatl in New Spain; the linguist Francisco Pareja developed the first Timuca writing system in Florida; in the Caribbean, Dominicans Antonio de Montesinos and Bartolomé de las Casas denounced the enslavement of the indigenous peoples resulting in New Laws to protect them (1542). The Jesuits

---

in the early Modern Atlantic (Philadelphia, PA: University of Pennsylvania Press, 2018).

[46] Recently retold by Laila Lalami from the point of view of a Moroccan slave survivor, the first Arabic-speaking African to land in what is now the USA. Laila Lalami, *The Moor's Account* (New York: Pantheon Press, 2014).

[47] Patricia Escandón, '"Esta tierra es la mejor que calienta el sol": La emigración española a América siglos XVI–XVII', in *Historia comparada de las migraciones en las Américas*, ed. by Patricia Galeana (Mexico, D.F: UNAM, 2016), pp. 19–31; Rosario Márquez Macías, *La emigración española a América 1765–1824* (Oviedo: Universidad de Oviedo, 1995).

founded settlements in present-day Argentina, Brazil and Paraguay where they learned the indigenous languages and taught their converts Latin.

To make sense of this hyper-hybrid population a racial taxonomy was invented, the *castas*, which ranked people according to birth, colour, race, ethnicity and physiognomy. Like the categories operating in *morisco* Spain, these New World *castas* had important legal, economic and social implications; the lower the *casta*, the more tax was paid. Purity of blood (*limpieza de sangre*), as applied to descendants of Muslims and Jews in Spain, was the most important factor in genealogy; the slightest variation from white Christian stained the family through generations. Only those with 'pure blood' could emigrate to the Indies. The highest *casta* was *español* (European born in Spain, or *criollo* born in the Americas), followed by *castizo* (mainly European, partly indigenous), *mestizo* (mixed-race European/indigenous), *indio* (pure indigenous), *pardo* (mixed-race European/indigenous/African), *mulato* (European/African), *zambo* (African/indigenous), *negro* (black African). Paintings to illustrate this taxonomy were commissioned in the eighteenth century under the Bourbons. The translingual and transcultural implications of these hybrid identities are profound. Undermining the apparent commonality in the cultures of the Hispanophone world, the taxonomic inclusion of these orders of difference would lead paradoxically to the progressive erosion of *castizo* and *pureza* (purity).

7. *French*. Following the costly War of the Spanish Succession (1701–1714), Philip V, born in Versailles, grandson of Louis XIV, ascended to the throne in 1700. The Spanish Crown thus passed from the Austrian Hapsburg dynasty to the French Bourbons, where it remains today.[48] The monarchs' domains extended to Naples, Sardinia, Sicily, Milan, Flanders and Luxembourg, as well as Spain and the Spanish Americas. The Bourbons tightened up and centralised imperial government and administration. The French language, culture and customs, considered by the elites to be superior to *castellano*, afforded high status. The influence of French on the languages and literatures of Spain was stifling, resulting in numerous one-way translations from French into Spanish and rule-bound translingual imitations. Throughout the eighteenth century and early nineteenth, whether ruled by Bourbon absolutism or Napoleon's First Empire, the Hispanic world was drawn into geopolitical strategies and disputes that favoured France (for example, Trafalgar in 1805 and the Peninsular War/Spanish War of Independence 1808–1814). Even the term 'Latin America' (rather than Hispano- or Ibero-America) was adopted

---

[48] Spain is a constitutional monarchy since 1833, apart from when it was a Republic in 1873 and 1931–1936/1939, and a military dictatorship (1939–1975).

in the 1860s to suggest the Indies were French-speaking and to erase the Hispanic colonial legacy.[49]

On the positive side, this being the Age of Enlightenment, the Bourbons, especially Charles III (1759–1788), cultivated learning and science (see Samson, Chapter 6; Ginger, Chapter 7). The Royal Academy of Spain was established in 1713 to standardise the Spanish language; the other Hispanic languages almost disappeared even from common speech. Scientific expeditions across the Americas culminated in the maps and scientific discoveries of Jorge Juan and Antonio de Ulloa, cartographer Bernardo de Miera y Pacheco and the Prussian scientist Alexander von Humboldt. Juan and Ulloa joined the French Geodesic Mission (French Academy of Sciences) sailing to Quito where they set the Equator and proved Earth was oblate not round. Juan later established the Royal Astronomical Observatory in Madrid. To encourage trade and extract maximum revenue for the Crown, the administration of the Indies was overhauled; French ships could enter the ports; intendancies replaced Vice-royalties; taxation increased. In 1767 the Society of Jesus (Jesuits) was expelled but Franciscans, such as Junípero Serra, were permitted to establish 21 missions, including San Francisco (1776) and San Diego (1769) in California, and San Antonio in Texas (1781), thus further extending *castellano* in north America.[50]

The tightening of imperial control (the 'Bourbon reforms') led to the most significant indigenous and mestizo uprisings in the Americas to date, the Tupac Amaru rebellion of 1780–1784 in Peru, in which hundreds of thousands of Quechua and Aymara-speaking peoples were killed. The *cacique* (chief) José Gabriel Tupac Amarú, self-styled Emperor of the Incas, was bilingual (Quechua-Spanish), but his wife, Micaela Bastidas, and most of his followers were not. Neither were the Spanish officials. Interpreters were needed at their trial before the entire family was brutally executed or imprisoned. Ultimately, it was under Bourbon rule that the Indies gained independence from the Bourbon monarchs and hence from Spain, not only due to the incompetence of the last of their absolutist kings, Charles IV and Ferdinand VII (1808; 1813–1833), but also to the aggression of another Frenchman, the Corsican

[49] Areas in which French is the majority/official language are Guiana, Haiti, six Caribbean islands and Quebec. Quebec is apparently part of Latin America.

[50] California remained Spanish speaking until the end of the nineteenth century with bilingual newspapers published in San Francisco and Los Angeles. See Leonard Pitt, *The Decline of the Californios. A Social History of the Spanish-speaking Caifornians 1846–1890* (Berkeley, Los Angeles, London: University of California Press, 1966), and Rosaura Sanchez, *Telling Identities. The Californio testimonios* (Minneapolis and London: University of Minnesota Press, 1995).

Napoleon Bonaparte. Bonaparte's invasion of Portugal and Spain resulted in the creation of the modern nation-states of both the Iberian Peninsula and Latin America.

8. *Spanishes, states and nation-states.* The Napoleonic invasion of the Iberian Peninsula (1807–1808), unprecedented since the Islamic invasions a thousand years earlier, removed Spain from Bourbon control and incorporated it into the French First Empire (1805–1814). The Holy Roman Empire was abolished in 1806. But Napoleon had neither the strength nor time to extend his authority to the Indies. Until Napoleon was defeated in the Peninsular War/Spanish War of Independence, Spain did not exist as an independent national political entity. The French armies occupied all Hispania and it was a northern kingdom, Asturias, which finally declared war seeking arms from Britain. The spirited reaction against Napoleon across Europe was fuelled by a new and potentially dangerous political ideology, nationalism.

Nationalism argued for the political and economic self-determination of a 'nation', a 'natural' community sharing a language, race, culture and religion forged through 'blood ties' and a common history. For the Prussian J. G. Herder, who coined the term, the connection with the mother-tongue of the 'homeland' or 'fatherland' was paramount. In *Treatise on the Origins of Language* (1772) Herder argued that language, the 'organ of thought', shapes the way we think, and that each language community interprets the world accordingly. Language creates national identities: 'a poet is the creator of the nation around him'.[51] J. G. Fichte wrote, 'Wherever a separate language is found, there a separate nation exists.'[52] But political nationalism aimed not only to 'preserve' a 'national' or cultural identity; it aimed also to actively create this identity 'where it is felt to be inadequate or lacking'.[53] In this view, the Hispanic languages had resisted the imposition of French and survived in oral traditions, such as popular (folk)song and ballads, which demonstrated the existence of distinctive language-defined Hispanic 'races'. Herder himself translated into German (though from a French source) the fifteenth-century Castilian-Arabic border ballad 'Romance de Abenámar'. In the nineteenth century, the impact of German Romanticism and nationalism, and European

---

[51] Johann Gottfried Herder, *Shakespeare*, ed. and trans. by Gregory Moore (Princeton and London: Princeton University Press, 2008 [1773]), p. 38.

[52] Quoted in C. A. Macartney, *National States and National Minorities* (Oxford: Oxford University Press, 1934), p. 99.

[53] Eugene Kamenka, 'Political nationalism. The evolution of the idea', in *Nationalism. The Nature and Evolution of an Idea*, ed. by Eugene Kamenka (London: Edward Arnold, 1976), p. 6.

interest in all things Hispanic (see Partzsch Chapter 14), prompted a revaluation of Hispano-Arabic cultures and medieval literatures, and a resurgence of the languages and identities of Galicia, Catalonia and the Basques.

In the Indies, the vacuum that followed the dissolution of imperial power allowed the Vice-royalties to establish their own governing bodies and, after some twenty years of civil war, to constitute themselves into 18 independent republics and sovereign nation-states. This process continued throughout the nineteenth century as borders were resolved. The Republic of Argentina, for example, was not invented with the name, capital and borders it has today until 1880. The federal Gran Colombia, established by Bolivar in 1819 comprising territories in present-day Colombia, Ecuador, Panama, Guyana and Venezuela, was dissolved in 1831. The United States of the Republic of Mexico ceded a third of its territory to the United States of America after US troops invaded in 1846. Not all the new states were sufficiently homogenous in cultures, languages and identities to be deemed 'nations' or nation-states. Paraguay, established in 1811 and consisting almost entirely of mestizo Guarani peoples, was an exception; Guarani, co-official with Spanish, is today widely spoken by the non-indigenous population and is an official language in Mercosur. Argentina, on the other hand, populated by waves of European immigrants (mainly Italians and Spanish), had to work hard to create a sense of national identity. Spanish has remained the official language in the former Spanish dominions, but the many other spoken languages have been standardised and given co-official status in the twentieth and twenty-first centuries. Since 2009, the Plurinational State of Bolivia officially recognises 32 living languages. Quechua, with its many dialects, has been transformed and is widely used in both rural and urban areas of the Andes (Howard, Chapter 4). Hispano-America is a multilingual, multiethnic, multiracial, multicultural society featuring local and supranational translingual practices within and across countries and communities, including the United States, and it is within this context that new forms of Spanish are emerging.

Without an Empire (although retaining overseas provinces Cuba and Puerto Rico until 1898, and a colonial presence in Morocco and Equatorial Guinea until 1968 and 1975, respectively), Spain reverted to the configuration of Visigoth Hispania. Since 1833 it has been an independent sovereign state, governed by a constitutional monarchy. But, as with the American republics, Spain has had to work hard to create a sense of Spanish national identity. The central government in Madrid (Castile) downgraded the 'historic nations' to provinces (on the French model) and repressed their languages, leading to two centuries of constant tension and war. Their political rights were acknowledged in the Federal Republic of 1873 and the Republic of 1931–1936/1939. They were finally granted political autonomy in the post-Franco Constitution of 1978. The languages of Galicia, Catalonia and the Basque country are now co-official and thrive in spoken and written form.[54] Andalusia is also an autonomous 'historic community', and although its language, Andalusi, has not been revived its culture survives in music (although see Llano, Chapter 8). Spain's status as a pluri-nation-state is the result of, and not a precursor to, its imperial history.

In conclusion, this overview of the development of the Spanish language in its historical and political context underscores that the Spanish-speaking world is, and always has been, translingual, transcultural, trans-imperial and transcontinental, and has supplied much of the foundation of Western modernity and globalisation. For this reason 'Spanish' studies are necessarily 'Hispanic' Studies, encompassing the cultures and languages of Spain (including Catalonia, Galicia and the Basque Country, and sometimes Portugal), of Spanish America (*Hispanoamérica*) (the nation-states of North, Central and South America, parts of the USA, the Hispanophone Caribbean, or *antillas*), as well as of Roman and Islamic Spain, pre-Colombian America and the Spanish and Spanish-American global diasporas. The terms Hispanic/Spanish/Iberian, and Spanish/Latin America Studies, have all been used and queried by scholars but the blurred lines between them demonstrate the extent to which the study of the Hispanophone world defies easy labels and challenges accepted categories and disciplinary norms. This is something to celebrate. Students should not be afraid to cross borders, even if this means honing their language skills or working through translations. To do full justice to Hispanophone cultures a translingual framework, approach and methodology (where possible) should always be a priority.

Part Two
Transnational Approaches to the Hispanophone World: Recent Theories and Debates

Given the geographical breadth and historical complexity of its object of study, as indicated above, 'Hispanic Studies' has always been something of an atypical discipline within Modern Languages, variously housed under 'Iberian', 'Spanish and Spanish American', 'Spanish and Latin American' studies, and internally distributed between 'Peninsularists', 'Latin Americanists', 'Golden Age specialists' and so on. The recent transnational 'turn' has unsettled these divisions, prompting engagements with the 'supranational'

---

[54] Spain is divided into 17 autonomous communities with their own executive, legislative and judicial powers, and two autonomous cities in North Africa, Ceuta and Melilla.

and 'trans-imperial' dimensions of so many heterogeneous Hispanophone cultures. Such a 'turn' stems in large part from engagements with critical theory by Spanish specialists in modern languages in the 1980s,[55] and particularly with theoretical interrogations of nationhood and nationalism in vogue at the time. Reworking Herder's (and later Ernest Renan's) view of the nation as 'a soul' or 'spiritual' principle, Ernest Gellner had already stressed in 1964 the discontinuity of nationalism and nationhood. 'Nationalism', he argued, 'is not the awakening of nations to self-consciousness: it invents nations where they do not exist'.[56] Benedict Anderson, more memorably, shifted Gellner's focus on 'invention' towards a definition of the nation as an 'imagined' political community. It was, he argued, '*imagined* because the members of even the smallest nation will never know most of their fellow-members, meet them, or even hear of them'; and imagined as a *community*, 'because regardless of the actual inequality and exploitation that may prevail in each, the nation is always conceived as a deep, horizontal comradeship'.[57]

Linking the spread of nationalism to 'print capitalism' – to revolutions in print technology that would facilitate the creation of vernacular fields of communication and exchange – Anderson's work offered Hispanists new ways of approaching literary texts, and significantly drew its examples from Hispanophone works like *El periquillo sarniento* (1816) by the Mexican José

---

[55] Jean Franco's studies of Latin American literature and culture were pioneering in this regard, particularly in their engagement with feminist and Marxist theory. See, for example, *Critical Passions: Selected Essays*, ed. by Mary-Louise Pratt and Kathleen Newman (Durham, NC and London: Duke University Press, 1999). Paul Julian Smith's *Writing in the Margin: Spanish Literature of the Golden Age* (Oxford: Oxford University Press, 1988) was pathbreaking in bringing Golden Age Spanish literature into dialogue with post-structuralist critical theory, as were his comparative readings of Spanish and Latin American literature in *The Body Hispanic: Gender and Sexuality in Spanish and Latin American Literature* (Oxford: Clarendon, 1992) and *Representing the Other: 'Race', Text and Gender in Spanish and Spanish American Narrative* (Cambridge: Cambridge University Press, 1993). In the 1990s, British Latin Americanists such as William Rowe, John Kraniauskas, Catherine Boyle (founders, with David Treece, and Daniel Balderston, of the *Journal of Latin American Cultural Studies* in 1992) and British Hispanists such as Jo Labanyi (founder in 1997 of the *Journal of Spanish Cultural Studies*) developed these theoretical interventions in the field, as did US-based scholars such as Alberto Moreiras, Mábel Moraña, John Beverley, George Yúdice, Brad Epps and others, who also contributed powerful critical reflections on the fields of Hispanism and Latin Americanism.

[56] Ernest Gellner, *Thought and Change* (Chicago: Chicago University Press, 1964), p. 168.

[57] Benedict Anderson, *Imagined Communities: Reflections on the Rise and Spread of Nationalism* (London: Verso, 1991 [revised edition]), pp. 5–6; p. 7. Italics in original.

Joaquín Fernández de Lizardi and *Noli me tangere* (1887) by the Filipino José Rizal. Without fully subscribing to Marxist critique, it also underscored how the nineteenth-century spread of nationalism across Europe and the Americas was inseparable from the inherently transnational dimensions of capitalism. Indeed, in 1848, in a prescient account of what we now call 'globalisation', Marx and Engels had already noted that capitalism, nothing less than a *world-system*, had stamped a cosmopolitan character on all production and consumption: 'The need of a constantly expanding market for its products chases the bourgeoisie over the whole surface of the globe. It must nestle everywhere, settle everywhere, establish connections everywhere.'[58] 'When money leaves the domestic sphere of circulation', Marx later wrote, 'it loses the local functions it has acquired there',[59] making talk of this or that 'national economy' sound curiously fetishistic. And as with material, so with intellectual production. Hence in the political sphere, Marx and Engels saw 'the executive of the modern state [as] but a committee for managing the common affairs of the whole bourgeoisie', and imagined, following Goethe, that in the sphere of culture 'national one-sidedness and narrow-mindedness' would soon give way to an emerging 'world literature' (*Communist Manifesto*, pp. 83–84).

Given the importance of the conquest and colonisation of the Americas to the emergence of capitalism, it is no surprise that the first critical engagements with nationalism in Hispanic studies should come from Latin American (literary) studies. Most memorable among these was Doris Sommer's *Foundational Fictions*, which cross-fertilised Anderson's work on nationalism with Foucault's history of sexuality in Europe to explore how the recurrent trope of inter-racial love (*mestizaje*) in nineteenth-century Latin American novels aimed to move readers with imaginary scenarios in which entrenched colonial hierarchies of regional, racial and political difference might be overcome.[60] In their citation and reworking of romantic works like Chateaubriand's *Atala* and Saint-Pierre's *Paul et Virginie*, she observed, these novelistic allegories of patriotism also sought to explore their nation's differences vis-à-vis their European and American intertexts. It would remain open to question, however, whether in reworking the tropes of this emerging 'world literature' these rewritings could shore up national differences in the

---

[58] Karl Marx and Friedrich Engels, *The Communist Manifesto*, with an introduction by A. J. P. Taylor (London: Penguin, 1985), p. 83.

[59] Karl Marx, *Capital: A Critique of Political Economy*, Vol. 1 (London: Penguin Books, 1976), p. 240.

[60] Doris Sommer, *Foundational Fictions: The National Romances of Latin America* (Berkeley and Los Angeles: California University Press, 1991), pp. 30–51.

face of the homogenising effects of the world-market, or whether, like Freud's 'narcissism of minor differences' – the feuding between neighbouring populations who share more in common than they normally admit – they betrayed more unsettling forms of emerging uniformity.[61]

If the novels analysed by Sommer presupposed the translatability of romantic into republican sentiments, they did so on distinctly unstable grounds. For allegory – romantic fiction's preferred form – inevitably petrified history in the form of a 'death mask', representing 'in the realm of ideas what ruins [were] in the realm of things'.[62] In the context in which Sommer's study was written – one marked by the aggressive (re)turn to free-market capitalism, the global dismantling of welfare states and the supplanting of literature by television and digital forms of communication as mediators of private sentiment and public opinion – the humanist 'pillars' around which the broader discipline of Modern Languages had historically been organised had also begun to crumble.[63] These included not only language – Spanish or *castellano*, understood as a unifying feature of Hispanophone culture – but also literature and history, its supplementary supports, whose principal aim had historically been to secure the link between literate populations and state power. It was as if, like Hegel's Owl of Minerva (which 'takes flight only when the shades of night are gathering'),[64] efforts such as Sommer's to explain the nation's cultural dimensions had grasped *in hindsight* a phenomenon now entering its historical twilight.

Raymond Williams once noted that the description and analysis of culture was 'expressed in an habitual past tense' that tended to reduce cultures to timeless 'fixed forms'.[65] It is from the rubble scattered around the remains of these seemingly immutable fixities – language, literature and history – that

---

[61] Sigmund Freud, *Civilization and its Discontents. Standard Edition*, Vol. 21 (London: Vintage, 2001), pp. 114–115.

[62] Walter Benjamin, *The Origin of German Tragic Drama* (New York and London: Verso, 1977), p. 178.

[63] These terms are from Jon Beasley-Murray's 'Beyond Hispanic Studies? Interdisciplinary approaches to Spain and Latin America', in *The Companion to Hispanic Studies*, ed. by Catherine Davies (London: Routledge, 2002), p. 166. His acknowledgement that its geographical scope made Hispanic studies something of an 'anomaly' within Modern Languages does not always sit comfortably with his alignment of Hispanism, at other points, with the altogether more monolingual areas of the discipline like German or Italian studies.

[64] G. W. F. Hegel, Preface to *Elements of the Philosophy of Right*, ed. by Allen W. Wood (Cambridge: Cambridge University Press, 1991), p. 23.

[65] Raymond Williams, 'Structures of feeling', in *Marxism and Literature* (Oxford: Oxford University Press, [1977] 2009), pp. 129–130.

engagements with new cultural formations have emerged, and with these, understandings of their lived transformations today. With these come new understandings not only of the dynamism of the post-national 'here and now', but also of the historic instability of the borders of the Hispanic world prior to and after the spread of nationalism. Globalisation, for example, may generate increased intermingling of languages, but this phenomenon forms part of the longer history of multilingualism and creolisation already mentioned, a history that unsettles chauvinistic and imperial histories of the Spanish language (see Pountain, Chapter 1). Likewise, expansion of the traditional 'Spanish' canon that began with studies of Latin American literature in the 1960s has now extended to include Chicano literature, Hispanophone African literature and myriad other forms of migrant, mass, minority and subaltern literacies. These new literacies in turn make us question whether literature – which has long since ceased to be the dominant cultural form – could ever bind populations to national state projects. With the global spread of digital communications, as Taylor and Pitman explore in Chapter 10, both the Hispanic world and Hispanic studies are being profoundly reshaped, and no longer only by lettered intellectuals.

This transnational turn in Hispanic studies both extends and invigorates what Jon Beasley-Murray, in his account of these changes, calls a 'post-Hispanism'. This is a Hispanism attentive to the 'traffic' circulating in and around the foundational 'pillars' of Modern Languages as a discipline. That 'traffic' is transnational, first and foremost, insofar as it indexes today's global flows of capital, commodities, information and people across permeable national borders. These flows have destabilized our imagination of the Hispanophone world as a static patchwork of sovereign nation-states, replacing the nation with the 'network' as the framework within which to understand cultural processes.[66] Circumventing the state's mediation of national identity, flows of culture and information now link producers and consumers, across national boundaries, to increasingly diasporic public spheres.[67] The upshot, as Arjun Appadurai argues, is that the reproduction of the nation as an 'imagined community' now confounds theories of identity that presuppose the nation-state as the key arbiter of national identity.[68] The availability, within such diasporic spheres, of a whole range of de-territorialized national narratives also allows national histories to be written in

---

[66] Manuel Castells, *The Information Age: Economy, Society and Culture*, Vol. 1 – *The Rise of the Network Society* (Oxford and London: Basil Blackwell, 1996).

[67] Arjun Appadurai, *Modernity at Large: Cultural Dimensions of Globalization* (Minneapolis: University of Minnesota Press, 1996), pp. 21–22.

[68] Appadurai, *Modernity at Large*, p. 4.

and through *other* histories. Works by Jorge Volpi and Ignacio Padilla of the Mexican 'Crack' generation, for example, evidence how 'Mexicanness' is being re-imagined through novelistic reworkings of Nazi German history, and in ways that bypass the hallowed rules of certain post-Revolutionary forms of cultural nationalism. As Baker argues in Chapter 11, these 'post-national' works go beyond earlier forms of cosmopolitanism, Borges's assertion, for example, that '[o]ur [Argentine] patrimony is the universe',[69] to render nationalism and its myths inoperable.

In addition to weakening the continuity that formerly existed between nation and state, capital's constant commodification of difference further confounds assumptions about the location of regional identity. In the relentless branding of 'lo latino' as a cipher of sensuality and the exotic in the marketing of everything from fast food to classy booze, even Latin America, as Swanson writes in Chapter 9, is torn from its once bounded, geographical contours. As Latinity goes viral – thanks to Hollywood, Netflix, 'world music' and magical realism (now as much a mass-produced export as bananas were at the turn of the previous century) – Latin America no longer sits 'down there, south of the Río Grande', but also 'up here, over here, everywhere'. Flows of money, people, information and culture introduce a whole new order of instability into the world that confounds such locations of culture. But not everything is in flux. For today's flows of capital and information also produce new forms of exclusion and localization, sometimes passing *over* regions in ways that suspend their populations in situations of structural *superfluity*.[70] Sklodowksa contends in her study of post-Soviet material culture in Cuba (Chapter 12), for example, that there are 'worlds of difference' between former First-World, Third-World and emerging Second-World nations' experiences of the post-Cold War period. Globalisation thus remains as much an 'imagined' entity as the nation itself,[71] resting on as much 'actual inequality and exploitation' as the imagined national community.[72]

Where 'post-Hispanism' has perhaps made its most significant contribution to the critical interrogation of the global order is in its contribution to

---

[69] Jorge Luis Borges, 'El escritor argentino y la tradición', in *Discusión* (Madrid: Alianza, 1995 [1951]), pp. 188–203, p. 201.

[70] Zygmunt Bauman, *Globalization: The Human Consequences* (New York: Columbia University Press, 1998); see Étienne Balibar's essay 'Violence, ideality and cruelty', in Étienne Balibar, *Politics and the Other Scene* (London: Verso, 2002), pp. 129–145; Achille Mbembe, 'Necropolitics', *Public Culture*, 15.1 (2003), 11–40.

[71] Néstor García Canclini, *La globalización imaginada* (México: Paidós, 1999).

[72] Anderson, *Imagined Communities*, p. 7.

post-colonial theorisations of modernity, and of modernity's emergence out of the imperial processes formative of trans-Atlantic capitalism.[73] The kinds of 'traffic' that Beasley-Murray traces in Steven Soderbergh's film *Traffic* (2000), for example – border-crossings by people and by the new liquidities of drugs and narco-capital – certainly blur essentialised differences between *hispanidad* and (in the film's case) Americanism ('Beyond Hispanic Studies', p. 165). They also evoke much earlier crossings that ended in shipwreck and in the shattering of religious and political worldviews. Cabeza de Vaca's *Naufragios*, for example, which is situated in and around the borderlands where Soderburgh's *Traffic* is filmed, narrates one such crossing as a series of calamities, with the noble Spanish adventurer shipwrecked, taken captive and enslaved by indigenous tribes. In short, it is a narrative about the quest to extend the possessions of Spanish empire that ends with the Spaniard dispossessed of his imperial power certainties.[74] By the twentieth century, the mutual transformation of coloniser and colonised in encounters like those narrated in the *Naufragios* – a process termed 'transculturation' by the Cuban ethnographer Fernando Ortiz – would become the stuff of countless fictions that query the stability of empire and nationhood and their foundations.

A key point of reference for understanding these post-colonial contributions to the transnational 'turn' in Hispanic studies is the work of the Latin American Subaltern Studies Group, founded in 1992 by Ileana Rodríguez and John Beverley. With their shared interest in interrogating (after Ranajit Guha) 'the logic of the distortions in the representation of the subaltern in official or elite culture; and uncovering the social semiotics of the strategies and cultural practices of peasant insurgencies',[75] its members explored the historic fragility of the creole or *criollo* Latin American intellectual's assumption of continuity between nation, state and 'people' ('Founding Statement', p. 112). They did so

---

[73] Works such as Helen Graham and Jo Labanyi, *Spanish Cultural Studies: An Introduction* (Oxford: Oxford University Press, 1995), Mabel Moraña, *Ideologies of Hispanism* (Nashville: Vanderbilt University Press, 2005), Joan Ramon Resina, *Del hispanismo a los estudios ibéricos: una propuesta federativa para el ámbito cultural* (Madrid: Biblioteca Nueva, 2009), and essays by Eduardo Subirats – see in particular 'Seven theses against Hispanism', in *Border Interrogations: Questioning Spanish Frontiers*, ed. by Benita Sampedro Vizcaya and Simon Doubleday (London and New York: Berghan Books 2008 [reprinted 2011]), pp. 246–259, offer critical reflections both on the history of Hispanism and on the fraught relationship between post-colonial studies and post-imperial Hispanic studies.

[74] Álvar Núñez Cabeza de Vaca, *Naufragios* ed. by Juan F. Maura (Madrid: Cátedra, 2013).

[75] Ranajit Guha, cited in 'Founding statement', *Boundary* 2: *The Postmodernism Debate in Latin America*, 20.3 (Autumn, 1993), 135–146, 111.

by recognising how state intellectuals in post-revolutionary Mexico, Cuba and Nicaragua (including the writers of the Boom) had occluded forms of subalternity, the lived experiences and knowledge of blacks, Indians, Chicanos, women and non-straight subjects, in their adherence to traditional Marxist understandings of class. With the crisis of Guevarism in Bolivia in the late 1960s, the rise of the student movements around the globe in 1968 (not just in France) and the development of the communications industries in the 1980s – the referents for an emergent field of Latin American Cultural Studies – the model of the revolutionary *criollo* intellectual had to be rethought, and particularly his role as the broker between people and state.

Yet if for the Latin American Subaltern Studies Group the nation remained haunted by its instrumentalisation as means to manage profoundly different ethnicities and subject them to the homogenising discourses of state power, the group's shared aim of epistemic *de-nationalisation* (the denationalisation of knowledge) – 'simultaneously a limit and a threshold of [their] project' ('Founding Statement', p. 118) – would generate very different approaches to the cultural field. Not all members of the Subaltern Studies Group, for one, understood the 'transnational' solely in terms of contemporary neo-liberal erosions of the nation-state by global flows of labour and capital. Such was the case in particular with proponents of the 'decolonial' turn. Walter Mignolo, for example, would insist with Aníbal Quijano that coloniality was *constitutive* of modernity: that the Western Renaissance or Enlightenment, could not be thought independently of colonialism, rather that they represented 'two sides of the same coin'.[76] The upshot would be a call to reorient critical thinking, from the point of view of this alignment of modernity and coloniality, towards epistemic and political decolonisation – to show that Eurocentric systems of knowledge constituted but one small part of a far larger, diverse array of epistemologies. 'Decoloniality', as much a political as an epistemic goal, represents a heuristic and an unfinished project aimed at rethinking the history of the former colonial 'periphery' from non-Western epistemologies (or systems of knowledge) developed outside of, yet simultaneously with, modern Eurocentricism.[77]

Building on the work of the Peruvian sociologist Aníbal Qujiano and the Argentine philosopher Enrique Dussell, decolonial approaches to Hispanic culture radically extend the call made by the Cuban Romantic José Martí,

---

[76] See Walter Mignolo, *Local Histories/Global Designs: Coloniality, Subaltern Knowledges and Border Thinking* (Princeton: Princeton University Press, 2000), and *The Idea of Latin America* (Oxford: Blackwell, 2005).

[77] See Nelson Maldonado-Torres's hugely informative overview of the 'Decolonial turn' in Poblete, *New Approaches*, pp. 111–127.

in 'Our America' (1891), to embrace a *different* America that is not only multi-, but also *inter*-cultural. This involves recognising that *criollo* thought, the inherited baggage of leaders of European descent who wear 'epaulets and professors' gowns in countries that came into the world wearing hemp sandals and headbands', must learn 'to fit liberty to the body of those who rebelled and conquered for it'.[78] It approaches the history of the Americas (North, Central and South), following Martí, in a way that places 'the Incas on the same footing as the Greeks'. Like the work of another forerunner, José Carlos Mariátegui, whose *Seven Interpretive Essays on Peruvian Reality* (1928) envisioned an Andean form of Socialism that would evolve in an organic relationship with the collective structures of the Incan Ayllu ('community'), decolonial thinking parts company with the millenarian pessimism according to which neo-liberal globalisation is the *only* goal towards which world history might progress. Instead of *multi*-culturalism – which involves a European-style state's management and containment of differences within a hegemonic neo-liberal framework – it strives for *inter*-culturalism, or the state's construction along the lines of distinct yet equally valued epistemologies.[79] The works of Silvia Rivera Cusicanqui and Joanne Rappaport have significantly developed these ideas in their studies (and promotion) of indigenous and intercultural Andean literacies (also addressed by Howard in Chapter 4).

Also significant among efforts to explore the traffic between cosmologies and epistemologies (although less anthropological and more traditionally literary-critical in its approach) is the work of Peruvian author and scholar, Julio Ortega, whose *Transatlantic Translations* brings literature produced on both sides of the Atlantic into dialogue with each other. Its aim is to examine 'how the new was perceived in terms of the already conceived, the different constituted by what was already known and the unnamed seen through what had already been read'. Ortega's approach maps 'a new "geotextuality"', studying 'cultural practices of *hybridization* and *mestizaje*' as they open up uncharted histories of cultural 'intermixing'.[80] His approach to this dialogical interplay advantageously avoids the reduction of colonial history to a narrative of victimisation while also steering clear of the sometimes fetishistic subsumption of 'native' epistemologies under the banner of decolonial *resistance*. The disadvantage with this approach, however, lies in its potential

---

[78] José Martí, *Nuestra América* (Caracas: Biblioteca Ayacucho, 2005), p. 10.
[79] See 'After "Latin" America', in Mignolo, *The Idea of Latin America*, pp. 95–148.
[80] Julio Ortega, *Transatlantic Translations: Dialogues in Latin American Literature*, trans. by Philip Derbyshire (London: Reaktion Books, 2006), p. 9. Emphases in original.

to overlook the violent origins and ongoing instrumentalizations of notions like *mestizaje* and *hybridity* by state power. For while signalling something like inclusivity, diversity and plurality 'from below', such notions remain tied to the 'top-down' incorporation of heterogeneous populations into national state processes, particularly under populism. As Gareth Williams argues, with Alberto Moreiras (both also members of the Subaltern Studies Group) fictions of *national* ethnicity constructed on the 'hybridity' thesis (most notoriously José Vasconcelos's interpellation of Mexicans as a *mestizo* 'raza cósmica' in 1925) often conceal and neutralise both the ethnic *and* class antagonisms generated by the nation-state's participation in global, neoliberal divisions of power and labour, no less so in today's Estado Plurinacional de Bolivia than in the context of post-revolutionary Mexico.[81]

As well as reminding us of the fragility and mutability of the Hispanic world's contours, works like the *Naufragios*, with its account of the years Cabeza de Vaca spent wandering around current-day Florida and Texas before crossing into modern-day Mexico, also underscore the tri-continental dimensions of the conquest and colonisation of the Americas: its entanglement of European, American and African subjects, and its transformation of the course of all three continents' histories. Numerous Africans also travelled on the disastrous Narváez expedition on which Cabeza de Vaca embarked, having been captured by Portuguese slave-traders and sold in Spain. Only one of them, 'Estevanico el negro', would survive. Although mentioned by Cabeza de Vaca, his story is eclipsed by Cabeza de Vaca in his alternately picaresque and messianic *relación*. Recent works such as Laila Lalami's *The Moor's Account*, which imaginatively retells Estevanico's story from the slave's point of view, remind us of the importance of black people within abstract narratives of the conquest as a defining moment in 'Western' modernity. Like Lalami's *The Moor's Account*, in which Estevanico (now identified as Mustafa ibn Muhammad ibn Abdussalam al-Zamori) is the first to set foot in what is now the USA,[82] they are reminders that the Atlantic world is also a *black* Atlantic built by those who endured the horrors of slavery and the middle-passage, and that trans-Atlantic capitalism has been, in Paul Gilroy's words, as 'rhizomorphic' and 'fractal' as it has been transcultural and international. Indeed, since Columbus's voyage (piloted by Pedro Nino, also an African),

---

[81] See Gareth Williams's discussion of these processes in *The Other Side of the Popular: Neoliberalism and Subalternity in Latin America* (Durham, NC: Duke University Press, 2002), pp. 23–70. See also José Vasconcelos, *The Cosmic Race: A Bilingual Edition*, trans. and annotated by Didier T. Jaén (Los Angeles: The Johns Hopkins University Press, 1979).

[82] Lalami, *The Moor's Account*.

the Atlantic has been 'continually crisscrossed by the movements of black people', and not only as commodities, but as subjects 'engaged in various struggles towards emancipation, autonomy, and citizenship'. The stories of their voyages, and of their struggles for autonomy and citizenship, make nation-centred approaches to location, identity and historical memory look decidedly provincial.[83]

Awareness of the ways in which the *black* Atlantic 'crisscrosses' histories of colonialism and trans-Atlantic capitalism indeed precludes what Gilroy terms 'cultural insiderism'.[84] It guards against a kind of '*Hispanic* insiderism' that would limit critical scholarship of Spanish imperial history to the recovery of only a 'two-way' traffic between Europeans, on the one side, and Americans on the other. The spread of the Spanish Empire to encompass not only the Americas but also parts of Africa, Asia and the Pacific, demands much wider-eyed approaches to Hispanophone culture. Outlining their own efforts to push beyond such 'insiderist' mappings, Brad Epps and Luis Cifuentes observe the repeated omission of Africa and Asia in most Spanish literary histories, and call for a relocation of Spanish literary history 'beyond' Spain.[85] Benita Sampedro's work on Spanish colonialism in Africa and Latin America, corrects such omissions, particularly in her focus on Equatorial Guinea, whose history is 'crisscrossed' by the lines of Portuguese and Spanish imperial history in Africa and America, and problematises traditional definitions of region, periodicity and nationality in Hispanic studies.[86] More recently, Jerome Branche's *The Poetics and Politics of Diaspora* pursues the ways in which the modern African diaspora interrupts and dislocates trans-Atlantic histories through 'scatterings' of poetic, literary and musical works from Cuba, Equatorial Guinea, Spain, the UK and Colombia. These scattered formations produce *relocations* of diasporic subjects, and through a poetics of '*malungaje*' that bind exile to new forms of kinship. They also set up important dialogues between studies of the Hispanophone and Lusophone world.[87]

---

[83] Paul Gilroy, *The Black Atlantic* (London: Verso, 1993), pp. 6, 7, 16.

[84] By 'insiderism' Gilroy refers to the blindspots of British Cultural Studies with its canonically English frames of reference, *The Black Atlantic*, p. 3.

[85] Brad Epps and Luis Fernández Cifuentes, *Spain Beyond Spain: Modernity, Literary History and National Identity* (Lewisberg: Bucknell University Press, 2005), p. 19.

[86] Benita Sampedro Vizcaya, 'Engaging the Atlantic: New routes, new responsibilities', *Bulletin of Hispanic Studies*, 89 (2012), pp. 905–922, and *Border Interrogations: Questioning Spanish Frontiers*, ed. by Benita Sampedro Vizcaya and Simon Doubleday (London and New York: Berghan Books, 2008 [reprinted 2011]).

[87] Jerome C. Branche, *The Poetics and Politics of Diaspora: Transatlantic Musings*

Other border-crossings add complexity to these re-locations of culture and kinship, moving across borders not only linguistic, economic and geographical but also corporeal and psycho-sexual. Cabeza de Vaca had witnessed many such crossings during his captivity among the Hans and Capoque peoples, in his account of indigenous 'homosexuality', in his cross-identification as a 'female' slave and in his later identification as a faith healer or *chamán*. More sobering works such as Chilean-born Roberto Bolaño's posthumously published *2666* (2004) now dwell on the Mexican–US border as the site of different forms of 'capture', this time of working-class subjects by intersecting forms of structural-economic dehumanisation. Here racially marked migrant women perform underpaid jobs in multinational *maquilas* (assembly plants), and typically wind up dead in the desert, discarded like the cheap throwaway products they churn out daily. Yet works by Chicano writers such as Gloria Anzaldúa, Cherríe Moraga and Sandra Cisneros remind us, like Partzsch in Chapter 14, that transnational forms of collaboration between women writers have also historically mitigated the marginalisation they experienced within patriarchal national(ist) frameworks. In so doing, they explore the converging lines of race, class, gender and sexual difference as these structure everyday experiences of exclusion among migrant women in the United States.[88] Discourses on the Caribbean have for a long time explored the maritime area's historically de-centred, de-centring relation to modern Atlantic history, its poetic relationality, its transculturation of subjects and its erosion of national borders.[89] Only recently though, as James discusses in Chapter 16, have Caribbean writers begun to inspect the intersecting racial and sexual dimensions of Caribbean discourse. And the profusion of 'littoral' and island spaces in contemporary

---

(New York and London: Routledge, 2015). See in particular, 'Introduction. *Malungaje*: Towards a poetics of diaspora', pp. 1–26, where Branche explains the Bantu origins of the term 'malungo', its interconnected meanings of brotherhood and consanguinity, oceanic transport, and misfortune, before exploring its later elaboration as a concept in colonial Brazil.

[88] See Gloria Anzaldúa, *Borderlands/La Frontera: The New Mestiza* (San Francisco: Anne Lute Books, 2007 [1987]) and *This Bridge Called by Back: Writings by Radical Women of Colour*, ed. by Cherríe Moraga and Gloria Anzaldúa (New York: State University of New York Press, 2015).

[89] See Antonio Benítez Rojo, *La isla que se repite* (Madrid: Editorial Plaza Nueva, 1989), Eduoard Glissant, *Poetics of Relation*, trans. by Betsy Wing (Michigan: University of Michigan Press, 1997) and Gustavo Pérez-Firmat, *The Cuban Condition: Translation and Identity in Modern Cuban Literature* (Cambridge: Cambridge University Press, 1989).

Latin American film, discussed by Hernández-Adrián in Chapter 13, further expands the geography of the Caribbean as we know it.

As they chart the expanding limits of the discipline and renew critical awareness of its occasional lapses into monolingualism, these critical 're-routings' of Hispanism add a second layer of meaning to the transnational 'traffic' explored within contemporary 'post-Hispanism', and one to which we have already alluded. This is concerned as much with questions of *spatial* mobility within the expanding territories of the Hispanic world – with the different degrees of freedom enjoyed by people of diverse origins, as underscored by stories of conquest and slavery, diaspora and exploitation – as it is with the interplay between the multiple forms of knowledge and subjectivity that converge at the crossroads of the Hispanophone world's multiple fractal histories. This 'traffic' is rarely if ever smooth, but subject to hitches and delays, jammings and collisions. As the work of post- and de-colonial scholars has shown (and as the rise of new forms of xenophobia daily remind us) some epistemologies do not travel at all. But scholarly engagement with the legacies of colonialism and imperialism, while giving the lie to oft-parroted discourses about Spain's exclusion from 'modernity' (a discourse engaged with critically in this volume by Thurner, Samson and Ginger), demand at the very least that we rethink the prejudicial view of modernity as a European project. It prompts us to explore what happens to modernity's core narratives when they enter the slippery 'contact zones' in which cultures come into contact with one another.[90] Explorations of colonial histories of contact also provide the basis on which to interrogate assumptions about the north–south travelling of identity-politics today, a topic explored by Quarshie in Chapter 17.

Exemplary of the ways in which Hispanic cultural studies have tried to bring together these different forms of 'traffic', two works stand out in particular. The first is Mario Santana's *Foreigners in the Homeland: The Spanish American New Novel in Spain, 1962–1974*, which redefines 'national' literature in a manner 'not restricted to the native production of citizens [...] but that also takes into consideration the wider spectrum of literary objects, both autochthonous and imported, available within the national literary market'.[91] This definition allows Santana to show how 'national literatures are both bound and open: limited by the configuration of the nation as a relatively distinct cultural, political, and economic entity, but also permeable, receptive to the appropriation of extrinsic elements' (*Foreigners*, p. 19). Nowhere is this clearer than in his account of

---

[90] The term is Mary Louise-Pratt's from *Imperial Eyes: Travel Writing and Transculturation* (London: Routledge, 1992), p. 2 and passim in 1992 edition.

[91] Mario Santana, *Foreigners in the Homeland: The Spanish American New Novel in Spain, 1962–1974* (Lewisburg: Bucknell University Press, 2000), p. 18.

the multi-sited genesis of the Latin American 'Boom'. Developing Swanson's insight that the 'Boom' was largely the product of publishing houses in Spain, Santana shows how, with their 'nationalisation' as an object of Spanish literary history and criticism, 'Boom' texts also 'provided and legitimized models (and countermodels) for the renewal of fiction in Spain' (*Foreigners*, p. 156).

The second work that exemplifies what genuine transnational Spanish criticism might look like is Lisa Surwillo's *Monsters by Trade: Slave Traffickers in Modern Spanish Literature and Culture*. Surwillo complements Santana's 'defamiliarisation' of the national by inviting us to read key nineteenth-century 'Spanish' literary works from the point of view of empire. Taking Mignolo's 'no-modernity-without-coloniality' thesis as a point of departure, she argues that it was the slave trade in Cuba that proved most influential in shaping Spanish modernity, and long after the slave trade was declared illegal.[92] Indeed, after the second decade of the nineteenth century, the figure of the slave trader in Spanish literature became 'simultaneously a symbol of Spanish defiance of British maritime ascendency, a conduit of wealth for the empire, the occult force behind the government, and an outlaw, in many ways beyond the control of Cubans or the Spanish government' (*Monsters*, p. 9). The same ambiguity shaped the 'Spanish-ising' of works such as Harriet Beecher-Stowe's *Uncle Tom's Cabin* (1853), the book to appear in more editions than any other imported novel in Spain before that point in the century, which was adapted and reworked in such a way as to support striking opposed political agendas ranging for apologies of *mestizaje* as 'racial annihilation' to positions for and against slavery and the slave trade itself (*Monsters*, pp. 31–65).

Few of the essays in this volume share the view that the nation ceases to offer a meaningful framework through which to read works art and literature, cinema or music in Hispanic studies. Even fewer are of the conviction that nationalism is any time soon likely to become a thing of the past. Indeed, as many of them show, the nation (like modernity, the broader framework out of which nationalism emerges) remains in Appadurai's words, very much 'at large'. What together the essays gathered here *do* offer are important insights into the multilingual nature of the Hispanophone world, into the multiple histories that have shaped its component nations and regions, into the ways in which the histories of these nations and regions are being geographically re-*routed* and into the proliferation of ways of seeing and feeling that have emerged at the crossroads of these multiple re-routings. And what we have sought to underscore in our final appeal to the terms 'routes' and 'reroutings' is that the languages, identities and cultures of the Spanish-speaking world

---

[92] Lisa Surwillo, *Monsters by Trade: Slave Traffickers in Modern Spanish Literature and Culture* (Stanford: Stanford University Press, 2014), p. 2.

remain as much 'on the move' today as they were prior to the moment in which 'Spanish' itself went global.

Section 1

Language

This first section focuses explicitly on language and may be usefully read alongside José del Valle's work on transnational languages, linguistic nationalism and linguistic imperialism.[1] Focusing on Panhispanism and *hispanofonía*, del Valle examines the political history and status of Spanish as an 'artifact in the service of emerging nation-States' and imperial expansion (Valle, p. 388). But he also highlights the tension between Spanish perceived as an instrument of imposition on the one hand and, on the other, Spanish as a key player in new globalising information flows that offer alternative cultural and economic communities that resist the hegemony of English. Some of these questions will be addressed throughout the book.

In the first chapter of Section 1, Christopher Pountain discusses important transnational features in the development of the Spanish language, both historical and current. He underscores the fundamental distinction between standardised, written language (pertaining to the literate elites) and the (until recently) undocumented languages of everyday speech and song. This distinction must be borne in mind throughout the reading of this book because, until the invention of recorded and broadcast speech, all reconstructions of past language use and associated cultural identities were based on the survival of material objects and the written word. As Pountain points out, this poses huge challenges for attempting to reconstruct any historical continuity between the Romance vernacular of Castile and the Spanish of today. For

---

[1] José del Valle, 'Transnational languages: Beyond nation and empire? An introduction' and 'Panhispanismo e hispanofonía: breve historia de dos ideologías siamesas', in *Sociolinguistic Studies*, special issue *Language Beyond the Nation: A Comparative Approach to Policies and Discourses*, 5.3 (2011), 387–397, 465–484.

Pountain the globalisation of Spanish was not a transnational phenomenon but an 'extended national phenomenon' since Castilian was implanted as the tool of imperial expansion, and linguistic unity was enforced in all written culture and religious instruction. Today, however, Spanish is diasporic and arguably transnational. It is an official language *de facto* or *de jure* in 21 countries yet, despite the emergence of *Spanglish/espanglish* and Spanish Creoles, it has not fragmented into different versions. A sense of belonging to a continuous language community remains strong.

L. P. Harvey's and James T. Monroe's chapters (2 and 3) discuss in detail the most intriguing and culturally complex epochs in the history of the Iberian Peninsula; its incorporation into the Arabic-speaking empires of Islam. The multiple variations of language use over 800 years in which Classical Arabic vied with Classical Latin as the language of letters, with colloquial varieties encompassing mutually unintelligible dialects of Arabic (Syrian, North African) and distinctive Romance vernaculars, notably the Romance spoken in al-Andalus (Andalusi-Romance or Mozarabic) have yet to be fully understood. Serious investigation did not begin until the 1940s with the discovery and identification of Romance-dialect songs written in Arabic (and Hebrew) script. So while Harvey discusses the Arabic writings of two authors born in Cordoba, Ibn Hazm – a canonical figure in Classical Arabic literature – and Ibn Quzman, who wrote colloquial Arabic surviving in Latin script, and *aljamiado* literature (Castilian texts written in Arabic letters), Monroe points us to tantalising glimpses of colloquial Romance (such as the word *culo*) captured in the lyrics of bawdy songs chanted by Arabic-speaking men. Monroe's broader argument is that popular Romance songs (sung by minstrels and passed on orally) eventually shaped Classical Arabic poetry (the *muwashshah*). Some of these Andalusi songs are still sung in the Arabic world today, passed on not by notation but improvisation. Reconstructing the 'mother-tongues' of Christians, Muslims and Jews in a constantly shifting translingual and multicultural context, with only scant evidence from surviving texts, is a challenge to be surmounted. The implications for theories of the 'transnational' have yet to be worked out.

Rosaleen Howard's chapter (Chapter 4) introduces further levels of complexity into a 'transnational' appreciation of the Spanish language: its contact and interaction with more than 420 indigenous languages in the Americas – non-alphabetic languages, without written texts, learned and shaped through oral traditions. Modern anthropologists and ethnographers have studied indigenous cultures in detail yet reconstructing historically the impact of the imposition of Spanish, the language of letters and the law, is more difficult. The 'voices of the conquered' may be retrieved in the archives through official documents, the writings of *mestizo* bilinguals, such as Spanish/Quechua Felipe Guamán Poma de Ayala and the works of the Catholic clergy who oversaw the compilation and translation of the rituals and beliefs of the indigenous peoples to facilitate conversion. Some indication of the subjective experiences of colonisation is gleaned through glyphs and images. But it is only in the late twentieth century, since recognition of the scientific value of oral 'testimonios', that the first-hand experiences of ordinary indigenous people expressed in their own language have been documented and studied. In the present century, since use of a mother-tongue is now a human right, most Latin American nation-states have been legally reconfigured as pluricultural and multilingual. The first to do so was Mexico in 2003; Howard studies in detail the impact of the Peruvian Indigenous Languages Act of 2011. Again, the implications of these developments for a transnational agenda, for example, the emergence of a Spanish-Quechua hybrid (as noted by Pountain) have yet to be fully explored.

1

Transnational Dimensions in the History of Spanish

Christopher J. Pountain

In this essay, I intend to look at a number of particular aspects of the history of Spanish that are relevant to the current attention being paid to the transnational dimensions of modern languages study. I set the scene with a critical consideration of what is meant by 'the Spanish language', a label that is often taken for granted, and the historical trajectory that has led it to achieve global status. Next, I attempt to correct the excessively nationalistic view of the evolution of the language that has prevailed until quite recently. I then look very briefly at the well-known phenomenon of lexical borrowing, and finally at a number of scenarios in which the interaction between speakers of Spanish and speakers of other languages has led to the creation of what are arguably new languages.

The 'Spanish Language': Some Problems of Definition and Status

The definition of 'Spanish' inescapably involves the question of the relation between language and nation. Spanish is often viewed historically as being simply one of the many particular developments of Latin in the Iberian Peninsula, which came to be accepted as an official language largely because of the historical accident of being spoken in the right place (Castile) at the right time (the political ascendancy of Castile as a result of being at the forefront of the so-called Reconquest of al-Andalus). In fact, however, things are much more complex. In the first place, although it is usual to assume historical continuity, even identity, between the Romance vernacular of Castile and the present-day de facto or de jure official language of 21 countries, languages that, like Spanish, are vehicles of a nation's business and culture (*Ausbau* or standardized languages in Kloss's 1967 terminology) are rather different in nature from vernaculars that are used only for everyday practical communication.[1] For use in national administration, the legal system, education, cultural expression and the media, two things have to happen. First, there must be agreement on a standard form of the language. The codification of that standard may vary in format and extent, but it will involve a series of sometimes arbitrary decisions on which of a number of coexisting variants are to be taken as part of the language, which means that the standard may either be modelled on the language of a particular social group, or may in fact not equate exactly to any pre-existing actual form of the language, a clear case of the latter being the eclectic standard of modern Galician.[2] Second, the language must be elaborated to cater for all the fields in which it is used, through the provision of specialised and technical terminology and sophisticated intellectual expression. This will mean that the range of the language exceeds the competence of any individual speaker. But it is this process of codification and elaboration that establish the identity of a language. When genealogical trees are drawn to show the relatedness of languages, the languages they refer to are usually the languages for which such *Ausbau* status has been achieved. A corollary of this, which is not often insisted upon, is that the achievement of *Ausbau* status is the only secure basis for establishing the beginning of these languages' existence: otherwise, as Wright points out, 'Any attempt to fix a starting point for the history or origins of the Spanish Language, or for any language other than a genuinely creolized pidgin, is necessarily artificial.'[3] Furthermore, if the processes of standardisation and elaboration began, as was the case with Spanish, some time ago, linguistic items and structures that have become obsolete will be included in the notion of 'Spanish'. Thus, the very notion of 'Spanish' is defined by the length of time it has had *Ausbau* characteristics as a result of being cultivated for essentially national purposes.

However, another way of defining 'Spanish' concerns the attitudes of speakers. Spanish has spread through the territories of Spain itself and the former Spanish Empire, and despite the many regional variations that have arisen in the course of this geographical diffusion, it is fair to say that throughout all these territories there is a sense of belonging to the same

[1] Heinz Kloss, '"Abstand languages" and "Ausbau languages"', *Anthropological Linguistics*, 9 (1967), 29–41.

[2] Christopher J. Pountain, 'Standardization', in *The Oxford Guide to the Romance Languages*, ed. by Adam Ledgeway and Martin Maiden (Oxford: Oxford University Press, 1967), pp. 634–643 (pp. 637–638).

[3] Roger Wright, 'Ramón Menéndez Pidal and the history of the Spanish language', in *Ramón Menéndez Pidal after Forty Years: A Reassessment*, ed. by Juan Carlos Conde (London: Department of Hispanic Studies, Queen Mary, University of London, 2010), pp. 145–162 (p. 154).

language community. This consensual attitude towards Spanish overrides the fact that Spanish is referred to by two names: *español* and *castellano*. *Español* excites passion precisely because of its nationalist implications (interestingly, in contrast to 'English'). Within Spain, *español* tends to be rejected by areas in which a different language is used. In the wider Spanish-speaking world, there is sometimes resistance to using *español* because it carries connotations of colonialism, but *español* and *castellano* denote the same linguistic reality.

The history of Spanish might at first sight, then, appear to be the antithesis of the transnational. The very notion of 'Spanish', like the notion of any language given a national name, implies that it is an appurtenance of a distinctive nationhood.[4] We can point to various key stages in the medieval nationalist dimensions of Castilian, the most important of which are the elaboration of a consistent written language, the *castellano drecho*, which was developed under the aegis of Alfonso X 'el Sabio' (reigned 1252–1284), and Nebrija's *Gramática de la lengua castellana* of 1492, which famously asserted in its dedication to Queen Isabella that 'siempre la lengua fue compañera del imperio' ('language has always been the companion of empire'), a claim that turned out to be much more significant than he could possibly have imagined with the discovery and colonisation of the Spanish Empire. This in itself is not actually a transnational phenomenon but an extended national phenomenon, Castilian being implanted as the official language of imperial expansion. Linguistic unity was insisted upon from an early stage. In 1550, a law of Philip II required that all indigenous inhabitants of the Empire should be taught 'nuestra lengua castellana', although the king also insisted on priests speaking the Indian language of their area. But his son Philip III went further in 1605, decreeing that all religious instruction should be given in 'la lengua espagnola'.[5]

The emancipation of the colonies from rule by Spain, the first phase of which came in the wake of the American and French Revolutions, might have resulted in the fragmentation of Spanish; but Spanish today displays a remarkable unity for a diasporic language, at least at the level of educated usage. The aspiration to such a standard (often now simply referred to as the *norma culta*) has a venerable and prestigious tradition both in Spain and in the

---

[4] See José Del Valle and Luis Gabriel-Stheeman, 'Nationalism, *hispanismo*, and monoglossic culture', in *The Battle over Spanish between 1800 and 2000. Language Ideologies and Hispanic Intellectuals*, ed. by José Del Valle and Luis Gabriel-Stheeman (London: Routledge, 2002), pp. 1–13.

[5] Pierre Achard, 'The development of language empires', in *Sociolinguistics: An International Handbook of the Science of Language and Society*, ed. by Ulrich Ammon, Norbert Dittmar and Klaus J. Mattheier, 2 vols (Berlin: De Gruyter, 1987), pp. 1541–1551 (p. 1544).

Americas. Del Valle identifies the highly significant role played by the towering figure of Ramón Menéndez Pidal, in legitimising, in such publications as his 1945 book, the notion of a pan-Hispanic standard.[6] Menéndez Pidal exalted the similar aspirations of a number of Latin American linguists, especially Andrés Bello (b. Caracas, 1781), who in the mid-nineteenth century had argued in his influential *Gramática de la lengua castellana destinada al uso de los americanos* (1847) that following the Spanish norm was the only way of avoiding a linguistic fragmentation that would be detrimental to the interests of the Spanish-speaking American republics.[7] Now nearly 200 years since the first wave of liberation, the 'language battle' (see Del Valle and Gabriel-Stheeman, 'Nationalism') appears to be going decisively in favour of what might be seen as a continuing unity (or, sceptics would claim, renewed imperialism, apparently cultural though the objectives could also be considered economic, on the part of the mother country).[8] However, the modern standard is of an interestingly convergent kind. It is laid down, not just by the Spanish Real Academia Española (RAE), but by the Asociación de Academias de la Lengua Española (ASALE), a body comprising the Academies of all the 21 Spanish-speaking countries plus those of North America and the Philippines, which is enshrined in a common orthography, dictionary and grammar. This standard is officially polycentric, the principle being that the educated usage of any Spanish-speaking country is accepted as standard provided that it does not militate against the unity of the language. While this may ultimately turn out to be a utopian expectation, this may truly be viewed as a transnational aspiration, and Spanish stands high in global language rankings, being second or third in terms of the number of its native speakers, one of the working languages of the United Nations and the Security Council, the World Trade Organization and the Fédération Internationale de Football Association (FIFA).[9]

---

[6] José Del Valle, 'Lenguas imaginadas: Menéndez Pidal, la lingüística hispánica y la configuración del estándar', *Bulletin of Hispanic Studies*, 76 (1999), 215–233, and *Estudios de Lingüística del Español*, 16 (2002), <http://elies.rediris.es/elies16/Valle.html>, accessed 6 August 2016. Ramón Menéndez Pidal, 'La unidad del idioma', in *Castilla, la tradición, el idioma* (Madrid: Espasa-Calpe Argentina, 1945), pp. 171–218.

[7] Andrés Bello, *Gramática de la lengua castellana destinada al uso de los americanos* (1847), ed. by Ramón Trujillo (Santa Cruz de Tenerife: Instituto Universitario de Lingüística Andrés Bello/Cabildo Insular de Tenerife, 1981 [1847]), p. 129.

[8] See, for example, Clare Mar-Molinero and Darren J. Paffey, 'Linguistic imperialism: Who owns global Spanish?', in *The Handbook of Hispanic Sociolinguistics*, ed. by Manuel Díaz-Campos (Malden, MA and Oxford: Wiley-Blackwell, 2011), pp. 747–764.

[9] Christopher J. Pountain, *Exploring the Spanish Language. An Introduction to its Structures and Varieties*, 2nd edn (London and New York: Routledge, 2016), pp. 278–285.

Approaches to the History of Spanish

Traditional approaches to the history of languages have tended to militate against any transnational perspective. The 'family tree' model of language evolution encouraged concentration on processes of change that were purely internal to languages (since the whole rationale for the family tree was the comparative reconstruction of a proto-language on the basis of its extant descendants). The historical linguist's task was construed as identifying regular changes that operate consistently within a single language, the implication of which is that each language is self-contained and evolves according to its own dynamics. Some of the most influential accounts of the history of Castilian/Spanish essentially follow this method.[10] Somewhat opposed to this reconstructional approach was that of the dialectologists, who rapidly realised that it was not a straightforward matter to associate languages, or 'dialects', with a circumscribed geographical area, since isoglosses (boundaries between linguistic variants) do not always obligingly cluster together.[11] They were also able to show that some apparent exceptions to sound changes may be the result of what we can call transdialectal diffusion.

To this general background we must add the particular contribution of those linguists who opened up the historical study of Spanish and in so doing created a research tradition the effects of which are still felt to a certain extent today. Menéndez Pidal (1950) had what Fernández-Ordóñez refers to as a 'Castilian nationalist vision' that saw the language of Castile (essentially, the Romance of Cantabria) as exhibiting revolutionary features that distinguished it from neighbouring languages and then spreading southwards as a result of the political hegemony of Castile, so breaking the east–west Romance dialect continuum of the Peninsula like a wedge (*cuña*).[12] The history of Spanish therefore came to be seen as no more than the history of Castilian, and Castilian as simply the Romance of a well-defined geographical area. There is now a considerable body of evidence to suggest that Menéndez Pidal's 'nationalist' view of the origin and spread of Castilian was flawed, and that the true situation is much more complex, involving, on the one hand, original variation

---

[10] Ramón Menéndez Pidal, *Manual de gramática histórica española*, 11th edn (Madrid: Espasa-Calpe, 1962).

[11] An example of such a patterning of isoglosses in the north of the Iberian Peninsula is discussed in Pountain, *Exploring the Spanish Language*, p. 141.

[12] Inés Fernández-Ordóñez, 'Menéndez Pidal and the beginnings of Ibero-Romance dialectology: A critical survey one century later', in *Ramón Menéndez Pidal after Forty Years: A Reassessment*, pp. 111–144 (pp. 120–124). Ramón Menéndez Pidal, *Orígenes del español. Estado lingüístico de la Península Ibérica hasta el siglo XI*, 3rd edn (Madrid: Espasa-Calpe, 1950).

within the Romance of the Castilian area, and, on the other, the role of that ongoing variation in the formation of the national standard. Fernández-Ordóñez argues, on the basis of the examination of the full data from the *Atlas lingüístico de la Península Ibérica* project now available,[13] that 'there is no such thing as a uniform Castilian in many respects', and that the varieties of Old Castilian shared certain features with Astur-Leonese to the west and Navarro-Aragonese to the east, some of which were propagated directly towards the south ('Menéndez Pidal and the Beginnings', pp. 134–139).

It is also likely that transdialectal levelling took place at a number of crucial points in the definition of the standard language. The Castilian of the great corpus of texts emanating from the scriptoria of Alfonso X, which is often represented as the first attempt to standardise the language, is not straighforwardly identifiable with the Castilian of any one locality, because it is the result of collaboration by translators, glossers and redactors drawn from a number of areas.[14] Levelling also took place in the sixteenth century, in the wake of the influx of new settlers from all parts of Spain to the new capital, Madrid, and the consequent creation of a linguistic *koiné* there.[15] Some of the characteristics of Latin American Spanish could similarly be attributed to levelling among early settlers who were drawn from different parts of Spain (*Variation and Change*, pp. 142–144).

We may also question whether Castilian is really distinctive through linguistic innovation in the way that Menéndez Pidal saw it. A broader, transnational view of the Romance languages shows that even those features of Castilian development that might be thought of as 'innovative' because they are not shared with Castile's immediate geographical neighbours are not especially unusual when viewed in the context of general tendencies in language change, and can even be found in more distantly related Romance languages. The so-called 'f>h' change, that is to say, the conversion of initial Latin /f/ in many contexts to /h/ and the subsequent loss of /h/ (for example, Lat. FOLĬA > Sp. *hoja*), indeed gives several Castilian words a dramatically different phonological form from that of their neighbouring cognates (cf. Fr. *feuille*, Pg. *folha*, Cat. *full*). But while this development may be considered distinctive within the

---

[13] David Heap, *Atlas lingüístico de la Península Ibérica. ALPI searchable database* (London and Ontario: University of Western Ontario, 2003), <http://westernlinguistics.ca/alpi/>, accessed 21 June 2017.

[14] Inés Fernández Ordóñez, 'Alfonso X el Sabio en la historia del español', in Rafael Cano, *Historia de la lengua española*, 2nd edn (Barcelona: Ariel, 2005), pp. 381–422.

[15] Ralph Penny, *Variation and Change in Spanish* (Cambridge: Cambridge University Press, 2000), pp. 42–48. *Koiné* is a standard language or dialect resulting from contact between mutually intelligible varieties of the same language.

Iberian Peninsula and among other national standard Romance languages, it also features in Gascon, where the descendant of FOLIA is *hoélhe*, and there are several areas of Italo-Romance in which a similar change has taken place.[16] When we adopt a comparative, transnational, perspective, we can see that the Castilian f>h change is by no means unique to Castilian and is a natural phonetic development of lenition, or consonantal weakening.

Lexical Borrowing

The international dimension of lexical borrowing has always been apparent and is universally acknowledged. But although in etymological dictionaries foreign loanwords are usually attributed to a specific source, that of the language to which they originally belonged, we may often suspect that some of these words had a transnational currency, since they are borrowed not only into Spanish but into many other languages, bringing about a degree of convergence between different languages. Nowhere is this clearer than in present-day borrowings from English: not only does English *telephone* provide the model for Spanish *teléfono*, but this word is paralleled in many other languages (and not only European languages).[17] We may suspect that the same is true of much earlier borrowings, although a precise trajectory of borrowing is often difficult to establish. For example, Ar. *sukkar* is the origin not only of Spanish *azúcar* and Portuguese *açúcar*, but is also generalised throughout Western Europe (cf. It. *zucchero*, Fr. *sucre*, Cat. *sucre*, Eng. *sugar*, Germ. *Zucker* and, for that matter, Medieval Latin *zucharum*). Since sugarcane was grown by the Arabs in Sicily and in the Iberian Peninsula, we may surmise that the Romance languages of these regions were the primary borrowers, and that the more northerly areas adapted the word from Italian, given that the Spanish and Portuguese borrowings are distinctively characterised by the incorporation of the initial Arabic definite article into the noun itself (here *as-*).[18] None the less, since the need for this borrowing was universal, it can be thought of in its various manifestations as a 'transnational' word.[19]

---

[16] Gerhard Rohlfs, *Grammatica Storica della Lingua Italiana e dei suoi Dialetti. Fonetica*, trans. by Salvatore Persichino (Turin: Einaudi, 1966), p. 206.

[17] See the entry for *telephone* in the *OED. Oxford English Dictionary* (<http://www.oed.com>, accessed 21 November 2016).

[18] See the discussions in *OED* under *sugar* and in *TLF* under *sucre*. *Trésor de la Langue Française informatisée* (Paris: CNRS Editions, 2004) and at <http://atilf.atilf.fr>, accessed 4 October 2016.

[19] The picture is complicated by the fact that the Arabic word is a borrowing itself from an Indian source, also reflected in (Classical) Lat. *saccharum*, Gk. σάκχαρον, Russ. *caxap*.

This transnational dimension of some loanwords assumes considerable importance in tracing the history of what are usually termed 'learnèd' lexical borrowings (*cultismos*, in Spanish) in the languages of Western Europe. The extent of contact between the vernaculars and the Latin that continued in active use as a language of the Roman Catholic Church, in academic and scientific contexts, and as a language of international diplomacy is often underestimated.[20] In the case of the Romance languages, it is important to distinguish the 'learnèd' impact of Latin from the 'popular' inheritance of the Latin from which these languages evolved in the first place. A simple indication of this distinction is the existence of doublet developments of Latin words, such as Lat. ARTĬCŬLU(M), which in Spanish has both the popular derivative *artejo* – 'knuckle' and the learnèd derivative *artículo* – 'article'. While the popular word has a physical meaning close to that of Latin – 'a small member connecting various parts of the body', the *cultismo* has the more abstract meaning associated with Latin 'part, division'. *Artículo* is almost certainly the result of imitation of Latin legal language,[21] and the impact of its borrowing is substantial: it has now significantly widened its meaning to include such general references as 'item of trade', 'section of a book or newspaper', and is much more common than *artejo*. But this process has transnational dimensions: there are parallel borrowings, with much the same extended meanings, in other languages too, which suggest a global development rather than a series of independent changes (compare Fr. *article*, It. *articolo*, Eng. *article*, Ger. *Artikel*).

The Interaction of Spanish with Other Languages

The final dimension of transnational contact to which I want to draw attention is the result of scenarios in which Spanish has been an input in the creation of new languages. The nature and status of such languages have often been misunderstood because they appear to be 'imperfect' forms of Spanish, but this attitude has largely been rectified and their study has become an important part of the history of Spanish.

---

[20] See Christopher J. Pountain, 'Latin and the structure of written Romance', in *The Cambridge History of the Romance Languages. Volume I: Structures*, ed. by Martin Maiden, John Charles Smith and Adam Ledgeway (Cambridge: Cambridge University Press, 2011), pp. 606–659.

[21] A common phrase in Latin legal documents of the northern Iberian Peninsula was *nec suadentis articulo* – 'nor with the instruction of anyone persuading [us]'. See Wendy Davies, *Windows on Justice in Northern Iberia, 800–1000* (London: Routledge, 2016), p. 142.

Creoles

The three best-known languages that are commonly referred to as Spanish creoles are the Papiamentu/Papiamento of Curaçao and Aruba, the Palenquero of El Palenque de San Basilio, Colombia and the Chabacano of Zamboanga in the Philippines. From the transnational point of view, what is significant about creoles is the number of languages that have contributed in various ways and at various times to their formation, and in this respect these three creoles are all different. Their base is generally thought to be the creation of a system of communication among slaves from many different parts of Africa and speaking many different languages who needed to communicate with both their masters and one another. This incipient lingua franca or pidgin then passed down the generations within their new communities as a native language, with words progressively supplied (a process known as lexification) by various languages. Palenquero was in origin the language of a group of slaves who escaped from Cartagena (Colombia) in 1603 and created a settlement in the remote interior, which became a haven for other runaways.[22] It was therefore mainly lexicalised by Spanish, and its speakers (now rapidly declining in number) are situated in an otherwise Spanish-speaking environment. The processes that produced Chabacano are more obviously complex,[23] and its subsequent lexification was by Malay, Spanish and Tagalog. Papiamentu, the most successful of these creoles in terms of the degree of its establishment as an *Ausbau* language, superficially looks the most like Spanish, but this is due to extensive further lexification from Spanish as the *Ausbau* process has progressed, since this creole is used extensively in the media and in official contexts. Historically, the fact that Papiamentu has been used in an officially Dutch-speaking environment since the seventeenth century has been the reason for a good deal of lexification by Dutch in addition to Portuguese and Spanish, and even some borrowing of Dutch grammatical features (Papiamentu is unusual among creoles in having a passive verb-form, for instance); the importance of the islands in international trade has also led to some borrowings from other languages.

Creoles are unambiguously new languages: they have a significantly different grammatical structure from that of their lexifying languages; there is no mutual intelligibility between a creole and its lexifying languages, and the creole-speaking community has a sense of distinctive linguistic identity.

---

[22] See the classic account by D. Bickerton and A. Escalante, 'Palenquero: A Spanish-based creole of northern Colombia', *Lingua*, 24 (1970), 254–267.
[23] See Keith Whinnom, *Spanish Contact Vernaculars in the Philippine Islands* (London: Hong Kong University Press and Oxford University Press, 1956), pp. 1–17.

Interference and Code-switching

Societal bilingualism occurs in areas where another language survives strongly: in the Spanish-speaking world this is the case especially in Catalonia, Galicia and the Basque Country in Spain, in many areas of Central and South America where indigenous languages continue to be used, and in the United States, where English is the dominant language. It may give rise to 'interference' between one language and another, which may take place on a number of levels, not just lexical. For example, in the Spanish of Catalonia, the future indicative rather than the present subjunctive is sometimes used in future-referring temporal clauses (*Cuando vendrás, iremos al cine*) rather than standard *Cuando vengas, iremos al cine*.[24] In such societies, oscillation between one language and another (code-switching) may also take place. This is very clear in the code-switching that takes place between Spanish and English in the US, which has been very extensively studied.

Can this kind of contact give rise to what might be regarded as a new language? In the case of contact between Spanish and English in the US, there is certainly no shortage of both wishful thinking and disapproving assumption that this is likely. Here, almost any kind of English borrowing, interference of English in Spanish, or code-switching between the two languages is referred to as *Spanglish/espanglish*, the latter being the term approved by the *DLE*,[25] while strenuous opposition to the practice of *Spanglish/espanglish* has come from the language regulators, who see it as a significant threat to what is perceived as the unity of Spanish, thus ironically giving credence to the notion of *Spanglish/espanglish* as a breakaway language.[26]

However, we must immediately distinguish two quite different phenomena. First, we can identify what might be referred to as 'linear code-switching' of the kind evidenced in the title of Poplack's landmark study, 'Sometimes I'll start a sentence in English Y TERMINO EN ESPAÑOL', where the two languages

---

[24] José Luis Blas Arroyo, 'El español actual en las comunidades del ámbito lingüístico catalán', in *Historia de la lengua española*, pp. 1065–1086 (p. 1075).

[25] On the undiscriminating use of this term, see Ricardo Otheguy, 'Espanglish', in *Enciclopedia lingüística hispánica*, ed. by Javier Gutiérrez-Rexach (London: Routledge, 2016), pp. 454–462. Real Academia Española, *Diccionario de la lengua española*, 23rd edn (Madrid: Espasa, 2014), abbreviated *DLE*, and <http://www.rae.es/obrasacademicas/diccionarios/diccionario-de-la-lengua-espanola>, accessed 31 July 2017.

[26] See José Del Valle, 'US Latinos, la hispanofonía, and the language ideologies of high modernity', in *Globalization and the Spanish-speaking World: Macro and Micro Perspectives*, ed. by Clare Mar-Molinero and Miranda Stewart (Basingstoke: Palgrave Macmillan, 2006), pp. 27–46.

are clearly being used alternately. It is now fairly conclusively established that speakers who engage in code-switching are confident speakers of both languages.[27] Second, in the Spanish of the US there has been more extensive integrated borrowing from English into Spanish than in many other areas of the Spanish-speaking world, as exemplified in the much-quoted sentence *Se me laqueó la troca* – 'I've locked myself out of my truck',[28] where Eng. *lock* and *truck* have been incorporated into Spanish and given Spanish morphological forms. Neither *laquear* (with this meaning) nor *troca* appear in the *DLE*; hence, they are not regarded as part of standard Spanish. However, we can easily see that they are not code-switches into English but have been fully integrated into Spanish. Their spelling indicates a pronunciation and morphology that conforms to Spanish: the American English /ɒː/ of *lock* has been adapted as Spanish /a/ in *laquear*, and the word has been given the verbal suffix *-ear* to turn it into a regular Spanish *-ar* verb; *truck*, as well as showing more significant modification of its vowel (American English /ʌ/ to Spanish /o/) in *troca*, has been assigned to the feminine gender (probably due to the parallel with the existing *camioneta*) and given the gender inflection *-a*. *Laquear* has the completely Spanish syntax of being used reflexively with an indirect object to indicate an accidental action, rendering what is actually quite a difficult notion to express in standard Spanish (the gloss originally given was 'la camioneta se quedó cerrada con las llaves adentro'); but the construction is not modelled on English, which treats *truck* as the object of the complex preposition *out of* (in Spanish, *troca* is actually the subject of *laquearse*).

Hispanic writers have envisaged *Spanglish/espanglish* as constituting a new language that is a symbol of Hispanic identity (*Exploring the Spanish Language*, pp. 267–268). There has also been cultivation of code-switching 'bilingual' poetry by US Hispanic poets since the 1960s,[29] and a number of popular Hispanic singers (for example, Ricky Martin, Shakira) code-switch in their lyrics:

> There's a lot of things
> That I'd do to please you

---

[27] Shana Poplack, 'Sometimes I'll start a sentence in English Y TERMINO EN ESPAÑOL: Toward a typology of code-switching', *Linguistics*, 18 (1980), 581–618 (p. 615). Ana Celia Zentella, 'Spanish and English in contact in the United States: The Puerto Rican experience', *Word*, 33 (1982), 41–57 (p. 47).

[28] <http://news.bbc.co.uk/hi/spanish/misc/newsid_4002000/4002783.stm>, accessed 10 July 2011.

[29] *Chicanos: Antología histórica y literaria*, ed. by Tino Villanueva (Mexico City: Fondo de Cultura Económica, 1980), pp. 53–54.

> Take you to the medico por el caminito
> They saw your girlfriend looking for me with a rifle
> 'Cause we're dancin' Mambo
> Oh, what she don't allow it?
> (https://genius.com/Shakira-loca-english-version-lyrics, accessed 11 April 2018)

One of the leading apologists for this position, Ilan Stavans, notoriously produced an exaggerated artificial version of the beginning of *Don Quijote* 'in *Spanglish*', which may be seen to be a mixture of code-switching and the extensive use of integrated borrowings (the glossary in this book is undiscriminating between those borrowings that are particular to US Spanish and anglicisms that have been more widely accepted into Spanish):

> In un placete de La Mancha of which nombre no quiero remembrearme, vivía, not so long ago, uno de esos gentlemen who always tienen una lanza in the rack, una buckler antigua, a skinny caballo y un greyhound para el chase.[30]

Code-switching therefore certainly represents a new mode of expression, but because it consists of extensive movement between one language and another that takes place for a multiplicity of reasons (the mood of the speaker, the need to accommodate to others, originality, playfulness, expressiveness and so on), it does not constitute a stable form, and so cannot be defined and codified (and hence learned) as a language.

However, if we are to consider *Spanglish/espanglish* as a variety of Spanish that has many more integrated borrowings from English than other varieties of Spanish, and a degree of interference from English that has affected phraseology and even morphology and syntax, then there is more of a case for thinking that a new language is likely to be created.[31] Although the United States has by some reckonings the fifth largest number of native

---

[30] Ilan Stavans, *Spanglish. The Making of a New American Language* (New York: Rayo, 2003), p. 253.

[31] Ricardo Otheguy and Ana Celia Zentella, 'Apuntes preliminares sobre el contacto lingüístico y dialectal en el uso pronominal del español en Nueva York', in *Spanish in Contact: Policy, Social and Linguistic Inquiries*, ed. by Kim Potowski and Richard Cameron (Amsterdam: Benjamins, 2007), pp. 275–295; Michelle L. Salazar, 'Está muy diferente a como era antes. *Ser* and *Estar* + adjective in New Mexico Spanish', in *Spanish in Contact: Policy, Social and Linguistic Inquiries*, pp. 343–353. Carmen Silva-Corvalán, 'Bilingualism and language change: The extension of *estar* in Los Angeles Spanish', *Language*, 62 (1986), 587–608.

Spanish speakers of the countries of the world, Spanish does not have official status, there is no regional standard as in other Spanish-speaking countries and it is not the language of the majority of citizens. Quite apart from the quantitative differences in terms of the borrowings and interference from English that already exist, how US Spanish is regarded by the wider Spanish-speaking world, and how firmly US Spanish speakers remain connected to this world, are critical factors in the future unity of Spanish. There are already some signs of a break: Urciuoli observed that US Spanish heritage speakers studying Spanish at school, where the Mexican standard is generally followed, end up as diglossic and regard the language spoken at home as inferior.[32] And in the history of Spanish we do have a striking example of what happens when the language loses contact with the broader linguistic community: Judeo-Spanish, the Spanish of late fifteenth-century Spain that was taken into exile with the Jews who were expelled from Spain in 1492 and settled in many other countries around the Mediterranean and eventually further afield. Judeo-Spanish is different in many respects from the Spanish of the rest of the world, not only because of the loanwords it took from the communities with which it came into contact, but because it has both survivals and innovations of its own that set it apart (see *Exploring the Spanish Language*, pp. 233–241). The status of US Spanish is thus likely to remain a burning transnational question.

Hybridisation

Despite the foregoing, a clear distinction between code-switching and what may be regarded as a genuine hybrid language is not always easy to draw. There is one apparently very clear example of a hybrid in which Spanish participates: the case of Media Lengua, described by Muysken, which is spoken in Salcedo, Ecuador, and is a hybrid of Spanish and Quechua.[33] In this language, the morphology and syntax is Quechua, but the lexis is Spanish; this is a systematic, stable feature of the language, and there is no linear alternation between the two languages as in code-switching:

---

[32] Bonnie Urciuoli, 'Whose Spanish? The tension between linguistic correctness and cultural identity', in *Bilingualism and Identity. Spanish at the Crossroads with Other Languages*, ed. by Mercedes Niño-Murcia and Jason Rothman (Amsterdam: Benjamins, 2008), pp. 257–277.
[33] Pieter Muysken, 'Media Lengua', in *Contact Languages: A Wider Perspective*, ed. by Sarah G. Thomason (Amsterdam and Philadelphia: Benjamins, 1997), pp. 365–426.

Media Lengua:	*unu*	*fabur-ta*	*pidi-nga-bu*	*bini-xu-ni*
Quechua:	*shuk*	*fabur-da*	*maña-nga-bu*	*shamu-xu-ni*
	one	favour	ask	come
		accusative	nominaliser	progressive
			benefactive	1st person singular
Spanish:		'Vengo a pedir un favor'		

('Media Lengua', p. 366)

Some of the older speakers of Media Lengua do not, in fact, speak Spanish, in contrast to the typical code-switching scenario in which speakers are bilingual in the two languages involved. On the other hand, another language that is often regarded as a hybrid, the *fronteiriço* of Uruguay, described by Elizaincín, is not so straightforward. In *fronteiriço*, switches between features of Spanish and Portuguese are very frequent, and can even take place within a word (so a form such as *chegó* shows the Portuguese lexical stem *cheg-* 'arrive' combined with the Spanish verb inflection *-ó*).[34] But as in code-switching in the US, the mixing is not systematic (for a detailed commentary on a sample of *fronteiriço* (see Pountain, *Exploring the Spanish Language*, p. 272), and *fronteiriço* cannot be codified as a stable language; Bottaro concludes that it is on a par with the 'interlanguage' that is characteristic of learners of a foreign language.[35] We can be even less certain about the status of some other potential hybrids we know to have existed in the past, especially since our knowledge derives largely from texts that are creative or playful in nature and almost certainly exaggerate the switching between languages. The massive influx of Italian immigrants to Argentina, and specifically to Buenos Aires, in the late nineteenth century and early twentieth, gave rise to a language known as *cocoliche*, a mixture of Spanish and Italian, which is today known to us mainly through the popular theatre of the time, where it was generally used as a source of humour, and was no doubt represented in a stereotypical, exaggerated way, and through some residue in present-day *lunfardo*, the 'slang' of Buenos Aires, which also has a presence in tango lyrics. Cancellier asks the interesting question of what *cocoliche* is <u>not</u>: *cocoliche* did not have a stable structure and so cannot be thought of as a variety of either Spanish or Italian (in this it is like *fronteiriço*); it is not a pidgin, since the two languages

---

[34] Adolfo Elizaincín, *Dialectos en contacto: español y portugués en España y América* (Montevideo: Arca, 1992).

[35] Silvia Etel Gutiérrez Bottaro, *O Contínuo Linguístico na Região Fronteiriça Brasil-Uruguai* (Master's thesis, University of São Paulo, 2002). Also available as Ebook Kindle at <https://www.amazon.com.br/contínuo-linguístico-região-fronteiriça-Brasil-ebook/dp/B017BPRQQC>, accessed 1 April 2020.

on which it is based are largely mutually intelligible, and it did not serve as a mother tongue to a community, as a creole can.[36] Following Ferguson and DeBose, she calls it a 'broken language'.[37]

Conclusions

There are a number of dimensions of the history of Spanish that inescapably involve engagement with a transnational dimension: the development of Spanish as a diasporic language with a consequent global importance; the nature of its unity as a speech community and the threats, actual and potential, to that unity, and the ways in which Spanish has interacted with other languages with which its speakers have come into contact, as a host language, a lending language or as a contributor to the formation of new languages. At the same time, some of the traditional assumptions about the history of Spanish and the nature of language change are ripe for re-evaluation from a transnational perspective: the reality of the continuum of development between the Romance of Castile and the national language of Spain and its empire, the precise origins of foreign loanwords and the complementarity of 'internal' and 'external' factors involved in language change.

---

[36] Antonella Cancellier, 'Italiano e spagnolo a contatto nel Rio de la Piata, I fenomeni del «cocoliche» e del «lunfardo»', in *Atti del XIX Convegno [Associazione ispanisti italiani]*: ed. by Antonella Cancellier and Renata Londero (Roma, 16–18 settembre 1999), Vol. 2 (Italiano e spagnolo a contatto), pp. 69–84, pp. 78–80. See <cvc.cervantes.es/literatura/aispi/pdf/14/14_073.pdf>, accessed 1 July 2017.

[37] Charles A. Ferguson and Charles E. DeBose, 'Simplified registers, broken language, and pidginization', in *Pidgin and Creole Linguistics*, ed. by A. Valdman (Bloomington, IN: Indiana University Press, 1977), pp. 99–125.

2

Arabic in the Iberian Peninsula

L. P. Harvey

The seventh century CE (Common Era or AD) saw that great move out from the Arabian Peninsula that took Islam, its culture and language, into the lands of the Fertile Crescent (Phoenicia, Assyria and Mesopotamia) to Palestine, Egypt and beyond, and with that culture spread the language of Allah's revelation, Arabic, which became the predominant language of the whole region. By the early eighth century the Islamic caliphate that had been established was in a position to expand further, beyond its already impressive conquests, both eastwards (into what is now Iran), and to the north-west, across from North Africa into the Iberian Peninsula. In both directions the invaders carried with them their language and their sacred text, the Qur'an, and in the conquered territories they encountered non-Semitic languages and cultures.

In the East there emerged relatively early, from the contact of Arabic with one of the Indo-European languages in use, a hybrid speech that contained a very high proportion of Arabic words in its vocabulary but the structural framework of which was still recognizably Indo-European. The original Indo-European pre-existing languages faded away and were replaced by this immensely successful new hybrid, predecessor of the Farsi (Persian) of today's Iran, one of the great languages of the Islamic cultural domain and itself the parent of, for example, the Urdu of the Indian sub-continent.

To the West, however, the outcome of that clash was quite different even though the dominant language that existed before the arrival of Arabic was Latin-based Indo-European. The dominant language did not become one single hybrid as in Persia (Iran). For Muslims in the Iberian Peninsula Arabic thrived, adopting only a relatively small number of Romance (Latin-derived) loanwords. In al-Andalus (the Muslim name for Roman Hispania), Arabic emerged both as a commonly spoken vernacular and as the predominant language of culture, whereas in many Christian communities (especially those of the northern fringe, Galicia, Asturias and Catalonia, for example) new Latin-based Romance vernaculars emerged. These might contain some loanwords picked up from the Arabic-speaking conquerors of most of the peninsula, but they continued to be in both grammatical structure and core vocabulary Romance languages (Galician, Castilian, Catalan and so on). The majority of the Islamic invaders of the very early period (the eighth century) were not in fact native Arabic-speakers (they were North African Berbers), with Arabic speakers flooding in slightly later. Arabic, however, came to predominate as the language of the rulers of the Iberian Peninsula. Al-Andalus thus became and continued for centuries to be in its culture an integral part of the Islamic world. One factor that anchored it there effectively was the obligation on all Muslims to go on Pilgrimage to Mecca if they could afford to do so. Clearly a majority never managed to fulfil this obligation, but Mecca remained a centre of the society's focus and served to anchor the society of al-Andalus in the Arabic speech domain. Al-Andalus remained predominantly Arabic-speaking throughout its long, five-hundred-year history, from the eighth to the thirteenth century predominantly, and in some regions (the kingdoms of Valencia and Granada) up until the expulsion of Muslims in 1609.

The sort of linguistic hybrid that flourished in the East (in the literature of outstanding masters, such as the Persian poet Ferdawsi), did not appear until much later in the far West. Among Christians, both for literary purposes and in forms of written expression, Latin predominated until it began to be supplemented for some non-ecclesiastical and secular purposes by the various Romance vernaculars. Thus, the two source cultures, Latin and Arabic, remained unmerged. Alongside the Arabic of the mosques and administration and some regions of the countryside, but separate from it, there subsisted and flourished the Romance dialects that were emerging from Latin, first for spoken purposes, and only later for use in writing. Latin unalloyed continued to function at least until the end of the Middle Ages for all serious written purposes, and beyond that up to the twenty-first century in some churches where it is not yet completely dead.

Alvarus of Cordova and the Martyrs at Cordova
(Christians in al-Andalus)

We know little about the speech of the Christians who lived in al-Andalus under Muslim rule (referred to as Mozarabs or 'Arabised'). Fortunately, we have one reliable piece of evidence: the text in the *Indiculus Luminosus*

(Shining Example) by Alvarus of Cordova (c.800–861), an author highly critical of the readiness of some of his co-religionists to embrace the culture of their religious enemies. In late ninth-century Cordoba some 48 Mozarabic Christians were executed by the Caliphal authorities, a sure indication of political and cultural conflict. The writings of the Christian polemicists who treat the subject, besides Alvarus, provide us with striking evidence of the stresses that were generated as the Arabic-language culture of the Islamic conquerors came up against the Latin-based culture of the Christian population. Nothing equally informative is available from other contemporary sources. In his *Indiculus Luminosus*, Alvarus inveighs against the readiness of the Christian youth of his congregation to adopt Arab ways and the Arabic language and to neglect the culture of their forebears:

> [There are] Christian youths, outstanding in status, eloquent, well-bred in their manners, stylish in their dress, who are accomplished in the scholarship of the Gentiles [here to be interpreted as 'Muslims'], notable for their knowledge of the Arabic language, and who devote themselves most keenly to the works of the Chaldeans [to be interpreted here as 'Arabs'], who read these texts with the closest attention, discuss them most avidly, are keen book collectors , going on to disseminate them to all and sundry, yet on the other hand they are ignorant of the language of the Church, and hold in contempt as below them those sources that spring from Paradise. Woe upon us! Christians who do not know their own religion! Latins who do not understand their own language! So much is this the case that in the community of Christians it is difficult to find just one man among four thousand who would be able to write a letter to his fellow in grammatical Latin. Yet very many are capable of explaining the rhetorical subtleties of the Arabs, and are better at versifying than [the Arabs] would be.[1]

It is easy to write off this passage from the *Indiculus luminosus* as a venerable sage sounding off at the feckless youth of his times, but for all its exaggeration the passage tells us that Arabic and Islamic culture were making significant

---

[1] *Corpus scriptorum mozarabicorum*, ed. by Juan Gil, 2 vols (Madrid: Antonio de Nebrija, 1973), Vol. I, pp. 55–124; *IL CSM* I, pp. 314–315 (author's translation). See also Kenneth Baxter Wolf, 'Muhammad as anti-Christ in ninth-century Cordoba', in *Christians, Muslims, and Jews in Medieval and Early Modern Spain: Interaction and Cultural Change*, ed. by Mark D. Meyerson and Edward D. English (Notre Dame, IN: University of Notre Dame Press, 2000), pp. 11–21.

inroads into what had once been the exclusive cultural territory of the Christian Church.

The complex events associated with the ninth-century outbreak of voluntary martyrdoms in Cordoba are so interesting and unusual that it is tempting to allocate them more space than they merit. There were no more than 48 martyrs executed by the *qadi*'s (magistrate's) swordsman, compared with the many hundreds who perished on both sides in the various campaigns and warfare of the period. However, an understanding of the circumstances of the martyrdoms is necessary for this period. As is well known, Islam in general and the Islam of al-Andalus explicitly grants toleration to Christians (although not to pagans or free-thinkers), but that toleration differs fundamentally from what we in the West mean by the word today. Such toleration does not imply equal treatment. This is made clear by the fact that Christians, although privileged in that they were permitted to remain alive, whereas other non-Muslims such as pagans were not, were first and foremost subject to a discriminatory annual tax, the *jizya*, payment of which entailed an additional humiliating ceremony. Muslims of course were exempt. This differential legislation may be defended if one bears in mind that the Muslims had to pay a different tax, the *kharaj*, while others did not, and that Muslims were liable to military service, others not. The general theme of such provisions of the Islamic law, the *shari'a*, is that Christians are always to be placed in a lower or less advantaged position, symbolically and in reality, so that a Christian might not ride on a horse while a Muslim walked, should not wear superior-grade clothing and so on. A mosque was expected loudly to summon folk to prayer, but churches might not sound their bells to summon the Christian faithful and new churches might not be built where there had been none before, whereas building a new mosque anywhere was an unambiguously meritorious action. In terms of personal relations, a Christian girl might marry a Muslim, but a Muslim girl was very firmly forbidden to marry a non-Muslim. A variant on the proposition that Islam must always come out on top arose in the case of converts *from* Islam, theoretically an utter impossibility of course, but it happened nevertheless. This led to only one legal outcome: classification as a traitor to the faith and so conviction for apostasy and therefore death. What was offered to the Mozarabic *dhimmi* (protected subject) was thus a very partial toleration, a second-class toleration. Unsurprisingly, this arrangement was resented but had nevertheless to be silently accepted without complaint by those Christians who wished to live as Christians in this society.

How the Christian 'martyr movement' came to emerge in Cordoba from merely a widespread feeling of resentment to the open voicing of discordant views is not known with certainty. Some Christian clerics in the Cordoba area, such as one Speraindeo, an abbot from the parish of Santa Clara, must have voiced in sermons a Christianity that was less flexible and some of the faithful began to act on such teaching by speaking ill in public against Islam and against its Prophet. If in an open *qadi*'s court an individual charged with 'apostasy' was to repeat his offence and publicly curse the Prophet, that placed the judge in an awkward situation. The law was quite specific: the 'apostate' should be beheaded (as we see on TV news today). After consulting the Caliph himself, one *qadi*, in a vain manoeuvre to arrive at a more merciful outcome, ruled that the offender must be insane (so not liable to capital punishment), but these Christian enthusiasts were determined to show their faith, not hide it. Escape was not that simple. The most severe part of the wave of martyrdoms lasted only ten years, and after 859 none are recorded, although this does not mean the protest movement was extinguished. We should bear in mind the paucity of sources, but with the execution of the 48 enthusiasts in the previous decade perhaps the Caliphal authorities managed to stifle what was no more than a minor protest movement.

Mozarabs elsewhere do not seem to have been moved to protest. It will be recalled that Alvarus had complained of the extent of acculturation, but he would be thinking of the urban Cordoba of his day; few of the protesters mentioned are identifiable as say mere field-labourers. Was the wave of 'voluntary martyrdoms' a phenomenon limited to the Mozarabic urban middle-class? The martyrs were not all men. Two young women, Flora and Maria, were jailed on the same day and both were put to death on 24 November 851. Although both were guilty of scandalously and publicly rejecting Islam, in Islamic law their cases were quite distinct. One, Maria, came from a devout Christian background, for we know her brother, Walabonsus, had been executed earlier. Flora, however, was from a mixed family – her father was Muslim and her mother Christian – and when she first appeared in court, her brother tried (unsuccessfully) to persuade her to retract. Flora's case reminds us that in practice a few individuals, in spite of the explicit provisions of the *shari'a*, did convert in the 'wrong' direction, *from* rather than to Islam. There were other martyrs of both sexes who followed these examples.

Evidence of a different kind operating in the opposite direction, that is to say evidence of the Christian penetration of Islamic culture, is to be found in the Arabic poetry of the newly created society of al-Andalus. Fragmentary but unambiguous indications of the impact of Romance models on compositions in Arabic shows that popular songs in the Romance vernacular were appreciated and even incorporated by Hispano-Arabic poets into their verse. But first it is necessary to briefly refer to the Arabic literary forms that existed in al-Andalus and that received such non-Arabic influences. The Holy Qur'an in the Arabic language was the pre-eminent text for all to study, to which might be added the prose literature associated with Islamic Studies: the Prophet's biography (*sira*) and so on. The early poetry of the pre-Islamic period, however, somehow escaped the ban that the pious wished to see applied to the culture of the *jahiliyya* ('ignorance', that is, pre-Islamic lore). The great Arab (and Arabian) poems of that early period were part of the culture of the well-educated man who would know by heart the works of pagan poets such as Imru'l Qais and Labid. The predominant form of this early poetry was the *qasida*, which is what Islamic Spain inherited as its Classical poetic model. The *qasida* was built on strict quantitative metres and repeated the same rhyme at the end of each line (perhaps 50 or more). The structure of the subject-matter was also governed by strict tradition, such as the convention of the nostalgic evocation by the pseudo 'Beduin' poet of the abandoned desert camp-site bringing memories of his beloved in better times. Some writers, born on the Iberian Peninsula, belong to the whole Arabic-speaking world. One such as Ibn Hazm of Cordova.

Ibn Hazm of Cordova (994–1064)
(Arabic Literature in al-Andalus)

Ibn Hazm's opus contains a great variety of material, all of it of the highest quality (about 40 books are extant but there was clearly very much more, although the figure of 400 books is difficult to accept). He wrote with authority on many erudite subjects, law, medicine, theology, some in multi-volume works any one of which would have secured his lasting reputation. An indication of the range of his work is the book *Al-Fisal*, which studies the belief system of the Hindus (Brahmans), Zoroastrians, Jews, Christians, religions and sects. But there is no doubt that his fame in modern times has been won by a charming treatise entitled *Tawq al-Hamamah* (c.1022) (The Dove's Neck-ring) with the subtitle 'Of Love and Lovers'. It deals with aspects of love systematically without being in the least exhausting. The general pattern in each of the 28 chapters is to open with a short analytical paragraph. In 'On Separation', for example, the poet points out that for the lover separation can occur even if the beloved is under the same roof, if access is denied. These reflective or analytical sections are broken up by passages in verse, translated from the Arabic with great charm by A. J. Arberry:

> In every minute of each hour
> To view her house is in my power,
> But she who in the house resides
> Eternally unseen abides.

What does this close propinquity
Of residences profit me,
Since spies are posted to forestall
My drawing nigh to her at all?

Alas, sweet neighbour dwelling near,
Whose every footstep I can hear,
And yet am conscious that Cathay
Itself is not so far away![2]

Another way in which Ibn Hazm varies his presentation in addition to his verses are the frequent prose passages of personal reminiscence. A good example is his chapter entitled 'On Falling in Love while Asleep'. He reports that a friend said to him,

> An extraordinary thing has happened to me, the like of which I have never heard [...]. Last night [...] I saw in a dream a young maiden, and on awaking I found that I had completely lost my heart to her, and that I was madly in love with her. Now I am in the most difficult straits possible, with this passion I have conceived for her.

This friend continued afflicted for more than a month; nothing would cheer him up. 'It is a vast mistake to occupy your soul with something unreal', Ibn Hazm tells his friend in reproof, 'you have very little judgment, -- if you are actually in love with a person whom you have never seen and does not exist in the world at all'. He continues, 'his case is to be explained as a pure fantasy of the mind and falls into the category of mental hallucination. I have expressed this situation actually in verse [...]' (*The Ring of the Dove*, pp. 24–25).

Ibn Hazm came from a distinguished family, part of the élite of the caliphal court in Cordoba, but in 1013 his privileged world was disrupted by the civil war launched by disgruntled Berber soldiery and he sought refuge elsewhere. The Caliphate descended rapidly into the chaos of the period we know as that of the Taifa Kings. The reports that Ibn Hazm knew 60 scholars who were put to the sword at this time might be well founded.

---

[2] Ibn Hazm, *The Ring of the Dove: A Treatise on the Art and Practice of Arab Love*, trans. by A. J. Arberry (London: Luzac Oriental, 1994 [1951]), p. 94. See also A. J. Arberry, *Aspects of Islamic Civilization: As Depicted in the Original Texts* (Abingdon: Routledge Library Editions-Islam, 1964); *El collar de la paloma: tratado sobre el amor y los amantes de Ibn Hazm de Córdoba*, ed. and trans. by Emilio García Gómez with prologue by José Ortega y Gasset (Madrid: El libro del bolsillo, 1997 [1952]).

That he was able in his *Tawq* to write in the same tone about both homosexual and heterosexual affairs has given rise to a false interpretation of his morals in the West. He is quite explicit in his condemnation of 'the sin of Lut', sodomy, but equally he condemns adulterous heterosexual conduct, everything the Qur'an condemns. His reading of Scripture is strict and literal, directed against 'The Vileness of Sin', and his approach is not in the least 'liberal'. There is clearly a risk in modern times that Ibn Hazm's independent viewpoint will be misunderstood and that he will be adopted as a prophet of some new morality. Such a reading is in my opinion misguided. It may be the view held by the cataloguers of the U.S. Library of Congress, who place Ibn Hazm alongside such established writers as Havelock Ellis, Kinsey and others. He does not belong in their company.

One feature that marks him off from many authors in al-Andalus and the Middle East is his sympathetic understanding of the situation of women and girls. He is aware that his attitudes are special. He explains this by telling us he had an unusual upbringing, largely confined to the harem: 'I have observed women at first hand and am acquainted with their secrets to an extent that nobody else could claim – I grew up among them and I knew no-one but them'. He continues, 'Women taught me the Koran, they recited to me much poetry; they trained me in calligraphy' (Arberry, 1964, p. 165). Although he was widely praised for aspects of his theological writings, his work was viewed by some with mistrust and even burnt. By the time he wrote his compendious *Kitab al-fisal fi'l-milal wa'l-ahwa'* (Book on Creeds and Sects) he was in the process of transiting in doctrine from Malikism (the most widespread of the theological schools in al-Andalus) to the literalist Zahirism to which he later adhered, which led to imprisonment. The fact that the doctrinal debates of the peninsula among Muslims were fully integrated into those of the world of Islam did not mean he was not conscious of what was distinctive about al-Andalus, and he produced a notable polemical treatise *Risala fadl al-Andalus* (On the Excellence of al-Andalus). The reputation of *Tawq al-Hamamah* and its success today provides us with a curious parallel with that of Omar Khayyam's *Rubaiyat*, also from the East. Both works enjoyed at first a modicum of success in their homelands until exceptionally fine translations into English appeared (Edward FitzGerald's version from Persian in the case of Omar Khayyam (London, 1859) and Arberry's of the *Tawq al-Hamamah*). These translations obliged native criticism, in Farsi for Omar and in Arabic for Ibn Hazm, to re-evaluate belatedly and upgrade the importance of the original works. Both works richly deserve the high rating they now enjoy in their native lands.

Ibn Quzman (1078–1160)
(Arabic Poetry in al-Andalus)

Like Ibn Hazm, Ibn Quzman was profoundly attached to his native Cordoba, but these authors were different in almost every way. Ibn Quzman is the most famous and one of the most original poets in al-Andalus, particularly known for his *zajal* (a traditional form of oral strophic poetry semi-sung in a colloquial dialect, popular today in Lebanon, Palestine and Jordan). Indeed, Ibn Quzman is thought to be the earliest recorded *zajal* poet. Unlike Ibn Hazm, who holds a secure place in the Arabic literature of the Islamic world, Ibn Quzman is not widely celebrated. One reason is that his work is not available, another is the bawdy character of his poetry and the absence of even a minimum of moralising. What are pious Muslim readers to make of an author who tells them: 'If there is anyone among men who is either a sodomite or a fornicator, in me both activities are included'? (*zajal* 30). No more than his frank delight in erotic themes or his celebration of the excellence of wine have recommended him to the pious. We can hear his delight as he rolls round his mouth the specific names of the vintages he appreciated (*zajal* 94), or the sounds of his actual boozing: 'Hardly is the wine poured out, jug jug/ When you see his mouth to the flask, glug glug/ As it descends into his stomach, slug slug' (*zajal* 96).[3] In modern times no printed edition was available on the market in the Arab world. A distinguishing characteristic is that he employs the metrical structure of the popular love song (*ghazal*) and uses predominantly the colloquial Arabic speech of his native city, not literary Arabic. That means incorporation of a relatively high proportion of Hispanisms.

As previously explained Ibn Hazm looked back nostalgically on the refinement of the Caliphal society of Cordoba at its peak, only to see it fragmented by the incursions of rebellious soldiers, so that much of his life was lived against the background of the political violence and confusion of the Taifas. A century later, Ibn Quzman's Cordoba was in the grip of the strict Islamic morality of the Almoravids (North African Berbers by ethnic origin), replaced as the poet grew older by the invading and 'reforming' Almohads (also North Africa-based and even more puritanical). The tension between the libertarian poet Ibn Quzman and his society surfaces in his verse, 'Only the unskilled fear a jurist/ Would I respect a jurist or flee his presence?/ I would shit on the mother of a man who does not drink/ Even if Al-Ghazali were before me' (*zajal* 22) (*The Mischievous Muse*, Vol. 1 p. 149); Al-Ghazali was one of the most influential philosophers and theologians of Sunni Islam.

---

[3] See James T. Monroe, *The Mischievous Muse: Extant Poetry and Prose by Ibn Quzman of Córdoba (d. AH 555/AD 1160)*, Brill Studies in Middle Eastern Literatures, vol. 39 (Leiden: Brill, 2017), vol. I, p. 191, p. 601, p. 615.

Perhaps Ibn Quzman will never be much read in the Arab world, but he is an accomplished poet. A sister genre to the *zajal*, a genre usually entirely in vulgar Arabic and in which Ibn Quzman was a skilled exponent, is the *muwashshah*. The *muwashshah* is also strophic, unlike the monorhyme *qasida*: in fact, its rhyme schemes can be extremely complex. The language of the body of these poems is Classical Arabic, with just one tiny but significant exception: the *kharja*. This, the final refrain, was predominantly worded in colloquial Arabic, not in the classical tongue, and even within that it sometimes contains snatches in a Romance dialect (Mozarabic) sung by an entertainer or singing-girl. These refrains preserved in the *kharjas* have elicited much interest, especially from European scholars. Although written in Arabic script (never in a Latin-based one), the *kharjas* appear to be the very earliest evidence from any part of Europe of a vernacular language recognisably differentiated from the parent Latin itself. Not surprisingly when first decrypted (they had long remained incomprehensible) they created a stir. Deservedly so, but the very originality of these discoveries by S. M. Stern in 1948 led to mention of them becoming almost obligatory in any treatment of the Arabic genre itself and of early poetry in Romance. The Romance element is a small part only of poems that are predominantly in Classical Arabic: the evidence is truly fragmentary. We do know that *muwashshahs* were performed with musical accompaniment in public entertainments, and the hypothesis that these were the lyrics of 'pop-songs' sung by musicians to entertain princelings seems highly plausible (see Monroe's chapter in this volume).

The word *muwashshah* is a participle derived from Arabic noun *wishah*, 'an ornamental belt', which would be decorated with a 'string' of motifs. The poem with its repeated decorative rhymes is envisaged as an ornamental sequence (and essentially different from the monorhyme classical *qasida*). A specimen of the Mozarabic *kharjas* is: '*Non kero non un khillello illa as-samarello*' where we can see that the interpenetration of the cultures reaches down to the level of the language itself. Arabic *khill/khalil* 'true friend' and *asmar* 'brown', 'swarthy', could easily have been written with traditional Arabic 'internal' diminutives, but the Romance diminutive terminations 'ello' are felt by the poet to be more expressive: 'The only special little friend I want is a swarthy one'. Or '*Ke fareyo o ke serad de mibi, habibi? Non te tolgas de mibi*', 'What am I to do, or what will become of me, darling. Never leave me'. There is a danger that our appreciation of the *kharjas* will get out of proportion. There is a far greater corpus of material available in Arabic written in Hebrew (rather than Romance) script, as well as Hebrew texts written in al-Andalus. Some of the vast number of extant works by the great Maimonides (Rambam – Rabbi Moses ben Moses 1135–1204) survive in Judeo-Arabic. The following point was argued by Maimonides himself:

If there are two muwashshahs on the same subject, one that arouses and praises the instinct of lust, and if one of these two muwashshahas is in Hebrew and the other is in either Arabic or Romance, why then listening to or uttering the one in Hebrew is the most reprehensible thing that one can do in the eyes of the Law [the Jewish law] because of the excellence of the Hebrew language for it is not appropriate to employ Hebrew in what is not excellent.[4]

The society of al-Andalus included a minority of Jews, many of whom had positions of importance, such as tax-gatherers, medics and administrators. We have no reason to think their vernacular was not the universal Hispano-Arabic, but they preserved Hebrew as their language of pubic devotion and scholarship. They wrote Arabic when convenient, using the Hebrew script for all purposes (both are Semitic languages and adaptation is not difficult). Forming a significant part of the intelligentsia of al-Andalus, Jews participated in the latest cultural trends, including the vogue enjoyed by the *muwashshaha* and its music. We have extant poems both in Arabic in a Hebrew script and others in Hebrew in Hebrew script but in both cases obeying the metrical rules of the Arabic *muwashshaha*. Some Jewish poets wrote original *muwashshahas* in Hebrew, with refrains in vernacular Arabic, and in these refrains a few words might occur in proto-Romance, as in the case of the Arabic poems. The feat of S. M. Stern in deciphering the Mozarabic *kharjas* was considerably facilitated by the fact that the exiguous repertory of Mozarabic-in-Arabic scripts that he had to work on could be eked out from the poems written by Jewish poets with the Mozarabic words in Hebrew script.

Ibn Tufail
(Arabic Writing in al-Andalus)

Consideration of Ibn Tufail (1105–1185) does not imply any disparagement of Ibn Bajja (Avempace to the Latins) (1085–1138) who was, in fact, Ibn Tufail's mentor. Both served in the secretariat of the Almohad caliphate. The principal point confirming Ibn Tufail's entitlement to esteem is his philosophical allegory or novel *Hayy Ibn Yaqzan* (Alive, son of Awake). This tale of how a man living in isolation on a tropical island (possibly Ceylon) comes to know and master the world where he is marooned (implying perhaps we are all marooned in our world) by studying everything

---

[4] Cited by James Monroe, 'Zajal and Muwashshaha: Hispano-Arabic Poetry and the Romance Tradition', in *The Legacy of Muslim Spain*, ed. by Salma Khadra Jayyusi, 2nd ed. (Leiden: Brill, 1994), pp. 398–419, p. 413.

methodically, not least the plants and the animals. The beloved antelope doe who at the beginning of the tale saved him from death by starvation does eventually die too. Quite unemotionally Hayy performs an autopsy on the animal, discovering the function of the internal organs. Indeed, his exploration of the whole world about him is worthy of a dispassionate modern scientific survey, one that takes in the wonders of the heavens too. He wanders alone, searching for a creature like himself, and fails, till one day he encounters someone who came to the island in pursuit of solitude: thus, Hayy meets his companion Asal. Later, in an expedition overseas to the land whence Asal came, Hayy attempts to propagate the knowledge he has acquired, the religion of Reason he arrived at on his island. He fails, for humankind, he concludes, cannot aspire to the higher truths to which he has attempted to introduce them. He understood 'the condition of mankind, and that the greatest part of them were like brute beasts, he knew that all wisdom, direction and good success consisted in what messengers of God had spoken, and the divine Law delivered; and that there was no other way besides this, and that there could be nothing added to it.'[5] So, the pair 'took their leave and left them, and sought for an opportunity of returning to their island, till it pleased God to help them to a conveniency of passing' (p. 177). The final message of Ibn Tufail appears to be that Hayy's personal esoteric, oneiric religious ideas are secret, 'which none can receive but those which have the knowledge of God' (p. 177).

Such a work about an entirely independent thinker who searches for himself the secrets of Creation proved of interest in the West. In the fifteenth century, Pico della Mirandola had a Latin version (based on a Hebrew version of the Arabic) made for himself but the work's wide impact in Europe in the Age of Enlightenment is to be ascribed to the Latin version published by Edward Pocock (junior) in 1671 and subsequent versions. The title Peacock chose, *Philosophus Autodidactus*, conveys the aspect of Ibn Tufail's work that fascinated him and his period. The first English version, by Simon Ockley, appeared in 1708.[6] It was certainly available therefore to Daniel Defoe whose novel *Robinson Crusoe* (London 1719) was about a man grappling all alone on his island, and rapidly became a best-seller in England, Holland, Germany and France.

---

[5] *The History of Hayy Ibn Yaqzan by Abu Bakr Ibn Tufail*, trans. by Simon Ockley, ed. with introd. A. S. Fulton (London: Chapman and Hall, 1929), p. 175.

[6] *The Improvement of Human Reason Exhibited in the Life of Hai Ebn Yokdhan*, newly translated from the original Arabic by Simon Ockley (London: E. Powell, 1708).

Aljamiado Literature

When the word *aljamiado* occurs in a modern text it simply means that a Spanish text is written in Arabic letters. Like most words, its history of development is more complex than that simple definition suggests, but for present purposes I will adhere to standard modern usage. The language in which such *aljamiado* texts occur is predominantly Castilian (often with some regional flavour), although with perhaps a larger admixture of Arabic items of vocabulary than the majority of texts. Nevertheless, any such *aljamiado* text is unquestionably to be classified as Hispanic and, in broad terms, Indo-European.

At the beginning of this chapter I mentioned the non-Hispanic languages that are at core Indo-European but regularly written in the Arabic script: Farsi and Urdu. There is, however, a profound difference between these two classes of linguistic hybrids: Farsi is the medium of expression of a whole large state (today Iran), and is used for administrative and all other purposes, whereas *aljamiado* texts could only circulate within Spain's Islamic Morisco communities and had to be kept away from prying eyes, especially those of the Inquisition and Spanish officialdom. To fail to keep the texts secret after the key dates of 1500 for Castile and 1526 for the lands of the Crown of Aragon, would probably lead to the proprietor's death. The script is occasionally found in earlier texts, from the fifteenth century, when its use did not risk such dire consequences, but to judge from the quite substantial number of extant *aljamiado* manuscripts, the phenomenon belongs almost exclusively to the sixteenth century. Yça b. Jabir, the *mufti* (Islamic scholar and jurist) of Segovia, with his substantial *Suma* (treatise), not to mention the Qur'an he produced with the Christian John of Segovia, was a pioneer in the use of the Castilian vernacular for Islamic devotional purposes, but we cannot be certain that what he wrote himself had been in the Arabic script. To judge from extant manuscripts of his works, Yça's productions did get copied in that form and transposed for use among his fellow-Muslims. If, as stated, the Inquisition came down heavily on those caught with *aljamiado* documents, it might seem remarkable that any have survived. What we have in our libraries is there in part thanks to the Inquisition itself. Its rigorous rules of procedure obliged it to bring into court relevant evidence, which would entail presenting *aljamiado* manuscripts if they had been impounded. Such documents were carefully archived and, with luck, remain on file to this day.

Another factor tending to bring about the preservation of some of the Morisco material has been the massive walls of some sixteenth-century houses. When the Moriscos learnt they were under sentence of expulsion (in the late sixteenth century and early seventeenth), they realised they could not take into exile manuscripts they prized. Rather than risk having them fall into the hands of infidels, they ingeniously constructed hidden cupboards inside the walls of their houses and so skilfully covered them up that even in the late twentieth century manuscript hoards were still coming to light as old houses were reconstructed. The most remarkable of such finds was in 1884 in Almonacid de la Sierra (Aragon): the catalogue drawn up by Ribera, Asín and others lists 101 items including many great codices. Among the impressively large manuscripts is one (of 472 folios), the *Tafsira,* by 'El Mancebo de Arévalo', who lived and wrote in the sixteenth century and by whom there survive two other large codices, the *Sumario de la relación y ejerjicio espiritual* (now in the Biblioteca Nacional, Madrid) and the *Breve Compendio de Nuestra Santa Ley I Sunna*, not at all brief (250 ff.), in the University Library, Cambridge.[7] They are each of great interest. I will end with an example from the Cambridge manuscript and quote, for obvious reasons, from the final colophon, Dd.9.49, folio 249:

> my source was such a famous man as Ali Sarmiento who occupied the professorial chair [catedrático] of the University of Granada [possibly he was the khatib of the community mosque], which city was lost in the time of this honoured leader, and he saw the Muslim banners paraded by the Infidels, and saw our noble maidens insulted, and the nobility brought low and desolate. I heard it said by trustworthy men that the poor Muslim maidens were put up for exchange, and that men gambled for them and sold them off in a public auction, this when once Granada had been the flower of nobility, there was none to equal it. The safe conducts that the unbelievers had given were of no use. Everything turned to bitter aloes.
>
> In the book entitled *Pattern for Prophets* [*Dechado de annabíes*] are to be found certain treatises on the subject of the Peninsula of Andalucia. Anybody who wishes to see them will find them there and have the greater cause to weep. May His Immense Goodness [Allah] direct towards the sad Muslims the grace of his good pleasure, may he not permit them to end in the hands of such cruel enemies, rather may the places of worship be rebuilt, so that the word of the true religion of Islam may be taken out of hiding and published abroad. *Ya rabb al-'alamin* [O Lord of Heaven and Earth].[8]

---

[7] *El Mancebo de Arévalo, Sumario de la relación y ejerjicio espiritual* (Biblioteca Nacional, Madrid, MSS/Res. 245); *Breve Compendio de Nuestra Santa Ley I Sunna* (University Library Cambridge University, Dd.9.49).

[8] *Breve Compendio de Nuestra Santa Ley I Sunna*, Dd.9.49, folio 249. Author's translation.

3

The First Chapter in Ibero-Romance Literatures

The *ḫarja-s* (kharjas)

James T. Monroe

In an article written some years ago, I pointed out that the diction used in the Andalusī-Romance[1] *ḫarja-s* (kharjas) is not only *formulaic*, in the technical, Parry-Lord sense of that word (thereby revealing the oral milieu in which those *ḫarja-s* were composed and flourished),[2] but that the very same formulas and themes found in those Andalusī fragments also surface

---

[1] The Romance, Latin-derived language spoken in the southern Arab-controlled part of the Iberian Peninsula during the Middle Ages was referred to by scholars as 'Mozarabic', a word derived from the Arabic term *musta'rab* ('Arabised'), and applied, by the mediaeval Christians inhabiting the north of the Peninsula to those among their coreligionists who inhabited the Arab-held territory of the south, which, in turn, was called Andalus by its inhabitants. But because this Romance language was spoken not only by Christians but also by the majority of Muslims and Jews in Andalus, in the present chapter I shall refer to it as Andalusī-Romance. Likewise, I shall refer to the area itself as Andalus, not Andalusia, in order to distinguish between the mediaeval, Islamic-controlled area of the Peninsula and the southern region of modern Spain. Put differently, the mediaeval Arab poet Ibn Quzmān of Cordova was an Andalusī, whereas the modern Spanish poet Federico García Lorca was an Andalusian.

[2] In oral-formulaic poetry poets use set 'formulas', such as set themes, phrases and rhythms linked together to rapidly compose verse. For a summary of Milman Parry and Albert B. Lord's groundbreaking theory concerning the oral-formulaic nature of the Homeric epic, see Albert B. Lord, *The Singer of Tales* (Cambridge, MA: Harvard University Press, 1964); for its application to classical Arabic *qaṣīda* poetry, see James T. Monroe, 'Oral composition in pre-Islamic poetry', *Journal of Arabic Literature*, 4 (1972), 1–53; Michael J. Zwettler, *The Oral Tradition of Classical Arabic Poetry: Its Character and Implications* (Ohio State University Press, 1978).

in the lyrical traditions of several different Romance languages, in all of which, ladies lament the absence or loss of their lovers, thus suggesting that they must all derive from a common Pan-Romanic source.[3] In addition to these findings, Guillermo E. Hernández pointed out the striking coincidence existing between such poetic formulas contained in the *ḫarja-s*, on the one hand and, on the other, certain expressions of lament for departed loved ones, that are to be found in Latin funerary inscriptions.[4] Finally, in a series of learned publications, Elvira Gangutia Elícequi showed that women's songs, of the type found in the Andalusī-Romance *ḫarja-s*, had antecedents that went from Latin, through Greek texts, all the way back to Sumerian, Akkadian and Phoenician verses sung during rituals performed, by women, in worship of the goddesses Inanna, Ishtar and Aphrodite, all three of whom had a lover (Dumuzi, Tammuz and Adonis, respectively) who was simultaneously viewed as being their son.[5] Gangutia Elícegui singled out three major themes that were common to all these lyrical traditions, namely those of the woman who, in her love-induced despair, (1) addressed her mother as her confidante, (2) announced the appearance of her lover at the main, entrance-door (Lat. [*porta*] *janua* > Andalusī-Romance *yana*) to her home and (3) often addressed that same lover as though he were her son. These three major themes are also to be found in the corpus of Andalusī-Romance *ḫarja-s*.[6] Gangutia Elícegui further provided evidence for the fact that the Greek poets of Antiquity had already adopted the custom of quoting lines from earlier songs in their own poems, to indicate the melody to which the latter should be sung, just as *muwaššaḥa* poets were to do centuries later.

---

[3] James T. Monroe, 'Formulaic diction and the common origins of Romance lyric traditions', *Hispanic Review*, 43.4 (1975), 341–350.

[4] See Guillermo E. Hernández, 'Some *Jarcha* antecedents in Latin inscriptions', *Hispanic Review*, 57 (1989), 189–202.

[5] Elvira Gangutia Elícegui, 'Poesía griega "de amigo" y poesía arábigo-española', *Emerita*, 41 (1973), 329–396; *Cantos de mujeres en Grecia* (Madrid: Ediciones Clásicas, 1994); 'Los "cantos de mujeres". Nuevas perspectivas', *Emerita*, 78.1 (2010), 1–31.

[6] For the lover as son, see, for example, 'Komo ši filiyolo 'alyéno, / Non maš adormeš a mew šeno' ('Like another's little son, / You no longer sleep at my breast'). For the lady confiding in her mother, along with the lover at the door, see, '¿Ké faré, mamma? / Meu l-ḥabīb ešt 'ad yana' ('What shall I do, mother? / My lover is at the door.'). See Emilio García Gómez, *Las jarchas romances de la serie árabe en su marco: edición en caracteres latinos, versión española en calco rítmico y estudio de 43 moaxajas andaluzas* (Madrid: Sociedad de Estudios y Publicaciones, 1965), p. 171, p. 388; Josep María Sola-Solé, *Corpus de poesía mozárabe: las harğa-s andalusíes* (Barcelona: Ediciones Hispam, 1973), p. 241, p. 252.

Whereas colloquial Arabic women's songs of the above type exist throughout the Arab world,[7] many of those embedded in the Andalusī *ḫarja-s* are largely, and, surprisingly, in Romance, in contrast to those placed in the mouths of men, which are predominantly in colloquial Arabic. An explanation for this differentiation between men, who are presented as being speakers of Arabic, and women who, in contrast, are portrayed as being speakers of Romance, is provided by Ibn Ḥazm of Cordova (AH 384-AD 994; AH 456–AD 1064).[8] In his *Jamharat Ansāb al-'Arab*, a treatise on the various Arab tribes settled in the Iberian Peninsula, Ibn Ḥazm provides geographic specifications as to where each tribe was settled and, in the process, he discusses the tribe of the Banū Balī in the following terms:

> The territory of the Banū Balī, in Andalus, is a place named after them, north of Cordova, where they still reside up to the present, settled according to their various lineages, while *neither their women nor their men* have any proficiency whatsoever in the Romance language (*laṭīniyya*), but only in Arabic. They are generous to their guests, and do not eat sheeps' tails up to the present day. They have another territory in the district of Mawrūr.[9]

The point here is that the Banū Balī were so conservative that, unlike most Arab settlers in Andalus, and as late as the eleventh century, they still adhered to their traditional Arab customs and, unlike other Arab conquerors who had long since intermarried with native, peninsular wives who spoke Romance, those of the Banū Balī had not. As a result, neither did their descendants,

---

[7] See James T. Monroe, 'Kharjas in Arabic and Romance: Popular poetry in Muslim Spain?', in *Islam: Past Influence and Present Challenge*, ed. by Alford T. Welch and Pierre Cachia (Edinburgh: Edinburgh University Press, 1979), pp. 168–187; Moneera al-Ghadeer, *Desert Voices: Bedouin Women's Poetry in Saudi Arabia*, Tauris Academic Studies (London and New York: I. B. Tauris, 2009).

[8] See *Biblioteca de al-Andalus: encyclopedia de la cultura andalusí* (Almería: Fundación Ibn Tufayl de Estudios Árabes, 2012), 8 vols, vol. 3, biog. [596], pp. 392–443 (henceforth *BA*). Here and below, all dates are provided, first according to the Islamic, Hijra calendar (AH), followed by the Christian one (AD).

[9] Ibn Ḥazm, *Jamharat Ansāb al-'Arab*, ed. by 'Abd al-Salām Muḥammad Hārūn, Ḍaḫā'ir al-'Arab (Cairo: Dār al Ma'ārif, 1962), vol. 2, p. 443. Here and below, all translations from the Arabic, unless otherwise indicated, are my own. The district of Mawrūr is 'currently Morón de la Frontera, in the province of Seville, to the south-east of the latter and of Carmona and to the south-west of Cordova'. See *Encyclopaedia of Islam*, 2nd edn, ed. by H. A. R. Gibb et al. (Leiden: E. J. Brill, 1979–2004), 12 vols, vol. 6, p. 898 (henceforth *EI2*), (italics mine).

including the female ones, speak Romance, a feature that Ibn Ḥazm considers so unusual as to warrant attention. However, Arab men often knew Romance as well, having learned it from their native, Romance-speaking mothers, and they used it on informal occasions, as the following anecdote indicates:

The Prince of the Faithful, the [Caliph] 'Abd al-Raḥmān al-Nāṣir [AH 300–AD 912; AH 350–AD 961] held a private session, in the company of his inner circle, among whom was Abū l-Qāsim Lope, whom he deemed willing to participate in wantonness and jesting, so he said to him: 'Ridicule 'Abd al- Malik ibn Jahwar, by satirizing him', referring to one of his viziers. But [Abū l-Qāṣim Lope] replied: 'I am afraid of him.' So [the Caliph] said to 'Abd al-Malik [ibn Jahwar]: 'Then *you* ridicule [Abū l-Qāṣim Lope].' But ['Abd al-Malik ibn Jahwar] answered: 'I fear for my honour, insofar as he is concerned.' So [the Caliph] replied: 'Then let you and me *both* ridicule [Abū l-Qāṣim Lope]', and he improvised the following verses [rhymed in *-ūlu*]:

Lope, Abū l-Qāṣim has such a long beard that Length [*ṭūlu*] itself is short in comparison with it.

To which 'Abd al-Malik [ibn Jahwar] added:

It is two miles wide, when measured, so that one's mind is maimed and exhausted [*maḥbūlu*] by it.

Then [the Caliph] Al-Nāṣir said to Lope: 'Now *you*, in turn, ridicule [Ibn Jahwar], since *he* has ridiculed you.' So [Lope] improvised:

God's agent in our times, [the Caliph], has declared that I have such a long beard, that Length [*ṭūlu*] itself is short in comparison with it,

And wretched Ibn Jahwar has added words, the edible part of which consists of *cardillo*[10] and beans [*fūlu*].

---

[10] Romance for 'Golden thistle', in this context, the variety known as *Scolemus hispanicus*, a biennial plant of composite genus, that grows both in sown and fallow fields. It bears yellowish flowers and prickly leaves with curly edges, while its fleshy stalk may be cooked and eaten when tender. See *Real Academia Española, Diccionario de la lengua española*, 23rd edn (Madrid: Espasa Libros, 2014), p. 437; *The Oxford English Dictionary*, 2nd edn (Oxford: Clarendon Press, 1989), 20 vols, vol. 6, p. 657.

Were it not that I am embarrassed by the presence of the Commander of the Faithful, I would thrust my prick up šū...[11]

At which point, he stopped and remained silent, whereupon Al-Nāṣir said: 'Complete the end of the verse.' But [Lope] refused to do so, whereupon [the Caliph] said for him: 'culo',[12] thereby completing the end of the verse. Then Lope said: 'Our lord, it is *you*, [and not I], who have ridiculed him', while Al-Nāṣir, along with those present, got the point and laughed, and [the Caliph] ordered [Lope] to be rewarded.[13]

One point illustrated by the above anecdote is that it depicts no less than an early tenth-century Andalusī Caliph as being so fluent in the Romance language of Andalus that he is spontaneously able to provide an obscene rhyme-word in that language, to end a poem that is in the process of being improvised in Arabic. A second point is that the assembled inner circle of the Caliph, made up entirely of men, is sufficiently versed in Romance to understand the allusion and laugh at it. A third, is that one of the participants in the above episode bears the Romance name Lope.

In 1948, S. M. Stern published an article in which he singled out twenty Hispano-Hebrew *muwaššaḥa-s* containing *ḫarja-s* that he identified as being in the Andalusī-Romance (Mozarabic) dialect. In so doing, he not only discovered the first chapter in the Romance literatures of the Iberian Peninsula, but also opened up a whole new field of study, the significance of which cannot be sufficiently stressed.[14] Stern's pioneering article was followed by the contribution of Emilio García Gómez who gathered together 43 Romance *ḫarja-s* contained in Arabic *muwaššaḥa-s* (*Las jarchas romances*). Josep María Sola-Solé, in yet a third, key publication, provided further, valuable refinements to our understanding of the *ḫarja-s* previously discovered (*Corpus de poesía mozárabe*).[15] Over the years, subsequent scholars

---

[11] Romance for 'his' (Span. *su*).
[12] Romance for 'bottom, anus'.
[13] Al-Maqqarī, Aḥmad ibn Muḥammad, *Nafḥ al-Ṭīb min Ġuṣn al-Andalus al-Raṭīb*, ed. by Iḥsān ʿAbbās (Beirut: Dār Ṣādir, 1968), 7 vols, vol. 3, pp. 617–618. Italics mine.
[14] Samuel Miklos Stern, 'Les vers finaux en espagnol dans les *muwaššaḥa*s hispano-hébraiques. Une contribution à l'histoire du *muwaššaḥa* et à l'étude du vieux dialecte espagnol "mozarabe"', *Al-Andalus*, 13 (1948), 299–346.
[15] For Arabic *ḫarja-s* in Hebrew poems see James T. Monroe and David Swiatlo, 'Ninety-three Arabic *Ḫarǧas* in Hebrew *Muwaššaḥs*: Their Hispano-Romance prosody and thematic features', *Journal of the American Oriental Society*, 97 (1977), 141–163. For two important recent editions including Arabic *ḫarja-s* in Arabic *muwaššaḥa-s*

have engaged in prolonged and often heated debates concerning the origin, metrics and literary nature of this poetic corpus of women's Andalusī songs. The present chapter is an attempt to synthesise the results of their investigations, from a comparative perspective, in order to provide an explanation for the origin and development of this genre of poetry.

Both the strophic genre known as *muwaššaḥa* as well as its related form, the *zajal*, as they are performed today in Arab lands, normally involve a soloist, who begins by intoning the initial *maṭlaʿ* or 'refrain' (Span. *estribillo*), which, in its simplest form, is rhymed (*AA*), thereby teaching it to his chorus. Then he solos the first *ġuṣn* (Span. *mudanza*), rhymed bbb, plus the first *simṭ* (Span. *vuelta*), the rhyme of which (*a* for the *zajal* or *aa* for the *muwaššaḥa*), alerts the chorus that they should repeat the refrain (*AA*). Then, the soloist sings the second *ġuṣn* (ccc) plus *simṭ* (*a* or *aa*), to which the chorus again responds by singing the refrain (*AA*), and so on, until the end of the song, which is normally from five to seven strophes long. In the *muwaššaḥa* the final *simṭ* is called *ḫarja* ('exit'). The following is a verse translation of a classical Arabic *muwaššaḥa* with a colloquial *ḫarja*, by Ibn Quzmān (d. AH 555–AD 1160), in which an attempt has been made to reproduce the overall rhythmic beat, number of syllables per line and rhyme scheme, including the internal rhymes in the caesuras (medial pauses) found in the original:

0. Critics by vocation, / Mine are moons ashining,
   Topping branches bending, / On their butts' foundation.

1. There is sin in blaming / Those you see love smiting,
   When full moons, inflaming, / Rise from reeds inviting,
   That are waists, each claiming / Hearts. Of these, I'm fighting
   Anklet-maid: creation / Of our Lord, assigning
   Her to be my rending / Pain and castigation.

2. At a lover wonder, / To his flame committed,
   Yet who's torn asunder, / Once he has submitted;
   Or when gossip's thunder / Adds to grace befitted:
   Woe! To my damnation, / All excuse declining,
   Did my foe, unbending, / Earn me her vexation!

see *The* Jaysh al-Tawshīḥ *of Lisān al-Dīn ibn al-Khaṭīb: An Anthology of Andalusian Arabic Muwashshaḥāt*, ed. by Alan Jones (Cambridge: Gibb Memorial Trust, 1997), New Series, No. 33; *The 'Uddat al-Jalīs of 'Alī ibn Bishrī: An Anthology of Andalusian Arabic Muwashshaḥāt*, ed. by Alan Jones (Cambridge: Gibb Memorial Trust, 1992), New Series, No. 31.

3. My one goal, in beauty, / Is beyond my clasping.
   Ne'er was such fair booty / Found in Eden's grasping.
   Death was but my duty / To her glance, agasping
   *(Dart-like penetration): / Charm, to death consigning
   Lions, each defending / Cubs from dire starvation.*

4. What to her's the moon, and / What to her's the sun?
   Mouth with pearls bestrewn, and / Lips so red, they stun:
   So wine-red I swoon, and / Doubt of that, there's none.
   *She's my mind's fixation, / With my thoughts entwining:
   My desires attending, / Sans humiliation.*

5. Warned she of our parting; / Sang she of my biting
   Of her breast, now smarting, / With my tears, affrighting
   Down my cheeks departing, / Raindrop-like alighting:
   'Gimme delectashun, / To wot's kind inclining.
   Gentle, unoffending / Be, in our relashun!'[16]

The following is an example of a colloquial *zajal*, also by Ibn Quzmān, and also adapted into English verse, in such a way as to imitate the metrical structure and rhyme scheme employed in the original. It is a love poem to a lady named Nujayma (diminutive of *najma* 'star'), in which the poet achieves the tour de force of rhyming all the poem's common rhymes with that name.

0. *Everywhere I love Nujaymie
   This time-ie*

1. Who won't die, should he adore you?
   If I'm killed, the blame's before you.
   If my heart could just ignore you
   It would never sing this rhyme-ie

2. Hey, you dunderhead, *chiflado*,
   You're a sad one, *apenado*.

---

[16] For the original Arabic text and a literal, prose translation see James T. Monroe, *The Mischievous Muse: Extant Poetry and Prose by Ibn Quzmān of Córdoba (d. AH 555/AD 1160), Edition, Translation, and Notes*, Brill Studies in Middle Eastern Literatures, vol. 39.1–2 (Leiden and Boston: E. J. Brill, 2016), 2 vols, part 1, vol. 1, pp. 994–999. For a literary analysis of the poem, see *ibid.*, part 2, vol. 2, chap. 15, pp. 1412–1431.

Full's the day (of doubt, no shadow);
Scant's the food you've had, meantime-ie

3. I declare, by Allah's greatness,
   I can't bear this wretched straitness!
   When I reach Green Mosque, sans lateness,
   Poplar Well you've left for – blimey!

4. Every party you adorn,
   Clever girl, and beauty born.
   Gold, your lap would oft have borne,
   Had you been a leper slimy!

5. All your lovers you've dejected;
   Babel's magic you've collected;
   Wonders are from you detected,
   For each word you say's sublime-ie.

6. Apples on your little breast;
   Cheeks as white as flour – the best!
   Pearly teeth, and for the rest,
   Mouth as sweet as sugar prime-ie!

7. If you banned our ritual fasting;
   From God turned us, Everlasting,
   In Grand Mosque would none be lasting,
   Save those bound with ropes that stymie!

8. You are sweeter far that candy;
   I'm your slave, my lord, and handy!
   All opposed, who would withstand me,
   Slap their necks for such a crime-ie

9. Until when will you abuse me?
   Until when will you accuse me?
   In a house, alone, God fuse me,
   With you – (a bouquet!) – sometime-ie.[17]

---

[17] James T. Monroe, *The Mischievous Muse*, vol. 1, pp. 72–75; vol. 2, chapter 3, pp. 1092–1119.

The alternation between a soloist, followed by choral intonation, as described above, is precisely what the Syrian scholar Ibn Ḥijja al-Ḥamawī (AH 767–AD 1374; AH 837–AD 1433) is referring to when he provides us with the following etymology for the term *zajal*:

> In classical Arabic, the word *zajal* means 'shout, roar'. One says: 'A cloud *zajal*-ed', when it thunders. One also uses the word *ṣawt* ['loud noise, echo'] and *zajal*, to describe the sound made by stones, iron, and metals. Similarly, one uses the above [term] to allude to the skill with which a public speech is begun, by saying: 'Praise be to God, Who raised the *zajal* ['chorus'] of the angels, in the world of the Kingdom of Heaven, with praise for Him'. This poetic genre was called *zajal* simply because it cannot be enjoyed, nor can the sections of its metres be appreciated, until it is sung [in solo recitation], and made to resound [chorally] out loud.[18]

In sum, the *zajal* is composed entirely in colloquial Andalusī Arabic, whereas the *muwaššaḥa*, with the exception of its colloquial *ḫarja*, is entirely in Classical Arabic. The earliest surviving Andalusī text to mention the genre of Arabic poetry known as *muwaššaḥa* is that of Ibn Bassām of Santarem (d. AH 542–AD 1147).[19] In his *Kitāb al-Ḏaḫīra*, he informs us that it was invented by a certain blind poet named Muḥammad ibn Maḥmūd of Cabra,[20] a town southeast of Cordova, adding that most of these poems were not in the quantitative, classical metres used in Arabic poetry (*Ḏaḫīra*, Part 1, vol. 1, *loc. cit*),[21] for which reason he chooses to refrain from citing any examples

---

[18] Ibn Ḥijja al-Ḥamawī, *Bulūġ al 'Amal fī Fann al-Zajal*, ed. by Riḍā Muḥsin al-Quraši, introd. by 'Abd al-'Azīz al-Ahwānī (Damascus: Manšūrāt Wizārat al-Ṯaqāfa wa-l- 'Inšād al-Qawmī, 1974), p. 128. *Cf*, Edward William Lane, *An Arabic English Lexicon* (London: Williams and Norgate, 1867), 8 vols, vol. 3, p. 1217. For more on this point see David Wulstan, 'The *Muwaššaḥa* and *Zajal* revisited', *Journal of the American Oriental Society*, 102 (1982), 247–264; James T. Monroe, 'The Tune or the Words? (Singing Hispano-Arabic poetry)', *Al-Qantara*, 8 (1987), 265–317.

[19] For his biography, see *BA*, vol. 2, biog. [395], pp. 573–592.

[20] Ibn Bassām al-Šantarīnī, *Al-Ḏaḫīra fī Maḥāsin 'Ahl al-Jazīra*, ed. by 'Iḥsān 'Abbās (Beirut: Dār al-Ṯaqāfa, 1978), 8 vols, part 1, vol. 1, pp. 468–470. See James T. Monroe, 'On re-reading Ibn Bassām: "Lírica Románica" after the Arab conquest', *Revista del Instituto Egipcio de Estudios Islámicos en Madrid*, 23 (1985–1986), 121–142. On Muḥammad ibn Maḥmūd of Cabra, see *BA*, vol. 4, biog. [751], p. 63. He lived at the end of the ninth century and beginning of the tenth AD.

[21] For a full description of the Arabic quantitative metrical system, which is based on regular, alternating sequences of long and short syllables, see William Wright, *A*

in his book. Elsewhere in that same work, and in a passage that has not, to the best of my knowledge, yet been noticed or assessed by specialists for its significance, he adds that the non-Arab, Romance speakers (*'Ajam*) of the Iberian Peninsula

> *do not possess quantitative poetry* or sound speech, whereas the language of the Arabs is ample in its phrases and pure in its expressions; it *does possess quantitative poetry*. (*Ḏaḫīra*, part 3, vol. 2, p. 739 [emphasis mine])

Putting two and two together, we have good reasons to suspect that those poems Ibn Bassām has excluded from his anthology were composed in the non-quantitative metres of the *'Ajam*. In contrast, and a century later, Ibn Sa'īd al-Andalusī al-Maġribī (AH 610–AD 1213; AH 685–AD 1286),[22] in his *Al-Muqtaṭaf min 'Azāhir al-Ṭuraf*,[23] and relying on Al-Ḥijārī's (AH 500–AD 1106; AH 549–AD 1155) lost *Mushib*,[24] claimed that the inventor of the *muwaššaḥa* was a certain Muqaddam ibn Mu'āfà.[25] Both Muḥammad ibn Maḥmūd and Muqaddam ibn Mu'āfà existed, both were from Cabra, and both were contemporaries, while only Muḥammad was blind. Later, the genre was adopted by Ibn 'Abd Rabbihi al-Andalusī (AH 246–AD 860; AH 328–AD 940),[26] who was the author of the *'Iqd al-Farīd*.[27]

According to Ibn Bassām and Ibn Sa'īd, the early *muwaššaḥa-s*, composed by their inventor and his followers, up to, and including, Ibn 'Abd Rabbihi, had no internal rhymes in their caesuras, and gradually disappeared, so that none had survived by their time. Then came a group of poets who added internal rhymes to the caesuras, while examples of such later poems had (and have) survived. It is significant to note, however, that examples of poems with unrhymed caesuras are documented in that similar Andalusī strophic genre known as *zajal*, thus suggesting that the *zajal* is the more primitive of the two genres, a point to which I shall return, below. Several other mediaeval authors also attest to the early existence of strophic poems

---

Grammar of the Arabic Language, 3rd edn (Cambridge: Cambridge University Press, 1967), 2 vols, vol. 2, pp. 350–390.

[22] On whom see, *EI2*, vol. 3, pp. 926–927.

[23] Ed. Sayyid Ḥanafī Ḥasanayn, *Al-Muqtaṭaf min 'Azāhir al-Ṭuraf* (Cairo: Markaz Taḥqīq al-Turāṯ, 1983), pp. 255–266.

[24] See, *BA*, vol. 1, biog. [157], pp. 454–456.

[25] See, *BA*, vol. 4, biog. [822], pp. 203–205. He also flourished at the end of the ninth century and beginning of the tenth.

[26] On whom see, *BA*, vol. 1, biog. [190], pp. 620–629.

[27] Ed. Aḥmad Amīn et al. (Cairo: Lajnat al-Ta 'līf, 1965), 7 vols.

in Andalus. Averroes (AH 520–AD 1126; AH 595–AD 1198) in his *Middle Commentary on Aristotle's Poetics*, states that imitation and representation may appear separately from each other, 'like tune in flute-playing; rhythm in dance; and representative utterances [...]. Or all three may be brought together – like what is found in the kind of poems called *muwaššaḥa-s* and *zajal-s*, these being the ones the people of this peninsula [Andalus] have devised in this tongue [Arabic]'.[28] Likewise, in his *Mishnah*, which was published in Old Cairo in AD 1168, Maimonides (1134–1204), in the process of referring to certain licentious *muwaššaḥa-s*, declares that 'if one of two *muwaššaḥa-s* is in Hebrew, and the other is either in Arabic or is in Romance, why then, listening to, and uttering the one in Hebrew is the most reprehensible thing one can do, in the eyes of the Holy Law'.[29] This passage clearly implies that at the time Maimonides was writing, strophic poems of the type we are considering existed in all three major Andalusī languages, namely Arabic, Hebrew and Romance.

Brian Dutton argued that Muqaddam ibn Muʿāfà, whom, of the two candidates, he is inclined to believe was the actual inventor of the *muwaššaḥa*, is an unusual name in Arabic. Literally, it would mean 'Praefectus, son of Salvatus', thereby suggesting that the former term, Muqaddam, is a title rather than a name.[30] This Arabic title was incorporated into Spanish as *almocadén*, and used to designate a leader, or captain of a troop of infantrymen (*Real Academia Española, Diccionario*, p. 42, p. 113). It was also adopted, as a loan translation, in the form of *adelantado* (Span. 'placed ahead, a leader' is a literal translation of Ar. *muqaddam*), who was, in mediaeval times, the military or political head of a frontier province ('Some New Evidence', p. 42).[31] If Dutton's very persuasive suggestion is correct, then the inventor of the *muwaššaḥa* may have been the son of a native Iberian convert to Islam (*Muʿ āfà* means 'forgiven', *salvatus*), and thus, a person more than likely to have been familiar with the tradition of Romance poetry. If so, we might conclude that the newly invented *muwaššaḥa* may have been based largely upon the syllabic metrical system used in Ibero-Romance poetry,[32] and not on the quantitative system

---

[28] Abū l-Walīd ibn Rušd, *Averroes' Middle Commentary on Aristotle's Poetics*, trans. by Charles E. Butterworth (Princeton: Princeton University Press, 1986), pp. 62–64.

[29] Maimonides, *Mishnah*, ed by Y. Qafih (Jerusalem: Mossad Harav Kook, 1963–1968), 6 vols, vol. 4, pp. 416–417.

[30] Brian Dutton, 'Some new evidence for the Romance origins of the *Muwashshaḥas*', *Bulletin of Hispanic Studies*, 42 (1965), 73–81.

[31] Joan Corominas and José A. Pascual, *Diccionario crítico etimológico castellano e hispánico* (Gredos: Biblioteca Románica Hispánica, 1980), 6 vols, vol. 2, p. 438.

[32] In the stress-syllabic, as opposed to the quantitative metrical system, all syllables are of equal duration, and some are stressed while others are not. In some cases, this

normally used in Classical Arabic (in fact the Arabic language lacks a word to express the concept of 'syllable').[33]

As far as the *zajal* is concerned, those scholars who were either Andalusīs, or had close ties to Andalus, all admit that the inventor of that genre was unknown to them. We have an extant fragment in that form preserved in Ibn Ḥayyān's *Muqtabis*[34] (the composition of which is dated to the year AH 300/ AD 912), and since it was a common practice for the *muwaššaḥa* to quote the initial refrain (*maṭlaʿ*), normally borrowed from an earlier *zajal*, at its end, as its *ḫarja* (whereas the *zajal* has no quoted *ḫarja*), in order to indicate the melody to which that *muwaššaḥa* was intended to be sung, we may reasonably conclude that the *zajal* came first; that it was originally an oral, popular genre, and flourished among minstrels in market places, whereas the more learned, classical *muwaššaḥa* was a later invention, based upon the *zajal*, of which it was a musical *contrafactum* (Monroe, 'Which came first?', pp. 46–47). The greater antiquity of the *zajal* with respect to the *muwaššaḥa* may be further confirmed by the existence of a Berber family named the Banū Zajjālī who settled in Andalus, in the district of Tākurunnā,[35] from whence they moved to Cordova,[36] and whose lineage can be traced back as far as the late eighth

---

stress follows regular patterns, but in Spanish popular poetry intended for singing, it is often the case that the musical beat imposes itself on syllables that are linguistically unstressed. For an extreme example, see the verses: 'Las mis penas, madre, / de amores son' ('My sorrows, mother, / are caused by love'), in which the underlined vowels are stressed, linguistically, as follows: ó o ó o ó o / o ó o ó, while they are actually sung to a melody that is stressed 'Las mis penas, madre, / de amores son' (o ó o ó o ó / ó o ó o), thereby entirely violating the natural, linguistic stress. A standard manual on Spanish metrics is that of Tomás Navarro Tomás, *Métrica española: Reseña histórica y descriptiva* (Madrid: Ediciones Guadarrama, 1972). However, that author tends to select only examples of regularly stressed and/or learned Spanish poetry, thus ignoring the vast corpus of popular songs in which the irregular linguistic stress is disguised by the musical rhythm to which such songs are sung.

[33] This conclusion seems obvious from another angle: any *zajal* in the Andalusī-Romance dialect could only have been composed in the syllabic system, since the Romance languages had long since lost the quantitative nature of the Classical Latin language. Hence, any Arabic poems based on that syllabic system can only be expected to have adhered to Andalusī-Romance norms.

[34] See, Ibn Ḥayyān (AH 377–AD 987; AH 469–AD 1076), *Kitāb al-Muqtabis*, vol. 5, at Monroe, 'Which came first, the *Zajal* or the *Muwaššaḥa*?', p. 48.

[35] The precise borders of this district are unclear, but its capital was the city of Ronda. See *EI2*, vol. 10, pp. 144–145.

[36] On whom, see, *BA*, vol. 7, biogs. [1881–1885], pp. 714–720, and the family tree on p. 716. The earliest datable member of that family is a certain Abū ʿAbd Allāh (d. AH 232–AD 846), who was preceded by his father Saʿīd, and grandfather [Abū Sulaymān]

century AD. Little is known about this family, but their name means, quite literally, 'sons of the man related to the *zajjāl* ("*zajal*-composer or reciter")', and when and where there were *zajjāl-s* there must have been *zajal-s*.

As time went by, this popular, oral, genre was adopted by learned, literate poets such as Ibn Quzmān, Ibn Ġurla, Mudġallīs and Ibn Rāšid (all of whom flourished in the twelfth century AD), among others.[37] This may be confirmed by the words of Ibn Quzmān himself, for in the anthology containing his colloquial, *zajal* poetry, he includes an introduction that is composed in classical Arabic rhymed prose of the most learned sort, indicating that he was no market-place minstrel. In that introduction, he refers to certain *zajal* poets from at least three generations immediately preceding his own (which clearly precludes any possibility that he or his contemporaries could have invented the *zajal*), and criticises them for committing what he considered to be the grave mistake of having introduced classical Arabic inflections (*i'rāb*) into their colloquial *zajal-s*, thereby 'contaminating' them. In the case of one poet from the generation immediately preceding his own, he writes:

> The poets of the previous generation did not really know the true way; for they strayed from the right direction, and wandered east and west, producing inane ideas, outlandish themes, and a diction whose inspiring demons were refractory, along with classical inflections (despite the fact that the latter are the ugliest feature to appear in a *zajal*, and more unpleasant than the arrival of death), as was the case when one of them said – may God pardon him:

> *qad takassara jināḥak wa-tabarrada muzāhak*
> Your wing broke and your joke backfired.[38]

Musà b. 'Īsà, both of whose dates are unknown. If we subtract the standard thirty years per generation from the year of Abū 'Abd Allāh's death, we might conjecture that his grandfather died *c*.AH 172–AD 786, whereas the Battle of Covadonga, in which Andalus was conquered by the Arabs, took place in AH 103/AD 722, some six decades earlier.

[37] Ibn Ġurla died *c*.AH 555–AD 1160. See *BA*, Apéndice, biog. [2147], p. 200. Ibn Rāšid lived during the twelfth century. See, *BA*, Apéndice, biog. [2331], pp. 372–373. Mudġallīs was roughly contemporary with Ibn Quzmān. See, Ṣafī al-Dīn Ḥillī, *Al-Kitāb al-'Āṭil al-Ḥālī wa-l-Muraḫḫaṣ al-Ġālī*, ed. by Wilhelm Hoenerbach (Wiesbaden: Franz Steiner Verlag, 1956), p. 16. Ibn Quzmān d. in AH 555–AD 1160. See, Monroe, *The Mischievous Muse*, vol. 1, p. 1.

[38] James T. Monroe, 'Ibn Quzmān on *I' rāb*: A *zéjel de juglaría* in Arab Spain?', *Hispanic Studies in Honor of Joseph H. Silverman*, ed. by Joseph V. Ricapito (Newark, DE: Juan de la Cuesta, 1988), pp. 45–56; *The Mischievous Muse*, vol. 1, p. 16. In the

In sum, the above sources indicate that the *muwaššaḥa* was invented by one of two specific poets from Cabra, both of whom flourished at the end of the ninth century and beginning of the tenth AD. In contrast, references and allusions to the existence of the *zajal* go back as far as the late eighth century, while no credible evidence concerning any inventor is provided in those sources, thereby suggesting that the genre may well have existed, on a popular, oral level, from time immemorial. In light of this evidence, we can only conclude that the *muwaššaḥa* was the daughter of the *zajal*, rather than its mother, and that the Arabic *zajal*, in turn, derived from a popular Romance form of which we have numerous later examples.

As mentioned above, in the *zajal*, the *simṭ-s* / *vueltas* (*a*) reproduce only half the rhymes of the *maṭlaʿ* / *estribillo* (*AA*), whereas in the *muwaššaḥa*, the *simṭ-s* (*aa*) duplicate the full set of rhymes found in the *maṭlaʿ*. This fact may be explained if we consider that the *muwaššaḥa* is built from the bottom up, as it were, beginning with the borrowed *ḫarja* that is placed at its end, and that will (in the interest of regularity) determine the number of corresponding rhymes in the *simṭ* of each preceding strophe, whereas the *zajal*, which is built from the top down, traditionally requires the *simṭ-s* to exhibit only half the rhymes of the *maṭlaʿ*. In other words, in the *muwaššaḥa* the rhymes of the *maṭlaʿ* and *simṭ-s* duplicate those of the borrowed *ḫarja*, whereas, in the *zajal*, there is no *ḫarja* to be duplicated, since the originally popular minstrels, in that tradition, knew their melodies by heart.

As we have previously noted, Ibn Bassām points out that the Romance-speaking inhabitants of the Iberian Peninsula did not have quantitative poetry, and refuses to include certain early *muwaššaḥa-s* in his anthology because they are based on an alien metrical system. Later on, the Egyptian scholar Ibn Sanāʾ al-Mulk (*c*.AH 550–AD 1155; AH 608–AD 1211) indicates that, as far as metre is concerned, there are several categories of Andalusī *muwaššaḥa-s*: (1) Some are in the regular, quantitative metres of the Arabs.[39]

---

above transliteration of the Arabic text, the two underlined a̱s represent a vowel that is required in the classical conjugation of the verb, but omitted in its corresponding colloquial form. Here, the literate poet has inserted them into an otherwise colloquial poem for the sake of the metre. To this evidence, let us add that, in *Zajal* 87:27, Ibn Quzmān declares: 'I grasped the inkwell; I seized the pen: / I gathered praise; I produced aphorisms, / My hand hit the page, and embroidered it; / I finished my poem, which proved to be a masterpiece!' By his own admission, the poet is a clearly literate, rather than an oral, composer. See Monroe, *The Mischievous Muse*, part 1, vol. 1, p. 545; pp. 995–999; pp. 1000–1014, for further fragments of his classical compositions in verse and in prose.

[39] See Ibn Sanāʾ al-Mulk, *Dār al-Ṭirāz fī ʿAmal al-Muwaššaḥāt*, ed. by Jawdat al-Rikābī (Damascus: no pub., AH 1378/AD 1949), p. 35.

(2) Others are in metres that, although regular, from a quantitative point of view, are not recognisable as any one of the sixteen specific metres identified by Ḫalīl ibn Aḥmad (d. *c.*AH 175–AD 791), the theoretician who established the fundamentals of Arabic prosody; these being the only metres normally used in the classical Arabic poetic tradition.[40] (3) Yet a third category, constituting the vast majority of poems belonging to this genre, is based upon metres that were unrecognisable to a mediaeval Arab prosodist, but that were perceived to be perfectly regular when sung (*Dār al-Ṭirāz*, p. 37). If the Andalusī *muwaššaḥa-s* derived from the more popular *zajal*, which, in turn, was based on a local, popular Romance tradition of syllabic poetry, this can only mean that the *muwaššaḥa* incorporated that non-quantitative, syllabic tradition into the high culture of Arabic poetry.

At this juncture, let us note that, in Old Irish literature, the epic known as the *Táin Bó Cúalnge* ('Cattle-Raid of Cooley'), contained in a surviving ninth-century manuscript, but committed to writing as early as the seventh century, includes two poems composed in the *zajal* strophic structure, one of which exhibits the basic rhyme scheme later to be found in Ibn Quzmān, while the other represents a slight variation on that scheme (*The Mischievous Muse*, part 2, vol. 2, pp. 1305–1308).[41] Since Ireland, after the fall of the Roman Empire, was the last outpost of Latin culture in Europe, a culture that Irish monks lovingly preserved in their monasteries, we have good reasons to suspect that the *zajal*esque poems preserved in Ireland were a reflection of the late-Latin poetic tradition, popular in nature that, along with its Greek, Sumerian, Akkadian and Phoenician antecedents, has been carefully described by Gangutia Elícegui, as mentioned at the beginning of this chapter, and that was simultaneously being cultivated, on an oral level, throughout Romania, where it was later to surface in the form of Galician-Portuguese *cantigas*, Castilian *villancicos*, French *rondeaux* and *virelais*, Provençal *dansas*, and Italian *laude* and *ballate*, all of which are composed in the same *zajal* form we find documented earlier in Arabic, and from the Andalusī-Romance variant of which *muwaššaḥa* poets often quoted refrains, in order to indicate the melodies to which their Arabic poems should be sung.

To conclude, taken as a whole, the above texts, along with the various scholarly studies based upon them, strongly suggest that the Andalusī-Romance *ḫarjas* are the oldest surviving examples of a tradition of women's songs derived from Latin. It further suggests that this Latin tradition has even

---

[40] On Ḫalīl ibn Aḥmad see *EI2*, vol. 4, pp. 962–964.
[41] For other Old Irish *zajal* examples, see Kuno Meyer, *A Primer of Irish Metrics* (Dublin: Hodges, Figgis, & Co, 1909), p. 25, and Gerard Murphy, *Early Irish Metrics* (Dublin: Hodges, Figgis, & Co, 1961), pp. 70–73.

deeper roots in Antiquity. If so, such texts constitute the first known chapter in Romance literatures to have flourished on Iberian soil. Subsequently, that early Romance tradition was imitated, both as to its metre and strophic structure, in colloquial Andausī Arabic, thereby giving rise to the *zajal*, after which that *zajal* genre was incorporated into the Classical Arabic tradition in the form of the *muwaššaḥa*. In turn, the latter, along with its parent *zajal*, spread back to the Eastern Arabic heartlands of the Mediterranean world, from whence it had originally travelled westward in Antiquity. In this sense the Iberian Peninsula amply repaid the debt it had initially incurred when it borrowed this valuable literary asset from the Middle East.

4

Indigenous People of the Andes through Language

Rosaleen Howard

In this chapter I will reflect on my research among indigenous peoples of the Andean highlands of Ecuador and Peru and the central valleys of Bolivia, all bordering on the western Amazonian uplands. Beginning in the mid-1970s and continuing today, this work has focused on peoples' use of language and verbal discourse as media through which indigenous people express their cosmovisions, deliberate on their history, negotiate their position vis-à-vis non-indigenous society and constitute their sense of identity. This period in Latin American history has witnessed momentous changes in the ways that indigenous people have been represented, and have represented themselves, to the wider world, and these changes in turn have affected the types of phenomena I have studied and the methods I have used.

Who are Andean indigenous people? How can we learn about them? What kinds of sources can we use? Whose point of view do the sources present? How should we interpret and understand them? What are the languages spoken? Who speaks them? What does it mean in sociocultural terms to speak one language or another? I will venture to explore these questions in what follows.

Academic studies of Andean indigenous people have adopted different disciplinary tools in order to describe and analyse their ways of life, socioeconomic conditions and cultural beliefs and practices. Anthropologists, for example, have made use of ethnographic methods to gain first-hand understanding of the cultural practices, technologies and ways of thinking of the diverse peoples who live from north to south along the Andean chain. Fast-flowing river systems and intermontane valleys separate their settlements from each other, a topography that has ensured they evolved their cultures and local ways of speaking in relative autonomy one from the other. Great diversity therefore exists between and within the indigenous languages in their spoken forms, as also within oral Andean Spanish, together with variation in storytelling traditions, vernacular literacies, music and dance, dress, food, craft techniques, traditional healing practices and other outward expressions of local and regional identity. All of these, furthermore, support systems of knowledge that run counter to the dominant frameworks of Westernized, more universalized, systems.

Anthropologists have also developed ways of interpreting their research findings that help us appreciate the social, economic, historical and political factors that shape Andean identities. Identity is best understood not as something existing outside of cultural practice, but rather as emerging, or being performed, in and through practice. From an inverse point of view, cultural practice can also be seen as constructing, or shaping, identity. Attention to language use gives particular insight into the ways that identity is culturally shaped, served by a combination of linguistic anthropological and critical sociolinguistic approaches, all of which make use of ethnography, as this discussion will show.

The juxtaposition and intermingling of Andean languages, vehicles of non-alphabetic and largely oral life ways, and Spanish, with its culture of letters associated with the realms of bureaucracy and the law, become an ever-present axis along which Andean peoples constantly repositioned themselves vis-à-vis the colonial authorities and down to the present day. This semiotic positioning provides a thread along which to trace the nature of Andean identities today, as constituted in their modes of language use and literacy practices.

'Representation' is a key concept that enables us to consider the different lenses through which a researcher, as cultural outsider, may look, in order to gain understanding of the viewpoints and life experiences of the peoples she or he studies. The postcolonialist cultural critic Gayatri Chakravorty Spivak drew our attention to the complexities of this concept as a means to explore how the experience of decolonisation finds cultural expression in emergent independent nation-states around the globe. She elaborates on Marx's distinction in German between *Darstellung* ('speaking about') and *Vertretung* ('speaking for'), which both translate into English as the one word 'representation';[1] furthermore, in his discussion of Spivak, Beverley explains that *Darstellung* is 'mimetic representation or representing as an object of disciplinary knowledge' while *Vertretung* is taken as the 'act of political delegation'.[2]

---

[1] Gayatri Chakravorty Spivak, 'Can the subaltern speak?', in *Marxism and the Interpretation of Culture*, ed. by Cary Nelson and Lawrence Grossman (Urbana, IL.: University of Illinois Press, 1988), pp. 271–313.

[2] John Beverley, *Subalternity and Representation: Arguments in Cultural Theory* (Durham, NC: Duke University Press, 1999), p. 169, n. 4.

Through their history, written representation of Andean cultures in the *Darstellung* sense has shifted perspective as the agents doing the representing have changed. The early historical record depicts the key events and processes of the Conquest from the point of view of the Spanish; they were the ones who mastered the technology of alphabetic writing and the institution of the archive for the purpose. From the second half of the twentieth century, however, ethnohistorians such as Miguel León Portilla for Mexico and Nathan Wachtel for the Andes made it their job to trace the indigenous voices to be found in that very same archive, depicting what these authors described as 'the vision of the vanquished'.[3] These voices find expression in the historical accounts, or 'chronicles', written by people of indigenous origin, speakers of native tongues who had learned Spanish and alphabetic literacy under the colony, the most notable of whom was the indigenous nobleman Felipe Guamán Poma de Ayala (c.1615).[4]

There also exists a single early colonial account written in Quechua, telling of pre-Columbian Andean myth, ritual and religious beliefs of southern Andean society in what is nowadays the province of Huarochirí in the department of Lima. An anonymous scribe compiled the so-called 'Huarochirí manuscript' (c.1600) in Quechua,[5] under instruction from a Spanish parish priest of the day whose aim was to learn about indigenous beliefs in order to assist the Church's mission of erasing them from people's minds and supplanting them with Christian doctrine. The Huarochirí manuscript is fascinating for many reasons, among them the fact that it arises from within a culture where the kind of knowledge it conveys had hitherto been largely transmitted in the oral medium or in ritual; setting the stories down in the linear fashion demanded by writing was not a straightforward task. The text also reveals the inner conflict and ambivalence that

---

[3] Miguel León Portilla, *Visión de los vencidos. Relaciones indígenas de la conquista* (Mexico City: Universidad Nacional Autónoma de México, 2007 [1959]); Nathan Wachtel, *The Vision of the Vanquished: The Spanish Conquest of Peru through Indian Eyes, 1530–1570* (Hassocks: Harvester Press, 1977).

[4] Felipe, Guamán Poma de Ayala, *Nueva corónica y buen gobierno* (Paris: Institut d'Etnologie, 1936 [c.1615]), ed. facsimile. Frank Salomon provides a study, of greater geographical and archival range, of South American indigenous people's testimonies to be found in the written historical record. See Frank Salomon, 'Testimonies: The making and reading of native South American historical sources', in *Cambridge History of the Native Peoples of South America*, ed. by Frank Salomon and Stuart B. Schwartz, 3 vols (Cambridge: Cambridge University Press, 1999), pp. 19–95.

[5] Frank Salomon and Jorge Urioste, *The Huarochirí Manuscript: A Testament of Ancient and Colonial Andean Religion* (Austin, TX: University of Texas Press, 1991 [c.1600]).

the Quechua narrator feels towards the colonised condition in which he and his fellow countrymen found themselves.

As Andean colonial society evolved, a powerful mestizo landowning class grew up in the southern Peruvian Quechua speaking highlands, particularly in the previous Inca heartland around Cuzco. This class was distinctive in its Spanish–Quechua bilingualism and in its use of written Quechua (using the Spanish alphabet) for literary purposes, a literature that extoled the idealised past of the Incas, from whom the authors claimed ascendancy. Thus, for example, a Quechua theatrical tradition developed, which had its heyday towards the end of the eighteenth century at the time of the Tupac Amaru indigenous uprisings.[6] The regional power of this mestizo bilingual elite was quashed by edicts from metropolitan Spain in reaction against the growing national independence movement, and Quechua was officially banned from institutions.[7] This Quechua–Spanish landowning middle class still persists, embodied in the Cuzco Academy of the Quechua Language founded in the early 1950s.[8] However, neither in the literary writings of their eighteenth-century ancestors nor in the puristic form of Quechua they write and speak today, can they be considered to represent the indigenous class, in the *Vertretung* or 'speaking for' sense. Theirs is a racialised ideology that differentiates the place in which they position themselves in regional Cuzco society from the position they attribute to the indigenous *runa* (Quechua people) of the countryside (Howard, *Por los linderos*, pp. 216–222); they do not advocate for the latter.

The mode of social positioning, and self- and other- representation of the Cuzco mestizo elite, finds echoes more widely in Andean society with the emergence of *indigenismo* in the early part of the twentieth century. *Indigenismo* was a political-philosophical movement that found literary expression in novels that depicted the impoverished and marginalised plight of the Andean Indian at the same time as they tended to a romanticised representation. In no way did their work lobby for emancipation of the indigenous sector in the real world, but rather the ultimate goal was assimilation of 'the Indian' through a civilising mission. Thus, the indigenist novels

---

[6] César Itier, *El teatro quechua en el Cuzco*, 2 vols (Lima: Institut Francais d'Études Andines, 1995).

[7] Bruce Mannheim, *The Language of the Inka since the European Invasion* (Austin, TX: University of Texas Press, 1991), p. 74.

[8] Rosaleen Howard, *Por los linderos de la lengua. Ideologías lingüísticas en los Andes* (Lima: Instituto de Estudios Peruanos/Instituto Francés de Estudios Andinos/Editorial de la PUCP, 2007), http://books.openedition.org/ifea/5275, accessed 7 April 2020; Serafín M. Coronel-Molina, *Language Ideology, Policy and Planning in Peru* (Bristol: Multilingual Matters, 2015).

represent the indigenous as other, 'speaking about' them in the *Darstellung* sense.⁹ At that period, there were few indigenous voices speaking for themselves or on behalf of their people.

This situation began to change from the late twentieth century onwards, with the emergence of what came to be known as testimonial literature, through which indigenous voices were directly heard. By their nature as a written form, these texts usually came into being as a result of an anthropologist or journalist collaborating with the indigenous narrators to bring an initially oral account to written publication. One of the earliest examples for the Andean region was the *Autobiografía de Gregorio Condori Mamani y su esposa Asunta*, the life story of two monolingual Quechua speakers, economic migrants from the countryside to the city of Cuzco sometime in the 1940s, told to two Peruvian anthropologists who befriended them in the 1970s. Ricardo Valderrama and Carmen Escalante recorded their account over many months, transcribing and translating it into Spanish.¹⁰ Since then the book has been translated into many languages, was recently published in a new edition in Peru, and a documentary film has been made about Gregorio's life.

Gregorio's story comes to us as a verbatim transcription of the voice, a text produced in the act of speaking then transcribed for dissemination to an audience beyond the immediate time and place of its production, translated into the languages of cultural outsiders to Gregorio's world. This is a quite different mode of circulation from that of literary texts that start life in written form. Thus it is with the ethnographic study of oral tradition more generally and in the work I have done, for example, on Quechua storytelling in central highland Peru. By applying the concept of performance to the analysis and interpretation of orally transmitted stories, we come to appreciate their status as a *Darstellung* from the inside, a locus of enunciation quite different from that of the indigenist novel. A performative approach to the study of face-to-face storytelling allows us to understand the stories' meanings as a function of the storyteller's personal identity, the time and place of his or her narration and the surrounding circumstances of their lives at that moment, which may lead them to put a particular spin on their version of a story. Like

---

⁹ Examples of *indigenista* novels are *Huasipungo* (1934) by Ecuadorean Jorge Icaza; *Tempestad en los Andes* (1927) by Peruvian Luis E. Valcárcel; *Raza de Bronce* (1919) by Bolivian Alcides Arguedas; for a critique see, for example, Antonio Cornejo Polar, *Writing in the Air: Heterogeneity and the Persistence of Oral Tradition in Andean Literatures* (Durham, NC: Duke University Press, 2013 [1994]).

¹⁰ *Gregorio Condori Mamani y su mujer Asunta. Autobiografía*, ed. by Ricardo Valderrama and C. Escalante (Cusco: Centro Bartolomé de las Casas, 1977).

the utterances of language itself, no story is ever told in quite the same way twice, and the storyteller's personal biography may well be at the root of the variations so produced.[11]

In the context of the politics of identity that has emerged among Latin American indigenous peoples since the turn of the 1990s, the concept of representation in the *Vertretung* sense becomes most salient. In the case of Andean-Amazonian peoples, the rise of the Confederation of Indigenous Nationalities of Ecuador (CONAIE) in the late 1980s, and the growth of the Aymara *Katarista* movement in Bolivia at about the same period, gradually led to indigenous political enfranchisement and protagonism on the national stage.[12] This is to mention but two examples of the many indigenous political organisations and social movements that have sprung up and, in the case of Bolivia, come to power since that time. Representation evolves from other- to self-representation as part of this process. Moreover, political representation changes from being 'represented by' to directly 'representing' on behalf of one's own group.

In the case of a politics of identity, however, the matter is more complex. Identity becomes a tool with which to assert one's claim for recognition in a bid for power. Language, dress, music and ritual all become a part of a semiotics of the political.[13] In this context we detect some intertwining of the different senses of representation. *Darstellung* in the sense of performing identity is invoked to serve the agenda of *Vertretung* in the sense of political delegation; the motivation that drives the first shifts its ground in order to support the second. To return to Spivak's argument, the conflation of these divergent meanings in a single term in English (and indeed in Spanish *representación*) opens up potential for ambiguity and misinterpretation, which could be put to disingenuous ends. In the Latin American context, where there are interest groups that seek to contain the rise of the indigenous movements, there is a sense that even when the latter appear to self-represent, they are prevented from claiming a fully autonomous voice by the structural conditions of coloniality that hold them back.[14] From the indigenous

---

[11] Rosaleen Howard-Malverde, *The Speaking of History. 'Willapaakushayki' or Quechua Ways of Telling the Past* (London: Institute of Latin American Studies, Research Papers 21, 1990).

[12] *Indigenous Movements, Self-Representation and the State in Latin America*, ed. by Kay Warren and J. Jackson (Austin, TX: University of Texas Press, 2002).

[13] Rosaleen Howard, 'Language, signs, and the performance of power: The discursive struggle over decolonization in the Bolivia of Evo Morales', *Latin American Perspectives*, 172, 37.3 (2010), 176–194.

[14] Aníbal Quijano, 'Coloniality of power, Eurocentrism and Latin America', *Nepantla: Views from the South*, 1.3 (2000), 533–580.

perspective, there is an inexorable tension between being spoken about and being able to speak for oneself.

So far, this essay has dealt with the relationship between Andean indigenous peoples and their identities from the perspective of language as 'voice' or representation. I will now turn to the relationship between Andean indigenous peoples and their languages as communicative codes properly speaking. I will address the question of what it means in a postcolonial multilingual society to speak one language as opposed to another, and the ways in which this is a significant sociocultural and political issue.

We can glean a sense of the high levels of multilingualism that prevailed in the Andean-Amazonian countries at the time of the Spanish invasion from this Spanish explorer's account, as he navigated the Magdalena River in the early sixteenth century:

> They speak so many languages, so different from each other that I believe there aren't numbers high enough to count them [...]. In many provinces one doesn't go a league without coming across another language, as remote and distinct from the first as Castilian Spanish from Basque, or from English, or from the African languages. (Cabello Valboa (1590) cited by Mannheim, *The Language of the Inka*, p. 36)

Today, despite great loss of languages and decline in numbers of those that are still spoken, Latin America constitutes one of the most linguistically diverse regions of the world, with an estimated 420 languages spoken across 21 countries.[15] For the Andean region, in addition to languages of the Chibcha family such as Nasa, spoken in southern Colombia, Aru languages such as Aymara spoken widely in southern Peru and western Bolivia, and the many varieties of Quechua spoken from southern Colombia down to northwest Argentina, other Andean languages, such as Jaqaru in southern Peru and Chipaya on the Bolivian high plateau, survive on a smaller scale. In addition, vestiges of Andean languages of the past such as Culli in northern Peru, Puquina in the Lake Titicaca region and Cañari in Ecuador, can be traced in place names, names of flora and fauna and even in people's family names. Despite relatively healthy numbers of speakers in the case of some of the indigenous languages, and some effective language revitalisation initiatives taking place, the predominant and ever-increasing trend has been towards Hispanisation.

---

[15] *Atlas Sociolingüístico de Pueblos Indígenas en América Latina*, ed. by Inge Sichra (Cochabamba: UNICEF/FUNPROEIB, 2009), pp. vii–ix.

From the earliest decades of the Spanish colony, Hispanisation fulfilled the function that Antonio de Nebrija had remarked upon in the preface to his *Gramática de la lengua castellana* (1492), with the much cited words 'siempre la lengua fue compañera del imperio' ('language was always the companion of empire').[16] Studies such as those of contributors to del Valle (Part III) give us insight into how this worked in practice in different geopolitical locations in Latin America at various periods of post-Hispanic history.[17] At its most basic, Hispanisation is a linguistic phenomenon, whereby the European colonising language gradually replaced the autochthonous ones, entailing many historically evolving features of language contact, to be observed in the surface of speech. However, not only does Hispanisation have linguistic effects, but also social and cultural dimensions. Linguistic colonisation has had far-reaching physical, material and political consequences for Latin America's native peoples. Many of them have become assimilated into the mainstream societies due to the acculturation that Hispanisation brings in its wake, losing not only their languages but also their distinctive identities. These assimilative processes became particularly entrenched in the Andean region.

In the remainder of this chapter, I will first examine some of the consequences of Hispanisation in the Andean countries from the subjective point of view of people's life experiences. Second, I will ask whether, and how, these often-alienating kinds of experience are being alleviated by language legislation and policy in present times. I begin with an extract from the autobiography of Gregorio Condori Mamani, mentioned earlier, in which he recalls his experience of military service, a memory dating back to sometime in the 1940s. Although Gregorio speaks Quechua, words relating to the Hispanising domains of military service and alphabetic literacy are derived from Spanish; these borrowings (in bold in the extract) are the only lexical resource at his disposal for describing this sphere of experience and the verbal exchange associated with it. Indeed, the extensive language mixture that characterises Gregorio's testimony is both a product and a symptom of the hegemonic process of linguistic colonisation that he and his *runa* ancestors have undergone through the ages (see also Howard, *Por los linderos*, pp. 159–165). These are his words:

Khaynan karan. **Cuartelta** haykoq kanki mana ñawiyoq, mana ñawiyoq lloqsimoq kanki, **porque** mana atiykoqchu **abecedario**

---

[16] Elio Antonio de Nebrija, *Gramática castellana* (Madrid: Fundación Antonio de Nebrija, 1992 [1492]), p. 99.

[17] José del Valle, *A Political History of Spanish: The Making of a Language* (Cambridge: Cambridge University Press, 2013), part III.

correcto lloqsimuy. Chhaynallataq mana simiyoq haykunki, mana simillayoqtaq lloqsimunki, apenas castellanoman simi t'okhashaq. Cuartelpin chay tenientekuna, capitankuna, mana munaqkuchu runa simi rimanaykuta. 'Indios, carajo! Castellano! neqkun. Chhaynatan a pura patada castellanota rimacheq kasunkiku clasekuna.

Así era. Se entraba al cuartel sin ojos y sin ojos se salía, porque no podías salir con abecedario correcto. También sin boca entrabas y sin boca salías, apenas reventando a castellano la boca. Hasta antes de entrar al cuartel no sabía castellano; ya en el cuartel mi boca reventó al castellano. En el cuartel esos tenientes, capitanes, no querían que hablásemos runa simi: - ¡Indios, carajo! ¡Castellano! – decían. Así, a pura patada, te hacían hablar castellano los clases. (Valderrama and Escalante, p. 45; translation by the editors)

(That's how it was. You went into the barracks without eyes and you came out without eyes, because you couldn't learn the abc correctly. You also went in without a mouth and came out without a mouth, with your mouth barely bursting into Spanish. Before I entered the barracks I didn't know Spanish; once I was in the barracks my mouth burst out in Spanish. In the barracks the lieutenants, the captains, didn't want us to speak Quechua: 'Indians, dammit! Spanish!' they said. In that way, the officers kicked you into speaking Spanish.) (Author's translation)

Gregorio likens his experience of being a monolingual non-literate Quechua speaker to being in a state of physical incapacity, unable to see ('without eyes') or speak ('without a mouth'). The racial violence with which his superiors in the barracks treated him and his fellow Quechua conscripts is evoked in the way his words are infiltrated by their remembered Spanish insults (*¡Indios, carajo!*), and he recalls the suppression of Quechua as a physically embodied experience ('the officers kicked you into speaking Spanish').[18]

Gregorio's account graphically evokes the problem of racism that pervades Peruvian society, and Andean society more widely, viscerally expressed through the army seniors' language, discourse and physical behaviour. As far as language is concerned, we note their use of the interpellation 'indios',

---

[18] See Rosaleen Howard, 'Papel de viento: procesos semióticos en el discurso literario quechua', in *Heterogeneidad y literatura en el Perú*, ed. by James Higgins (Lima: Centro de Estudios Literarios Antonio Cornejo Polar, 2003), pp. 127–155, for further discussion of the cultural significance of Gregorio's testimony on this point, pp. 146–148.

a racially charged epithet that carries highly negative connotations, and the expletive 'carajo!' Regarding discourse, their exhortation to the *runa* conscripts to speak Spanish, accompanied as it is by negative language and physical admonition, speaks to a discriminatory linguistic habitus whereby social exclusion is exercised, among other channels, along lines of linguistic difference (Cornejo Polar, *Writing in the* Air, p. 160).[19]

The kind of linguistic racism that Gregorio describes was symptomatic of the society of his day, revealing of problems of non-recognition of indigenous rights and linguistic human rights along with them, that were only beginning to be expressed in terms of 'rights' at that time. Furthermore, this example gives us insight into the workings of linguistic hegemony, whereby Hispanisation is both the product of and has helped to reproduce the forms of discrimination that indigenous people suffer due to their cultural and linguistic difference. Such discrimination, as my own research and that of others has shown, produces feelings of shame and inferiority in speakers, who may opt to speak only Spanish to their children in the interest of what they see as the best path to social mobility (Howard, *Por los linderos*).

Since Gregorio's day, following the tenets laid down in the landmark (1989) Convention 169 'Concerning Indigenous and Tribal Peoples in Independent Countries' of the International Labour Organization (ILO), the majority of Latin American nation-states have responded to the indigenous movements' growing demands, reformed their political Constitutions so as legally to recognise the pluricultural and multilingual nature of the modern nation-state,[20] and approved legislation and policy that attend to educational reform for speakers of indigenous languages and to the principle of language rights as a dimension of human rights in the case of speakers of minority and indigenous languages.[21]

Mexico led the way with its 2003 *Ley General de Derechos Lingüísticos de los Pueblos Indígenas,* and other countries to have been passed language rights Acts in recent years include Paraguay, Colombia, Peru and Bolivia. However, implementation of legislation that demands recognition of minority language rights and sanctions non-adherence to such a law is a drawn-out process, as the necessary accompanying shift in discriminatory attitudes in society tends to lag far behind. In recent years, though, Peru has provided a proactive example of implementation of state-led policy on language rights,

---

[19] Pierre Bourdieu, *Language and Symbolic Power* (London: Polity Press, 1991).

[20] *Multiculturalism in Latin America. Indigenous Rights, Diversity and Democracy*, ed. by Rachel Sieder (London: Palgrave Macmillan, 2002).

[21] Stephen May, *Language and Minority Rights* (London and New York: Routledge, 2012).

backed by its Indigenous Languages Act (Law 29735, passed in 2011).[22] I will now discuss some features of the implementation of this Act that can be read as positive examples of the *Vertretung* dimension of indigenous representation.

The task of implementation of the Peruvian Indigenous Languages Act is the remit of a division of the Ministry of Culture. One of their first actions after the passing of the Act was to administer a programme of training for bilingual indigenous people to become accredited translators and interpreters, with their names entered into a National Register, able to apply their skills in public service settings.[23] The training courses, which run over three intensive weeks and have been conducted in ten iterations since 2012, in addition to their pedagogical value, generate conditions that favour the personal and professional development of the indigenous participants, speakers of many of the country's estimated 48 indigenous languages including several varieties of Quechua. The training programme reinforces their self-confidence and sense of worth as indigenous members of society, representatives of their communities and organisations, and many of them move on to professional work in which, increasingly, their indigenous identities are relevant and recognised.

One of the spin-offs of the training programme was an initiative on the part of the Ministry to invite some of the trainees to translate the text of the Indigenous Languages Act into their mother tongues; this was duly done and more than 20 different language versions of the Act were published in written and audio CD format for dissemination to the regions where the languages are variously spoken. In the translation process, the translators confronted many challenges, of which the problem of linguistic equivalence was perhaps the least problematic.[24] The following example illustrates how the issue of

---

[22] The full name is *Ley que regula el uso, preservación, desarrollo, recuperación, fomento y difusión de las lenguas originarias del Perú* ('Act that regulates the use, preservation, development, recovery, promotion, and spread of the indigenous languages of Peru').

[23] The indigenous translation and interpreting training experience was the object of a recent Arts and Humanities Research Council (AHRC)-funded collaborative research project ('The legislated mediation of indigenous language rights in Peru'). See Rosaleen Howard, Luis Andrade and R. De Pedro Ricoy, 'Translating rights: The Peruvian Languages Act in Quechua and Aymara', *Amerindia. Revue d'Ethnolinguistique Amérindienne*, 40 (2018), 219–245. Luis Andrade Ciudad, Rosaleen Howard and R. de Pedro Ricoy, 'Traduciendo culturas en el Perú: los derechos lingüísticos en la práctica', in *Lenguas en contacto: desafíos en la diversidad*, ed. by Marleen Haboud (Quito: Centro de Publicaciones de la PUCE, 2019), pp. 513–554.

[24] More detail is provided in Howard et al., 'Translating rights: the Peruvian Languages Act in Quechua and Aymara' (2018).

representation became salient as the translators sought strategies to resolve the difficulties.

The example relates to the nature of the Indigenous Languages Act as a discursive genre, that is, a legal statute expressed in the impersonal, abstract and often indeterminate language of the Law.[25] For the most part, the translators recognised that their indigenous language translations would not carry the weight of law; the original Spanish version was the one that was legally binding. Rather, their translations were intended to perform the quite different discursive function of informing peoples in the indigenous communities of the content of the Act in a language they could understand, as the translator into the Chanka variety of Quechua spoken in southern Peru explained: 'El objeto era comunicar y hacer que la gente también se apropie de la Ley, o sea esta es una ley que defiende nuestros derechos' ('The aim was to communicate [the content] and enable people to take ownership of the Act, for this is a law that defends our rights') (interview with Chanka Quechua translator, Lima, November 2014).

In support of this aim, a strategy we identified in our analysis of the Quechua translation, supported by the explanation the translator provided us with in interview, was the shift from third-person singular to first-person plural in certain declarative phrases that express the basic tenets of the Act. So, for example, the Chanka Quechua translation of Article 1.1 begins: *Kay leymi lluqsimun kikinchikpa siminchikkunapi rimananchikpaq derechunchikkuna qawarichinapaq* ('This Act is passed in order to make visible our rights for us to speak our own languages'). The inclusive first-person suffix *-nchik* appears on various key words in the translation, while the original Spanish glosses as follows: 'The aim of this law is to clarify (people's) rights and guarantees in linguistic matters, as established in Article 48 of the Political Constitution of Peru'.[26] The shift from this impersonal register to a personalised one establishes a radical discursive shift between the original text and its translation, by constructing the Quechua-speaking translator and her interlocutor as collective subjects of the utterance; the communicative effect of the inclusive 'we' is to personalise the text and involve all parties in emitting its message. In the spirit of this Quechua translation, at least as far as some of its Articles are concerned, the law can be taken not only to represent the people it is designed to serve, but actually to emit their own voice.

---

[25] John Joseph, 'Indeterminacy, translation and the law', in *Translation and the Law*, ed. by M. Morris (Amsterdam and Philadelphia: John Benjamins, 1995), pp. 13–36.

[26] Rosaleen Howard, Luis Andrade and R. De Pedro Ricoy, 'Translating rights: The Peruvian Languages Act in Quechua and Aymara', *Amerindia. Revue d'Ethnolinguistique Amérindienne*, 40 (2018), 237–238.

In this chapter I have taken the concept of 'representation' as a theme to help trace the positions from which indigenous peoples in the Andes have been constructed in their colonial and postcolonial history, and how this outsider construction has gradually shifted to the position we find today, whereby indigenous peoples, through their political organisations and their cultural practices, acquire the power to speak for themselves. This overview has placed particular emphasis on indigenous people's use of their languages in speaking and writing.

Section 2

Temporalities

As Tony Porter reminds us, temporalities (conceptions of time) are constructed socially.[1] Temporal systems, described as 'assemblages that bring together temporal artefacts such as clocks and schedules, the temporalities of the natural world and the body, and social practices involving agency, power and organization' (Porter, p. 270), are developed to suit particular interests. The interaction of temporal systems, especially since the emergence of world standard time, constitutes and intensifies globalisation. In modernity, time is abstracted from space and segmented 'into atomised units susceptible of measurement and quantification', which are 'driven by the forces of merchant, industrial and finally speculative finance capital'.[2] This Eurocentric conception of time has occluded alternative temporalities, such as those in Pre-Colombian America. Since the 1980s temporalities have been 'spatialized' into numerous, often conflicting, temporalities that challenge the European project of modernity and the historicist, colonialist conception of time as a linear, universal progression through 'stages' of development from 'savagery' to 'civilization'. Even today the increasing acceleration of time driven by the digital economy, has resulted in a 'world of the perpetual present';[3] in fact, instantaneous communication across space is what makes transnationalism possible.

---

[1] Tony Porter, 'The strategic manipulation of transnational temporalities', *Globalizations*, 1, 13.3 (2016), 270–284.

[2] Russell West-Pavlov, *Temporalities* (London and New York: Routledge, 2013), p. 175.

[3] George Vassilacopoulos and Toula Nicolacopoulos, 'Radical change in the era of the perpetual present', 21 February 2003. <http://www.ethicalpolitics.org/seminars>, accessed 5 January 2019.

This second section explores temporalities and the social construction of time in relation to our understanding of the Spanish-speaking world and terms such as 'transnational' and 'modern' in this context.[4] Focusing on the early modern period (sixteenth and seventeenth centuries) Mark Thurner develops ideas sketched out in the introduction arguing that the term 'transnational' is too 'shallow' to encapsulate the complex histories of the Hispanophone world that has 'long been global'. He points to the fragility of names such as 'Spain', 'Peru' and 'Tawantinsuyu', the Quechua name for the Inca Empire. What did these names signify? How have their meanings changed over time? By approaching a history of 'Spain' from the perspective of 'Peru', as did the Peruvian scholar Pedro Peralta de Barnuevo (1663–1743) for whom 'classical' Spain was to Peru what Rome was to Spain, Thurner suggests that both 'Spain' and 'Peru' are 'transnational inventions'. He asks, furthermore, what 'nation' might mean in the context of an Empire in which a 'Spanish nation' coexisted with an 'Indian nation', later divided into, respectively, a 'nation' of European and American (Creole) Spaniards on the one hand, and a 'nation' of distinct American *castas* on the other.

Alex Samson argues that the drive to measure time and space in the early modern period (1500–1800) propelled scientific and technological advancement across the Spanish world (which included most of Western Europe and the Americas) to an unprecedented degree. The Empire was 'the engine-room of progress and invention' on a global scale. The obsession with precision in the measurement of time and space, leading to ground-breaking inventions such as the pendulum clock (in the Spanish Netherlands),[5] made it possible to map and navigate with exactitude and to fix otherwise porous boundaries in the newly discovered, unmapped territories. European precision technologies displaced the cyclical, ritual time and dating systems of indigenous peoples in the Americas, ushering in urbanisation and 'transnational' modernity. But if transnational communication became speedier and more reliable, promoting global flows of itinerant capital, commodities, people and knowledges, for a long time the Empire would find significant obstacles to temporal standardisation in its encounter with diverse indigenous understandings of time itself.

Andrew Ginger considers what 'the modern', 'modernity' and 'modernism' might have meant in a post-imperial Spanish-speaking world and concludes

---

[4] See also, for example, Joanna Page and Ignacio M. Sánchez Prado, 'Temporalities in Latin American film', *Arizona Journal of Hispanic Cultural Studies*, 16 (2012), 203–10.

[5] The states of the Holy Roman Empire in the Low Countries governed by the Spanish Crown (1556–1714).

that it is almost impossible to pinpoint their meanings. The debates in nineteenth- and twentieth-century Spain and Latin America about whether and in what ways the newly formed states were 'modern' and how they compared to other countries is so embedded in language games that, in Ginger's view, poetry – the creative use of language – may be the only way of grasping and articulating the complex heterogeneity of the modern Hispanic world. Ginger's model is José Martí's *Nuestra América* (Our America) (1891), the celebrated, poetic manifesto for a post-colonial Latin American future, still influential today. Martí (1853–1895), the 'Apostle of Cuban Independence' from Spain, envisaged a non-Eurocentric, organic and ethical conception of modernity for a transnational Spanish America.

Finally, Samuel Llano presents what might be considered a transnational anachronism: the attribution of a professionalised art form, the 'Spanish' musical style flamenco, to a historical period and ethnic genealogy to which it does not belong. His chapter underscores the dangers of inventing history to explain present-day transnational phenomena without due evidence. Manipulation of the past to legitimise (or undermine) interpretations in the present must be resisted. The aim of this book is precisely to query the unnuanced application of the currently fashionable term 'transnational' to the Hispanic world. Llano rehearses the long-standing debates about whether flamenco 'belongs to' the cultures of medieval Islam, Spanish Roma/*gitanos* or nineteenth-century cafés, concluding that the history of flamenco is 'a fictional space', constructed in narratives 'cobbled together' for a specific purpose. The purpose was political, to create a 'national dance' in order to consolidate a national Spanish identity during the authoritarian regime of Francisco Franco (1939–1975) and, later, a distinctive Andalusian regional identity in a Spain of 'autonomous communities'. The chapters in this section prompt us to be aware of the manipulation of temporalities in relation to the Spanish-speaking world, often for national or imperial political purposes.

5

The Names of Spain and Peru

Notes on the Global Scope of the Hispanic

Mark Thurner

Before the nineteenth-century reduction of 'Spain' and 'Spanish' to a trademark tongue born of Iberian soil and sun, the scope of 'the Hispanic' had long been global and 'transnational', albeit in ways that now require historical explanation. Politically speaking, 'the Spanish Monarchy' did not exist as such before 1812, and the Spain we think we know today was at that time (and perhaps still is) far off in the future. For most of its history, the Crown was known instead as 'la Monarquía Hispánica' and 'Indiana'. The distinction between 'Hispanic' and 'Spanish' was subtle and inconstant but in the end crucial, for although 'Hispanic' was in certain contexts interchangeable with 'Spanish' its meaning was for many in the empire akin to 'Roman', that is, it signified a sort of modern, global and improved edition of the Roman empire. Tellingly, the long and variable titles of dominion of the Hispanic throne's dynastic incumbent shifted according to the context and moment of its iteration. As Juan Solórzano Pereira noted in his *Politica Indiana* (1647) (Book I, Chapter VIII) the titles were so long and contingent that they consumed many pages, and so Charles V was content with the elegant, all-encompassing 'Plus Ultra', while his son Philip II was called by 'Supreme Catholic Majesty King of Kings', or simply 'Sun King', as well as 'Emperor of the Indies'.[1] Philip IV was known as the 'Planet King', and the Bourbons were generally called 'King of the Spains [las Españas] and Emperor of the Indies'. These titles were relatively speaking, not pompous exaggerations, since the scope and complexity of the Hispanic Empire far outstripped all previous known empires, including the Egyptian, Persian, Chinese and Roman.

---

[1] Juan Solórzano Pereira, *Politica Indiana* (Madrid: Diego Diaz de la Carrera, 1647).

When the 'Spanish Nation' and the 'Spanish Monarchy' finally was constituted in 1812 as an all-inclusive, unitary concept under the plural name of 'The Spains', its scope was not limited to a contiguous territory but was instead a transoceanic commonwealth of 'Spanish' citizens and nationals that included those formerly classified as 'Indians' and 'Mestizos'. Although this global, Constitutional Spanish Monarchy of The Spains was short-lived as an effective political unit, its ambiguous, transoceanic cultural effects endured, in part because the 1812 Constitution of Cádiz served as a blueprint for many of the national constitutions of the 'Hispanic American republics'. It was not until the very late nineteenth century – that is, after the loss in 1898 of the few remaining 'Ultramarine' island provinces (Cuba, Puerto Rico) of the once vast and far-flung 'Empire of the Indies' – that the primary referent of 'Spanish' and 'Spain' became 'national' in the limited, territorial sense in which the term is widely understood today, such that 'The Spains' could now only refer to intra-Peninsular variations. At about the same time, the neologism 'Latin America' began to catch on among elites in certain parts of the Americas and north of the Pyrenees, although this new name did not become popular until the twentieth century. Instead, 'Hispanic America' or simply 'America' were more commonly used throughout the nineteenth century. In the early twentieth century concerted efforts were made to impress the hyphenated, transoceanic names of 'Hispano-America' and 'Ibero-America' in popular parlance as well. These names remain in use today, as does the more recent term, the 'Americas'.

In sum, and like most 'new' academic concepts that would push the horizons of research and learning, the otherwise promising project of 'Transnational Spanish Studies' begs a little history. In the first place, the notion of 'transnational' is too shallow for the Hispanic world if we understand 'national' in today's limited, territorial terms or via such notions as 'diaspora'. The 'national' in the sense understood today did not exist before the late eighteenth century, when other senses of the term prevailed. Before we run with the concept, we should first ask ourselves a few critical, historical questions: When, where and how was 'Spain' and 'the Spanish' and 'the Hispanic' fashioned, and in relation to what other concepts or names did they emerge (for example, 'Iberia', 'Europe', 'Indies,' 'New Spain' or 'Rome')? What useable meanings adhered to those concepts in this, that or another context? What changes or inflections did those concepts suffer across space and time? The same questions must be posed to such concepts as 'nation' and 'empire', without which 'transnational' would only appear to be impossible. The point being that the entangled histories of these names of history are not merely of academic interest to philologists and *curiosos*: common usages in the streets of Madrid, Mexico City or Lima today betray their indelible traces.

'Spain' itself is not necessarily the best place from which to engage the history of these traces, particularly if we are interested in their global dimensions. Consequently, here we will focus primarily on 'Peru', understood as a key component of the *Plus Ultra* Indo-Hispanic world.[2]

Before 1812 one could speak and write of 'the Spanish nation' or 'the Spanish language' not only or even primarily in relation to 'foreigners' (such as the French, Germans, Chinese, Turks and so on) but instead in terms of intimate others, that is, vis-à-vis 'nations' and 'tongues' *within* the Peninsula and the Indies. This is particularly true when we consider the meaning of 'Spanish' beyond the Peninsula and Europe, that is, in the *Plus Ultra* realm of 'the Empire of the Indies'. But it frequently holds just as well for more proximate parts of the Hispanic world, including the Iberian and Italian peninsulas and much of 'Austrian' or Central and Eastern Europe. The making of 'Spain' and 'Spanish' was largely a Castilian project, and thus strongest in Castile and the Indies. Other parts of Peninsular 'Spain' spoke other languages, although 'Castilian' could serve as a lingua franca. Eventually, and this is as true today as it was in the eighteenth century, the majority of 'Castilian' speakers never set foot in Castile or even Europe, and they did not speak like *madrileños*. Global 'Spanish' was and remains today largely an American or 'Indian' invention

A recent controversy is illustrative. The current Spanish government has sought to market Spanish as a 'global language' via the Cervantes Institute, but within the Brand of Spain (*Marca España*). This act is reminiscent of the Cortes de Cádiz, who in 1812 declared a global Spanish empire of 'Spaniards'. In 1812 this could, at least temporarily, attract adherents. Today, it is roundly rejected by the American academies and speakers of Spanish, who demand a 'Panhispanic' approach to the language. It is evident that today 'Hispanic' is not quite consonant with 'Spanish' or 'Spain'. The addition of the prefix 'pan-' (more or less equivalent to 'trans'), however, draws attention to the ambiguity of the term. It still seems to require a prefix, whereas in the imperial past it did not.

'Spain', 'Spanish' and 'Hispanic' in History

What things could 'Spain' and 'Spanish' mean in the twelfth, sixteenth or eighteenth centuries? Since the conquest of Toledo in 1085 under King Alfonso VI of Castile and the imperial coronation of his successor in Leon

---

[2] *Plus Ultra* (Lat. further beyond) is the national motto of Spain. The motto of the Holy Roman Emperor and King of Spain, Charles V, was *non terrae plus ultra* (no land further beyond).

in 1135, where Pope Innocent II bestowed the extraordinary title of 'King of Kings', Castile and Leon's kings had demonstrated imperial and crusading pretensions that rivalled those of the Germanic Holy Roman Emperors. A century hence, Alfonso X *El sabio* (reigned 1252–1284) made an unsuccessful bid for election as Holy Roman Emperor. His bid for universal Christian rule was buttressed by the writing of an imperial 'History of Spain'. It was not the first time that a peninsular or Iberian 'king' had deployed the name 'Espanna', although it was surely the most memorable to date. Although or perhaps because it was unfinished, the *Estoria de Espanna* left its mark on subsequent Hispanic historiography both in the Peninsula and the Indies. The *Estoria* emphasized the legacy of Roman Empire in the Iberian Peninsula, and it sang the epic story of the heroic military campaigns to expand Christian 'Spain' against Islam. Notably, this vernacular history of Castilian kings and knights engaged in the Reconquista helped establish in historical discourse the imagined, unitary subject of history named 'Spain'. This image drew upon Roman and Phoenician 'Hispania' and 'Hispalis' (early gloss for the city that later became Seville) found in the writings of Isidore of Seville (c.560–636). 'Spain' was thus configured as an expansive desire for Christian realm that could trace its venerable genealogy to Roman 'Hispania'. This history was addressed to notables, the church and other European courts, and it was written 'in the name of Spaniards'.

The much-heralded union of 'the Supreme Catholic Monarchs' Ferdinand and Isabella did not make a single 'Spanish Kingdom' or nation but instead united, in dynastic alliances, several kingdoms and cities within and without the Iberian Peninsula, the strongest being Castile and Aragon, with the latter including Sicily and Naples.[3] Two centuries later, their grandson and Burgundian prince became 'Charles I of the Hispanic Monarchy'. Charles realized Alfonso's dream when in 1519 he was elected 'Germanic Holy Roman Emperor'. Taking the title of Charles V and the emblem of *Plus Ultra* (signifying dominion beyond the Pillars of Hercules, in Cádiz), his reign as 'King of Rome and Emperor of the World' represented the early modern apex of Catholic empire, in effect uniting, if only partially and by force of arms, the Germanic and Romanic worlds on the eve of their longstanding divorce. Critically, Charles V's universal reign coincided with the successive 'conquests' or Catholic 'accession' into Christendom and the transfer of sovereignty of the 'monarchies' and 'rich lands' of the Occidental Indies, 'Mexico' and 'Peru', soon to become very profitable Viceroyalties. Charles V's claims to world dominion were promoted in Miguel de Ulzurrum's *Catholicum*

---

[3] See Antonio Feros, *Speaking of Spain: The Evolution of Race and Nation in the Hispanic World* (Cambridge, MA and London: Harvard University Press, 2017).

opus imperiale regiminis mundi (1525).[4] Philip II effectively hispanised this imperial 'Roman' tradition, in part by erecting El Escorial, near Madrid, as a Salomonic temple and tomb for his father and the future of his dynasty in Spain, in part by collecting sacred relics from around Spain and the heretical North. Under Philip II, the original 'Sun King' and 'Emperor of the Indies', and continuing under Philip III and Philip IV, the famous 'Planet King', the imperial 'history of Spain' begun by the Alphonsine historians now fully encompassed 'the Indies' east and west. This global expansion during the long reign of the Philips generated a network or 'red columnaria', that is, a Catholic 'Monarquía Hispánica' whose twin symbolic pillars were no longer those of Hercules (the mythical founder of Cádiz) at the Mediterranean mouth of the Atlantic but those of 'the Spains' and 'the Indies'.

Early modern 'Spain' understood as 'Iberia' or the 'Peninsula' (that is, as *país*) consisted of several 'nations' and 'kingdoms' and cities, including Catalonia, Barcelona, Portugal, Valencia, Castile, Leon, Toledo, Cordova, Sevilla, Murcia, Aragon and Navarre. Belonging by right to a 'nation' in the Peninsula was generally defined by birth and descent, such that one could be a *vecino* or *ciudadano* of a nation such as Castile or Valencia, and thus be called Castilian or Valencian. Castile was most identified with the name of 'Spain' and 'Spaniard', however. Since the Indies were ruled by the Crown of Castile via the Council of the Indies, many of the migrants were initially Castilian and Basque, although, notably, in the Indies they were generally called 'Spaniards'. Indeed, it is in the Indies that 'the Spanish nation' emerges in official discourse and administration in juxtaposition to an 'Indian Nation'. Nevertheless, within the Indies it was still possible to distinguish transplanted Peninsular 'nations' of Spaniards (that is, Catalonians, Galicians, Asturians, Basques and so on). That is, 'nation' came to mean two things in the Indies: a legal and fiscal category separated from the Indian, within which it was possible to recognise cultural distinctions, also called national, derived from the Peninsula. The critical distinction between 'Spanish Nation' and 'Indian Nation' would unravel and enter into crisis in the second half of the eighteenth century, when the 'Spanish Nation' was split into 'European Spaniards' and 'American Spaniards'. The 'Indian Nation' also unravelled, split by tensions between *originarios* (local natives) and *forasteros* (migrant natives) and between the several *castas* of mixed blood. The Bourbons would eventually abolish the distinction, creating the new category of *indígena* or natives. Finally, the 1812 Constitution of Cadiz would abolish the Bourbon *indígena*, making

[4] Roberto J. Gonzalez-Casanovas, *Imperial Histories from Alonso X to Inca Garcilaso: Revisionist Myths of Reconquest and Conquest* (Potomac, MD: Scripta Humanistica, 1997).

all eligible inhabitants of the Indies 'Spaniards' or 'Ultramarine Spaniards'. The revolutions of independence would abolish 'Spaniard' and also 'Indian' (although that had already been done by the Bourbon regime), in favour first of the continental name of 'American' and, a few years later, of national names like 'Peruvian' or 'Mexican'. Nevertheless, the Bourbon name and category of *indígena* would return in most of the Hispanic American republics.

In Peru, 'Spaniards' were also generally called 'Wiracocha' (Quechua for people from across the sea) until the eighteenth century, and indeed appear as such in official census records. Still, both in the Peninsula and the Indies the Castilian language, with many local variations, became the dominant vernacular of the empire, over time becoming, from the perspective of the Peninsula, modern 'Spanish'. In Peru, however, this name change was not accepted. The language is still routinely called 'castellano' in Peru, and in the colonial period it was often called *cristiano*. It should be noted that in central and southern Mexico, Central America, the Andes, Amazonia and Patagonia the majority of inhabitants, including Creoles and Mestizos, spoke in native tongues or a hybrid or 'Creolised' manner. In Peru, Quechua served as the lingua franca of social communication until the late nineteenth century. As a result, Peruvian Castilian was highly variable, ranging from a high Castilian in certain barrios of Lima to a heavily Andean Castilian in the highlands and Amazonia, marked by code-switching and Quechua and Aymara (among other native tongues) intonations and forms of address, vocabulary and syntax.

The Names of Peru and Spain

The date 23 April is World Book Day. Although it is unlikely that all three died on this date, the bookish celebration ostensibly commemorates or markets the passing in 1616 of Miguel de Cervantes Saavedra, William Shakespeare and Inca Garcilaso de la Vega. In the UK Shakespeare steals the show. Spanish institutions in the UK, particularly the Instituto Cervantes, obviously do celebrate Cervantes but UK interest is only slight. Inca Garcilaso de la Vega is almost totally ignored, or if mentioned appears only as a token, supporting player who no-one seems to know anything about. This is due in part to the fact that today Shakespeare and Cervantes are celebrated as 'universal' authors, and that both wrote fiction and drama that is still widely read and performed. The 'universal' superlative is not bestowed on Inca Garcilaso, who moreover did not write fiction, or at least not in the sense in which that term is understood today. Unlike Cervantes and Shakespeare, Inca Garcilaso was a translator and historian, and pretty much only Peruvians and scholars read his work today and then, sadly, normally not as history but as 'literature'.

Nevertheless, although not 'universal' the modest Inca Garcilaso de la Vega was quite probably more 'global' and pioneering than the two giants who, every 23 April, dwarf him.

In the *Plus Ultra* domain of the Hispanic, the fictional characters of *El Ingenioso hidalgo Don Quixote de la Mancha* strangely tread as 'Spaniards' where its Castilian author could not. Indeed, it is tempting to speculate that the first modern novel was written in no small part *because* its future author was denied passage to the Peru of his desire, ostensibly for wounds suffered at the Battle of Lepanto. In contrast, the author of *Los Comentarios Reales de los Incas* (The Royal Commentaries of the Incas) penned his history of the Incas while in Andalusian exile, as he watched his Peru's precious metals sail up the Guadalquivir.[5] After soldiering for His 'Sacred, Catholic, Royal Majesty, Defender of the Faith [and] King of kings' in Peru and Andalusia, the Peru-born and baptised Gómez Suárez de Figueroa (1539–1616) retired to a monkish life near Cordova, adopting, in a genealogical and poetic gesture authorised by patriarchal custom, the pen name of 'Inca Garcilaso de la Vega'.[6]

Gómez was the son of the union of captain Sebastian Garcilaso de la Vega y Vargas and the niece of the Inca Huayna Capac (the twelfth 'Capac' Inca who apparently fell victim to smallpox before Pizarro's arrival in the Inca realm), baptised Isabel Suárez Chimpu Ocllo. Gómez was born out of wedlock, since at the time Crown policy prohibited marriage between 'Indians' or 'New Christians' and 'Old Christians' or 'Peninsulars'. Sebastian later married Luisa Martel, arranging for Chimpu Ocllo to be wed to the commoner Juan del Pedroche. Gómez sailed to Spain in 1560, and three years later adopted his father's aristocratic surname and the titular and matrilineal 'Inca'. Some scholars have suggested that he favoured his father's surname for its literary prestige: Garcilaso de la Vega (1503–1536) was a celebrated Golden Age poet-soldier. In his work the author of the global age's first antipodal mestizo history would thus present himself to the world of letters as an 'Inga yndio' or Indian Inca with a prestigious Spanish surname of resonant literary fame. But is his two-part history of Inca civilisation and 'Roman' *traslatio imperii* or 'Spanish' conquest best understood as a literary gem of 'the Spanish Golden Age'?

Los Comentarios Reales was by contemporary standards 'history' or 'historical commentary' or 'chronicle', not 'literature', 'fiction' or 'fable' as it is often read today. Those anachronistic markers were applied to the text by

---

[5] *Los Comentarios Reales de los Incas* (Lisbon, 1609) (The Royal Commentaries of the Incas).

[6] See the royal dedication in Inca Garcilaso de la Vega, *La traducción del indio de los tres diálogos de amor de León Hebreo* (Madrid: Pedro Madrigal, 1590).

critics centuries later. In its general design, *The Royal Commentaries* may be characterised as a providential, Neoplatonist or exegetical dynastic history, or what at the time was known, after the Old Testament and classical traditions of royal genealogical history, as a 'Book of Kings'. It clearly distinguishes, via the exegetical or etymological method and with considerable erudition, between 'fable' and 'similitude', the latter being the measure of truth in early modern historiography. In this account, the Inca or Capac dynasty uncannily parallels the Roman, and it is no coincidence that there are twelve Incas before the dynasty's fall, as in the 'Twelve Caesars' of Suetonius.[7] The bloody and providential finale of the dynasty also echoes the storied travails of the late imperial tetrarchy and, in particular, of Constantine as narrated by Eusebius. Nevertheless, it is not a mere aping of Roman history, and it does not present itself as a 'Spanish' account. Still, it would not be incorrect to argue that in certain respects it was an ingenious 'imitation' of Roman history in the early modern sense of that word, when a well-executed 'resemblance' implied a genial artifice that could improve upon and thus exceed, its original. Indeed, and like other accounts of the period, Garcilaso's Inca empire exceeds the Roman in every way but one: the written word.[8] By writing a providential history of the Incas based primarily on the exegesis of Inca and other native oral sources, complemented by the observations of trustworthy eyewitnesses and early chroniclers, our Peruvian author provided, in a retrospective gesture of mourning that opened a new future, that missing element. On paper, at least, the 'Peruvian empire' of the Inca's pen could now compete with and indeed surpass the ancient Roman empire of Virgil and Suetonius, the same that had conquered and civilised 'Hispania'. Decisively, that great empire of the book now had its antipodal and mestizo 'Inca' historian. On 23 April we may celebrate the Inca as the author of the first truly 'global' or antipodal history book.

The name 'Peru' first appeared, as Peruvian historian Jorge Basadre noted, 'with a loud crash' in 'an abyss of history' at 'the edge of the world' in the early 1500s.[9] But it was Inca Garcilaso's exegesis of the event of naming that established for posterity 'the origin and principle of the name of Peru'. As Basadre noted and Raul Porras Barrenechea confirmed, the news of Peru

---

[7] Gaius Suetonius Tranquillus, *De vita Caesarum* (AD 121), known as The Twelve Caesars, consists of 12 biographies of Caesar and the 11 emperors. A similar structure is evident in *Los Comentarios Reales*.

[8] See David Lupher, *Romans in a New World: Classical Models in Sixteenth-century Spanish America* (Ann Arbor, MI: University of Michigan Press, 2003).

[9] Jorge Basadre, *Meditaciones sobre el destino histórico del Perú* (Lima: Huascarán, 1947), pp. 104–105.

was resounding, even euphoric: 'her name resonated universally as a fascinating announcement of riches and well-being'.[10] In the sixteenth-century, the name 'Peru' evoked dizzying images of El Dorado. The proverbial *poseer el Perú* (literally, 'he's got Peru') was applied to extraordinarily wealthy men of influence, and it anticipated by more than two centuries that more remembered Spanish proverb about the New World: '*hacer la América*' ('do America'), that is, 'to get rich abroad'. Even more exhilarating was the exclamation, still heard in Peru and neighbouring countries today, of '¡Vale un Perú!' (That's worth a Peru!). This phrase appears to have initially evoked Francisco Pizarro's fabulous 'gift' of 'Peru' to the Holy Roman Emperor Charles V, which included the supposed 'crown' or feather headdress of the Inca, the *maskaypacha*, which for the monarchy would symbolise the transfer or accession of imperial sovereignty. Notably, Pizarro's gift to the titular 'Emperor of Rome' was made possible by an earlier, more fantastic one: the 'king's ransom' or 'palace full of gold' rendered to Pizarro by the captive Inca Atahualpa c.1533. In his *General History of Peru* (1617), also known as the *Second Part of the Royal Commentaries of the Incas*, Inca Garcilaso would meticulously crosscheck and quantify Atahualpa's ransom (his figure was slightly lower than Blas Valera's kipu-based accounting of 4,800,000 ducats), comparing the figures with those presented by French jurist and historian Jean Bodin for European ransoms. He concluded that not only was the Inca's ransom the greatest the world had ever seen but it was also the principle material cause of Spain's greatness 'for', he wrote, 'it was well established' that prior to the conquest of Peru, 'Spain had little money'.

At the same time, the Inca's prideful reckoning of Atahualpa's record-breaking ransom is an exercise in a work of mourning that is a colonial critique and, in the eyes of those later 'Peruvian' reading subjects whom Inca Garcilaso's history founds, a melancholy anticipation of a shared colonial misery. Writing some 70 years after the event, Inca Garcilaso noted that Atahualpa's unprecedented ransom now seemed like a paltry sum to his fabulously rich 'Spanish' readers, since '10 or 12 million ducats worth of gold and silver now sail up the Guadalquivir each year, sent by my land to all of Spain, and to all of the Old World'. Peru's gold and silver, he added, had 'revealed herself to be a cruel stepmother (*madrastra*) to her own sons, and the passionate mother of foreigners'.[11]

---

[10] Jorge Basadre, *La Promesa de la Vida Peruana y otros ensayos* (Lima: Mejía Baca, 1958), p. 14; Raul Porras Barrenechea, *El Nombre del Perú* (Lima: Villanueva, 1951).
[11] Inca Garcilaso de la Vega, *Segunda Parte de los Comentarios Reales de los Incas o Historia General del Peru* (Cordova, 1617), Libro I, Capitulo XXXVIII, folio 31. My translation.

Since Inca Garcilaso's early, motherless reckoning of the wages of empire in exile, the 'king's ransom' of the Inca cannot help but evoke the stepmothered patria of a colonial history whose subjects shared a similarly displaced condition. But Inca Garcilaso's *Royal Commentaries* was itself a 'king's ransom' of another kind, for it purchased in the world of letters riches of the soul (converted to Catholicism) for living and future Peruvians. At the same time, however, this ransoming of the soul would recognise the loss and curse of the 'riches of the body' remitted to Spain and 'all of the Old World' (as is well known, Peruvian silver underwrote the emerging, global system of banking with centres in Genoa, Amsterdam and London, and it provided the means in the form of the *peso columnario*, for commerce with China and India). The Incas were reinvented in Inca Garcilaso's exiled history as the 'Kings of Peru that were'.[12] Nevertheless, this dynastic reinvention that placed Peru in a supreme position on the global map of history had at its heart the founding figure of the barbarian 'Indian'. Although this figure was mentioned in earlier accounts of the naming of 'Peru' including that of José de Acosta, it was Inca Garcilaso who canonised and Peruvianised 'Beru', with these memorable words:

> One [of the ships sent down from Panama by Blasco Nuñez de Balboa] sailed farther than the others down past the equator, navigating along the coast, and as it went on its way it caught sight of an Indian fishing at the mouth of a river like those many rivers that flow into the Ocean there [...] The ship passed before the Indian [...] By way of signs and words the Spaniards [...] inquired of him: 'What land was this and what was it called?' By their facial expressions and gestures the Indian understood that they were questioning him, but he did not understand what they were asking him, and to those whom he understood to be questioning him, responded he with haste (before they could do him harm) by naming his proper name, saying 'Beru,' and then he added another [name], saying 'Pelu.' What he meant to say was: 'If you ask me what I am called, then I call myself Beru, and if you ask me where I was, then I say I was in the river [...]' The Christians understood in accordance with their desire, imagining that the Indian had understood and so responded appropriately, as if he and they had spoken in Castilian. Ever since that time, which was in 1515 or 1516, the Spaniards – corrupting both names as they have almost all the words

---

[12] The foundational chronicle is Francisco de Xerez, *Verdadera relación de la conquista del Peru y de la provincia del Cuzco llamada la Nueva Castilla* (Seville: Casa de Bartholomé Pérez, 1534).

they take from the language of the Indians of that land – [...] have called that rich and grand Empire [...] that the Inca Kings [...] had conquered and subjected, 'Peru.' That is the origin and principle of the name of Peru, so famous in the world, and rightly so, for she has filled the world with gold and silver, pearls and precious stones. (*Primera Parte de los Comentarios Reales de los Incas*, Libro 1, Capítulos IV-V)

For the antipodal or bi-worldly Inca ('transnational' is too feeble a term to encompass his gesture), the name of Peru was both evidently wrong and manifestly true, for it was a predictable corruption of words made irresistibly true by the history of the usage of words. By the early 1600s the origin of the name of Peru had become confused by the corruptions of translation, the repetition of error and a widening gulf of ignorance. Among the early accounts of the origin of the name the most notable and informed was that of the 'ghost chronicler' and intrepid mestizo Jesuit, Father Blas Valera.[13] Blas Valera had argued that the name was not 'proper' to Peru but instead a Spanish corruption of the Quechua term *pirua* (granary). Despite his great admiration for Blas Valera's historical writings (apparently the lost source of much of his own history), Inca Garcilaso rejected this view on historical and linguistic grounds. 'Pirua' could not be the origin of 'Peru' since at the moment of coinage (*c*.1515 or 1516) the Spaniards had not yet penetrated into the Inca-ruled, Quechua-speaking interior and so could not possibly have encountered this word or the thing it named. The first boatloads of Spaniards, the Inca noted, had landed in the northern reaches (today southern Ecuador and northern Peru) of the 'barbarian' Yunga-speaking coastal region.[14]

Shifting the ground of the controversy to the linguistic probabilities of the first act of utterance of the name, Inca Garcilaso offered an alternative account based, apparently, on his second-hand knowledge of the 'Yunga' (lowland) or 'Chimu' tongue. Since 'in the language of that distant coastal province, Pelu is an appellative name that means river in general', and since historical accounts suggested that the Spaniards had come ashore near the mouth of one of these rivers, it was likely that this Yunga name for river was implicated in the event of Spanish discovery. But that was insufficient proof, for how could the Spaniards, unschooled in Yunga, have known that 'river' was called 'Pelu'? At the mouth of some such 'Pelu' the Spaniards must have

---

[13] On Blas Valera, see Sabine Hyland, *The Jesuit and the Incas: The Extraordinary Life of Padre Blas Valera* (Ann Arbor: University of Michigan Press, 2003).

[14] This is Inca Garcilaso's contention. Other contemporary accounts of first contact place the mythical river of 'Viru', 'Veru' or 'Pelu' closer to Panama, where Yunga was not spoken. The Inca's version has become the accepted truth.

encountered a stunned, Yunga-speaking 'Indian' (indio) barbarian and taken him aboard. The proper name of this barbarian was surely 'Beru'. In short, 'Peru' was, in the first instance, the événemential conjuncture of the utterance of the words 'Beru' and 'Pelu' in the mouth of 'Beru' (the barbarian) in the mouth of 'Pelu' (the river's mouth at the sea) in the ears of wayward Spanish navigators.

Following the Jesuit chroniclers Blas Valera and José de Acosta, Inca Garcilaso confirmed that 'in Peru' the names 'Peru' and 'New Castile' (in the early sixteenth century these names were often applied interchangeably, although the measurable dominion granted to Pizarro as the Emperor's *adelantado* was rather less extensive than the still imaginary Peru) were uttered only by Spaniards. Although the resounding 'Peru' was the preferred name in Europe, the name 'Peru' was still uncommon among the provincial natives 60 years after contact, because in their language they did not have a generic name for the union of the kingdoms and provinces of the Natural Lords (kurakas or ethnic chiefs) that ruled over them, as when one says Spain, Italy or France, which hold within themselves many provinces. They were accustomed to naming each province by its own proper name and they did not possess a proper name that signified the entire realm (*Primera Parte de los Comentarios Reales*, Libro I, Capítulo IV). Things were different for the Quechua speakers at the high centre of the Inca Realm, however. In Inca Garcilaso's lingua franca (Quechua), that realm or 'union' was called 'Tawantinsuyu, which means the four quarters of the world' conquered and 'united by the Inca kings' (Libro I, Capítulos IV–V). Nevertheless, within or under each of the imperial 'quarters' the many 'provinces' retained their local names in so many languages, and these were all that were known to the provincial natives of the provinces. By an accident of geography and history, then, 'Peru' had 'resonated famously' in Europe well before the Spanish conquistadors had encountered Inca elites and granaries (or, rather, the appellative names of 'Inca' and 'granary') in the interior provinces of their civilised realm, named 'Tawantinsuyu' in Quechua.

But it was not just a question of mistaken identity. 'Tawantinsuyu' was not, strictly speaking, a proper name for a land but instead a universal imperial gloss for the civilised or conquered world that, as Inca Garcilaso explained, resonated from the top and the centre, for Cuzco, 'the navel of the world', was the place where 'the four quarters of the world' had once converged. But as he wrote his history from Andalusian exile this was no longer true: Cuzco was no longer 'the navel of the world'. Lima, the new 'City of Kings' was now the emerging centre and lifeline of the 'Viceroyalty' or 'Kingdoms and Provinces' of 'Peru'. Via Lima, the 'New World' to which 'Peru' belonged was now conjoined with the much vaster 'Universe' of Christendom ruled first by 'The

King of kings' (Jesus, although the Castilian kings also held this title, granted by the pope), second by the Pope and third by 'our Kings of Castile'. The age of the limited universe named Tawantinsuyu had come to a providential close that in turn opened out onto the truly global age of Peru. Between the old but (it was now revealed) false universality of Tawantinsuyu and the new and true one of Christendom, a new global history would emerge. The historical subject named 'Peru' was one of the first fruits of this new, global historical imagination. As in the ancient age of Alexander the Great and the Hellenistic 'universal historians', the palate of the Mediterranean historical imagination had suddenly expanded.[15] Now, the expansion was, for the first time, truly global.

As Peruvians are fond of pointing out, the eventual author of *El Ingenioso Hidalgo Don Quijote de la Mancha* (1605) responded to the marvellous call of Peru's name but was apparently turned down because of his wounds. History's loss was in this case literature's gain. And yet, as art historian Thomas Cummins has noted, Cervantes's fictional creations showed up in Peruvian history. Leaving their author behind, Sancho Panza and Don Quixote made the Atlantic crossing to Panama and from there down the Pacific or South Sea, arriving in Peru in 1607, where they were soon pressed into action as theatrical figures in what must have been splendid performances of the street plays called 'Christians and Indians', or the 'Spanish conquest of the Incas', which in Peru was staged as a New World parallel to the 'Christians and Moors' spectacle, still performed today in Andalusia, albeit with significant twists of plot.[16] All of this was no chivalric fable.

But the eponymous 'Beru' was also a fiction, or rather, a 'hermeneutical necessity'. As Acosta tried to explain in his brilliant but frequently misread *Historia Natural y Moral de las Indias* (1590):

> Among us the word 'Indias' is general since, in our tongue, when we say 'Indias' we refer to far away and rich lands that are very different from ours. Thus, we Spaniards call Peru and Mexico, China, Malaysia, and Brazil 'Indias' even though said lands and dominions are very distant and diverse one from the other. One can also not deny that the name 'Indias' was taken from Oriental India, because for the ancients that other India was celebrated as a very remote and rich land so far

---

[15] See Raoul Mortley, *The Idea of Universal History from Hellenistic Philosophy to Early Christian Historiography* (Lampeter: Edwin Mellen Press, 1996).

[16] Thomas Cummins, 'La fábula y el retrato: imágenes tempranas del inca', in Thomas Cummins et al., *Los incas, reyes del Perú* (Lima: Banco del Crédito, 2005), pp. 1–41.

away that it seemed to be at the ends of the earth. And so, those who reside at the ends of the earth are called 'Indians'.[17]

In short, during the early modern period of *Plus Ultra* the classical proper name of 'India' had become the appellative colonial Renaissance name of 'Indias'. The name 'India' had gone global, for Charles V had 'pushed' the limits of Mediterranean empire to the ends of the earth. That 'Peruvians', 'Mexicans' or 'Chinese' were now 'Indians' was not the mindless repetition of a mistake by Christopher Columbus. Quite the contrary: the dispersion of 'Indians' marked the repeating threshold and horizon of a global modernity that has not yet reached its limit. The founding trace of this global colonial modernity was the 'Indian'. But to become the proper subjects of proper history (that is, to become 'Peruvians'), the recipients of this modern colonial dispersion (that is, 'Indians') would, according to an ancient custom, require a founding speech act or baptism. The history of that 'custom' of naming would later be traced by the Peruvian polymath Pedro de Peralta Barnuevo (1663–1743). Acosta had written that

> during the discovery of the New World it had been the custom to name lands and ports after the occasion of their discovery, and this is how the naming of Peru is commonly understood to have occurred. The opinion here is that, taking the name of the river where they first landed, called Piru by the natives, the Spaniards gave title to this entire land. This is confirmed by the fact that the native Indians of Peru do not use, nor do they know, the name of their land. (*Historia Natural y Moral*, p. 91)

But the wise Padre was, according to Inca Garcilaso, mistaken on one small but critical etymological point: the original utterance could not have been 'Piru' since that was not the correct name for 'river in general' in the language of the coast. In assuming that Peru got its name from a river that was the site of its discovery, Acosta was following a historiographical convention of Neoplatonist origin, and Inca Garcilaso followed the same tradition. The name of Father Acosta's 'other India' had been derived from the Indus River, that is, from the Sanskrit appellative name 'Sindhu', which may be translated as 'river in general'. This 'river in general' had written her name on the rich land of 'India' and also on the wide sea that swallowed her effluents. The same 'custom' and verisimilar truth had also revealed itself in the ancient history

---

[17] José de Acosta, *Historia Natural y Moral de las Indias* (Madrid: Dastin, 2003 [1605]), pp. 92–93.

of 'Iberia', for that peninsula had taken her name from the Iberus (Ebro) River named by the Greeks, and likely uttered by a native speaker of Basque.[18] Similarly, Inca Garcilaso's exegesis had revealed that 'Pelu' – the name uttered by 'Beru' in the place of the Spaniard's first landing – meant 'river in general' in the Yunga tongue. The Inca's verisimilar or Neoplatonist solution, which certainly agreed with what was known, was to put 'Pelu' in the mouth of 'Beru' and to place him in 'the river in general'. It was the founding 'speech act' of 'Peru'.

As the hybrid and conjunctural offspring of Beru's anxious utterance of his own proper name and the name for 'river' in the Yunga tongue, the Inca's 'Peru' was both 'imposed' and 'natural'. In *De lingua Latina*, which was apparently known to Inca Garcilaso, Roman scholar Marcus Terentius Varro had 'distinguished between names imposed on things by a person's fiat or will, and names arising from nature'. Thus, Varro wrote, 'there are only two kinds of origin of words, imposition and inflection; the first is like the fountain, the second like the river'.[19] 'Peru' was imposed by Spaniards, but only to the extent that it resonated with an authentic proper name inflected in an oracular, natural place in the original language and upon the 'occasion of discovery'. Resonant with such classical notions, Inca Garcilaso's account of the name became the canonical version.

In effect, Inca Garcilaso's exegesis and subtle literary turning of the words of the primal scene of contact returns authorship of the name of Peru to a paper conjuncture between the fictive proper name of a misread and misspoken Indian barbarian who is the original eyewitness of the abysmal event, and the global site of his modern colonial utterance: the oracular river-in-general at the edge of the world that was now the repeating horizon of world history: 'Indias'. This ends-of-the-earth conjuncture was now 'properly heard' and written by the antipodal and now global 'Inca' (Indian and European) historian. As the hearing 'receptor' of Beru's utterance and as 'commentator' on imperial Spanish history, Inca Garcilaso moved between the time of Beru's utterance and the time of his own discourse. In tying these two times together he made the name of Peru 'verisimilar' in the idioms both of Classical and Renaissance historiography. At the same time, he retrospectively reclaimed at one and the same time, both the 'Peruvian' origins of the name in an Indian barbarian named 'Beru' and, not least, his own true Patria: that two-part history book that allowed him to bridge his life and worlds. Consequently, the colonial eclipse of 'Tawantinsuyu' and the draining of her

---

[18] Pedro de Peralta Barnuevo, *Historia de Espana Vindicada* (Lima, 1730), s/n.
[19] Cited in Sabine MacCormack, *On the Wings of Time: Rome, the Incas, Spain, and Peru* (Princeton, NJ: Princeton University Press, 2006), pp. 192–193.

mineral riches was compensated by the hopeful prospect of an enlightened, literate 'Peruvian empire' (*On the Wings of Time*, p. 193).

This prospect and burden were shouldered with gratitude by subsequent generations of Peruvian historians, chief among them the Creole polymath and rector of Lima's University of San Marcos (founded 1551), Pedro de Peralta Barnuevo. If Inca Garcilaso de la Vega was the mestizo Herodotus of Peru who surpassed the Greek father of history and lies by founding a new global history of colonial origin, Pedro de Peralta Barnuevo was her unsung Creole Vico. But if Vico blazed the trail of a 'new science' of history inspired in a critical and poetic reading of classical antiquity, Peralta pioneered another poetic trail forward towards a brilliant new age guided by the lights of 'History'. As the first and perhaps only colonial American subject to write a history of Spain and Spanish antiquity, Peralta was a pioneer. He also wrote a history of Peru in verse, *Lima fundada o Conquista del Peru* (1732), an erudite 'heroic poem' that was read aloud, and that updated the prosaic content of Inca Garcilaso's history of the Incas.

Peralta's *Historia de España vindicada* (1730) is ostensibly a defence of Spain and its empire, intended to deflect European and particularly French attacks. But he wrote his Spanish history in a critical and comparative spirit that opened new vistas for the Peruvian historical imagination. French historians had charged that Spain was a mongrel empire of Asian, African and Indian elements that lacked the cohesion afforded by a venerable antiquity or genealogy, and so would soon disappear from the face of the earth, leaving little mark on history. The true subjects of Peralta's history are 'the Political Ship of the Name of Spain' and 'the country' named 'Iberia', but these subjects are interpolated from a 'Peru' and a 'History' that is in many ways both Spain's double and future.

Peralta's defence is brilliant, but it failed to exercise much influence in 'enlightened' Europe where, by the late eighteenth century, Spanish Empire was condemned as an 'Oriental' despotism, where for the most part its image remains. Indeed, modern historiography is what it is today in part because Peralta failed to convince its European masters that Spain and Peru were vanguards of world history. Peralta's forgotten history countered the European charges with a deep genealogy that traced in detail and with abundant footnotes 'the name and political ship of Spain' back to Noah's Ark (this was not unusual). True, Spanish Hapsburg imperial historians had written similar 'mythic' genealogical histories in the sixteenth century, but they had done so with less rigour. Moreover, those Spanish imperial chroniclers were susceptible to the Enlightenment's favourite slight that 'official' history was tainted by patronage and the sin of *amor propio* or vanity. But as a colonial subject stationed in enlightened Lima and thus far removed from

European polemics and rivalries, Peralta could present himself as free of those vices that dogged either side of the European debate, for he was neither a French 'hypocrite' nor a Spanish 'zealot'. His comparative researches led him to conclude that Spain was indeed the most ancient and singular empire the world had ever seen, for it was the only empire to 'unite two worlds'. Peralta also unites the two worlds of Peru and Spain in a defence that puts Peru in the driver's seat of world history.

Peralta's was a bold enterprise of *traslatio studii* (transfer of the site or 'seat' of knowledge from Spain to Peru) that addressed the 'ancient history' of Spain from the perspective of a Peru that was now Spain's light and future, for Spain was to ancient Rome what Peru was to Spain. Once an outer western province of Rome, Spain had subsequently outstripped Rome when she 'united two worlds'. In turn, Peru and the city of Lima had exceeded Spain's achievement by 'making of two empires, one'. That is, although Spain had united the Old World with the New and thus opened the flood gates of modern global history Peru, led by the 'City of the Kings of Peru' founded by Pizarro, had united the Inca and Spanish Empires, thereby producing the next (and last?) step in the westward-moving history of world empires. Peralta's Lima was the 'Political Phoenix' of its own modern mestizo empire, a new 'seat' of historical knowledge. Peralta thereby freed 'History' from 'the Prince' by making History the Prince of the world. Peralta's project is now revealed: to reclaim the rhetorical arts of the ancient poets and to place them at the service of a modern Lima that would lead the way into the brave new world of hybrid empires ruled by the Prince of princes, History itself.

In 1791, the editor of Lima's *El Mercurio Peruano* announced that the primary task of his enlightened periodical would be to counter European ignorance of Peruvian history. It is important to note that for the editor and his Peruvian and Spanish colleagues, 'Europe' did not then include Spain, Portugal, most of Italy, or Greece. Moreover, and since at the time the 'Spaniards' of Spain and the Indies or Americas formed one 'Spanish nation', Spaniards were not 'foreigners' in Peru. Peninsular- and Peruvian-born historians alike were fellow 'national historians'. Given the rising importance of hostile, northern European opinion, however, it was now necessary to combat the damages inflicted upon the image of Spain and the Indies, most of it based on misinformation or simple ignorance.

European *philosophes* had obliterated the very existence of the 'Peruvian' or native origin of the founder of the Inca dynasty, Manco Capac. Because of the influential writings of, among others, Raynal, Diderot and, later, the Prussian naturalist Alexander von Humboldt, the founder of the Inca dynasty was increasingly seen in Europe to be either of white European (as Voltaire speculated) or, more likely, Oriental origins. Manco was the cornerstone of the accepted genealogy of Peruvian sovereignty and the key figure in the Inca's narrative of the accelerated rise of Inca civilisation, which had neatly outstripped the achievements of millennial Rome in a mere two hundred years. In short, 'enlightened' European critiques now threatened 'Peruvian' (and, by implication, Spanish imperial) dynastic sovereignty in its very point of origin.

To the rescue of Manco Capac and the deep history of Peruvian sovereignty came many Peruvian historians. The most brilliant defence was elaborated by José Hipólito Unanue, an anatomist and shining light of the Peruvian enlightenment. Taking Montesquieu's experimental method to other shores and another conclusion, Unanue observed that the particular 'genius' of circumequatorial 'American genius' was the sensory product of diverse 'influences' exercised on the nerve endings by the splendid Andean clime, where an unparalleled range of altitudinal gradients mediated the effects of the blazing and otherwise enervating equatorial sun. Consequently, the 'imagination' of Peruvians was more rapid firing than the relatively dull European mind, which Unanue characterised, in accordance with the dark and damp climes of the north, as relatively slow to act and inclined to monotony. Based on controlled experiments, statistics and field observations, Unanue argued that Manco Capac must have been 'Peruvian', for only a talented native son of genius with hyperactive nerve endings could have grasped the nature of the Peruvian world in such a clear way as to launch Peru on its accelerated climb to the heights of world civilisation.

Unanue's experimental and 'physiological' proof was a defence of Inca Garcilaso de la Vega's thesis of the Inca dynasty's acceleration of history inaugurated by Manco Capac. This rapid rise made Cuzco superior to Rome, except in one sense: Cuzco lacked the written word. Inca Garcilaso's purpose was to remedy that absence in exemplary historical fashion, thereby surpassing, via a critical, retrospective gesture, *The Commentaries* of Julius Caesar. Key to that gesture was *The Royal Commentaries of the Incas*, which permitted the Inca Herodotus of modern global history to assume a critical position vis-à-vis classical universal history. Now, Unanue assumed a similar position vis-à-vis the dubious judgments of so-called enlightened Europe's 'Tribunal of History'.

Unanue's critique of Europe's 'Tribunal of History' was founded on a deeply experimental and historicist understanding of 'the name of Peru' as a microcosmic realm favoured by nature. This vision would enable him to assume a key role in two, seemingly contrasting, projects in the early nineteenth century, the one leading to Peruvian integration as an equal partner in a global 'Spanish monarchy' vis-à-vis the Cortes de Cádiz and its Constitution of 1812, to which Unanue was elected a delegate but was unable to arrive before the proclamation. The Cádiz Constitution created a unified, global 'Spanish nation' (*nación española*) of citizens and, for the first time, a constitutional 'Spanish Monarchy' (*monarquía española*). It also displaced the name of 'America' with that of 'Ultramarine Spain'. Thus, 'Peru' became, as Unanue noted in the inaugural issue of *El Verdadero Peruano*, the successor periodical to the *Mercurio Peruano*, 'la España Ultramarina' (Overseas Spain) and all its citizens, including Indians and most *castas* (after heated debate, those of African descent were denied full citizenship), were now 'Spaniards'. The new Constitution was, in Unanue's words, a 'heroic act of great wisdom' that went well beyond both ancient and modern precedents, creating the world's first global, unified nation of civil equals among metropolitans and colonials, uniting 'two worlds ruled by a single order'. When this project failed, Unanue assumed a leading position in the new Peruvian Republic, established in 1821. His critical views of Montesquieu played a role in the definition of the form of the new Republic. That Republic banished 'Spaniards' for 'Peruvians' but retained the Catholic faith and Castilian language, although most Peruvians still spoke Quechua. As the republican nineteenth century advanced, the Catholic church and Castilian were largely nationalised or 'Peruvianised', while Quechua was increasingly 'Castilianised' as a lingua franca, particularly in the provinces. In addition, the 'indigenous' population expanded, becoming the clear majority by the close of the nineteenth century. Only in the twentieth century would the 'mestizo' and 'white' populations come to form a majority in Peru.

What have we learned, or better, unlearned with these Peruvian registers and iterations of 'Peru', 'Spain' and 'Spanish'? First, it is likely that 'Spain' as a unified concept was at times more important in the Indies than it was in the Peninsula, and the same must be said of 'Spaniard'. Nevertheless, the trace of 'Castile' and 'Castilian' runs deep. In addition, it is clear the notions of 'Spain' and 'Spaniard' emerge in relation to the names of 'Indias' and 'Indians', as well as 'Peru' and 'Peruvians'. The names 'Europe' and 'America' are in play here, most acutely in the eighteenth century. We could conclude that 'Spain' and 'Peru' are transnational inventions, but, if we did, we would have to qualify, in historical and not merely theoretical terms, what we mean by 'national'. This is, more or less, what we have tried to do in this chapter.

6

Time, Empire and the Transnational in the Early Modern Spanish World

Alexander Samson

Una España de copernicanos, relojes, instrumentos, mappamundis, epistemologías alternativas quedaría por siempre sumergida entre imagénes de santos, místicos, penitentes y cruzados.[1]

(A Spain of Copernicans, clocks, instruments, mappa mundi, alternative epistemologies, was for ever submerged beneath images of saints, mystics, penitents and Crusaders.)

This plaintive lament over Spain's persistent exclusion from narratives of the rise of science and modernity reminds us, as does the frontispiece of the *Nova reperta* or *New Inventions of Modern Times* from 1590, that far from being marginal, the early modern Spanish world was at the heart of developments in metallurgy, botany, astronomy, cartography, instrumentation and medicine. It was the engine-room of progress and invention. This series of engravings illustrating the greatest recent scientific and medical discoveries of the period were produced in Antwerp in the Spanish Netherlands by Johannes Stradanus, after images by Jan van der Straet, with additional designs from Theodoor Galle and Jan Collaert. The collection included the frequently reproduced depiction of a printer's workshop, the infamous image of Amerigo Vespucci encountering a naked America, alongside other less

---

[1] Jorge Cañizares-Esguerra, 'La memoria y el estado: la monarquía de España en el siglo XVI', *Iberoamericana*, XIV.54 (2014), 177–185, p. 178.

128   Alexander Samson

familiar images of the manufacture of gunpowder and a workshop fabricating large-scale clocks.[2]

The decorative frontispiece, introducing the series, confects an image of travel and discovery, the modern art of war, printing, medicine and the precise measurement of the passing of time, with roundels commemorating Christopher Columbus and Vespucci, and Flavio Amalfitano, alleged inventor of the compass, alongside images of a cannon, printed sheets drying above a handpress, guayam wood for curing syphilis, alembic jars, a pestle and mortar, a saddle, a tree with silk worms (an indigenous industry ravaged by flooding, frost, locusts and drought between 1646 and 1666) and, important for our purposes, a clock with the key below: 'Rotisque iugis indita hora ferreis' (the hour is marked by the perpetual turning of iron wheels) (Figure 1).

For the creators of this series, modernity, technology and science were companions of empire. The belatedness that haunts the Spanish-speaking world is absent from this heterogenous conception of science and its construction of the new.[3]

Time was the greatest enemy of Spanish Empire. Its world on which the sun never set, a place of perpetual illumination, was overthrown by what Fernand Braudel identified as the insuperable 'obstacle of distance'.[4] Despite the medal struck in 1585 glorifying the Hispanic Monarchy with the motto *Ultra anni solisque vias* (Beyond the course of the year and the sun), time remained rooted in locale, rooted in geographical difference.[5] The simultaneity of the nation state remained a distant dream. This essay explores the historically rooted nature of time and the competing temporalities that undermined imperial control: the inability in the early modern period to reduce colonial experience across a global empire to a synchronous, legible and authoritative time, resolved itself in multitemporal heterogeneities.[6] Time

---

[2]   See Michel de Certeau's use of this image to inaugurate his *The Writing of History*, trans. Tom Conley (New York: Columbia University Press, 1988), Preface, pp. xxv–xxviii and Part II: Productions of Time: A religious archaeology, pp. 115–206.

[3]   Paul Julian Smith's conclusion to *Writing in the Margin: Spanish Literature of the Golden Age* (Oxford: Clarendon Press, 1988) suggests that Spain is the place of marginality, forever displaced but impossible to exclude, see especially pp. x–xx.

[4]   Fernand Braudel, *The Mediterranean and the Mediterranean World in the Age of Philip II*, trans. Siân Reynolds (Glasgow: Fontana, 1990), vol. 1, p. 374.

[5]   Humfrey Butters, 'Conflicting attitudes to Machiavelli's works in sixteenth century Spain, Rome and Florence', in *Comunes and Despots in Medieval and Renaissance Italy*, ed. by John Law and Bernadette Paton (London: Routledge, 2010), pp. 75–87.

[6]   This may foreshadow the 'heterogeneidad multitemporal' of the postmodern Latin

Figure 1. *Nova reperta* or *New Inventions of Modern Times*.

infected and inflected by locale, dependent on variegated forms of memory, historical writing and religion observance.

Clocks were a key metaphor for political control in early modern Spain, figuring, for example, in the much translated work of political philosophy by Antonio de Guevara, the *Relox de principes* (1529) (or *Diall of Princes* in the four English translations printed between 1557 and 1619), whose chapter 'La vida del príncipe no es sino relox que concierta a toda la república' expanded on this conceit by connecting virtue with the harmonious workings of a clock's mechanism: 'la vida del emperador virtuoso no es sino un relox que concierta o desconcierta al pueblo'.[7] A century later Diego Saavedra Fajardo picked up on this image in the 11th (*Ex pulsu noscitur*) and 57th (*Uni reddatur*) emblems of his *Idea de un Príncipe Político Cristiano representado en Cien Empresas* (1642), departing from an image of the church bell to reflect: 'Así el príncipe es un reloj universal de sus Estados, los cuales penden del movimiento de sus palabras: con ellas, o gana, o pierde el credito, porque todos procuran conozer

American city analysed by Néstor García Canclini in *Culturas híbridas: estrategias para entrar y salir de la modernidad* (Mexico, DF: Grijalbo, 1990), p. 72.

[7] Antonio de Guevara, 'Relox de Príncipes', in *Obras Completas de Fray Antonio de Guevara*, ed. by Emilio Blanco (Madrid: Biblioteca Castro, 1994), vol. 2, pp. 265–266.

por lo que dize, su ingenio, su condicion, i inclinaciones'.[8] The second emblem, illustrated by a clock, used the metaphor to reflect on the relationship between princes and their councillors and favourites (Figure 2). Only the hand can signal the hours, while the latter needed to work unseen in concert, correspondence and harmony: 'Unos y otros sean ruedas del reloj del gobierno, no la mano' (*Idea de un principe politico christiano*, fol. 413, sig. Fff3r).

At the heart of these variations on the metaphor are the concepts of 'concertar', 'corresponder' and 'armonía', a harmonious interaction of moving parts alongside the maintenance of proportion and relation, and the reciprocal reflection of mutual benefit.

Attempting to hold so many disparate and distant moving parts together led the Emperor Charles V to suffer a nervous breakdown in 1553. Incapacitated by melancholy, gout, catarrhs and haemorrhoids, by September, Francisco Duarte reported:

> las emerroidas se le hinchan y atormentan con tantos dolores que no se puede rodear syn gran sentimiento y lagrimas y estas cosas juntadas con las pasiones del espiritu. que an sido muy grandes y ordinarias le an mudado la condiçion y buena gracia que solia tener y la afabilidad y se le a todo conuertido en tanto humor malencolico que es siempre diz que esta pensatiuo y muchas vezes y ratos llorando tan de veras y con tanto derramiento de lagrimas como sy fuera una criatura

> (his haemorrhoids swell and torment him with so much pain that he cannot move without great emotion and tears and these things together with the passions of the spirit that have been great and quotidian have changed his condition and the good grace and affability he used to have and caused in him so melancholy a humour that they say he is pensive and cries often and for long periods of time so earnestly and with such shedding of tears as if he were a small child)

and 'ni quiere oyr negocios ni firmar los pocos que se despachan, entiendo y ocupandose dia y noche en ajustar y concertar sus relojes, que son hartos, y tiene con ellos la principal quenta' (he does not wish to hear business nor sign the little that is dispatched, I understand he spends day and night adjusting and synchronising his clocks, which are many, they are what matter most to him).[9] It is an evocative and suggestive form for his deep

---

[8] Diego Saavedra Fajardo's XIth emblem in *Idea de un principe politico christiano representado en cien empresas* (Milan: n.p., 1642), fol. 73, sig. K1r.

[9] AGS E 98, fols. 274–275. 'Memorial que embio Francisco Duarte de lo que le dixo

Figure 2. Emblem 11 *Ex pulsu noscitur*; Emblem 57 *Uni reddatur*.

depression to have taken, following the series of setbacks that began with his flight from Innsbruck in the face of Maurice of Saxony's advancing army, a complete reversal for the triumphant Christian paladin, who had defeated the Schmalkaldic League at Mühlberg, commemorated famously by Titian. The overwhelming problems of ruling Spain's global empire led to his unprecedented abdication three years later in 1556 in favour of his son. Tellingly, the earliest clock in the collections of Spain's Patrimonio Nacional (National Heritage) is 'el Candil', so named for its built-in oil lamp, meaning that it was designed for the nocturnal use of the unflagging workaholic Philip II, battling an informational overload in part of his own creation. The clock, dated 1583, was made by Hans de Evalo, a Flemish artisan, who had arrived at court in 1572 and was named royal clockmaker in 1580, a post he occupied until the king's death.

Clocks from the period possessed just one hand to mark the hours. Although tricky to calibrate, by the sixteenth century the best available mechanical escapement chronometers were accurate to within fifteen minutes a day or a margin of error of about 2 per cent. By the seventeenth century with the pendulum used as a regulator, the measurement of time became accurate to within seconds a day – a remarkable achievement of precision engineering. Accurate portable watches were even available to the very rich by the second half of the sixteenth century, normally worn as necklaces or pendants. Clocks and watches were luxurious objects conceptualised frequently in relation to complex decorative schemes reflecting on the nature of time. The most famous of all early modern clocks is perhaps the Strasbourg Clock, a scale reproduction of which from 1589 is found in the British Museum.

Apocryphally described as the first clock, the original timepiece appeared in 1352. By the sixteenth century it had stopped working and was replaced by the famous Renaissance clock, begun in 1547 but not finished until 1572, twenty-five feet wide at the base and sixty feet tall. The decorative scheme of the device included the three Fates, Urania the goddess of Astronomy, Colossus and a portrait of Copernicus. The base panels represented the four monarchies of the world Assyria, Persia, Greece and Rome. There were scenes of the Creation, Resurrection and Last Judgement, emblems of Vice and Innocence. The automated astronomical devices included a calendar dial with holy days, an astrolabe with signs of the zodiac and the planets, a mechanism displaying the lunar phases, while trains of automata including gods of the days of the week riding in chariots, the four ages of man striking the quarters of the hour, Christ and Death duelling on the hour, the Saviour losing all but

Nicolas Nicolai, September 1553'. *Cal. Span.*, XI, pp. 221 ff, see reference to Azevedo on p. 226.

the last battle and the cockerel from the old medieval clock shaking its tail and crowing at midday accompanied by the six-note carillon. The unfortunate cock was struck by lightning and ceased to work in 1640. The theatre of the world and morality play enclosed within this remarkable device had been designed by the professor of Mathematics, Conrad Dasypodius, and made in collaboration with clockmakers, painters and musicians. This marvel linked human temporality to the supernatural sphere of eternity and the struggle of man's salvation (Figure 3).

Nevertheless, the use value of time pieces was highly limited until the standardisation of mean time against which to set the proliferation of devices that grew from the fifteenth and sixteenth centuries. The ringing of bells and church clocks that determined how people measured or shared a sense of time. As late as the nineteenth century, not only did different time zones affect the setting of clocks but different times existed in different parts of a country. The revolution standardising time, tying it to a unique common referent, was produced by the exigencies of the railways that extended across the whole of Britain by the middle of the nineteenth century. A timetable only made sense if the time in Durham was the same as the time in London. Before this London time ran four minutes ahead of time in Reading, seven and a half minutes ahead of Cirencester and 14 minutes ahead of Bridgewater, following the sun as it slowly crept its way across the surface of the earth. In the 1840s railway companies sought to standardise time, unfortunately each company doing so according to its own referent. The Grand Junction Company, for example, sent an employee with a watch on the train from Euston to Holyhead so that the time could be coordinated. Eventually the Railway Clearing House led the companies to cooperate and agree to use Greenwich Time, which had been in use for shipping and navigation since the seventeenth century.[10] In 1880 railway standard time in Britain became general standard time. Germany followed in 1893. The world was divided into four time-zones at an international conference in Washington in 1884. Modernity is about a growing imperviousness to nature, the replacement of agricultural, cyclical and ritual time with the uniform and precise time of the industrial world. Specialisation in the world of work transformed labour into a fragmented, sequential set of distinct operations, rather than an organic whole, the artisan's workshop replaced by the assembly line. Timetable spread from the parade ground to the factory, school, shop and government department.

---

[10] Wolfgang Schivelbusch, *The Railway Journey: The Industrialization of Time and Space in the 19th Century* (Berkeley, CA: University of California Press, 1986), pp. 43–44.

134 *Alexander Samson*

Figure 3. Strasbourg Astronomical Clock, first erected 1352–54.

While the average working day in the pre-modern world may on the face of it have looked longer than today, the comparison is false, since labour was not disconnected from other fields of activity. The concepts of leisure, free time, work and labour arise out of urbanisation and industrialisation and the birth of legal frameworks determining their times and durations. Time before this stretched out and contracted with the seasons. For those fortunate or unfortunate enough to enjoy a monastic life, the eight canonical hours beginning at midnight, continuing with Matins, Lauds, Vespers and so on, appear to have left little time for a good night's sleep, a maximum of three hours at a stretch. The saints' days and religious calendar, the link between weekly sermons and biblical stories shifting with the time of year filled each moment with spiritual significance. If the modern sense of time is intimately related to speed, the problem posed by exactitude and precision in the measurement of space typifies what has changed.

The measurement of longitude of course depended on accurate chronometers; even astrological readings relied on the time when the measurements were taken. That most modern science cartography, the lines of longitude that divided the earth, from the Treaties of Tordesillas (1494) to Zaragoza

(1529), depended on the measurement of distances on the basis of equations of time and approximate speed. The very definition of territories, where they were, their frontiers, boundaries and situation, depended in this way on huge inexactitudes for centuries. New techniques in surveying overlapped with older ways of dividing up the land according to symbolic objects, memory and evolving topography. Time eventually moved from being providential to become a product of precision engineering and eventually a mathematical abstraction, implicated in the most complex theoretical physics of General and Special Relativity, merged into the new concept space–time.

In *Capital* Karl Marx proposed that '[m]oments are the elements of profit', contrasting pre-modern legislation to lengthen the working day (from the first Ordinance of Labourers promulgated by Edward III in 1349 to the Elizabethan Statute of Artificers from 1563) with legislation limiting the working day passed between 1833 and 1864, which had sought to end the exploitation of industrial workers in England's factories. At the start of the Tudor period work for labourers and artificers from March until September was to last from 5am until 7pm or 8pm and in winter from dusk until dawn, with three hours for meals. By the end of the seventeenth century, according to William Petty, workers were putting in ten hours a day.[11] By 1833 the British Parliament saw the need to limit the working day of children between thirteen and eighteen years of age to twelve hours. Marx railed that the modern worker was 'compelled by social conditions [...] to sell his birthright for a mess of pottage' (Marx, *Capital*, p. 382). The introduction of relays, night shifts and differing timetables allowed owners to keep machinery constantly running, but the differing hours for minors under thirteen, children between thirteen and eighteen, and female workers required factory clocks to 'regulate, with military uniformity, the times, the limits and the pauses of work by the stroke of the clock'; capital hounded the worker 'hither and thither, in scattered shreds of time' (*Capital*, pp. 394, 403).

Our eight-hour day, the 'modest Magna Carta of the legally limited working day', followed proposals put forward in 1866 by America's General Congress of Labour and then the Congress of the International Working Men's Association, the latter drafted by Marx himself (*Capital*, pp. 415–416). It was E. P. Thompson who originally argued that the quantification of work by time was produced by industrialisation and a new centrality of the clock.[12] The biggest white-collar employer in the late eighteenth century, the Bank of England, as a result of specialisation, co-ordination and scrutiny, was heavily

---

[11] Karl Marx, *Capital: Vol. 1* (London: Penguin, 1990), p. 352 and note 29, pp. 383–384.
[12] E. P. Thompson, 'Time, Work-Discipline, and Industrial Capitalism', *Past & Present*, No. 38 (1967), pp. 56–97.

dependent on the clock, as work in its different offices needed to be 'timed to ensure accurate record-keeping and consistent service to the public': it 'begun the process of transforming irregular working patterns long before the cotton mills of the mid nineteenth century'.[13]

Michel Foucault in turn traced the way '[t]ime penetrates the body and with it all the meticulous controls of power', invoking the concept of an 'anatomo-chronological schema of behaviour' in order to understand the way the discipline of the cloister and military spread from the seventeenth century to every aspect of life, transforming speed into a virtue 'for turning to ever-increased profit or use the movement of passing time [...] capitalizing time'; 'a linear time whose moments are integrated, one upon another, and [...] orientated towards a terminal, stable point; in short an "evolutive" time'.[14] The discipline of ever more complex exercises transformed bodies through 'linear, continuously progressive organization' into perfectable individuals, engines of social progress.

In early modern Europe, time invested bodies with significance, shaping them through ritual in the context of providential and eschatological frameworks, tending inexorably towards the ultimate end of life – salvation or damnation. Its discipline foregrounded the avoidance of idleness, as an inducement to sin, *ocio* being linked to all manner of vice, notably in the picaresque. Empire, however, posed a challenge to Christian conceptions of time. In New Spain, the Mexica calendrical system presupposed fundamentally different ways of organising the past, identity and the body. Exploring the clashing conceptions of history and memory incarnated in the *Relaciones geográficas*, Philip II's grandiose information-gathering project, Serge Gruzinski argued that these colonial questionnaires, by seeking to make sense of Nahau history from the perspective of Christian time, engaged in transculturation making translation between the two systems possible. Tepeaca, near Puebla, for example, in their response, produced two different foundation dates, one using their own calendrical system, the other counting backwards 313 years. Much is lost in translation. The significance of names derived from their position within astronomical or ritual 260-day cycles, each day name/glyph and its symbolic associations with a totem animal or god combining with 13-day numbers, in 13 groups of 20 days or 20 groups of 13

---

[13] Anne Murphy, 'Clock-watching: Work and working time at the late eighteenth century Bank of England', *Past and Present*, 236 (2017), 99–132 (pp. 101–102, p. 116, p. 122).

[14] Michel Foucault, *Discipline and Punish: The Birth of the Prison*, trans. Alan Sheridan (London: Penguin, 1991), Part 3: Discipline, pp. 135–169 (pp. 152–153, p. 157, pp. 160–161).

days. The 365-day solar year was structured in relation to agriculture and a series of feasts that also had religious functions.

This complexity was compounded by indigenous groups using different dating systems, taken from distinct starting points. Both contrast with the universality of European systems of dating, tied to the birth of the saviour, inaugurating the time of Christian cosmology. Although there were linear aspects of indigenous constructions of the past, territorial divisions, the origins of tribute rights and successions of caciques, their cyclical conception of time in 52-year cycles meant their responses to questions about the past were often fragmentary and multivectoral. Memory in the world of the Mexica depended on oral tradition, alongside the painted codices of the *tlacuilos*. Visual representations of the past, with origin myths, toponymy, feast days and the computation of time, showed both the past and 'memories of things to come'.[15] Each moment, through the actions and rituals associated with it and its place in agricultural, political and religious cycles, retold multiple pasts and foretold manifold futures. Sacred caves, mountains and lakes connected the ever-present time of creation and the gods to human time, places that linked different temporal planes and allowed a form of time travel, landscape revealing the memory of an inescapable presence. Time was not beyond manipulation. Iztcoatl, one of the first Aztec kings, gathered together the painted books from the valley of Mexico and had them burnt, in order to mould the destiny of his new dynasty, altering the past in order to determine the future.[16] The fate of ordinary people was dictated by the day of their birth, which was often taken as their name.

Bernardino de Sahagún recorded in 1578–1580 the native aphorism: 'What used to be done a long time ago and is done no longer will be done again. It will thus be once again as it was in the past. Those who live today will live again, they will be anew', commenting 'this proposition is Plato's and it is the devil who taught it here for it is wrong, completely false and contrary to the faith!' (Gruzinski, *The Conquest of Mexico*, p. 90). The individual, health, cosmic and social harmony were determined by an inescapable present. Missionaries' attempts to record the indigenous past were quickly hampered by vertiginous demographic decline. Time after the conquest was cloven into before and after, as the indigenous population was decimated by epidemic disease, with smallpox carrying off as many as eight million in the 1520s, and

---

[15] Serge Gruzinski, *The Conquest of Mexico* (Cambridge: Polity Press, 1993), pp. 70–97.

[16] John E. Clark and Arlene Colman, 'Time reckoning and memorial in Mesoamerica', *Cambridge Archaeological Journal*, 18 (2008), 93–99 (p. 93).

the mysterious *cocolitzli* killing a further 12 to 15 million in 1545 and another two million in 1576.[17]

The speed of collapse, following severe drought in both cases, produced destabilising, dislocating effects on memory and the past. Its very legibility faded as older interpreters disappeared along with the codices that had guided their stories. The origins of sickness were often located in the breaking of prohibitions, which led numerous communities to revert to their old sacrifices, such as the Zapotec of Ocelotepec in 1577. The fact that argument was made in the presence of colonial officials half a century after the conquest underlines the tenuous nature of imperial control and evangelisation beyond metropolitan centres. Acknowledging the singularity of the conquest and waves of epidemics that had followed indexes the infiltration of Western linearity into indigenous consciousness that possessed 'a comprehensive conception of temporality that orchestrated all human activities':

> the Spanish administration with its chronological landmarks, its periodization, its sense of event, its criteria and requirements; and that of the indigenous tradition, more concerned with the parallelism of facts than with an analysis of their succession and for which, with the passage of human time, the strata of events were superimposed [...] Spanish liturgical time was cyclical in its way, while Nahau tradition not only knew a minor linearity but still more cherished the idea that a cycle was inscribed in a temporality irremediably doomed to degeneration and disappearance: the Fifth Sun was perishable, and it was the last. (*The Conquest of Mexico*, pp. 90, 97)

The Aztec Calendar stone blended space and time; divided spatially into sky, upper world and underworld; the year marked at the top, 13 Reed, corresponding to the year of the creation of the present sun. Humans existed to assist the gods in completing calendrical time and its renewal. Past was always present as a founding act, a constant affiliation between the moment and myth. The stone represented the life and death of present time or the world. Past, present and future were undifferentiated in Nahau conceptualisations of time, founded on repetition, the cyclical and symbolic association of death and renewal. Every religious festival was a reactualisation of a sacred event from 'the beginning', a

---

[17] *Cocolitzli* is unidentified, but may be some form of indigenous viral haemorrhagic fever. Ebola is a form of viral haemorrhagic fever. A recent scientific study has suggested enteric salmonella as another possibility. It is estimated the population of central Mexico fell from 25.2 million to 16.8 by 1532, to 6.3 by 1548, 2.6 in 1568, reaching 1.9 by 1585. See Gruzinski, *The Conquest of Mexico*, p. 81.

mythical past. Three planes interacted in any given moment, a primordial time of supreme deities, the time of the gods or myth, and human time.[18]

Pre-Hispanic codices, through their narratives of the past, forms of memorialisation, their preservation and rewriting, reveal much about Mesoamerican conceptualisations of history. The Nuttall-Zouche Codex, a Mixtec Codex dating back to the twelfth century, telling the story of Eight Deer Jaguar Claw, exemplifies the mystery and fascination of Mesoamerican historical writing. Recent research has shown the Codex had been repainted at some point. It was probably among the very first gifts of Moctezuma II to Cortés, which he had duly dispatched to Spain in July 1519. The Mixteca were the dominant group in the mountainous region of northern Oaxaca, from the eleventh century, and had resisted Aztec advances in the fifteenth century, following initial attacks on Coixtlahuaca in the 1460s, before a full-scale invasion by Moctezuma II in 1511–1512.[19] It seems likely that the codex was a spoil of this latter war. One explanation as to why the screenfold had been preserved in Tenochtitlan is Eight Deer's wearing a Toltec nose ornament, identical to ones represented on glyphs of Moctezuma.[20]

The identification with a former ruler and establishing an affinity with a hero of a former age is suggestive and resembles the ways in which historical 'documents' were used in Western Europe, tracing, for example, the genealogy of the Habsburgs back to Aeneas. As Gordon Brotherston has written, 'the notorious eleventh century tyrant Eight Deer Jaguar Claw's (AD 1011–1063) life and times are a central focus of post-Classic Mixtec history' and Zouche-Nuttall, an annal moving from one year date to the next with 'narratives that may concentrate on migration, military conquest and tribute rights, genealogy', also offers a 'biography [...] of Eight Deer, from his father's first marriage to his own, at the age of 40'.[21] The unusually detailed and elaborate picture of Eight Deer's adventures may be related to his subversion of Mixtec inheritance patterns, the genealogical edifice upon which this world's social stability depended. On the other hand, Four Wind, the son of Lady Six Monkey, who Eight Deer had murdered and usurped, reunited the competing dynasties by marrying the daughters of his mother's killer. But why was Eight Deer not written out of history with the return of the

[18] Mutsumi Izeki, 'The concept of time in pre-Hispanic Nahau culture with special reference to "fire" as a manifestation of time', *MA Dissertation*, Institute of Archaeology, UCL, 1996, Chapter 4, pp. 39–63.

[19] Colin McEwan, *Ancient Mexico in the British Museum* (London: British Museum Press, 1994), pp. 62–63.

[20] Robert Williams, *The Complete Codex Zouche-Nuttall: Mixtec Lineage Histories and Political Biographies* (Austin, TX: University of Texas Press, 2013), p. 15.

[21] Gordon Brotherston, *Painted Books from Mexico: Codices in UK Collections and the World They Represent* (London: British Museum, 1995), p. 15.

succession to its usual lines? His story survived for more than four centuries before entering the Hispanic world, coming down to us.

Essentially a biographical narrative dramatising a change of dynasty, the screenfold possesses a number of mysterious features. Eight Deer's story follows his life from boyhood until the zenith of his achievements as ruler of Tilantongo and Teozacoalco, but omits his death. It mixes the natural and supernatural in one single plane, many of the encounters in the screenfold are with spiritual beings, 'supernaturals', mixing chronicle and annal, with religious story. The culminating episode of Nuttall-Zouche sees Eight Deer and his rival Four Jaguar staring into the underworld from atop a temple platform (see below, page 142 Figure 4).[22]

The direction of individuals' glyphs has meaning, reversing to stand against the current of time, for example, when a figure's story comes to an end. This is also apparent in gesture, particularly pointing, which can indicate gifts or relationships. How should we read the hand gestures shared by Eight Deer and Four Jaguar? Labelling of figures throughout a codex appears to be superfluous, given the fact that they are undoubtedly characterised: Eight Deer is recognisable throughout. His transformations, most importantly after the nose piercing that elevates him to the priestly/royal caste, do come with representational transformations, differences costumes and associated symbolic objects. So, the glyphs function partly representationally. His hand drawn back holding the *atlatl* denotes a posture of war or attack. The war spear stuck into a place glyph signifies violent conquest.

There are also of course phonetic aspects to this system of communication with certain glyphs representing an idea or spoken word, or place names resembling the sounds of objects concatenated together. These ancient stories entwined history and myth, and appear to be particularly associated with supporting the dynastic and spiritual claims of particular places. They possess a certain linearity, being read directionally from right to left, boustrophedon style, with red lines indicating the direction of the patterning of events. In some sense this synchronic narration overlaps with chronology whose central significance is underlined by the constant presence of calendrical glyphs indicating when events took place.

---

[22] There are two facsimile editions: Zelia Nuttall, *Codex Nuttall: Facsimile of an Ancient Mexican Codex Belonging to the Lord Zouche of Harynworth England* (Cambridge, MA: Harvard University Press, 1902) and Arthur Miller, *The Codex Nuttall: A Picture Manuscript from Ancient Mexico: The Peabody Museum Facsimile Edited by Zelia Nuttall* (New York: Dover, 1975). The codex is available online: <http://www.britishmuseum.org/research/collection_online/collection_object_details.aspx?objectId=662517&partId=1>, accessed 16 March 2018.

The unidirectionality of Christian time, its tending towards one apocalyptic end, the Last Judgement, salvation or damnation, lent the study of chronology enormous intellectual seriousness in early modern Europe, incarnated in the works of thinkers like Joseph Scalinger.[23] The arrow of time, notions of time flying and depictions of Father Time often represented with wings, underline time's irreversibility in a Christian context, in contrast to its plasticity in ancient Mexico, the possibility of return. The Aztec calendar had led Michel de Montaigne to conclude that indigenous peoples must be civilised. However, they were less interested in order and succession than in the way moments could be tied to particular symbolic, ritual and religious associations. When Diogo Cao erected the Cape Cross in Namibia in 1485, he inscribed it with the date of his arrival – 6,685 years since the creation of the world. A number arrived at by adding the 5,200 years since the creation of the world given in the Vulgate, to the year 1485. The Hebrew calendar gave the lower figure of 4,000. Scalinger found a document in 1602 with a list of Egyptian dynasties dating back to before the flood. Similarly, the Jesuit Martino Martini, who had studied with Athanasius Kirchner, produced a chronology based on Chinese sources of history dating their origins back to before the universal flood.[24] Kirchner believed that time had begun in Egypt and that the Chinese were Egyptians since they both had hieroglyphic languages.[25] So while Friars in the New World confronted systems of time-reckoning that seemed heretical and pagan, intellectuals in Europe took on the challenge of chronology and histories from other parts of the world that posed similar challenges to their understanding of time. The mania for *memento mori*, along with the rise of diaries, sharpened awareness of the passage of time and fomented introspection and the religious disciplining of the soul. But at the same time indigenous and the variegated temporalities of the globe facilitated new possibilities for time. Fictional narratives loosened the rigid structure and vice-like grip of Christian chronology, moving backward and forwards, overlaying events to produce different aetiologies in relation to the course of a life, someone's soul, resisting exemplary or counter-exemplary resolutions.

[23] Anthony Grafton, 'Joseph Scalinger and historical chronology: The rise and fall of a discipline', *History and Theory*, 14 (1975), 156–185, p. 170.

[24] Nicolas Standaert, *The Intercultural Weaving of Historical Texts: Chinese and European Stories about Emperor Ku and His Concubines* (Leiden: Brill, 2016), Chapter 2 'Jesuit ccount of Chinese history and chronology and their Chinese sources', pp. 94–164. Original text is Martini Martinii, *Sinicae Historiae Decas Prima* (Munich: Johannes Wagner, 1658).

[25] Anthony Grafton, '7 – Kircher's chronology', in *Athansius Kircher: The Last Man who Knew Everything*, ed. by Paula Findlen (London: Routledge, 2004), pp. 171–187, esp. p. 172 and p. 184.

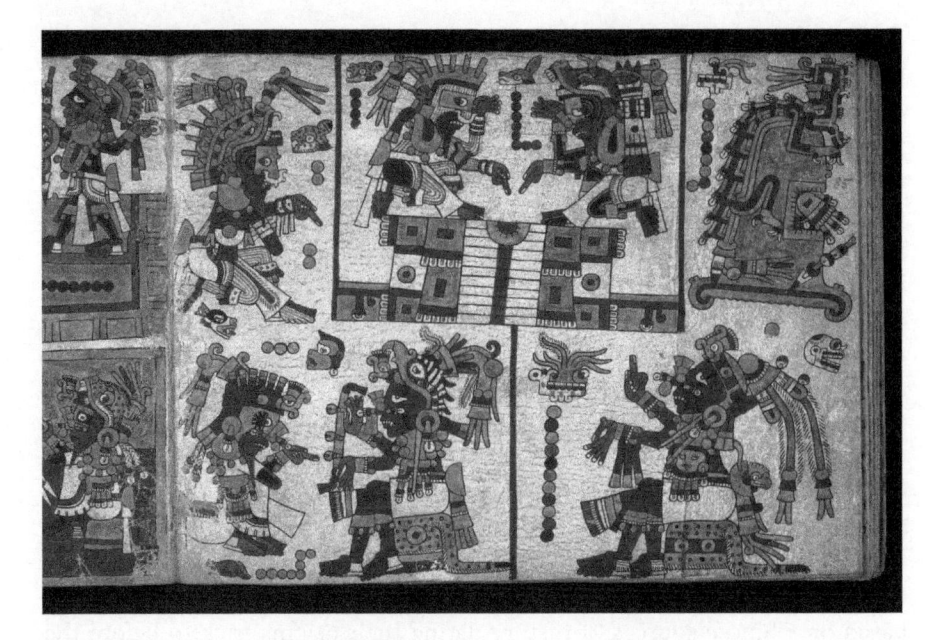

Figure 4. Eight Deer and Four Jaguar.

As mentioned, Braudel's *Mediterranean* emphasised the way in which geographical distance – the length of time that missives took to circulate bearing crucial information – was the greatest challenge to the existence and persistence of Spain's polycentric monarchy. Distance was time. Events could only become simultaneous with speed, the only truly modern sensation. Before trains, cars and air travel, the fastest humans travelled at 30 to 40 miles an hour on horseback. Information was materially embodied and so limited to this. The telegraph, along with the railway, revolutionised this, making possible the simultaneity of information of the newspaper, unifying geographical space, which Benedict Anderson saw as the precondition for the existence of the modern nation state.[26] Implicit within our conceptualisations of political entities, like the modern state, therefore, is this radically new temporality. While the cyclical, ritual elements of indigenous and Christian calendrical systems provided a point of contact, attempts to understand the past and history of Mesoamerica displaced an eternally returning present enclosing past and future with a providential and eschatological temporality, pointing towards the end of times. The latter was slowly displaced in turn by a time that is genetic and organic, evolutive time, linked to the maximisation

---

[26] Benedict Anderson, *Imagined Communities: Reflections on the Origins and Spread of Nationalism* (London: Verso, 2006), pp. 22–36.

of utility, especially of the body itself, through the disciplines of a progressive series of exercises. The ways in which time evolved from the Renaissance were profoundly influenced by global encounters, attempts to write the histories of colonial subjects and understand and evangelise civilisations in the East. In the early modern transnational Spanish empire subjects were rooted in an oppressive succession of events that has eventually been displaced by our equally oppressive simultaneity and sequences, a time broken into and breaking us into smaller and smaller fragments. As Richard II laments:

> I wasted time, and now doth time waste me;
> For now hath time made me his numb'ring clock;
> My thoughts are minutes, and with sighs they jar
> Their watches on unto mine eyes, the outward watch,
> Whereto my finger, like a dial's point,
> Is pointing still, in cleansing them from tears.[27]

---

[27] William Shakespeare, *Richard II*, ed. by Peter Ure, Arden Shakespeare (London: Routledge, 1994), Act 5, Sc. 5, ll. 49–54.

7

Modern, Modernity, Modernism and the Transnational; Or, Goodbye to All That?

Andrew Ginger

Similarity

Was the Spanish-speaking world 'modern', was it part of 'modernity', did it contribute to 'modernism'? If so, to what extent? These have been defining questions, both for Spanish-language writers and artists, and for scholars writing about them. One way to answer such enquiries is, first, to establish clearly and precisely what being 'modern' involves, and then to investigate whether the Spanish-speaking world measures up to the standard or is aligned to it. Crudely speaking, it is possible to imagine that 'modernity' is a social, economic and political system, featuring, for instance: European-style states corresponding to nations (nation-states), European imperialism and its legacy, industrialisation, the rise of cities (urbanisation), capitalism, the dominance of a 'bourgeoisie', an age of liberal revolutions, measurement of time and space and so forth. Likewise, it is possible to suppose that there was a radical change in the arts and literature that put them onto an entirely new footing ('modernism'). In turn, it is possible to try to relate the cultural system and the social, economic and political system, in one gigantic systematic account.

In practice, this has proved an extremely challenging endeavour. It is less than clear: (a) that we have clear definitions for these various notions; (b) that the notions actually correspond to historical realities; and (c) that they are intricately related to one another as part of a single system. Writing in the volume of essays *When was Latin American Modern?*, the historian Alan Knight states bluntly: 'The notion of "modernity" embodied in late twentieth-century modernization theory [...] is not historically much use.' The concept 'lumps' things together, Knight observes, when they are actually disparate.[1] In 2009, Jürgen Osterhammal published his vast and much-admired tome, *The Transformation of the World*, one of only a few global histories of the modern world seriously to cover Spanish-speaking peoples. Osterhammel tries to provide a panoramic and thematic view of the 'transformation', taking into account the many different perspectives and nuances of the nineteenth-century world.[2] His book is at once a monument to layered and textured nuance, and a (perhaps involuntary) testament to how rapidly such efforts, however subtle, come undone. 'The concept of modernity has to this day remained enigmatic,' Osterhammel affirms (*The Transformation of the World*, p. 836). On the one hand, the nineteenth century was an age of revolutions; on the other, there were hardly any in Europe for much of the century (*The Transformation of the World*, pp. 514–517). Despite centuries now of thinking about global economic change, 'investigation and reflection by the very best minds in history and the social sciences has not produced any kind of general theory of industrialization' (*The Transformation of the World*, p. 637). While talk of nationhood seems to have been important, 'the nineteenth-century was not an "age of nation-states"' (*The Transformation of the World*, p. 407).

In this chapter, I will take a rather different approach. I will take a step back and explore the ways in which people have posed such questions and responded to them. In particular, I will look at the language people have used when they have engaged in these debates. In practice, I will argue, we can see from how people have used such words that it is hopeless to look for a clear definition of the modern, modernism or modernity. My principal interest, though, lies beyond this negative conclusion. Through this chapter, we will explore how the larger debate is and was framed in language. As we do so, we come to understand that the discussion looks more like a vast poem than it does a painstaking search for definitions and facts. The poetic use of words associated with the terms *modern*, *modernity* and *modernism* is a way of evoking complex similarities across and beyond the Spanish-speaking world. This is something that many Spanish-language writers have championed.

Habitually, the form in which key questions have been cast has both a national and a non-national dimension. In that sense, they are apparently 'transnational' enquiries. On the one hand, people's phrasing often indicates

---

[1] Alan Knight, 'When was Latin America modern? A historian's response', in *When Was Latin America Modern?*, ed. by Nicola Miller and Stephen Hart (New York: Palgrave Macmillan, 2007), p. 106.

[2] Jürgen Osterhammel, *The Transformation of the World: A Global History of the Nineteenth Century*, trans. by Patrick Camiller (Princeton, NJ: Princeton University Press, 2014 [2009]), pp. xxi–xxii.

that we are assessing a series of nation-states: was Mexico modern, was there a Spanish modernism, for example? On the other hand, reference to a generalised term such as *modernity* indicates a wider phenomenon, unconfined by national borders. It suggests that what matters above all is the degree of resemblance to other places. While the notion of similarity has consequently been pervasive in debates about the 'modern' in Hispanic Studies, it has rarely in practice been brought to the fore as the central intellectual question in and of itself. What is it to say that Spanish-speaking countries do (or do not) *resemble* other 'modern' states? What is going on when we employ that verb, or, for that matter, words such as *similar* or *like* (or *dissimilar, unlike*)? To a significant extent, the answer lies in the ways in which a wide variety of words are or might be used. To give a simple example, if we say that the early writings of the famous Argentine author Jorge Luis Borges are or are not modernist, we are self-evidently deploying the term *modernist* in a particular way. How we do so expresses our approach to similarity in that case. The meaning of the word, the philosopher Wittgenstein famously said, is often its use.[3]

I will explore the varying ways that people formulate comparisons between the Spanish-speaking world and the 'modern', and the specific vocabulary that has arisen as a result. To know these words is crucial to being a 'Hispanist', just as the recurrent use of certain 'keywords' characterises modernity, modernism and the 'modern' more broadly.[4] I will investigate how people have used those words to explore similarities with the 'modern', and the challenges and problems that arise when they do so in relation to very different situations. Finally, I will dwell on the consequent awareness in the Spanish-speaking world that such key words are more like poetry than like dictionary definitions.

The Complex of Resemblances

Across so vast a series of territories and populations as the Spanish-speaking world, there are many layers to how people make such comparisons. In that sense, the 'Hispanic' side of the comparison is itself inherently 'transnational'. We might group together all those peoples and places by using a term such as *hispano*. Then we might place, for instance, *modernity* or other places and peoples on the other side of the comparison. For example, the Spanish historian

---

[3] Ludwig Wittgenstein, *Philosophical Investigations*, trans. by G. E. M. Anscombe (Oxford: Blackwell, 1968), §43.

[4] Melba Cuddy-Keane et al., *Modernism Keywords* (Hoboken: Wiley-Blackwell, 2014).

José María Portillo Valdés examines debates concerning the first modern political constitution of the vast territories governed by the Spanish monarchy, the 1812 Cádiz Constitution. In much of Europe, he says, 'modernidad' took shape in nation states. Conversely, he argues, debates in 'los Congresos del *mundo hispano*' ('the Congresses of the Hispanic world') [my italics] pointed to 'otras posibles formas de modernidad' ('other possible forms of modernity').[5] Sometimes writers emphasise, on the one hand, differences between particular Spanish-speaking regions, and, on the other, the notion that some of these areas might more resemble some place elsewhere that was 'modern'. So, according to the influential *Facundo; o, La civilización y la barbarie* ('Facundo; Or, Civilization and Barbarism') (1845) by the Argentine thinker and politician Domingo F. Sarmiento, a newly independent Argentina needed to split from the legacy of Spain's control of the River Plate region, so to become more like north-western Europe. In another formulation, the countries of the Spanish-speaking Americas are all taken together as one side of the comparison, leaving out other countries where Spanish was a privileged language (principally Spain and its colonies in Guinea (1778–1968), in various configurations in parts of North-West Africa and Morocco (1885 to 1975), and in the Philippines before US occupation after 1898).[6] Relatively new terms such as *Latinoamérica* and *Hispanoamérica* have been used to this end (according to Google's Ngrams, which measures the frequency with which words are used, *Latinoamérica* is hardly used before 1900, and usage of *Hispanoamérica* soars after 1910). Such is the effect of the word *our* in the Cuban revolutionary José Martí's celebrated essay 'Nuestra América' ('Our America') (1891) where he sets out an agenda for Latin Americans in the modern world. In turn, the term *Hemispheric* is used by scholars such as María del Pilar Blanco to explore 'modernity' through 'the common experiences as well as stark discrepancies in countries north and south' across the Spanish- and English-speaking Americas.[7]

As the comparison is framed in different ways, so the patterns of transnational similarity shift. This also happens within given countries. Here the population and localities could be divided up or combined in diverse fashions, and variously described as more or less modern. Such formulations are a response to the heterogeneity of the Spanish-speaking world, a phrase that,

[5] José María Portillo Valdés, *Crisis atlántica: Autonomía e independencia en la Monarquía Hispana* (Madrid: Marcial Pons Historia, 2006), p. 127.

[6] *Facundo; o, La civilización y la barbarie*, ed. by Roberto Yahni (Madrid: *Cátedra*, 1990).

[7] María del Pilar Blanco, *Ghost-watching American Modernity: Haunting, Landscape, and the Hemispheric Imagination* (New York: Fordham University Press, 2012), p. 12.

for that reason, is more than a little misleading. From Galician and Catalan in Spain to Quechua in the Andes or Tagalog in the Philippines, multilingualism was widespread. So was the presence, alongside Spanish-descended 'criollos', of peoples of manifestly different descent, from the indigenous inhabitants of the Americas to the late nineteenth and early twentieth-century Italian immigrants in Buenos Aires or the Chinese in Mexico, to black slaves and their descendants from Colombia to Cuba. In Spain itself, many still voiced an ambiguous sense of connectedness to Islamic north Africa, a consequence of the long history of Islamic Iberia.[8]

In societies where discrimination and racism were widespread, some groups, notably the 'criollos', could be grouped within the 'modern' period, such that they resembled Europeans and Anglo-Americans, whereas others – notably the indigenous and black populations, and even supposedly uncivilised whites such as the Argentine *gauchos* – might be associated with a pre-modern era and dubbed 'primitives' or 'Orientals'.[9] Over the centuries, sexual intercourse and reproduction between people of diverse descent – miscegenation or *mestizaje* – had been far more common in Spanish than British governed territories. Where this had occurred, as in Mexico, intellectuals pondered how a *mestizo* (mixed) population group might properly be deemed to resemble other 'modern' peoples and grouped with them.[10] The question arose likewise whether, in states that often claimed people were equal before the law, the various 'races' were or were not like one another, and, in turn, together or apart, like or unlike the 'modern'. In the Peruvian artist Francisco Laso's painting *Las tres razas (La igualdad ante la ley)* ('The Three Races (Equality before the Law)') (c.1859), we see a triangular composition with three children come together to play cards, presumably in Lima. At the apex is a boy whose outfit could place him anywhere from New York to Paris. He is joined by an indigenous girl in an Andean outfit, and a young, black woman in clothes similar to those worn in parts of Africa and whose recent ancestors would have arrived as slaves. We are left to ponder whether or not the apparent differences have in fact been triangulated, both among these individuals and across the globe. In Spain, there were those who questioned if people could be part of the modern

---

[8] Susana Martín Márquez, *Disorientations: Spanish Colonialism in Africa and the Performance of Identity* (New Haven, CT: Yale University Press, 2008).

[9] On the many nuances, see Carlos J. Alonso, *The Burden of Modernity: The Rhetoric of Cultural Discourse in Spanish America* (Oxford: Oxford University Press, 1998), p. 62 and Mary Louise Pratt, *Imperial Eyes: Travel Writing and Transculturation* (London: Routledge, 1992), pp. 186–197.

[10] Marilyn Grace Miller, *The Rise and Fall of the Cosmic Race: The Cult of Mestizaje in Latin America* (Austin, TX: University of Texas Press, 2004).

nation if they did not use Castilian, or were (like many Galicians) emigrants or (as so often happened) forcibly exiled. Conversely, some debated whether such people might not be *more* modern: an advanced Catalan nation for example, or leftists exiled in mid-twentieth-century Mexico, or artists like Luis Buñuel and Salvador Dalí, directors of the most influential Spanish modernist film, *Un chien andalou* ('An Andalusian Dog') (1929), made in France and in French. In its own way, all this could involve pondering whether diverse peoples and languages might better resemble the 'modern' if they were mixed together.[11]

If the claim to be 'modern' supposed transnational resemblances, the effect of invoking similarity was to cut across and along the many borders of the Spanish-speaking world, carving it into a multitude of possible formations that mirror varying chunks of other places and other times. The effect, beheld – as it were – from a distance, is of ever-mutating and re-aligning reflections.

Vocabulary and Translations

The challenge of articulating these shifting patterns of resemblance and difference has produced its own rich vocabulary and turns of phrase. To study the 'modern' period in the Spanish-speaking world has habitually involved learning such words and debating their usage. We have seen several instances thus far, from *Hispanoamérica* to *mestizo* and *mestizaje*. The latter term has become a major focus for debates, not least in the Argentian anthropologist Néstor García Canclini's influential *Culturas híbridas*.[12] Likewise, when Sarmiento wrote about the relationship between Europe, the modern and the multiple peoples of the southern cone, he spawned a long discussion around the terms *civilización* ('civilisation') and *barbarie* ('barbarism'). *Barbarie* for Sarmiento included the indigenous peoples, *gauchos* and aspects of the Spanish legacy, whereas *civilización* involved transatlantic links to France and what he deemed the right sort of European immigration.

Precisely because these debates seem peculiar to the Spanish-speaking world, discussions of the 'modern' often come down to the question: are

---

[11] Brad Epps and Fernández Cifuentes, *Spain Beyond Spain: Modernity, Literary History, and National Identity* (Lewisburg: Bucknell University Press, 2005), pp. 23–33; Inman Fox, *La invención de España* (Madrid: Cátedra, 1997), p. 12, p. 45, pp. 69–87; Kirsty Hooper, *Writing Galicia into the World: New Cartographies, New Poetics* (Liverpool: Liverpool University Press, 2011), pp. 1–3, pp. 17–25; Mari-Paz Balibrea, 'New approaches to Spanish Republican exile: An introduction', *Journal of Spanish Cultural Studies*, 6.1 (2005), 1–24.

[12] Néstor García Canclini, *Culturas híbridas* (Mexico: Grijalbo, 1990).

these words equivalent in some way to those used elsewhere to talk about the 'modern'? Is the vocabulary simply a straightforward translation? A case in point is the debate around *modernism*, a term used internationally to describe much experimental culture of the early twentieth century. Histories of Spanish literature in this period are often constructed around the term *generación*, indicating that groups of writers and artists arose in relation to important events. We have the *generación del 98* because of the *desastre* of 1898 when Spain lost Cuba, Puerto Rico and the Philippines to the USA, and the *generación del 27* because of enthusiasm for the seventeenth-century poet Luis de Góngora in his centenary year (1927). A great deal of the debate has involved questioning whether the local terminology (for example, *generación de 98*) impedes us from correctly describing these writers as *modernist*.[13] In turn, the British Hispanist Richard Cardwell debated with Donald L. Shaw, among others, whether *noventayochismo* (the 1898 movement) was actually distinct from what Spanish-speakers call *modernismo*, or whether both were manifestations of a Europe-wide notion of Decadence.[14]

The overriding preoccupation here might be described as a concern with normalisation: that is, identifying close resemblances with what is assumed 'normal' for a 'modern' country. Scholars have gone to great lengths to set up checklists of characteristics of modernism, showing that features of the movement found elsewhere are seen in Spain.[15] Such normalisation can entail disruption. That is to say, that by including the distinctive vocabulary of the Hispanic world in the 'normal' picture of modernism, we effectively change the latter dramatically. For example, Hispanists were trained to think that we should not use *modernism* to translate *modernismo*.[16] *Modernismo*, we were told, refers to a localised movement originating in Latin America in the late nineteenth century, notably featuring the Nicaraguan poet Rubén Darío. Conversely, some intellectuals argue that *modernismo* is vitally important to

---

[13] For example, Pedro Cerezo Galán, *El Mal del Siglo* (Madrid: Biblioteca Nueva, 2003), pp. 18–40; Ricardo Gullón, *La invención del 98 y otros ensayos* (Madrid: Gredos, 1969), pp. 7–15.

[14] Richard Cardwell, 'Deconstructing the binaries of *enfrentismo*: José-María Llanas Aguilaniedo's *Navegar pintoresco* and the finisecular novel', in *Spain's 1898 Crisis: Regenerationism, Modernism, Post-Colonialism*, ed. by Joseph Harrison and Alan Hoyle (Manchester: Manchester University Press, 2000), pp. 158–159.

[15] For example, John Macklin, *The Window and the Garden: The Modernist Fictions of Ramón Pérez de Ayala* (Boulder, CO: Society of Spanish and Spanish-American Studies, 1988), pp. 1–39.

[16] See Aníbal González, *A Companion to Spanish American Modernismo* (Woodbridge: Tamesis, 2007), p. 1.

modernity: it not only gave us the word *modernism* but presented a vision of Latin America as a source for world literature.[17] Its powerful assertion of Latin American prestige effected an 'inverted conquest' of European culture by Latin Americans.

Over a long time-period, Spanish-language writers have coined terms and phrases so as to create what we might call 'disruptive resemblances'. A classic (and controversial) instance is the phrase *Raza cósmica* ('Cosmic Race'), originally used in 1925 by the Mexican José Vasconcelos in his book of that title, and closely associated with the terms *mestizo* and *mestizaje*.[18] In the face of Anglophone dominance of the modern world, Vasconcelos predicts that the mixed 'races' of Latin America will attain ultimate superiority as a 'cosmic race'. This will not simply do away with the existing global order, but rather bridge it, draw on it and in so doing surpass it. Latin Americans will thus become the supreme moderns. In turn, Spanish-language cultures, and Hispanic Studies, have developed rich vocabularies to articulate how resemblance to the 'modern' does or does not occur. Historically, there has been a widespread insistence on the terms *retraso* ('delay') and *atraso* ('backwardness') to assert that Spanish-speaking countries are not sufficiently similar to the 'modern' world. The term *fracaso* ('failure') has been introduced, notably by the economic historian Jordi Nadal in *El fracaso de la revolución industrial en España* ('The Failure of the Industrial Revolution in Spain'), to nuance the phrasing.[19] A *fracaso* is not a *fallo* (outright failure) but rather a marked effort to imitate the modern, which then falls short. It is an imperfect form of resemblance. It is in this spirit that literary critic Noel Valis encourages use of the nineteenth-century word *cursi* (loosely 'kitsch') as something not entirely negative. What she calls *The Culture of Cursilería* expresses a creative tension, caught between being alike and unalike to the modern, belated and up-to-date.[20] Equally, many historians have sought to reverse Nadal's phrasing, most obviously in the Spanish-language title of David Ringrose's *España 1700–1900: El mito del fracaso* ('Spain 1700–1900: The Myth of Failure').[21] Here the language of normalisation reaches its peak: we study the

[17] Recently Alejandro Mejías-López, *The Inverted Conquest: The Myth of Modernity and the Onset of Transatlantic Modernism* (Nashville, TN: Vanderbilt University Press, 2009); Mariano Siskind, *Cosmopolitan Desires: Global Modernity and World Literature in Latin America* (Evanston, IL: Northwestern University Press, 2014).

[18] José Vasconcelos, *La raza cósmica: Misión de la raza iberoamericana* (Madrid: Aguilar, 1967).

[19] Jordi Nadal, *El fracaso de la revolución industrial en España, 1814–1913* (Esplugues de Llobregat: Ariel, 1975).

[20] Noel Valis, *The Culture of Cursilería: Bad Taste, Kitsch, and Class in Modern Spain* (Durham, NC: Duke University Press, 2002), pp. 1–30.

[21] David Ringrose, *España 1700–1900: El mito del fracaso* (Madrid: Alianza, 1996).

Hispanic world to show how similar it is to elsewhere, and shed words that emphasise its differences.

More assertive phrasing articulates the creativity involved in wrestling with notions of resemblance given the heterogeneity and specificities of the Spanish-speaking world. The influential Uruguayan intelectual Ángel Rama promoted the phrase *Transculturación narrativa en América Latina* ('Narrative Transculturation in Latin America').[22] This terminology describes a process in which a supposedly universal 'modernidad' and distinctively 'regional' Latin American cultures transform each other into something utterly new. The Argentine thinker Beatriz Sarlo likewise speaks of *Una modernidad periférica* ('peripheral modernity') and 'una cultura de mezcla' ('a mixed culture'). In her view what makes the great writer Jorge Luis Borges so supremely Argentine is that he seeks to be a cosmopolitan, alike to a wider modernity, in a place that at once seeks to embrace but is unlike the 'modern'.[23] In turn, the US-based academic Carlos J. Alonso rejects claims either that Latin America is alike to a wider modernity, or that it is defined by its failure to be as modern as other places. Coining instead the phrase *The Burden of Modernity*, Alonso echoes Martí's forceful use of the word *our*: 'To paraphrase José Martí: our modernity may be a conflicted modernity, but it is our modernity nonetheless' (*The Burden of Modernity*, p. 48).

Of Context

Underpinning many of the discussions we have reviewed is an assumption about language. The supposition is that words like *modernity* are properly used when they match a specific historical 'context', that is, a set of circumstances in a given place and time. On this account, to describe the Hispanic world, or part of it, as 'modern' is to say that it exhibited the same social, economic, political and cultural characteristics as a place that supposedly exemplified 'modernity'. For it not to have all those features, is for it to be *retrasado* or *fracasado* or *periférico*. More subtly, it is often assumed that (a) different contexts will give rise to distinct cultures, and, yet, that (b) the latter may, in some fashion, share fundamental features. As a consequence of (b), we may properly describe apparently divergent contexts as 'modern', because they are deemed, in some manner, to share something at root in common. This is what is implied, for example, in Alonso's assertion of 'our

---

[22] Ángel Rama, *Transculturación narrativa en América Latina* (Buenos Aires: Siglo XXI, 2004).

[23] Beatriz Sarlo, *Una modernidad periférica: Buenos Aires 1920 y 1930* (Buenos Aires: Editorial Nueva Visión, 1988), p. 15, pp. 28–29.

modernity'. A classic example is to be found in the British Hispanist Jo Labanyi's groundbreaking study *Gender and Modernization in the Spanish Realist Novel*.[24] Labanyi argues that Spain's economic circumstances were distinctive: plagued by a weak fiscal situation, and dependent on speculative finance, the country issued paper money that was not linked to the value of gold. This means that the symbol (a bank note) did not depend on an underlying secure thing to which it referred (the value of a precious metal). In classic accounts of capitalism and 'modernity' (for example, by the German thinker Walter Benjamin), symbols and words appear to be detached from any underlying reality and meaning.[25] So, Spain's distinctive failure to be 'modern' (lacking a robust capitalist economy) enabled it to be fundamentally 'modern' in another sense (symbols are detached from meaning and material reality).

A sceptical observer might ask: if the proper use of the word *modernity* requires it to match with a specific context, are we not actually using it in a completely different way from (say) Benjamin? If we really insist on the importance of context, there can be no such thing as 'our modernity' in a strong sense: there is either a definable set of circumstances properly called *modernity* or there is not. A similar problem afflicts the oft-touted notion that there is not one modernity, but plural 'modernities': we could only be sure that each of these was a 'modernity' if we had a single definition of that term. Indeed, one might wonder: would anything important be lost in Sarlo, Alonso, or any number of other writers (including myself) were we never to have used the word *modernity* at all? What if we simply said (for example) that late nineteenth-century Spanish novelists lived in somewhat different economic circumstances from Parisians, and, in their own situation, wrote texts that had interesting things in common with the French?

Alternatively, we can recognise that attempts to link the 'modern' to a 'context' are, at best, misleading, and, at worst, bogus. All that is really going on is that the word *modernity* is being deployed in a variety of circumstances and fashions, in such a way as to suggest that situations and outcomes are similar or dissimilar. To use words such as *modern*, *modernity* and *modernism* is a creative way of exploring patterns of resemblance that cross national borders and weave their way through the highly variegated globe and the heterogeneous Hispanic world. These words appeal because their use seems to certify the importance of Spanish-speaking peoples in recent developments in the

---

[24] Jo Labanyi, *Gender and Modernization in the Spanish Realist Novel* (Oxford: Oxford University Press, 2000).

[25] Walter Benjamin, *Charles Baudelaire: A Lyric Poet in the Era of High Capitalism*, trans. by Harry Zohn (London: Verso, 1973).

wider world (the 'modern world'). Its use may assert a claim that something offers 'accelerated change'.[26] The word *modernity* is grasped at as if it were a trophy. What gives the words this power is precisely their capacity to be used and re-used again and again in relation to such divergent circumstances and such different things. I have argued elsewhere that this is the only useful way in which we can talk of a 'modernism' stretching across the Atlantic world to include Spanish-speaking countries.[27]

Of Slippery Definitions and Strategies

After all, historically, the words *modern*, *modernism* and *modernity* have meant a range of different things. In her study of Spanish modernism, the academic Mary Lee Bretz offers '10 basic positions' with 'contradictory goals and methods'.[28] In the nineteenth century, *modern* could as easily signify the entire Christian era as it could something 'up-to-date'. In 1829, for example, the Spanish intellectual Juan Donoso Cortés used the word that way when urging people to break with the legacy of ancient Greek and Roman culture (classicism).[29] If we sample Mexican newspapers and journals of the year 1904 we find that *modernismo* refers variously to a tendency of British women to adore animals (*El Contemporáneo*, 26 January), an attempt to integrate indigenous peoples in the education system (*La Opinión*, 11 June), and the literary style of a Colombian poet (*El Tiempo Ilustrado*, 10 July). In its 1 January 1901 edition, the Spanish journal *Álbum Salón* considered *modernidad* to involve 'ese vago sentir y ese misterioso esperar' ('that vague feeling and that mysterious longing'), whereas for *La Ilustración Española y Americana* on 30 September 1890 it was defined as 'el don de la imaginación caprichosa en la observación exacta' ('the gift of the capricious imagination in exact observation').

Modern, *modernism* and *modernity* are extremely elastic words. So much is this so that historians often use them in ways that few people in the past would have recognized. Among academics, there has been a vast amount of recent discussion of *modernity*. The Spanish Biblioteca Nacional registers 760 works

---

[26] Susan Friedman, *Planetary Modernisms: Provocations on Modernity across Time* (New York: Columbia University Press, 2015), p. 94.

[27] Andrew Ginger, 'The origins of Atlantic modernism and the Spanish-speaking world', in *Theorizing the Ibero-American Atlantic*, ed. by Harald E. Braun and Lisa Vollendorf (Amsterdam: Brill, 2013), pp. 175–198.

[28] Mary Lee Bretz, *Encounters across Borders: The Changing Visions of Spanish Modernism, 1890–1930* (Cranbury, NJ: Associated University Presses, 2001), p. 39.

[29] Juan Donoso Cortés, *Obras completas*, ed. by Gavino Tejada (Madrid: Imprenta de Tejado, 1854), vol. I, p. 1, p. 14.

with the word *modernidad* in the title between 2000 and 2017, many of them discussing the past. This might lead us to think that *modernidad* mattered to people historically. Yet, a search of the Biblioteca Nacional's digitised periodical holdings suggests the word was used just once in the Spanish press in 1900. By 1920 we find a more promising 147 mentions, but this is dwarfed by more dominant terms like *socialismo* (1,279 instances). The real role of *modernity*, as used by historians, is to group together under a single heading a series of supposedly interrelated phenomena and terms in the past.

At the same time, the elastic vocabulary of the 'modern' is stretched to certain specific ends in discussions of the Hispanic peoples, so as to assert their fundamental significance, for good or ill, in the development of the wider world. In his book *Local Histories/Global Designs*, the Argentine theoretician Walter Mignolo points out how 'modernity' has habitually been discussed in terms of English-, French- and German-language culture from the eighteenth-century 'Enlightenment' onwards. This cuts out and hides away what he calls 'the colonial legacies of the first modernity' that gave us 'the economical foundation of the world system': that is to say, the Spanish conquest of a sizeable part of the Americas and the establishment of transoceanic commerce and government, with often brutal long-term consequences. That dark side of modernity begins in the Americas in 1492.[30] With a more positive spin on the legacy of Imperial Spain, the great work of literature *Don Quijote* by Miguel de Cervantes is often proclaimed the 'first modern novel'.[31] That would situate modernity's origin back in Madrid, 1605–1615, thus reclaiming Spanish Golden-Age literature's centrality in world culture. The *generación del 27* and Latin American writers' adoration of the difficult verse of Góngora might likewise place the beginnings of poetic modernism in the seventeenth century.[32]

It is often now forgotten that the massive participation of Spanish-speaking peoples in the wider Catholic Church meant the words *modernismo* and *modernista* could become strategic weapons in large-scale culture wars. From its promulgation by Pope Pius X in September 1910 until its derogation in 1967, all Catholic clergy had to take *The Oath Against Modernism*.[33] By this

---

[30] Mignolo, Walter, *Local Histories/Global Designs: Coloniality, Subaltern Knowledges, and Border Thinking* (Princeton, NJ: Princeton University Press, 2012), p. 131.

[31] For a recent example, see Rachel Schmidt, *Forms of Modernity:* Don Quixote *and Modern Theories of the Novel* (Toronto: University of Toronto Press, 2011), p. 9.

[32] See Crystal Anne Chemris, *Góngora's* Soledades *and the Problem of Modernity* (Woodbridge: Tamesis, 2008), pp. 104–106.

[33] Frank K. Flinn, *Encyclopedia of Catholicism* (New York: Infobase Learning, 2007), p. 519.

was meant, not the poetry of Rubén Darío, but rather non-Catholic trends in philosophy since the eighteenth century. That use of *modernism* is often to be found in Spanish-language writings of the late nineteenth century and early twentieth. For example, in the heyday of literary *modernismo*, the *Voz de México* of 23 February 1908 deploys that same word to denounce heretical theology. The aim is to deny similarity between Catholics and key elements of the modern world and reinforce Catholic resemblance to much longer, orthodox tradition. This could potentially make of the transnational Catholic communion a community apart.

Poetic History – Or, Goodbye (and Hello) to All That

Was the Spanish-speaking world 'modern', was it part of 'modernity', did it contribute to 'modernism'? If so, to what extent? These, I said at the outset, have been defining questions, both for Spanish-language writers and artists in the past, and for scholars writing about them. In turn, the defining illusion has been that those questions could actually be answered. More specifically, the deception is that anyone has a definition of *modern* or *modernity* or *modernism* that could be used to test whether the Hispanic world was indeed 'modern', 'modernist' or part of 'modernity'. We can, if we wish, persist in the endeavour, and assert that our particular usage of such words is the correct one. Or we can simply recognize the situation for what it is: we can let go, and say 'goodbye to all that'.

In conclusion, *Modern, modernity* and *modernism* are used to trace resemblances and dissimilarities across national borders. They open up vistas of ever-shifting and re-aligning reflections across a multitude of possible geographical formations. They are articulated through rich and varying vocabularies with which to make complex comparisons, but they are not definitively linked to any particular historical context or circumstances. Their sense is elastic and they are deployed to varying ends. They nestle among conglomerations of other words. The very beginning of the 'modern' shifts about in place and time, from the origins of Christianity to 1492 in the Americas to 1605 in Madrid or late nineteenth-century Nicaragua. What we have here is not a rigorously analytical pinning down of terms, nor an incontrovertible description of historical contexts. Contemplated head on, it all looks rather more like poetry: a creative use of language, stretching loose from prior definitions or given facts. This is not to trivialise matters. The poetic vocabulary of the 'modern' has been used for high stakes: the fate and dignity of millions of people in the 'Spanish-speaking' world and their relationship to others.

Historically, many influential 'Hispanic' writers have embraced this view. That ought not to be surprising: they have looked out across the vast heterogeneous complex of the Hispanic world, contemplated its intricate and contested relationship with the rest of the world and experienced the shifting ways in which language is used to articulate such things. A case in point is José Martí's previously mentioned essay, 'Nuestra América', a work often invoked in discussions of Hispanic modernity, and from which the words *modern*, *modernity* and *modernism* are entirely absent. Martí is seeking to evoke the similarity of all peoples despite apparent ethnic differences: 'No hay odio de razas, porque no hay razas' ('there can be no racial animosity because there are no races').[34] He tries to do so while attending to the local conditions of Latin American countries and resisting the threatening rise of the United States. At the same time, he seeks to draw on new ideas emerging in Europe to avoid being merely hostile to the US, and even to assert ultimately 'la identidad universal del hombre' ('man's universal identity') (*Antología*, p. 22). Even as he says this, he observes in Latin America 'la fatiga de acomodación de elementos discordantes y hostiles' ('the tiresome task of reconciling the hostile and discordant elements') (*Antología*, p. 19) derived from elsewhere. To juggle these considerations requires an intricate working through differences while attaining an overarching impression of resemblance. Yet Martí does not really advance a rigorous line of argument, a flowing discussion or a philosophical position: 'Nuestra América' is nothing like a coherent treatise.

Rather, the real key to expressing resemblances lies, not so much in what Martí says, but in how he says it. The prose has a jagged rhythm, assembling manifestly disparate pieces. It throws out curt philosophical assertions ('Pensar es servir' ['the thought is father to the deed'], *Antología*, p. 22); it conjures arresting imagery ('No hay proa que taje una nube de ideas' ['there is no prow that can cut through a cloudbank of ideas'], p. 16). There are down-to-earth references ('Estos tiempos no son para acostarse con el pañuelo a la cabeza' ['these are not times for sleeping in a nightcap'], p. 16) kept company by almost magical metaphors ('Ya no podemos ser el pueblo de hojas, que vive en el aire' ['we can no longer be a people of leaves living in the air'], p. 16). Statements pile up in a carefully stacked jumble of discordant elements, not at all unlike the 'composición singular y violenta' ('unique and violent character'), p. 17 that is Latin America itself. The final call, not just to

---

[34] José Martí, *Antología: Selección y estudio sobre 'José Martí, Amistad Funesta'*, ed by Reinaldo Sánchez (Montevideo: Editorial Ciencias, 1980), p. 22. For the contemporary English translation (*La Revista Ilustrada*, New York, 1 January 1891) see <https://writing.upenn.edu/library/Marti_Jose_Our-America.html>, accessed 7 April 2020.

a Pan-Latin-American identity, but to a shared humanity, flagrantly mixes up time scales, cultural references and images of disparate origin:

> Porque ya suena el himno unánime; la generación actual lleva a cuestas, por el camino abonado por los padres sublimes, la América trabajadora; del Bravo a Magallanes, sentado en el lomo del cóndor, regó el Gran Semí, por las naciones románticas del continente y por las islas dolorosas del mar, la semilla de la América nueva! (p. 22)

> (with a single voice the hymn is already being sung; the present generation is carrying industrious America along the road enriched by their sublime fathers; from Rio Grande to the straits of Magellan, the Great Semi, astride its condor, spread the seed of the new America over the romantic nations of the continent and the sorrowful islands of the sea!)

If we could use language like this, not like a philosopher or a painstaking historian, Martí suggests, we could experience how the Hispanic world, might, in complex, contested ways, and in all its vast heterogeneity, be similar to the rest. This is how language might be employed – its 'use', in Wittgenstein's terms – to articulate a way of connecting the specificities of a Hispanic nation or nations, others elsewhere, and the things they have in common: it would be both and at once 'national' and 'non-national'. It is poetry that takes us across borders, not a debate about the meaning of terms.

8

Flamenco as Palimpsest

Reading through Hybridity

Samuel Llano

There is hardly a musical style with a genealogy as disputed as that of flamenco and yet capable of evoking a more wide-ranging set of cultural associations.[1] Nearly every ethnic group that has settled in the Iberian Peninsula since the Middle Ages or held any contact with its pre- and post-1492 diasporas has been given some credit in the formation of this music. The genealogy of flamenco is shrouded in ambiguity due to the lack of conclusive sources dating from before the mid-nineteenth century. Amid calls for caution, the 'standard' scholarly narrative links flamenco back to what is variously referred to as Medieval Andalusian music, Arab-Andalusian music or Andalusi music. This music, the standard narrative goes, is a hybrid arguably formed by traditions that developed in the Iberian Peninsula up to the eighth century, plus the music of the Arabian Peninsula and Northern Africa brought to Spain from 711 by the Arabs, Egyptians and Berbers. Andalusian music subsequently developed in different geographical and aesthetic directions: it influenced European music and led to the birth of the lute and bowed instruments; it spread across the Southern and Eastern Mediterranean, reaching as far as Iraq and Yemen, and followed the Sephardic diaspora across Arab-speaking territories;[2] and it continued to develop in the Iberian Peninsula, where it entered into contact with the contributions of Gypsies (who purportedly started to arrive in the fifteenth century), Christians, Jews and Moriscos, evolving into what is known

---

[1] I would like to thank Matthew Machin-Autenrieth for his comments on an earlier version of this text.

[2] Dwight F. Reynolds, 'Jews, Muslims and Christians and the formation of Medieval Andalusian music', in *Musical Exodus: Al-Andalus and its Jewish Diasporas*, ed. by Ruth F. Davis (Lanham: Scarecrow Press, 2015), pp. 1–24 (pp. 1–4).

today as flamenco.[3] A more recent trend in scholarship of Arab-Andalusian music is sceptical of this account. Jonathan Glasser defines Andalusi music as a modern revival project constructed around the idea of 'loss', or, in other words, a nostalgia-driven scholarly and performance practice fuelled by the illusion that the music of Medieval Iberia, of which only vague documentary references remain, must be restored to its former glory.[4] In a similar vein, Jonathan H. Shannon posits that 'Andalusian music', considered as a 'unified musical practice with a fixed repertoire and a traceable genealogy' is both a 'colonial artifact' and a construct perpetuated to create continuity with the past in order to serve and promote contemporary political and commercial projects.[5] The similar sonority found in certain music from Spain to the Levant nowadays, both authors contend, is mostly due to the diasporic contacts and exchanges developed after the fall of Granada in 1492.

The most firmly established scholarly narrative today is that, through a relatively obscure process, all or most of the aforementioned influences coalesced around the mid-nineteenth century into a repertoire of *cantes* performed at *cafés cantante* in Andalusia.[6] This repertoire consists of approximately two dozen types of basic song known as *palos*, distinguished by meter, tempo, harmony and melody ('Modal harmony', p. 74).[7] Flamenco may be sung *a palo seco*, without instrumental accompaniment, but the guitar is a standard in flamenco recitals. The flamenco ensemble or *cuadro* usually includes a singer or *cantaor*, a guitar player or *tocaor* and one or more dancers (*bailaores*).

The characteristics of 'modern' flamenco are testimony to its multicultural history. The harmonic and melodic material in flamenco is organised according to a principle of 'modal harmony'. Chords act as basic units and their mutual relationship is governed in most cases by a modal – rather than a tonal – system ('Modal harmony', pp. 70–71). Although the prevalence of the

---

[3] Christopher Paetzold, 'Singing beneath the Alhambra: The North African and Arabic past and present in Contemporary Andalusian music', *Journal of Spanish Cultural Studies*, 10.2 (2009), 207–223, p. 208; Peter Manuel, 'Modal harmony in Andalusian, Eastern European, and Turkish syncretic musics', *Yearbook for Traditional Music*, 21 (1989), 70–94 (pp. 71–72).

[4] Jonathan Glasser, *The Lost Paradise: Andalusi Music in Urban North Africa* (Chicago and London: University of Chicago Press, 2016), pp. 4–7.

[5] Jonathan Holt Shannon, *Performing Al-Andalus* (Bloomington and Indianapolis: Indiana University Press, 2015), pp. 22–42.

[6] Gerhard Steingress, *Sociología del cante flamenco* (Sevilla: Signatura Ediciones, 1991), pp. 365–372.

[7] See also Peter Manuel, 'Flamenco in focus: An analysis of a performance of Soleares', in *Analytical Studies in World Music*, ed. by Michael Tenzer (New York: Oxford University Press, 2006), pp. 92–119 (pp. 95–99).

'E' mode in most *palos* may relate flamenco to the Phrygian mode of Western music,[8] the tension between chordal and modal structures is most probably a legacy of the Arab modal system or *maqâms* ('Flamenco in focus', p. 96).[9] That the *maqâms* are used nowadays all across the Southern and Eastern Mediterranean explains why the music from these geographies may recall the flamenco sonority (Modal harmony', pp. 75–79).

Unfortunately, ever since flamenco scholarship emerged in the 1860s, the multicultural richness of flamenco is also the reason why this music has been used to support a range of conflicting ideologies and competing narratives of national identity in Spain.[10] The widely shared assumption that it originated long before the word 'flamenco' started to be used in about the mid-nineteenth century has generated further uncertainty about its origins and genealogy. Constructions of flamenco's history that emphasise continuity with an uncertain past are used as the foundation of present 'certainties' and identity projects. Yet which ethnic group most contributed to the development of flamenco over history, or who flamenco 'belongs' to, is still greatly disputed.[11] Through these contested arguments scholars instrumentalise history in order to redefine their position relative to the different ethnic groups that conform the tapestry of Spain's multicultural past.

In this respect, flamenco scholarship is similar to writings on Spain's history. Historians have also debated which ethnic groups have contributed most to the formation of Spain. These arguments can be described as a struggle for hegemony in which the different factions involved have used a fictionalised version of the collective past to fashion a convenient image of themselves and the ideologies they adhere to. An extreme example of this divisive practice is the rewriting of Spanish history in Catholic terms.[12] Marcelino Menéndez y Pelayo (1856–1912), and, following his lead, Francoist historians, have associated the periods of Spanish colonial expansion and imperial splendour with the rise of Catholicism. They have consequently

---

[8] The Medieval Phrygian mode consists in a diatonic scale extending from E to an octave above. Its most distinctive feature is a semitone between its first (E) and second (F) degrees.

[9] The *maqâms* are the modes or 'scales' used in most music from the Southern and Eastern Mediterranean. Pitches are organised differently in each *maqâm*, but their most distinctive common feature is the presence of quarter tones.

[10] Sandie Holguín, Flamenco Nation: the Construction of Spanish National Identity (Madison, WI: The University of Wisconsin Press, 2019).

[11] Lou Charnon-Deutsch, *The Spanish Gypsy: The History of a European Obsession* (University Park, PA: The Pennsylvania State University Press, 2004), pp. 202–210.

[12] Henry Kamen, *Imagining Spain: Historical Myth and National Identity* (New Haven and London: Yale University Press, 2008), pp. 74–95.

cast Muslim rule in the Iberian Peninsula as a period of decadence and a temporary diversion from Spain's 'true' Catholic destiny.[13] The celebrated confrontation between a pluralistic and an eminently Catholic reading of Spanish history upheld by Américo Castro and Claudio Sánchez Albornoz respectively is another example of the extent to which the history of Spain has been subjected to manipulation.[14]

Spanish historiography and flamenco scholarship, although similar on many counts, present important differences. Performance is an essential means through which flamenco has articulated constructions of ethnicity and negotiated the place of musicians in society. This is partly responsible for the fact that dominant flamenco scholarship of the nineteenth century cultivated a more positive view of the Muslim legacy in Spain than mainstream historians of the same period. Unlike history, flamenco scholarship used predominantly oral testimony. The paucity of written sources opened up flamenco to being attributed to, and appropriated by, groups whose main form of communication is not writing. In the 1960s, *cantaor* Antonio Mairena articulated an influential account in which flamenco was presented as a *gitano* invention, to which non-Gypsies (*payos*) had contributed nothing of worth.[15] The orality attributed to flamenco and its use of performance to negotiate identities have facilitated attribution to a wider range of ethnic groups. This has had the positive effect of empowering minorities and recognising their role in the making of Spain, but it has not helped to undermine the power of ethnicity to structure narratives of identity that generate exclusion. Flamenco scholarship has thus been linked to both power and resistance. The best, and possibly the only way to end with flamenco being linked to strategies of marginalisation and oppression is by revealing its transcultural nature, and by exposing the biases and motivations underpinning accounts that restrict its ethnic background.

Flamenco, Hybridity and Ethnicity

The transcultural study of flamenco took off in the 1990s, coinciding with a rise in interest in hybridisation and popular music. Hybridisation is both a manifestation and a catalyst of transcultural processes. Studying hybridity

---

[13] Carolyn P. Boyd, *Historia Patria: Politics, History, and National Identity in Spain, 1875–1975* (Princeton, NJ: Princeton University Press, 1997), pp. 232–272.

[14] Hisham D. Aidi, 'The interference of al-Andalus: Spain, Islam and the West', *Social Text*, 24.2 (2006), 67–88, pp. 70–71.

[15] William Washabaugh, 'Ironies in the history of flamenco', *Theory, Culture & Society*, 12 (1995), 133–55 (pp. 136–137).

exposes the arbitrary politics of exclusion and appropriation underpinning most flamenco scholarship up to the 1990s. Hybridisation, or hybridity, for that matter, can be defined as the 'sociocultural processes in which discrete structures or practices, previously existing in separate form, are combined to generate new structures, objects and practices'.[16] The term 'hybridity' stems from the field of biology and was at first derogatory. Throughout the nineteenth century, the term was used to argue that the offspring of humans from different 'races' was inferior to their 'pure' forebears.[17] Even though 'hybridity' helps to account for complex transcultural processes it has often been misused to distinguish between 'pure, traditional' music genres and 'hybrid' ones, and, based on that distinction, to denigrate 'hybrid' cultures.[18] This distinction does not hold up, however, because 'the so-called discrete structures' that form a hybrid are 'a result of prior hybridizations and therefore cannot be considered pure points of origin' (*Hybrid Cultures*, p. xxv). The belief that certain cultural manifestations are 'pure' has persisted, despite its lack of rigour, because of a widespread perception that there is political gain in conceiving of identity as a fixed set of characteristics rather than as a process. According to Homi Bhabha, because 'the terms of cultural engagement, whether antagonistic or affiliative, are produced performatively', we 'need to think beyond narratives of originary and initial subjectivities and to focus on those moments or processes that are produced in the articulation of cultural differences'.[19] It would be appropriate to conclude that 'the object of study is not hybridity but the process of hybridization' (*Hybrid Cultures*, p. xxv).

The obscure and contested genealogy of flamenco bears the marks of the erasure of transcultural processes. Agendas of racial and aesthetic purity generate exclusion and lead to the production of myths and contradictions in flamenco scholarship, what Washabaugh calls 'ironies'. It is only recently that the study of flamenco has fully come to grips with this music's transnational history.[20] The earliest scholarly work on flamenco, dating from

[16] Nestor García Canclini, *Hybrid Cultures: Strategies for Entering and Leaving Modernity* (Minneapolis, MN and London: University of Minnesota Press, 1995), p. xxv.

[17] Robert Young, *Colonial Desire: Hybridity in Theory, Culture and Race* (London: Routledge, 1995), p. 8.

[18] Margaret Kartomi, 'The processes and results of musical culture contact: A discussion of terminology and concepts', *Ethnomusicology*, 25.2 (1982), 227–249, p. 228.

[19] Homi Bhabha, *The Location of Culture* (London and New York: Routledge, 1994), p. 1.

[20] Gerhard Steingress, 'Flamenco fusion and new flamenco as postmodern phenomena: An essay on creative ambiguity in popular music', in *Songs of the*

the late nineteenth century, aimed to establish links between flamenco and constructed racial categories. Early scholars debated the amount and quality of the contributions made by Gypsies and Andalusians to the flamenco tradition. In the 1880s, Antonio Machado y Álvarez, alias *Demófilo* (meaning 'friend of the people') and Francisco Rodríguez Marín, regarded the contribution of Gypsies as a primitive form of song from which a more sophisticated Andalusian *cante* had emerged. In contrast, their contemporary Hugo Schuchardt accused Gypsies of having corrupted Andalusian flamenco and of turning it into 'degenerate' music.[21] This latter view was widely aired from the 1910s on by anti-*flamenquista* Eugenio Noel in his numerous publications and peripatetic conference activity (*Discordant Notes*, pp. 67–77). In the 1920s, the composer Manuel de Falla and poet Federico García Lorca were the first to rescue the image of the Gypsy from the abuse committed by these scholars and the media at large. Falla and Lorca aimed to counter the effect of modernisation on tradition, which, they thought, was in danger of extinction. To that end they organised a competition in Granada in 1922, in which they showcased *cante jondo*. They conceived of this form of flamenco as the primitive root from which all *cantes* had emerged and presented it as an antidote against the 'commercialised', modern flamenco of the *cafés cantante* (Steingress, *Sociología*, pp. 31–53; *The Spanish Gypsy*, pp. 205–208).[22]

Demófilo, Marín, Falla and Lorca disagreed notably about the weight and value of the Gypsy contribution to flamenco. Their differences reveal, first and foremost, the difficulties of defining and studying the 'Gypsy', since all approaches (biological, ethnic, cultural, behavioural) generate exclusion

---

Minotaur: Hybridity and Popular Music in the Era of Globalization, ed. by Gerhard Steingress (Münster: Lit Verlag, 2002), pp. 169–216; see also Steingress, 'La hibridación transcultural como clave de la formación del Nuevo Flamenco (aspectos histórico-sociológicos, analíticos y comparativos)', *TRANS. Revista Transcultural de Música*, 8 (2004) <http://www.sibetrans.com/trans/articulo/198/la-hibridacion-transcultural-como-clave-de-la-formacion-del-nuevo-flamenco-aspectos-historico-sociologicos-analiticos-y-comparativos>, accessed 7 April 2020 and Steingress, *y Carmen se fue a París: Un estudio sobre la construcción artística del género flamenco (1833–1865)* (Córdoba: Almuzara, 2006).

[21] Samuel Llano, 'Public enemy or national hero? The Spanish Gypsy and the rise of Flamenquismo, 1898–1922', *Bulletin of Spanish Studies*, 94.6 (2017), 977–1004 (pp. 987–992); and Samuel Llano, *Discordant Notes: Marginality and Social Control in Madrid, 1850–1930* (New York: Oxford University Press, 2018), pp. 32–47.

[22] Michael Christoforidis, 'Manuel de Falla, Flamenco and Spanish identity', in *Western Music and Race*, ed. by Julie Brown (Cambridge: Cambridge University Press, 2007), pp. 230–241 (pp. 232–234).

and violence (*The Spanish Gypsy*, pp. 129–170).[23] The way to overcome these difficulties is not to deny the existence of a *gitano*/Gypsy or Roma ethnicity, as some have intended,[24] but, as with 'flamenco', to move beyond conceptions of the 'Gypsy' as a category with a fixed set of characteristics. The Gypsy can be more broadly and productively conceptualised as a set of 'diasporic modalities' that are more or less fragmentary and appeal to local kinship, communitarian identity (defined by parameters such as religion or extended musical practice) or universal ties to the world's Roma population.[25]

Beyond their differences, Marín, Lorca and Falla subscribed to the view that Gypsies and Andalusians, despite having shared certain cultural expressions, most notably flamenco, were separate groups. This view reinforced the marginal position of Gypsies in Spanish society from the Early Modern ages. The emphasis given by Falla and Lorca to aesthetic purity and tradition, and their rejection of any signs of change and modernisation are another form of essentialism. Their conception of flamenco could indeed be considered an example of 'invented tradition', a view subscribed to by several scholars (*Sociología*; *Flamenco Deep Song*).[26]

Underlying the debates about the ethnic composition of flamenco were anxieties about the role and suitability of the Gypsy as Spain's internal Other.[27] Scholars of the late nineteenth century and early twentieth had a strong desire to capitalise on flamenco's growing capacity to negotiate the tensions between Andalusia and Castile in the making of Spain. These tensions emerged as Andalusia started to dominate in foreign perceptions of Spain from the early nineteenth century on. They were also manifested in the reaction to this dominance by intellectuals in the orbit of the so-called

---

[23] Annemarie Cottaar, Leo Lucassen and Wim Willems, *Gypsies and Other Itinerant Groups: A Socio-Historical Approach* (Basingstoke: Macmillan, 1998), p. 19.

[24] Timothy Mitchell, *Flamenco Deep Song* (New Haven: Yale University Press, 1994).

[25] Paloma Gay y Blasco, 'Gypsy/Roma diasporas: A comparative perspective', *Social Anthropology*, 10.2 (2002), 173–88 (p. 174).

[26] For 'invented tradition' see Eric J. Hobsbawn and Terence O. Ranger, *The Invention of Tradition* (Cambridge: Cambridge University Press, 1997 [1992]). See also Enrique Baltanás, 'The fatigue of the nation: Flamenco as the basis of heretical identities', in *Songs of the Minotaur: Hybridity and Popular Music in the Era of Globalization*, ed. by Gerhard Steingress (Münster: LIT Verlag, 2002), pp. 139–168 (pp. 151–155) and Timothy Dewaal Malefyt, '"Inside" and "outside" Spanish flamenco: Gender constructions in Andalusian concepts of flamenco tradition', *Anthropology Quarterly*, 71.2 (1998), 63–73.

[27] Lou Charnon-Deutsch, 'Travels of the imaginary Spanish Gypsy', in *Constructing Identity in Contemporary Spain: Theoretical Debates and Cultural Practices*, ed. by Jo Labanyi (Oxford: Oxford University Press, 2002), pp. 22–40.

Generation of 1898.[28] These intellectuals considered Castile to be a more suitable repository of images and tropes than Andalusia for Spain's social and cultural regeneration. They hoped that Spain would overcome the end-of-Empire post-1898 *desastre* sentiment of crisis. They associated Andalusia with Gypsies, bullfighters, bandits and other tropes that cast a backward, pre-modern idea of Spain. The prevalence of Andalusia in constructions of Spain thus run contrary to their intention of modernising and 'regenerating' society. Such tensions were suspended, although not resolved, by the Franco regime (1939–1975). Francisco Franco used his power to impose cultural and political centralisation through measures that included the repression of the Catalan and Basque languages and cultures. Music was instrumental in helping Francoism bring about Spain's centralisation. On one hand, the *coros y danzas* (choirs and dances) department of the women's Sección Femenina, together with the government research body CSIC (the Consejo Superior de Investigaciones Científicas), published collections in which folklore from the different regions was presented as a local variant of a national essence.[29] On the other hand, flamenco was repackaged as an icon of Spain that held no particular ties to Andalusia. This strategy was labelled *nacionalflamenquismo* (national flamencoism) by scholars writing after Franco's death.[30] *Nacionalflamenquista* tactics were used in tandem with the widely publicised mantra 'Spain is different' in order to attract tourism into Spain.[31] By so doing, Francoism capitalised on the long-standing stereotypical conflation of Gypsies, Andalusia and Spain dominant in foreign perceptions of this country since at least the time of Prosper Mérimée's novella *Carmen* (1845).[32]

Notably absent from the history of scholarship and the cultural politics of flamenco outlined above is discussion of this music's transnational ties. This absence could be a consequence of the aforementioned anxieties over

---

[28] Inman E. Fox, 'Spain as Castile: Nationalism and national identity', in *The Cambridge Companion to Modern Spanish Culture*, ed. by David T. Gies (Cambridge: Cambridge University Press, 1999), pp. 21–36.

[29] Carmen Ortiz, 'The uses of folklore by the Franco regime', in *The Journal of American Folklore*, 112.446 (1999), 479–496; Eva Moreda Rodríguez, *Music Criticism and Music Critics in Early Francoist Spain* (New York: Oxford University Press, 2017), pp. 103–130.

[30] William Washabaugh, *Flamenco: Passion, Politics and Popular Culture* (West Sussex: Berg Publishers, 1996), p. 162.

[31] Sasha D. Pack, 'Tourism and political change in Franco's Spain', in *Spain Transformed: The Franco Dictatorship 1959–1975*, ed. by Nigel Townson (Basingstoke and New York: Palgrave Macmillan, 2007), pp. 47–66.

[32] José F. Colmeiro, 'Exorcising exoticism: "Carmen" and the construction of Oriental Spain', *Comparative Literature*, 54.2 (2002), 127–144.

Spain's relationship with its internal Others (Gypsies) and concerns about its cohesiveness and structure, thus relegating flamenco's transnational roots to a secondary position in discussions from the late nineteenth century onwards. The probing of Spanish identity through flamenco was mostly, if not completely, inward-looking. The 1898 *desastre* prompted certain intellectuals, including Miguel de Unamuno and José Ortega y Gasset, to call for the opening up of Spain to foreign influences.[33] But these intellectuals did not consider the cultures of Northern Africa as suitable models for Spain, and looked instead towards France and Germany. The rekindling of debates between *aliadófilos* and *germanófilos* during the First World War, debates that were mainly aimed at breaking Spain's neutrality, further stressed the tendency to look north for the sources of Spain's 'regeneration'.

Flamenco, Race and the Black Legend

In this context, it is hardly surprising that the intellectuals who strove for Spain's 'regeneration' regarded the Muslim remnants in Spanish culture as a liability. Scholars of the Arab world (*arabistas*) construed al-Andalus as the peak of civilisation in the Middle Ages, but their voices were smothered by conservative historians who regarded al-Andalus as an interference or anomaly in Spain's 'natural' Christian course of history ('The Interference of al-Andalus', p. 68). By emphasising the bygone splendour of al-Andalus, *arabistas* not only ran counter to increasingly dominant Catholic readings of Spanish history, but they also raised unintended and uncomfortable associations with the Black Legend. Most visitors to *Andalusia in the time of the Moors*, the Spanish pavilion at the 1900 Universal Exhibition in Paris, left with the impression that the rise of Christianism in Early Modern Spain, through which the foundations of modern Spain were established by the Catholic Kings, had wiped out the high-point of European Medieval civilisation.[34] This perception might have revived a longstanding Black Legend prejudice, according to which British and French colonialism were qualitatively superior to that of Spain.

The world of music was likewise sensitive to the way in which Spanish culture was imagined abroad. Musicologists and composers such as Felipe

---

[33] Carol A. Hess, *Manuel de Falla and Modernism in Spain, 1898–1936* (Chicago and London: The University of Chicago Press, 2001), p. 15, p. 41.

[34] Roger Benjamin, '*Andalusia in the Time of the Moors*: Regret and colonial presence in Paris, 1900', in *Edges of Empire: Orientalism and Visual Culture*, ed. by Jocelyn Hackforth-Jones and Mary Roberts (Malden, MA and Oxford: Blackwell Publishing, 2005), pp. 181–205 (pp. 184–185).

Pedrell and Francisco Asenjo Barbieri reacted vehemently against the ongoing foreign perception that Spanish music amounted to little more than popular and church music, a perception that Judith Etzion attributes to the persistence of the Black Legend.[35] In his writings Pedrell either denied Arab influences on flamenco, or regarded them as a subsidiary element. He thought they represented a primitive stage in the development of modern Andalusian song, which he regarded as more sophisticated (*Manuel de Falla*, p. 175).[36] Pedrell conceived of the Moor as primitive stock with which to give certain forms of flamenco a patina of 'authenticity' and a link to a mythical, idealised past. This role was analogous to the one that *Demófilo* and Rodríguez Marín gave to the Gypsy. In this context, discussing the aspects that flamenco shared with other Mediterranean and Middle Eastern musical traditions, such as the Phrygian semitone between the first and second scale degrees ('Flamenco in focus', pp. 96–97), could not only bring into question the autonomy of flamenco but also complicate the racial makeup of nation-building in Spain. In addition, it could reinforce associations with the Arab world that jeopardised Spain's endeavours to dispel the Black Legend.

In the same way that the Gypsy was the object of either idealising or demonising portrayals in literature, scholarship and the arts (Llano, 'Public enemy'), the Moor was either glamorised or denigrated. This changing view of the Moor intersected in different ways with foreign perceptions of Spain, and with the reactions of Spanish intellectuals to these perceptions. For all its complexity, this interlocking produced a single, monologic narrative of flamenco in which the Arab influence featured only as a secondary influence. Falla and Lorca, although they contradicted Pedrell by acknowledging an ancestral Arab influence in flamenco (*Manuel de Falla*, pp. 174–175), credited *gitanos* with giving *cante jondo* its definitive form, and placed them at the centre of discussions on the ethnic background of flamenco.[37]

The Moor and the Gypsy, although imagined in different ways, were both used with a similar purpose, namely, to oppose modernisation. Unlike the Gypsy, however, the Moor was no longer an Other 'among us', following

[35] Judith Etzion, 'Spanish music as perceived in Western music historiography: A case of the Black Legend?', *International Review of the Aesthetics and Sociology of Music*, 29.2 (1998), 93–120 (p. 94).

[36] Cristina Cruces Roldán, *El Flamenco y la Música Andalusí: Argumentos para un encuentro* (Barcelona: Carena, 2003), p. 11.

[37] Federico García Lorca, 'Importancia Histórica y Artística del Primitivo Canto Andaluz, Llamado "cante jondo"', in *Manuel de Falla y el "cante jondo"*, ed. by Eduardo Molina Fajardo (Granada: Universidad de Granada, 1998), pp. 177–208; and Manuel de Falla, 'El "Cante Jondo" (Cante Primitivo Andaluz)', in *Manuel de Falla y el "cante jondo"*, pp. 209–226.

the forced conversion of Muslims to Christianity (1492), and the subsequent expelling of Moriscos (1609–1914). The *Pragmática sanción* (1767), by which Charles III forced Gypsies to be culturally, linguistically and legally assimilated into Spanish society, meant that the marks that made Gypsies recognisable and quantifiable were, if not completely wiped out, at least harder to trace.[38] At the same time, in nineteenth century the image of the Moor and al-Andalus became shrouded in nostalgia mainly thanks to the contributions of foreign writers, as was the case with the Gypsy. Testimony to the nostalgic re-imagining of the Moor are Washington Irving's *Tales of the Alhambra* (1832) and François-René de Chateaubriand's *Le Dernier des Abencerrages* (1826), the latter of which inspired an opera (1874) by Pedrell (*Performing Al-Andalus*, pp. 125–133). Nostalgia contributed to perceptions that the figure of the Moor was in the distant past; several centuries separated the splendour of Andalusi music and flamenco, and the lack of reliable information on their mutual influence turned discussions about their relationship into a matter of high speculation, almost a 'profession of faith' (*El Flamenco*, p. 14).

However, a more vivid and menacing image of the Moor returned with force in the wake of the Spanish defeats of 1909 and 1921 in Morocco. These North African campaigns triggered a new wave of introspective and self-deprecatory diagnosing of Spain's ills by Spanish intellectuals and a re-examination of Spain's 'western-ness' ('The interference of al-Andalus', p. 67). Until the Civil War (1936–1939), during which Moroccan soldiers fought in Franco's army, the Moor lurked as a mysterious and fascinating yet also slowly encroaching presence in Spanish culture. The implications of discussing flamenco's links with the Arab world far exceeded the field of musicology. These debates could raise uncomfortable questions about Spain's relationship with its colonial past or undermine Spain's imperialistic ambitions in Northern Africa.[39]

It was not only racial bias against Spain's southern neighbours that accounts for the reluctance of Spanish musicologists to discuss transnational elements in flamenco. Even the influence of France, a country many Spanish intellectuals regarded as a beacon of civilisation, was also denied or glossed over. Steingress has documented the impact of classical French ballet and cabaret in the development of flamenco dancing via the Spanish troupes returning from performances in Paris. This influence, Steingress argues,

---

[38] Bernard Leblon, *Les Gitans d'Espagne: Le Prix de La Différence* (Paris: Presses Universitaires de France, 1985), p. 101.

[39] For Spain and North Africa, see also Eric Calderwood, *Colonial al-Andalus: Spain and the Making of Modern Moroccan Culture* (Cambridge, MA: Harvard University Press, 2018) and Susan Martin Márquez, *Disorientations: Spanish Colonialism in Africa and the Performance of Identity* (New Haven: Yale University Press, 2008).

reconfigured salons in Spain as 'spaces of artistic hybridisation' (*y Carmen se fue*, p. 67). Although popular with the public, these spectacles did not go down well with traditionalist intellectuals. The success of *ópera flamenca*, a genre that drew inspiration from French cabaret, upset Falla and Lorca, and prompted them to organise the *cante jondo* competition (Washabaugh, 'Ironies', pp. 135–136). Other contemporary critics were uneasy about France playing a decisive role in the development of Spanish identity through its influence in popular music. Ironically, Falla was himself the object of similar criticism when *The Three-Cornered Hat* was performed at Madrid's Teatro Real in 1921, following successful performances in London (1919) and Paris (1920). As Hess has demonstrated, Falla was attacked by the conservative Spanish press, which accused him of selling out Spain, and himself, to the French.[40] The greatest concern about French influence on flamenco and on 'Spanish music', however, was that it was due to an interest in the 'exotic' aspects of Spanish culture,[41] manifest, for instance, in Bizet's opera *Carmen*.[42]

Patrimonialisation and Heritage

In the face of flamenco's thoroughly transcultural history, claims that the age of flamenco's hybridisation began in the mid-twentieth century need to be reexamined. Peter Manuel celebrates 'the panoply of flamenco-related hybrids that have flourished' from the 1960s on thanks mainly to the contributions of *tocaor* (guitarist) Paco de Lucía and *cantaor* Camarón de la Isla.[43] This period witnessed Spain's opening up to foreign capital and cultural influence, first during the late Franco regime, and later during the early transition to democracy (Pack, 'Tourism').[44] It has also roughly coincided with the expansion of the recording industry and the media in Spain.[45] The celebration

---

[40] Carol A. Hess, 'Manuel de Falla's *The Tree Cornered Hat* and the right-wing press in pre-Civil War Spain', *Journal of Musicological Research*, 15.1 (1995), 55–84.

[41] Samuel Llano, *Whose Spain?: Negotiating 'Spanish Music' in Paris, 1908–1929* (New York: Oxford University Press, 2012).

[42] Elizabeth Kertesz and Michael Christoforidis. 'Confronting Carmen beyond the Pyrenees: Bizet's opera in Madrid, 1887–1888', *Cambridge Opera Journal*, 20.1 (2008), 79–100; Michael Christoforidis and Elizabeth Kertesz, *Carmen and the Staging of Spain: Recasting Bizet's Opera in the Belle Epoque* (New York: Oxford University Press, 2019).

[43] Peter Manuel, 'Andalusian, Gypsy, and class identity in the contemporary flamenco complex', *Ethnomusicology*, 33.1 (1989), 47–65 (p. 47).

[44] See Mary Vincent, *Spain, 1833–2002: People and State* (Oxford: Oxford University Press, 2007), pp. 182–183.

[45] Héctor Fouce and Fernán del Val, 'La Movida: Popular music as the discourse of modernity in democratic Spain', in *Made in Spain. Studies in Popular Music*, ed. by

of hybridity as a modern phenomenon has thus played into the hands of certain economic interests, especially in view of the considerable commercial success of flamenco fusion bands such as Ketama, Pata Negra and Kiko Veneno.[46] Yet, as Steingress has argued, 'despite the current diversification of flamenco resulting from its fusion with other traditional musics, the whole history of flamenco is characterised by this same phenomenon' ('La hibridación transcultural'). The impression that flamenco's hybridity is recent surely rests on the perception that the deliberate fusion of styles and traditions existing in separate form in the popular imagination, such as Arab-Andalusian music and flamenco, or jazz and flamenco, is a recent phenomenon; but it is also a result of a longstanding practice of neglecting this music's transcultural roots.

The persistence of this neglect does more to favour certain economic and political interests than it does justice to history. One would expect that, with the increasing recognition of flamenco's transcultural ties, and in the face of industry's celebration of hybridity, the (self-appointed) cultural and political institutions responsible for the promotion and diffusion of flamenco would eagerly jump on the bandwagon of transculturalism. Instead, the Junta de Andalucía (Andalusian Government) has chosen to patrimonialise flamenco in order to fuel their demands for political autonomy. In so doing, they construe an 'invented' tradition as the 'natural' foundation of modern forms of local political organisation. Article 68 in the reformed Andalusian Statute of Autonomy (2007) grants Andalusia 'competencia exclusiva en materia de conocimiento, conservación, investigación, formación, promoción y difusión del flamenco como elemento singular del patrimonio cultural andaluz'.[47] This declaration represents a reversal of the aforementioned politics of *nacionalflamenquismo* under Franco. The Statute aims to stop flamenco from being used as an icon of Spain that holds no particular ties to Andalusia.[48] But this 'exclusive' appropriation also testifies to the recurrence and convenience of narratives that sideline or deny transcultural elements, in this context those originating in other regions within Spain. The Statute attaches no significance to the fact that by the 1880s Madrid was arguably the locale with the liveliest flamenco scene in Spain.[49] Transculturalism is clearly an anomaly or even a liability in the framework of region-making in post-Franco Spain.

Silvia Martínez and Héctor Fouce (New York: Routledge, 2013), pp. 125–134 (p. 128, p. 132).

[46] Enrich Folch, 'At the crossroads of flamenco, new flamenco and Spanish pop: The case of rumba', in *Made in Spain. Studies in Popular Music*, pp. 17–27 (pp. 24–25).

[47] *Estatuto de Autonomía para Andalucía* (Sevilla: Parlamento de Andalucía, 2007), pp. 40–41.

[48] William Washabuagh, *Flamenco Music and National Identity in Spain* (Farnham: Ashgate, 2013), pp. 5–8.

[49] José Blas Vega, *El flamenco en Madrid* (Córdoba: Almuzara, 2006), p. 107.

In 2010 the United Nations Educational, Scientific and Cultural Organization (UNESCO) declared flamenco Intangible Cultural Heritage of Humanity, adding complexity to the already dense web of political interests and institutional manoeuvring that defines the politics of flamenco ownership in Spain. For one thing, UNESCO's declaration 'has served to consolidate [flamenco's] status as a symbol of regional culture', as it has reinforced the Andalusian Government's efforts to patrimonialise flamenco.[50] But if this regional patrimonialisation of flamenco sanctions the reemergence of one of Spain's 17 Autonomous Communities from the stark centralisation to which it was subjected under Franco, it cannot be plainly considered as a movement of resistance against power exercised from above, or from the centre for that matter. The exploitation of flamenco for political and economic gain in Andalusia is alienating a considerable number of Andalusian residents who do not identify with this music or who disapprove of the way in which it is being repackaged for tourist consumption. The Andalusian Government needs to address realities that shake the foundations of regional identity politics. Some residents of Granada, Almería and Jaén have formed the *Plataforma por Andalucía Oriental* to express opposition to the notion that Andalusia is defined by a unitary culture, and to reject the identification of flamenco with Andalusia (Machin-Autenrieth, *Flamenco*, pp. 77–96).[51] The *Plataforma* challenges the making of identity from above and shows that there are limits to the extent to which flamenco can be used as a political tool in Andalusia, at least under the exclusive terms set out in the Statute.

Conclusions

The history of flamenco is a fictional space, a playground where narratives of Spanish history and identity are conveniently cobbled together to serve a range of interests. Parts taken from previous accounts are used and rearranged with less rigour than intention, leading to damaging disputes about flamenco's ethnic background. Underlying these debates is the recognition that music is a powerful instrument of identity politics linked to the construction of memory. Depending on how it is conceived and performed, flamenco can either be a site for the negotiation of ethnic conflict or a tool of exclusion and marginalisation. It seems difficult to prevent certain peoples and institutions

---

[50] Matthew Machin-Autenrieth, *Flamenco, Regionalism and Musical Heritage in Southern Spain* (Abingdon and New York: Routledge, 2017), p. 10.

[51] See also Matthew Machin-Autenrieth, 'Flamenco? Algo Nuestro? (Something of ours?): Music, regionalism and political geography in Andalusia, Spain', *Ethnomusicology Forum*, 24.1 (2015), 4–27.

from appropriating flamenco at the expense of others, or that hatred of this music leads to abuse of the groups most commonly associated with it. The writing of flamenco's history can help critique forms of appropriation by exposing the ironies inherent in the production of identity. Scholarship must work through the layers of interpretation that have been piled upon flamenco. Flamenco is a palimpsest and its study will not yield access to truth nor reveal an original, primitive form, but will uncover the motivations behind the politics of identity of which it has been an object.[52] Each of these interpretations claims to be closer to a purported truth. It is easy to see with hindsight how many of these readings fail to meet the standards of rigour and objectivity that they claim to live up to. The memory battles over the meaning and events of the Spanish Civil War (1936–1939) remind us that we remember for present purposes.[53] They also teach us that there is no such thing as historical truth. Perhaps, the biggest irony of all is that the transcultural elements that have placed flamenco at the centre of debates on Spanish identity and history have been neglected by most parties involved in these debates.

---

[52] Sarah Dillon, 'Reinscribing De Quincey's palimpsest: The significance of the palimpsest in contemporary literary and cultural studies', *Textual Practice*, 19.3 (2005), 243–263.

[53] José F. Colmeiro, 'Canciones con Historia: Cultural identity, historical memory, and popular songs', *Journal of Spanish Cultural Studies*, 4.1 (2003), 31–45, pp. 31–33; Ángel Loureiro, 'Pathetic arguments', *Journal of Spanish Cultural Studies*, 9.2 (2008), 225–37 (pp. 226–227).

Section 3

Spatialities

The transnational is inherently spatial or, to put it another way, 'space is constitutive of transnationality'.[1] If, as we have seen, transnationalism involves 'multiple ties and interactions linking people or institutions across the borders of nation states',[2] then clearly all forms of transit, connection, exchange and mobility across the world in real time operate through space. This 'planet-spanning yet common – however virtual – area of activity' (Vertovec, p. 447) leads to new and intensified forms of human interaction, new imaginary spaces and a blurring of boundaries between space and place. Transnational connectivity gives rise to reconfigurations of place-defined identities, especially among and between diasporas 'dispersed' and 'scattered' across the globe, although neat dichotomies between nation and belonging on the one hand and rootless de-territorialisation on the other are misleading (*Transnational Spaces*, p. 4).

The five chapters in the following section all discuss the impact of globalisation, transnationalism and space in relation to Latin America (including Brazil) in the late twentieth and twenty-first centuries. As Philip Swanson argues, today the label 'Latin American', or 'Latin', is a brand circulating in the global consumer economy and the global imagination as a fusion of a popular Latino/a identities as experienced by the Hispanic diaspora in the

---

[1] *Transnational Spaces*, ed by Peter Jackson, Philip Crang and Claire Dwyer (London and New York: Routledge, 2004), p. 1. See also David Featherstone, Richard Phillips and Johanna Waters' helpful 'Introduction: Spatialities of transnational networks', in the special issue of *Global Networks*, 7.4 (2007), 383–391.

[2] Steven Vertovec, 'Conceiving and researching transnationalism', *Ethic and Racial Studies*, 22.2 (1999), 447–462.

USA. Citing a medley of examples of 'imaginary Latin America', from the Las Iguanas restaurant chain, magical realist fiction, blockbusters such as Zorro, and Latino celebrity Jennifer Lopez (born in New York to Puerto Rican parents), he asks, 'Where is Latin America?' The answer is, 'It's everywhere', and therefore nowhere. In the mass imaginary, 'Latin America' is a trendy de-territorialised brand mobilised to sell services and commodities globally.

For their part, Claire Taylor and Thea Pitman explore how the digital economy and social networking in Latin America afford new forms of negotiation between the local and the global, prompting revisions of ideas of place and challenging fixed identities. 'Latin America' is not a given, and neither are 'Hispanism' and 'Latin Americanism'. In fact, the very concept of an 'Area Studies' discipline is troubled by new transnational digital cultures. Drawing on examples including Digital Zapatismo, artistic activism on the US–Mexican border and the blogosphere of Cubans in Cuba, the United States and elsewhere, they argue that Latin American online culture and practice is post-regional, pushing us to rethink what we mean by local, national and regional in today's global network economy and to reconfigure disciplinary boundaries.

In her study of literary globalisation, Emily Baker also queries the concept of 'Latin American' literature, drawing attention to the recent declaration by Mexican novelist Jorge Volpi that 'Latin American literature does not exist'. The writers of the Crack Manifesto group refuse to write novels that contribute to 'great Latin American literature', to use 'magical realism' to merely satisfy market demand and to consolidate the nation-states they deplore. By engaging with other realities such as Nazi Germany and the Holocaust, with no mention of Mexico or the Americas, Volpi and fellow Mexican novelist Ignacio Padilla condemn all forms of 'closed and violent formation' that underpin a territorial approach to community and, indirectly, forms of oppression in their own country.

Elzbieta Sklodowska explores the extent to which the term 'Special Period', used to describe 1990s post-Soviet Cuba, is meaningful in cross-disciplinary, transnational analysis. She compares the *ostalgie* of post-Soviet Europe to Cuban *estalgia* by studying the way everyday objects and artefacts are repurposed and manipulated differently in each area to fit preconceived frames of analysis and allegiances. Through the life-stories of objects she traces commonalities that cross Cold War divides (East/West, First/Third/Second Worlds) and the differences that have emerged locally, particularly in the nostalgic reframing of objects and their commercialisation and collectability.

Finally, Francisco J. Hernández Adrián addresses representations of transnational archipelagos in recent Latin American cinema, noting particularly how islanders connect, communicate and network on, off and between remote and isolated islands and mainlands. He argues that islands (floating, peripheral enclaves relating to both land and water) might be conceived of as borderless 'space machines' that produce space–time transformations. Focusing on four recent films by directors from Colombia, Mexico and the Dominican Republic he discusses their shorescapes and islandscapes as imaginary spaces that transcend local material realities, transformed into transitional spaces of dreams, escape and longing that beckon to the future and the unknown. All the chapters in this section aim to overcome restrictive nation-centred approaches (hence their common use of Latin America to include Brazil), and to reconceptualise places as sites or nodal points in networks and flows rather than fixed locations. This perspective is recurrent throughout the book.

9

Where is Latin America?

Imaginary Geographies and Cultures of Production and Consumption

Philip Swanson

In many ways, 'Latin America' has long since departed from the parameters of its physical, geographical boundaries and become part of the global (especially Western or Northern) imagination. Manifestations of the phenomenon include: the popularity of a perceived 'new' Latin American cinema (*Amores perros* (2000), *Y tu mamá también* (2001), *Cidade de Deus* (2002)) and the transitioning of its directors to US film industry success; the transnational stardom of actors and singers like Gael García Bernal, Ricky Martin and Spain's Enrique Iglesias; the impact of 'border' movies from, for example, *Traffic* (2000) to *Sicario* (2015), and the popularity of drug war TV shows like *Narcos*; the rise of *regaeton* and the ubiquity in 2017 of a song like *Despacito*; the North American recreation of hit telenovelas in the shape of *Ugly Betty* or *Jane the Virgin*: the growth in exotic coffee culture by day and the unmissable presence by night of so-called '*salsa*' (often accompanied by glamorous-looking rum cocktails); the Caribbean and Latin American tourism boom with its socially oriented yet voyeuristic Rio *favela* tours and its fetishisation of supposed Havana decadence (a byproduct being the projection abroad of The Buena Vista Social Club). 'T'was ever thus', of course: one has but to think of gold and silver, much of the implicit content or subtext of *The Tempest* or *Don Quijote*, the cocoa, sugar or tobacco trade, Alexander von Humboldt's packed nineteenth-century lecture theatres or Good Neighbour Era Hollywood to realise just how long this exportation of the colonial exotic has been going on.

The rise of social media has accelerated this process to a feverish degree, but globalisation was already catalysing it in the later twentieth century and early twenty-first (the main focus here). One instance of Latin-inflected globalisation is the UK restaurant and bar chain Las Iguanas. The chain, which started out in 1991, aimed to bring what the company called 'our own brand of Latin magic' to presumably hitherto culturally deprived Britons, describing itself as Restaurant and Cachaçaria, and advertising salsa music and tapas, providing 'that all essential Latino atmosphere any time of day or night'. Though the chain's general manager was once quoted as claiming that 'our restaurants ooze [...] authenticity', the mixture of elements on offer just cited seems to mix notions of Spanish America, Brazil, the Hispanic USA and European Spain in an undifferentiated jumble of Latin otherness. The notion of Latin America (or, better, all-purpose Latinity) that is projected is, of course, positive, but based on the clichés of cultural assumption. For example, their website used to promise an experience involving 'passionate people', 'intoxicating Latin rhythms', a 'soundtrack of sultry salsa' and even 'the rich colour palette of the southern hemisphere'. Behind the upbeat projection, then, there seemed to lie a peddling of inconsistent stereotypes in which the Latin other could be conceived as liminal, dark, libidinous and unbridled.

However, there does appear to be a self-consciously politically correct element thrown in too to appeal to the relative cultural awareness of the liberal-minded British eating and drinking public. A degree of association with the popular classes was created by the description of their one-time 'signature dish', *xinxim*, as 'Pelé's favourite'. Plus, in an image that conjures up the notion of fair trade, one is reassured that the cachaça one consumes is produced by our friend 'João Luiz' (who nonetheless appears generic enough not to require an identifying surname), a master cachaça maker from a town near Rio, who 'looks after our field of Las Iguanas sugar cane, harvests it, distils and bottles it before shipping it to us in the UK'. The drinker's conscience is further soothed by the eco-friendly reassurance that, among the many 'Latin American things' that can be seen in Las Iguanas restaurants, are 'our mosaic table-tops [...] made for us in Brazil from sustainable woods'. So, while indulging oneself, one can at least feel that one is doing something to save the rainforest. One might feel slightly more uneasy about the anthropologising gaze that can risk appearing to reduce the people of Latin America to exotica not much different to the subcontinent's exuberant flora and fauna. An early version of the website teases the customer with the following prospect: 'you might also find a few life-sized Latinos if you know where to look'. In its July 2004 news release entitled 'Las Iguanas say HOLA! To Nottingham', the chain quotes one reviewer's characterisation of the restaurant as 'as loud and proud as Joaquin Cortez's [sic] Cuban heels, as intense as Antonio Banderas' gaze and as brazenly sumptuous as J-Lo's curves'. Of course, Cortés may wear Cuban heels, but he is from Andalucía not Cuba, Banderas is Spanish and based in Hollywood and J-Lo is a North American from the Bronx.[1]

---

[1] Las Iguanas has repeatedly modified and updated its website over the years. The

A trip to Las Iguanas, then, where you can have epicurean or libationary adventures, enjoy exotic new experiences and maybe – if you are lucky – even spot a life-sized Latino or two, sounds rather like going on a safari. And the safari cliché is rife in Northern/Western consumer culture in everything from tourism to shopping. One example is the US clothing company Banana Republic. Founded in 1978 and purchased by GAP in 1983, its name obviously plays on the cliché of political instability in Latin America (and elsewhere in what used to be called the 'Third World'). Moreover, its full original name, Banana Republic Travel and Safari Clothing Company, suggests that shopping there becomes a species of adventure or safari in which the Latin American other is projected as sexy but risky, as exciting but as frisson-inducing as an exploration in the jungle or hunting for jaguars. Paul Smith has quoted the founders of the company as saying they had the whimsy of imagining their business as a kind of republic of their own, the merchandise being a reflection of the surplus uniforms of supplanted military dictators.[2]

More bizarre still was the 2004 campaign of British clothing company FatFace. FatFace described itself then as an Active Lifestyle Clothing Brand, selling fashion gear, to quote from their company philosophy, to those who like to 'ski, surf, sail, climb, fly, mountain bike, play tennis or just love getting amongst it'. The 2004 campaign, trading presumably on the long-standing idea of the New World as place of space, excess, grandiose landscape, discovery, adventure and exploration, ran under the mystifying slogan '100% Ecuador' – together with the pun 'Es Todo sobre la Altitud' (It's all about altitude). What these versions of Latin America show is that imaginary geography is much more powerful than real geography and that, in the globalised system, true knowledge of Latin America has often been substituted by an imaginative Latin world existing in the minds of Northern and Western consumers.

Jon Beasley-Murray has drawn attention to the example of Bacardi, the consumption of which reveals a pattern of de-territorialisation of Latin America and the fabrication of imaginary versions of it abroad.[3] He notes that, although the Bacardi label carries the legend 'Established Cuba, 1862', it

most recent manifestation at the time of writing is: <https://www.iguanas.co.uk/>, accessed 10 December 2017.

[2] Paul Smith, 'Visiting the Banana Republic', in *Universal Abandon: The Politics of Postmodernism*, ed. by Andrew Ross (Minneapolis, MN: University of Minnesota Press, 1989), pp. 128–48 (p. 130).

[3] Jon Beasley-Murray, 'Latin American Studies and the global system', in *The Companion to Latin American Studies*, ed. by Philip Swanson (London: Arnold, 2003), pp. 222–238. In the same volume, Gareth Jones' essay on 'Latin American Geographies' is also a thought-provoking reflection on Latin America and imaginative geographies.

was founded by a Catalán, had its assets confiscated by Castro and saw the Bacardi family relocate to the USA and enter a drawn-out lawsuit over the rights to the name. The Headquarters of Bacardi re-located to the Bahamas, but with distilleries in Brazil and Mexico, its ingredients coming from those companies and Puerto Rico. Moreover, this quintessentially Cuban product underwent a campaign of de-Latinisation by the company in the Cold-War fevered USA of the 1960s and 1970s, with a new emphasis on the product as a mixer. The idea was to reduce the colonial, Latin and Cuban associations of Bacardi as rum, and re-present it as an American mixer drink in a big joint advertising campaign with Coca-Cola. Bacardi is Cuban, then, but also from nowhere. In a sense it is an image of the vacuousness of globalisation. It is literally just a name and, ironically, this, the name, the company's most precious asset, has been held, as Peter Foster observed in 1990, in a lawyer's office in Liechtenstein.[4]

However, the growing fashion of Latin food, music, films and holidays in the 1990s led to a vigorous but equally displaced and amorphous re-Latinisation campaign and Beasley-Murray noted in particular the promotion in the late 1990s of the Bacardi Breezer. He examined examples of the UK TV advertisements for the product. One is built around an imaginary opposition between staid Britishness and Latin sensuality, the formality of a British job interview set against the freedom and fun of a Latin carnival setting. But there is an important shift here, too. The difference between the two cultures is no longer one of simple binary opposition. Rather, the one now exists within the other. 'There's a bit of Latin spirit in every/one', the tag line says. The pun suggests that inside every bottle of Bacardi Breezer there is an explosive Latin experience just waiting to burst out ('there's a bit of Latin spirit in every *one*'). It also suggests, though, that that Latin spirit exists potentially in all of us and that Bacardi Breezers are a kind of psycho-social lubricant that will allow us to set that spirit free ('there's a bit of Latin spirit in *everyone*'). In other words, and this is Beasley-Murray's important point when he talks about 'viral *latinidad*', Latinity has become the cultural unconscious of the West and the North. It is interesting that one of the other adverts in the series depicts a young woman who is lying on a psychiatrist's couch. When asked by the stiff-bearded and bespectacled English doctor to tell her the first thing that comes to her head, the girl's mind appears to cut to a memory or fantasy of raunchy excess with a muscly dark-skinned man partly on the bonnet of what looks like a 1950s Cuban vintage automobile photographed against an obviously sweaty Latin backdrop. The Latin is the unconscious other – dark, dangerous

---

[4] Peter Foster, *Family Spirits: The Bacardi Saga* (Toronto: MacFarlane, Walter and Ross, 1990), p. 247; quoted by Beasley-Murray, p. 230.

and desirable, but a useful escape valve for the hard-working 'First-World' yuppie. Moreover, Latin America has burst its boundaries it seems and is, in many ways, now as much over here as it is over there, a fully fledged part of the mental landscape of modern Britishness.

Latin America increasingly exists – as it always has done – for the benefit of the gaze of the outside world, either as source of ogling wonderment or as source of exploitative possibility. With the rise of the movie industry in early twentieth-century California, the Latin look, as it was called, became extremely popular in the USA and Latin American actors became particularly popular (especially in the early silent movies where they enjoyed the advantage of not having to speak and thus mark their otherness). However, these actors quickly tended to become separated from their ethnicities. The original 'Latin lover', Rudolf Valentino, was actually Italian, while later stars of the 1930s, such as Ramon Novarro and Dolores del Rio, had the accents dropped from their names and were presented in publicity material as 'Latin' or 'Spanish', thus avoiding the sordid low-class connotations for North Americans of the term 'Mexican'. Also, such actors often played not Mexicans but other kinds of foreigner. This de-Latinisation of stars soon became something of a norm.

The most famous example is Margarita Carmen Cansino, the daughter of a Spanish male dancer and immigrant to New York. She started off playing Mexican señoritas in American B movies, but her big break came in 1941 when, in a tremendous stroke of de-ethnicisation, she was re-named as Rita Hayworth and cast in the title role of *The Strawberry Blonde*. This trend towards ethnic invisibility continued through to the 1960s and 1970s with the re-packaging of Latin actors such as Anthony Quinn and Raquel Welch. It perhaps continued into the twenty-first century with actresses such as Cameron Diaz, who, despite the surname, does not conspicuously embody Latinity. Moreover, pan-Latin othering continued to be rife as Brazilian or Mexican characters around the turn of the millennium were regularly portrayed by Spaniards such as Penélope Cruz or Antonio Banderas – although this as an improvement on the browned-up portrayals of Mexicans by, for example, Marlon Brando in *Viva Zapata* (1952) or Charlton Heston in *Touch of Evil* (1958).

These observations on Latinos in Hollywood are all in Clara Rodríguez's authoritative account. Here she also opines that, in the 1960s, 1970s and early 1980s, more notoriously negative images of Latin Americans or US Hispanics became the norm, particularly with the rise of the Spaghetti Western and the urban crime drama focusing on gangsterism and drugs. The growth and integration of the Latino population in the USA did eventually bring more positive role models in the 1980s and 1990s in the form of producers, actors and directors such as Salma Hayek, Robert Rodriguez and Andy Garcia (the situation has noticeably improved much further by the mid-twenty-first century). For some an iconic, if not very good, film that sums up this trend is the 2003 Jennifer Lopez vehicle *Maid in Manhattan*. The title may be taken as a pun indicating both the humble status of the Latina chamber maid and the possibility that Latinos can do well for themselves in the Big Apple of the twenty-first century: here, J-Lo's character 'makes it', but without having to relinquish her identity as a Latina.[5] All of which brings us on to the vexed question of Jennifer Lopez's bottom, which has received huge press attention and a fair bit of academic attention, too. Frances Negrón-Muntaner offers an informative perspective.[6] The furore probably began with or was most marked by the Puerto Rican American's being cast in the title role of Gregory Nava's 1997 tragic Mexican-American pop-star bio-pic *Selena*. With the movie expected to become a landmark of popular Hispanic American cinema, the casting was controversial because it was thought by some to collapse cultural specificities by positing a Caribbean identity as equivalent to a Mexican one, while others celebrated the casting as a masterstroke gesture towards the Hispanic USA's reclamation of a common Latina/o experience. One thing that was seen as marking out Lopez's Caribbean ethnicity was the sizeable shapeliness of her 'butt', a feature often considered in mainstream popular culture as constitutive of chicana identity. Jennifer herself made quite a big deal out of this and gave a large number of interviews for the media. Talking of the curvaceous Selena, J-Lo, commented that, unlike stars of an earlier generation, 'Selena could be who she was and, as for me, for once, I could be proud of my big bottom.'[7] In terms of conventional clichés of male heterosexual proclivities the 'big butt' has often been presumed to be fashionable or attractive in Latin American culture, while another cultural cliché emphasises the North American (or European) fascination with large breasts. In this unfortunately conceived debate, Jennifer Lopez has been credited with initiating a seismic cultural shift of emphasis in North America from breast to bottom, corresponding to a healthy Latinisation of North American culture. Is J-Lo's 'butt' an example of the de-othering of Latinity in the so-called 'First World'? Perhaps. The relentless focus on her bottom may be little more than the othering of the foreign and darker female body. Rodriguez claims that,

---

[5] See Clara E. Rodríguez, *Heroes, Lovers and Others: The Story of Latinos in Hollywood* (Washington, DC: The Smithsonian Institute Press, 2004), p. 228.

[6] Frances Negrón-Muntaner, 'Jennifer's butt', in *Perspectives on Las Américas*, ed. by Matthew C. Gutmann, Félix V. Matos Rodríguez, Lynn Stephen and Patricia Zavella (Malden: Blackwell, 2003), pp. 291–298.

[7] Mel Vincent, 'Lopez is bursting into Hollywood spotlight', *The Virginia Pilot*, 22 March 1997, E8. Quoted by Negrón-Muntaner, p. 294.

as Jennifer entered the cultural mainstream and became an A-list American star, she actually chose to reduce the size of her bottom, either by surgery or exercise (*Heroes, Lovers and Others*, p. 227). The more 'American' she became, the more she was de-Latinised à la Hayworth or Welch. Maybe not much was changing after all in the 2000s and Latinity remained disguised or had its specificity erased in 'First-World' popular culture, remaining a generic other that encapsulated the desires and fantasies of a non-Latin public.

Surely, one might think that in the modern era, especially after the PC explosion of the late 1980s, there would be many liberal portrayals of Latin American experience that sought to deliver a more authentic or sympathetic viewpoint. If one thinks of 1980s American movies such as *Missing* (1982), *Under Fire* (1983), *Salvador* (1986) or *The Milagro Beanfield War* (1988), one can see that this is, in fact, the case. The problem is, though, that, despite the liberal gesture, even apparently revisionist treatments from the more developed world inadvertently repeat the stereotypes and use Latin America as a backdrop for the exploration of Northern/Western concerns.

Roland Joffé's 1986 film, *The Mission*, appears to defend indigenous culture and attack European colonialism. It is set in a frontier area around the borders of Paraguay and Brazil in 1750 and deals with Jesuit priests' attempts to protect the innocent Guaraní Indians from the threat of the Brazilian slave trade, by keeping them in their missions at the time of a transfer of sovereignty from Spanish to Portuguese control. *The Mission* opens with a quotation that seems to present the film as a historically accurate account, yet is riddled with historical inaccuracies. Jean Franco and James Schofield Saeger have documented these problems.[8] The spectacular opening scene is of a crucified Jesuit crashing over the top of a gigantic waterfall. There is, apparently, no historical record of Jesuits being martyred as in this scene, but it certainly looks good. Later, one mission appears to be led by a Guaraní priest, but the indigenous population was excluded from the Jesuit order (what is worse, he is played by a Cambodian actor).

In a sense, such inaccuracy is to be expected, because this film remains an essentially European or North American *version* of Latin America. The arresting martyrdom of the opening puts the Jesuits, the white-skinned Europeans, at the heart of this drama, not the 'Indians', and the real heroes are

---

[8] Jean Franco, 'High-tech primitivism: The representation of tribal societies in feature films', in *Mediating Two Worlds: Cinematic Encounters in the Americas*, ed. by John King, Ana M. López and Manuel Alvarado (London: British Film Institute, 1993), pp. 81–94. James Saeger, '*The Mission* and historical missions: Film and the writing of history', in *Based on a True Story: Latin American History at the Movies*, ed. by Donald F. Stevens (Wilmington, NC: Scholarly Resources, 1997), pp. 63–84.

the Jesuit priests played by Robert de Niro and Jeremy Irons. Moreover, even in its sympathetic portrayal of the indigenous peoples, it simply reinforces another myth – that of the noble savage living in harmony with nature. The Indians, constantly photographed naked in connection with waterfalls and lush vegetation, are indistinguishable from 'nature' and denied human specificity or even agency as they play the role of naïve innocents, too simple to understand their situation and dependent on the priests for protection. The utopian context of the missions freezes time and stifles the possibility of change, turning the Indians into some kind of abstract emblem of timeless beauty and peace. Franco ('High-tech primitivism') takes this view and has taken the argument a stage further, suggesting that, although set in the past, the film is really about the present. Like the historical Jesuits, the film seeks to preserve the Indians in a kind of New Age limbo of harmony and love, reflecting the modern fascination with multiculturalism and the ideal of the colourful rainbow community of peoples living together side by side. Given the abundance of rainforest imagery in the film, despite the fact that it is not set in the rainforest, is this story of the corruption of Eden or Utopia little more than a manifestation of 1980s Western anxiety over ecology and the rainforest, a distorted reflection of the ideal world 'civilisation' is losing and must preserve? Ultimately, the planet *is* Europe and North America, hence the implied setting for *The Mission*, the rainforest, becomes interesting only when it affects other parts of the world.

In 1990 Universal Pictures boldly released Sydney Pollack's film about the Cuban Revolution, *Havana*. A flop as it turned out, there was nonetheless tremendous advance interest in the film because of its cost and because it was to re-launch the career of that idol of liberal Hollywood, Robert Redford. Much of the buzz in Hollywood in the late 1980s was about who would play Redford's love interest, Roberta. Roberta is the wife of a revolutionary leader who comes under the spell of Redford's charming but irresponsible poker player, Jack Weil, enjoying the easy sex, booze and gambling available to American visitors in the 1950s Batista-era Havana. With the film dwelling on sleaze and corruption supported by US business and government as the regime collapses, Weil does the right thing and sacrifices everything, including all his money and the biggest poker game of his life, to save Roberta's husband from certain execution, allowing the happy couple to stay and work for the Revolution while he returns to Florida. An unusually generous vision from a mainstream Hollywood film on Cuba, then. But the first surprise came with the casting of Roberta. The part did not go to a Cuban or even a Latina, but to Swedish actress Lena Olin. In fact, the only Cuban-born actor in the film was Tomas Milian, who played, of course, the villain, General Menocan. Add the blonde American hero, the glossy production values and the romanticisation of both Batista-era nightlife and the Revolution, and any political charge is pretty much neutralised. Indeed, the revolutionaries are barely seen, and their ideology never explained, and the hero is fundamentally apolitical.

The movie's echoing of *Casablanca* (1942) is obvious (love triangle against conflict-ridden background, with seemingly venal American ex-pat losing out personally by doing what is best for the cause because of the woman he loves but can never have), but what this shows is that Weil's character is linked not to reality but to fiction, romance and adventure. Hence, his motivation is love and general decency rather than politics. Roberta's husband tells Weil at one stage that 'politics is what your life is all about' and that if you want to get rid of Batista, 'you cannot do that nicely'. This seems to be a reference to that which the film and liberal Hollywood romance are forced to suppress, the centrality of hard politics and the extremely brutal reality of political revolution. The revolutionary ventures to Weil, whom he calls 'innocent', 'perhaps you believe in beautiful women', and Jack's friend, the Professor – old, wise and source of instruction – comments: 'women are perfect, the rest is bullshit'. Weil does undergo a species of political education (illustrated filmically, by the intercutting of his soulless three-in-a-bed romp with a couple of young American tourists and the tracking down and arrest of innocent Cubans, including a pretty young girl). But that education is neutralised and de-politicised. When Bobby, as Roberta prefers to be called, finally explains her political ideals to Jack, she says: 'It isn't an idea – it's a feeling inside you.' Real politics is overridden by feely-touchy goo. So, Weil is reduced to a kind of modern chivalric hero and the movie ends with him back in the USA commenting, in a voice-over dated 1963, that 'we've got our own kind of revolution going'. Given the film's multiple allusions earlier to Vice President Richard Nixon as an enemy of Latin America and justice, this seems to be an approving reference to JFK. But, of course, Kennedy was ferociously anti-Cuba and fiercely anti-Castro, sanctioning invasion and assassination attempts. The liberal revisionism cannot take on board the reality of revolution or the myth of Latin America as space for the exploration of European adventures and heroisms, and, despite its initial promise, the film ends up effectively denying history.

Films like *Havana* and *The Mission* show just how porous the borders of imaginary Latin America are as it seeps into the broader Western liberal imagination. Such seepage also has to do with the rise of so-called Magical Realism on the back of the Boom of the Spanish American novel in the 1960s. This latter phenomenon (coupled with the ambiguous allure of the Cuban Revolution) was what made Latin America interesting to the educated reading public of the world and was at the core of the development of Latin

Americanism as an academic discipline within Hispanic Studies. One of the reasons the new critical establishment sometimes appears to be keen to write the phenomenon out of cultural history is precisely because the Latin American Boom did not, in a sense, take place in Latin America, but in Europe. It is well known that most of the major figures of the Boom were based in Europe, that their novels were mainly promoted by Spanish publishing houses such as Seix Barral and their high-profile conferences and literary prizes (especially the Biblioteca Breve Prize), that interest in the Latin American novel was whipped up mainly by magazines in France and the USA and that it was translations that turned a number of the Boom authors, such as Gabriel García Márquez, into superstars. Critics nowadays routinely bemoan eurocentrism and the perceived reduction of modern Latin American literature to a game of formal catch-up with Europe, but it seems an undeniable fact of literary history that the sense of modernity in the New Novel is profoundly associated with the absorption of European and North American models and that the emergence of the New Novel is linked to forces of cosmopolitanism and the international market.

A key factor in the success of the international marketing campaign was the sobriquet of Magical Realism, a term that became so loose in the 1980s that it came to be associated with a generalised sense of innovative or colourful fiction from Latin America implicitly of appeal to a foreign audience. Magical Realism is a hugely contradictory business. The standard line is that it is a way of privileging an essentially 'Third-World' and specifically Latin American version of reality in a world dominated by eurocentric perspectives. But Cuban author Alejo Carpentier's original notion of *lo real maravilloso*, the marvellous real, was based on French Surrealism and European ideas of the unconscious, and, in any case, while seeking to vindicate an inherently Latin American world view, seems actually to be based on an invitation to gawp at the wondrousness of Latin American reality as if an outsider.

The global star of Magical Realism was Gabriel García Márquez and the famous opening of his masterpiece *Cien años de soledad* is *the* quintessential Magical Realist moment. The founding father of Macondo introduces his children to the most dazzling and beautiful diamond on earth – actually, the previously unknown substance ice. Now it is usually claimed that by presenting ice, films, false teeth and phonographs as bizarre and levitating priests, rains of butterflies and girls ascending into heaven as normal, that the novel is striking a blow for authenticity and Latin Americanness by inscribing events from the perspective of a remote rural community. But the reader *knows* that the beautiful diamond is only ice and must inevitably be engaged in a relationship of ironic complicity with the implied narrator. Thus, implied reader and narrator are, if anything, posited as 'First-World'.

Just as the character Gabriel (surname Márquez (hint hint)) leaves Macondo to go to Europe, so too does the Magical Realist experiment seem to be departing Latin America at the very moment of projecting its own Latin Americanness.

This leads to one final example. At about the turn of the millennium, some (by no means all) Latin American novelists and their novels had indeed departed from Latin America. Two of the leaders of the Crack generation of Mexico, Jorge Volpi and Ignacio Padilla, produced two of the best Latin American novels of the last decade of the preceding century, *En busca de Klingsor* (1999) and *Amphitryon* (2000), yet both are set against the background of Nazi and post-Nazi Europe and have nothing to do with Latin America.

Then there is the powerful case of another figure, with whom the Crack generation would certainly not like to be associated and who many critics would be quick to disown: Isabel Allende. Allende is by some measures the most successful Latin American writer of all time and yet (perhaps for the very reason of her success) she is routinely dismissed for naivety, a tendency towards stereotyping that runs counter to feminism and oppositional politics, an emotional idealism that shows little understanding of the reality of social problems, and, in general, the perpetuation of bourgeois norms. She is also perhaps implicitly criticised for leaving Latin America and settling and enjoying life in the United States. Snobbery aside, it seems self-evident that, if her novels are less rich as an aesthetic or literary experience than those of, for example, García Márquez, they are actually very effective politically in that they communicate pretty directly and meaningfully to masses of ordinary people in a way that professional practitioners of subaltern criticism could never hope to. Moreover, they do not appear to seek to be primarily Latin American in a conventional or limited sense. Allende's novels are now published more or less simultaneously in Spanish and English, first in New York. Many novels are set partly or entirely in North America and celebrate the melting pot and opportunity culture as well as critiquing them. If we take the example of her trilogy of children's fiction, only one has a Latin American setting. The young protagonist is an American and the novels appeal implicitly to a 'First'- rather than 'Third-World' reader. The adventures that teenager Alexander Cold enjoys with the primitive Amazonian People of the Mist, for example, are clearly designed to produce lessons of liberal moral instruction on environmentalism and cultural relativism for 'First-World' teenagers more usually glued to reactionary video games. Indeed, Alexander returns to the USA at the end of the first and final novel, ready to apply the lessons he has learned from his Amazonian, Himalayan and African outings, and emerges as a kind of ideal liberal 'First-World' teenage hero empathetic to the South and the values implicit in it.

One of Allende's post-millennium literary treatments is the perfect embodiment of the Latin in America: Zorro, in the 2005 novel entitled *Zorro*. The idea of the novel came to be the filling in of the background to Zorro, the character's life story from birth to the assumption of his role as masked freedom fighter in Spanish California. Diego, a *mestizo* in Allende's version, undergoes a double initiation ritual. The first is at the hands of the Native American Indians when, alone in a forest wilderness, he reaches a new plane of reality and comes face to face with what is revealed to be his totemic animal, *el zorro*, the fox. This primitive nature-orientated Native American initiation is complemented, however, by the more metropolitan European one in a secret lodge in big-city Barcelona. At its conclusion, Diego unhesitatingly assumes his new codename: Zorro, the Fox.[9] The point is, though, that despite the seeming differences, the Native American wisdom behind the first ritual is not at all dissimilar to the intellectual currents of late eighteenth- and early nineteenth-century Europe that motivate the second. The vast part of Diego's education (and the novel's narrative) takes place in Europe and, when he returns to California to save the day, he does so fuelled by ideas of the European Enlightenment. Moreover, the correction of the myth of colonial 'civilisation' is promoted via the idea of Independence. Diego learns to admire the United States for securing freedom from the English yoke and begins to dream of a similar future for the Spanish colonies. The implied audience for this novel does not seem to be some imagined anti-eurocentric Latin America, but rather the Hispanic USA and the wider global market. The Latin American writer and her fiction is now circulating freely in a transnational environment: she and it have become as much North American or European as Latin American. A new borderless Latin America, freed from geographical boundaries, is thus imagined.

Perhaps Zorro is a good place to end because it returns us to the mass cultural imaginary of porous borders evoked at the beginning of this chapter. Zorro's first outing, in the 1919 North American serialised novel *The Curse of Capistrano* by Johnston McCulley, was the spark for a massive pop cultural industry, especially following the masked man's transition to the silver screen in films such as *The Mark of Zorro*, with idols Douglas Fairbanks in the original 1920 movie and Tyrone Power in the 1940 talkie remake. Almost 40 movies have been made, recently two featuring Antonio Banderas, while the television series – begun in the 1950s – was the biggest-budget Western production of its time, and it spawned numerous imitations. Perhaps even more significantly for the development of a modern icon, the Disney series sparked a merchandising craze that continues to this day. There have even

---

[9] Isabel Allende, *Zorro* (New York: HarperCollins, 2005), p. 160.

been musicals (at least eight, with a West End London musical, based partly on Allende's novel and featuring music by the Gipsy Kings, running for nine months in 2008). The Gipsy Kings are a French band, often thought to be Spanish, and their music is regularly played in Latin American-themed restaurants. Indeed, returning to my starting point, the first time I visited the peculiar mix that is a Las Iguanas venue, the Gipsy Kings were playing. To mix it all up a bit more, I could have popped over to Italy's CanevaWorld Movie Studios (now re-launched as Movieland as part of the CanevaWorld resort) where they boasted a fabulous Zorro restaurant and show set in 'a real Mexican Fazenda'. Real? Mexican? *Fazenda*? And on a Californian theme in Italy ... Where is Latin America? It is not just up there or over there anymore. It is up here, over here and everywhere.

10

Digital Culture and Post-regional Latin Americanism

Claire Taylor and Thea Pitman

In this chapter, we explore how the rise of digital forms of communication and dissemination in the Spanish-speaking world raises important questions about the shape of the discipline, and contributes to understanding the transnational in new ways. Starting from the discussions that have shown how digital technologies both trouble our relationship to place, and yet are frequently employed by users as a re-embedding mechanism that re-connects them to physical place, we argue for how digital culture contributes to a re-thinking of some of the central notions underpinning Hispanism. We posit that an engagement with digital culture studies offers us not an outright overthrowing of the idea of 'the national' or 'the regional', but a critical lens through which to re-think some of the key issues underpinning these ideas.

As research over the past decade or more has shown, Latin American online cultural producers and activists make use of digital technologies to re-connect with physical place, or to encourage a re-thinking of the usual assumptions regarding place. For instance, the harnessing of globalised technology for local projects (as seen in the tactics of the Mexican Zapatistas) or the uses of digital technologies to give expression to a place that does not fit neatly within nation-state borders (such as the artivists working on the US–Mexico border) are examples of how digital technologies can afford new forms of negotiation between the local and the global, the hegemonic and the subaltern, and encourage not the complete jettisoning of place, but its re-thinking.

The new and hybrid digital genres, platforms, forms of circulation and modes of activism do not render the notion of a *Latin American* online culture redundant; rather, they suggest new ways of forming and understanding local, regional and transnational affiliations that go beyond the conventional boundaries of the nation-state. For this reason, we argue that digital culture studies is a particularly apt way of approaching notions of the transnational. As we set forth below, an understanding of, and approach to, Latin American digital culture must be framed within the notion of 'critical regionalism', which encourages us to re-think the regional (and national) assumptions underpinning notions such as 'Hispanism', 'Latin Americanism' or 'Spanish' studies. We take our cue from recent debates within Latin Americanism that have problematised area studies, and we argue that this questioning is an enabling way through which to view Latin American online practice.

In 1995, Neil Larsen argued that the 'seemingly natural and spontaneous availability of Latin America as a subject for discourse' is in fact 'partly a holdover from the colonial past', with the resultant implication that Latin American studies as a discipline may involve the (unwitting) perpetuation of colonial impositions.[1] Larsen's warning serves as a critique of any reductive stance that would take 'Latin America' as a given or as a passive object of study, and highlights the potential neo-colonial implications of doing so. In a similar vein, Idelber Avelar has set down the urgency of interrogating the history of Latin Americanism, arguing that in its very constitution it is based on exclusionary practices. For Avelar, it is thus essential that Latin Americanism be interrogated via exploring 'how and through what process the postulate of a continental identity creates a field of inclusions and exclusions, assigns positions, interpellates and constitutes subjects'.[2] In this respect, the project of Latin American studies itself is troubled and cannot be taken as an unproblematic given; instead, the very postulate of a continental identity must be interrogated.

Walter Mignolo reminds us that area studies (Latin American studies is one such area) emerged as a consequence of the 'hierarchical division into First, Second and Third worlds' in the second half of the twentieth century.[3] Mignolo's questioning of the geopolitics of area studies as a discipline again suggests a further and problematic hierarchical imposition at the heart of Latin American studies as a project. In a similar fashion, Daniel Mato has explored this concept, arguing that Latin American cultural studies is

---

[1] Neil Larsen, *Reading North by South: On Latin American Literature, Culture, Politics* (Minneapolis, MN: University of Minnesota Press, 1995), p. 1.

[2] Idelber Avelar, 'Toward a genealogy of Latin Americanism', *Dispositio/n*, 49 (2000), 121–133 (pp. 122–123).

[3] Walter D. Mignolo, *Local Histories/Global Designs: Coloniality, Subaltern Knowledges, and Border Thinking* (Princeton, NJ: Princeton University Press, 2000), p. 221.

'epistemologically, ethically, and politically loaded with the history of the application of the US and Western European hegemonic concept of area studies to Latin America'. For Mato, area studies is suspect, since it is 'historically marked by the interests of imperial and other forms of transnational and international dominance'.[4]

The issues raised by these scholars have direct relevance for Latin American digital culture studies. The troubling of the project of area studies, and of Latin American studies specifically, represents a potential troubling of the very foundations on which, ostensibly, Latin Americanists base our research, demanding a reassessment of what it means to engage in Latin American studies in our contemporary, globalised world. This problematic – the ways in which the project of area studies is troubled, and the fact that the notion of 'Latin America' is no longer closely mapped out onto discrete regional and geographical contours – is, we argue, central to Latin American cultural practice online and to our own critical approach to it. This is because the issue of location, the extent to which the objects of study themselves can be defined as *Latin American* in the first place, is central to the very nature of this emerging discipline. To talk of Latin American digital cultural practice is, thus, not an outright paradox, but rather emblematic of new forms of Latin Americanism that are resonant with the critiques raised by the scholars above. Digital cultural works, involving the construction, performance, circulation and consumption of parts or the whole of the work online, trouble clear-cut notions of location since a work may be produced by authors/creators from a variety of different geographical locations, hosted in others, re-circulated to others and consumed/re-created by users in yet other ones. That is not to say that location ceases to matter; rather, it means that Latin American online practice by its very nature requires a Latin American cultural studies that takes into account the problematisation of area studies. In this way, Latin American digital culture studies is one such sub-discipline that allows us to think through the transnational dimensions of Spanish Studies.

In order to negotiate these transnational dimensions of Latin American digital culture studies, we must engage with what scholars working in Hispanism in a variety of contexts have developed as regards the postnational, the postregional and critical regionalism. Borrowing Helena Miguélez-Carballeira's phrasing in which the postnational means that the 'concept of the "classic nation" (not necessarily the concept of "nation" altogether) has been superseded', we argue that it is not the concept of the region per se that has been superseded, but that what has been troubled is the 'classic' concept

---

[4] Daniel Mato, 'Latin American intellectual practices in culture and power: Experiences and debates', *Cultural Studies*, 17.6 (2003), 783–804 (p. 793).

of the region in which identity, territory and citizenship were tightly bound together.[5]

Román De la Campa's notions of the postnational are particularly relevant for Latin American digital culture studies, since he posits in postnationalism a possible solution to the problem of attempting to sustain areas of study through 'single meta-signifiers', such as Hispanism or Latin Americanism, particularly given the 'plethora of conflictive elements' contained by the latter term.[6] De la Campa crucially links emerging discourses of the postnational to precisely the 'crisis' of Latin Americanism (and Hispanism more broadly) referred to above. In its place, De la Campa argues for a 'postnational understanding of Hispanism' that would mobilise 'post-Hispanist discourses' (De la Campa, 'Hispanism', p. 302, p. 306); this involves understanding that we are witnessing 'not, therefore, an end of the nation in a rigorous sense, as many have augured, but rather a symptom of its dispersal' ('Hispanism', p. 306). In other words, the nation-state as arbiter of cultural capital may indeed be waning, but this does not render the notion of the national or Hispanic identity valueless; rather, Hispanic identity and discourse must be understood within the context of global flows, diasporic communities and the intricate crossings of nation-state borders.

De la Campa's exhortations for a post-Hispanism echo those of Alberto Moreiras who has argued that if the 'classic' model of Latin Americanism is no longer valid (the conventional area-studies-based Latin Americanism), then a 'second Latin Americanism' is possible via the notion of 'critical regionalism'. Moreiras's call for a critical regionalism that entails 'simultaneously thinking through the contradictory totality of global integration and fragmentation', and that involves the study of the 'historical fissures [and] the aporias of identity formation' that are constitutive of Latin Americanism, shares many concerns with De la Campa's vision of post-Hispanist discourses.[7] Moreiras's argument that Latin Americanism should involve a regionalism that must be critical is particularly fruitful, highlighting the importance of maintaining a critical stance towards the very notion of the unproblematic or 'classic' region itself.

---

[5] Helena Miguélez-Carballeira, 'Throwing stones at our own roof: Approaching metacritical concern in Anglo-American Hispanism', *Bulletin of Hispanic Studies*, 84 (2007), 162–178.

[6] Román De la Campa, 'Hispanism and its lines of flight', in *Ideologies of Hispanism*, ed. by Mabel Moraña (Nashville: Vanderbilt University Press, 2005), pp. 300–310 (p. 302).

[7] Alberto Moreiras, *The Exhaustion of Difference: The Politics of Latin American Cultural Studies* (Durham, NC: Duke University Press), p. 75.

By highlighting these discourses that question the nation-state, we do not endorse in its place a discourse of multiculturalism that, while apparently celebrating difference, ultimately works to trivialise local, national and regional differences, nor do we support a discourse of globalisation that works in the service of flexible accumulation and multinational capital. Rather, we argue for an understanding of the troubling of the nation and of the region by the digital, envisaging how such a questioning may be facilitated by what are admittedly globalised technologies, while at the same time maintaining a critical stance vis-à-vis the colonising tendencies of neo-liberal globalisation. Here we endorse Arturo Escobar's arguments about the 'double character of the struggle'[8] – that is, the need for artists and activists (he sees a very close relationship between the two groups in this context) to 'fight fire with fire', outsmarting the dominant groups who provide new technologies by turning those technologies against them 'through the production of cybercultures that resist, transform or present alternatives to the dominant virtual and real worlds'.[9] This, according to Escobar, involves an 'ongoing taking back and forth between cyberpolitics (political activism on the Internet) [...] and place politics, or political activism in the physical locations at which the networker sits and lives' ('Gender, place and networks', p. 32). Ultimately, Escobar argues, 'Cyberspatial practices need to contribute to the transformative defence of place and cultural difference (as resistance to the normalizing logic of hierarchies), even as they create novel forms of trans-local interaction and communities' (Escobar, 'Other worlds', n.p.), and he finds that women and environmental and ethnicity-based social movements are particularly well suited to effecting this task.

What we take from these debates on the postnational, the post-Hispanist and the post- or critical-regionalist, together with the theorisation of resistant cyberpolitics, is the interrogation of the 'classic' nation-state and, for the purposes of Latin Americanists, the interrogation of the 'classic' region, and the interrogation of the 'classic' model of Hispanism/Latin Americanism.[10] We propose that the study of Latin American digital culture can be one way of studying the fissures in, as well as the re-mobilisations of, certain 'Latin

---

[8] Arturo Escobar, 'Other worlds are (already) possible: Cyber-internationalism and post-capitalist cultures', *Textos de la CiberSociedad*, 5 (2005), <http://www.ciberso-ciedad.net/textos/articulo.php?art=18>, accessed 17 July 2017.

[9] Arturo Escobar, 'Gender, place and networks: A political ecology of cyberculture', in *Women@Internet: Creating New Cultures in Cyberspace*, ed. by Wendy Harcourt (London: Zed Books, 1999), pp. 31–54, p. 32.

[10] By 'classic' we mean the notion of the region and of Latin America as fixed, unproblematic and uninterrogated, or, to use Larsen's terms cited above, as 'seemingly natural and spontaneous' (Larsen 1995: 1).

American' cultural values and discourses. In this way, we can understand Latin American online culture and critical practice as 'postregional'. If, in the formulations of Arjun Appadurai and others, the postnational relativises and moves beyond the national narrative, then 'postregional' Latin American practice relativises and moves beyond the master narratives of 'Latin American-ness', while simultaneously mobilising, reworking and critiquing those narratives. This, we argue, is the positionality *par excellence* of Latin American online cultural production: arising precisely through the very contradictions and tensions of the medium itself – that is, from the problematic, and unresolved tensions in online interaction between the local and the global, between expression uncoupled from geographical specificity, and re-territorialisation. Latin American online culture plays upon these contradictions and tensions, and thus becomes a 'postregional' Latin American cultural practice. As 'Latin American postregional practice', Latin American cultural practice online is thus a practice that works through the dismantling of the conventional conceptualisations of 'Latin America', while taking up, engaging with and reworking, tropes and discourses of 'Latin American-ness'. At the same time, this 'postregional' practice also allows for moving beyond the 'classic' region without negating the value of regionalism altogether. In this way, Latin American online cultural practice plays with presence and absence enabled by new media technologies, and we can find within it both a tactical use of online fluidity and border-crossings, and moments of re-territorialisation, re-affirmations of place and re-workings of locality. Latin American online practice can be thus defined as a postregional practice in that the works of artists and activists often involve making us re-think place, as well as engaging directly in place-based concerns or protests, participating in struggles for the meaning of particular locales and attempting to critique or offer alternatives to the dominant socio-political norms associated with these locales.

Digital Art–Artivism–Activism

The study of Latin American digital cultural products and practices, artistic, activist, and quite frequently 'artivist', can thus be a particularly useful way to engage with debates on transnational Spanish studies and to understand new ways of thinking about local, national and regional identities. One example of critical, artistic work, not without its own tensions and internal contradictions, are the various artists and artivists who work in the US–Mexico border region and whose work challenges the expression of nation-state identities, as well as provides a critique of the late capitalist conditions of the border economy. There have been many festivals and interventions on the border, including the Borderhack festivals initiated in 2000 by Fran Ilich that aim to

Figure 1. *Turista Fronterizo.*

protest 'the inequalities and dangerous conditions' that Mexican immigrants face, and the Tijuana Calling online exhibition, which made use of new media technologies to explore the concerns of the border and to investigate the ways in which technologies, often put to use to police these very borders, may be re-encoded in a resistant fashion.

One example of a work exhibited in the Tijuana Calling festival is *Turista Fronterizo*, a collaborative work by Cuban-American performance and multimedia artist Coco Fusco and media hactivist Ricardo Domínguez (Figure 1). Taking the format of an electronic boardgame, *Turista Fronterizo* is based loosely on the *Monopoly* boardgame format but situates the physical localities and properties on the San Diego–Tijuana border.[11] When we play the game, as we move our avatar to a new square, a short animation appears in the centre of the board, commenting on the socio-political realities associated with each particular location and frequently making reference to real-life controversies, disputes and human rights abuses that have taken place within the border region.

---

[11] Coco Fusco and Ricardo Domínguez, *Turista fronterizo* (2005), <https://www.thing.net/~cocofusco/StartPage.html>, accessed 3 August 2017.

Figure 2. Geography of Being.

Another example is the work of Latino artist Ricardo Miranda Zúñiga, and his recent project, *A Geography of Being* (2012),[12] an interactive installation consisting of a video game along with sculptures that contain electronic circuits and react to the game (Figure 2). The video game is a resistant game that, far from drawing the user into a purely ludic, pleasurable world, encourages him or her to reflect on social issues. The game narrates the experiences of undocumented young immigrants in the US, positioning the player in the role of one such immigrant. The player needs to negotiate the game and learns about the hardships these young people face.

Perhaps one of the most high-profile cases of the creative use of digital technologies to contest dominant neoliberal logic and enable cross-border identities is the 'tactical media' project, the *Transborder Immigrant Tool* (2010), created by members of the Electronic Disturbance Theater (EDT), Ricardo Domínguez, Brett Stalbaum, Micha Cárdenas and Jason Najarro. The project involves the creation of a mobile phone app that uses global positioning system (GPS) to aid undocumented migrants to find sources of water when crossing the US–Mexico border, as well as showing the location of the nearest US Border Patrol stations and other landmarks on both sides of the border. Rather than the production of a utilitarian object (although it

[12] Ricardo Miranda Zúñiga, *A Geography of Being/Una Geografía de Ser* (2012), <http://ambriente.com/gob/>, accessed 3 August 2017.

has not yet been confirmed whether the app has ever actually been used by migrants to cross the border)[13] this project is more concerned with raising awareness and attempts to bring to light important issues about inequalities and access in the border region.[14] In these and many other projects, artists and activists working on the US–Mexico border, or taking border crossings as their subject matter, provide a nuanced and complex take on life in the border region, and explore identities that transcend the boundaries of the conventional nation-state.

All these digital artist projects owe something in their conceptualisation to the Zapatista movement, an indigenous-based campaign for autonomy and alternatives to mainstream politics that started with an armed uprising in Chiapas in 1994 but quickly evolved to become a globally renowned example of activism that took advantage of networked digital technologies to harness global attention for the group's cause and hence impede the Mexican government from crushing it on the ground while the international media were watching, or at least reading, online. Early artistic acts of digital civil disobedience in direct support of the Zapatistas included the EDT's design of tools to provoke websites to crash by flooding them with requests for information, and over time this artivist approach has come to be known as 'Digital Zapatismo'. In the opinion of Ricardo Domínguez, a key goal of the more creative examples of Digital Zapatista 'disruption' is not to effect physical/material or even syntactic (code-breaking) damage (the targets of more destructive hackers) but to provoke semantic disruption 'engaging and undermining the discursive norms and realities of the system as a whole'.[15]

Nonetheless, while such creative work does offer a disruptive poetics and can raise questions about the validity of the nation-state or the region as conceptual frameworks, these artivist projects are still a very niche product, 'avant-garde pyrotechnics' in the eyes of some,[16] with a circulation that might be global but that is also largely limited to the art world. Only a very few projects break out of this circuit, the public furore around Domínguez's use

---

[13] Mark C. Marino, 'Code as ritualized poetry: The tactics of the *Transborder Immigrant Tool*', *Digital Humanities Quarterly*, 7.1 (2013), <http://www.digitalhumanities.org/dhq/vol/7/1/000157/000157.html> accessed 10 August 2017.

[14] Cynthia Weber 'Design, translation, citizenship: Reflections on the virtual (de)territorialization of the US–Mexico border', *Environment and Planning: Society and Space*, 30 (2012), 482–496.

[15] Gloss of Domínguez in Jill Lane, 'Digital Zapatistas', *The Drama Review*, 47.2 (2003), 129–144 (p. 136).

[16] See Carlos Jáuregui, 'Writing communities on the Internet: Textual authority and territorialization', in *Latin American Literature and Mass Culture*, ed. by Debra A. Castillo and Edmundo Paz-Soldán (New York: Garland, 2001), pp. 288–300, p. 289.

of public funds to develop the *TBT* being a case in point.[17] In what follows we turn our attention to social movements and more loosely organised contestatory practices that have used the global reach of the Internet to defend local communities and create transnational ones to support them, picking out just three of the most notable examples.

While the successful use of new technologies for social protest espoused by the Zapatistas themselves is the most obvious example, it has received such extensive attention that we prefer to focus here on alternative, but no less impressive examples.[18] In Colombia the Asociación de Cabildos Indígenas del Norte del Cauca, an organisation representing the Nasa (Páez) people, are credited with having set up the first indigenous-led website in the country and for having been most innovative in the way in which digital technologies have been appropriated into a wider communicative framework. The organisation had a page on the Centro Internacional de Agricultura Tropical website from 2002 when they were part of an internationally funded project run by that institution. The website became semi-independent in 2003, and fully indigenous-led from 2004.[19]

The website is just one of the outputs of what the organisation refers to as its Tejido de Comunicación y Relaciones Externas para la Verdad y la Vida (Network/Weaving of Communication and External Relations for Truth and Life), a 'communication weaving', a deliberately awkward expression for the work of the team that brings together different media, both new and traditional, into a web where there are 'nudos' (knots) (people, communicators and/or recipients of communication), 'hilos' (threads) (the different media and communications strategies used to link those people) and 'huecos' (gaps) (the topics that need to be addressed, or gaps in the social fabric). There is a clear tacking back and forth between on- and off-line media, with the communication team members selecting different media for different purposes: radio and other oral forms of communication work well to spread information within the communities, whereas the website was originally

---

[17] Alex Dunbar, 'Follow the Gps, Ése', *Vice*, 2 November 2009, <https://www.vice.com/en_us/article/gqdg9x/follow-the-gps-225-v16n1>, accessed 21 July 2017.

[18] See Thea Pitman, 'Latin American cyberprotest: Before and after the Zapatistas', in *Latin American Cyberculture and Cyberliterature*, ed. by Claire Taylor and Thea Pitman (Liverpool: Liverpool University Press, 2007), pp. 86–110.

[19] Asociación de Cabildos Indígenas del Norte del Cauca / Çxhab Wala Kiwe, Territorio del Gran Pueblo (ACIN) (2003–2008), <http://www.nasaacin.net/>, 2008–, <http://www.nasaacin.org/>, accessed 5 July 2017. For detailed study of the ACIN website over time, see Thea Pitman, 'Warriors and Weavers: The Poetics and Politics of Indigenous Appropriations of New Media Technologies in Latin America', *Modern Languages Open*, 1:14 (2018), 1–31, https://doi.org/10.3828/mlo.v0i0.207.

designed to share information with the global community and attract support for their cause, as well as forge links between their cause and other related causes. For example, the group has had long standing links with the Basque international solidarity group Mugarik Gabe, and international non-governmental organisations (NGOs) such as FIAN International and Nobel Peace Prize winners, such as the Argentinian Adolfo Pérez Esquivel, have spoken out in their support over the last twenty years. As some of the main 'tejedores' (weavers) have argued,[20] they see their work as moving beyond Manuel Castells' concept of local, place-based 'resistance identity' to become a transnational 'project identity' where 'the building of identity is a project of a different life, perhaps on the basis of an oppressed identity, but expanding towards the transformation of society'.[21] It is here that the openness of the ACIN to collaboration via networked digital media with not just other indigenous groups, but also other projects and causes across the world that are also seeking to challenge hegemonic power structures and achieve autonomy and/or 'el buen vivir' (good living) is key.

This 'weaving' process has been massively successful. The version of the site active from 2004 until early February 2017 indicates that it had more than 15 million hits, and since the early 2010s the site has also had links to the organisation's presence on social media sites such as Facebook, Twitter and YouTube, indicating its ongoing willingness to modify its communication strategies to keep up with the times. And while the organisation itself has won international prizes for its assertion of indigenous autonomy and alternative approach to development (they were awarded the United Nations Development Programme's Equator Prize for their approach to sustainable development in 2004), the Tejido de Comunicación has also won significant international prizes for their innovative use of new media to support the indigenous movement (the Spanish Casa de las Américas' Bartolomé de las Casas prize in 2008).

While the above is evidence of a very local, ethnicity-based community working through its established organisational structures to appropriate new media in order to benefit from the affordances of global solidarity that such media can bring, our next example focuses on the impact of new media in

---

[20] Vilma Almendra, Gustavo Ulcué, Diana Giraldo et al., 'Resistir para salvar la vida: creatividad política y educación. El caso de la asociación de cabildos indígenas del Norte del Cauca', in *Ciberciudadanías, cultura política y creatividad social*, ed. by Rocío Rueda Ortiz, Andrés David Fonseca Díaz and Lina María Ramírez Sierra (Bogotá: Universidad Pedagógica Nacional, Doctorado Interinstitucional en Educación, 2013), pp. 115–135 (p. 124).

[21] Manuel Castells, *The Information Age, II: The Power of Identity*, 2nd edn (Malden, MA: Wiley-Blackwell, 2010 [1997]), p. 10.

terms of the way it supports diasporic communities and creates new ways of imagining and relating to local place. While diaspora have existed for millennia, contemporary diasporic communities, whatever their background, are arguably unthinkable without the affordances of new technologies, to stay in touch with loved ones, to send remittances back home and to circulate more widely information about conditions either at home or in the diaspora, possibly with a view to effecting social change. The latter is particularly important where the diaspora's raison d'être is, in large part, motivated by political conditions 'at home' and that nation-state's antagonistic relationship to members of that diaspora.

Cuba has generated a significant diaspora in the years since the 1959 Revolution, as 'waves' of Cubans have sought to leave the island either because of direct repression of dissenting views or simply because of hunger and lack of opportunities. The 2010 US census data identifies nearly 1.8 million Cubans and their descendants living there,[22] and there are of course large numbers of Cubans and their descendants living elsewhere in the world, particularly in Spain. During this period the island has been quite cut off from the outside world, particularly from Western democracies, yet the development of new information and communications technologies in those same parts of the world has started to have an impact on that isolation. Internet connectivity in Cuba was famed in the mid-2000s for being the least extensive in the whole of the Americas, lagging behind Haiti even, with the most reliable estimates on direct connectivity for 2007 embracing a mere 3 per cent of the population.[23] Although growing ten-fold in seven years, a report from 2015 still characterised Cuba as 'hav[ing] some of the most restrictive internet access in the world'.[24] Yet despite limited direct access, limited bandwidth and blocks on numerous sites, Cubans on the island have found many ruses to access the Internet for themselves. Since the advent of user-friendly blogging software in the late-2000s there has been a boom in blogging. This island-based blogging activity, together with significant amounts of blogging about Cuba from Cubans located in the diaspora (at a ratio of *c*.1:3) has created what has come to be referred to as 'la blogosfera cubana'.[25]

---

[22] Sharon R. Ennis, Merarys Ríos-Vargas and Nora G. Albert, 'The Hispanic population: 2010', *2010 Census Briefs* (Silverhill, MD: US Census Bureau, 2011), p. 2, https://www.census.gov/prod/cen2010/briefs/c2010br-04.pdf, accessed 27 August 2018.

[23] Carlos Uxó, 'Internet politics in Cuba', *Telecommunications Journal of Australia*, 60.1 (2010), 12.1–12.16 (p. 12.9).

[24] Freedom House, *Freedom on the Net 2015: Cuba* (2015), <https://freedomhouse.org/sites/default/files/resources/FOTN%202015_Cuba_0.pdf>, accessed 17 July 2017.

[25] See *Buena Vista Social Blog: Internet y libertad de expresión en Cuba*, ed. by Beatriz Calvo Peña (Valencia: Advana Vieja, 2010).

In comparison with the work of bloggers in the diaspora, island-based bloggers tend to be more plural in terms of political positions and more dialogic in their enactment of their politics, focusing on sharing information and experiences.[26] Bloggers on the island are also less aware of those blogging about Cuba elsewhere in the world ('Estado de la blogosfera cubana', p.76), instead tending to read each other's work, despite the Cuban government's attempts at censorship. However, the network created through blogging, and the way in which the outside world has come to look to island-based bloggers for information and critique, has allowed those based in Cuba an important means of breaking out of their physical confinement on the island and, like the Zapatistas before them, of shielding themselves from the worst excesses of governmental repression through the publicity afforded by their appeal to international support networks.

On the island itself, one of the most notorious bloggers is Yoani Sánchez, who started her blog, *Generación Y*, in early 2007 in order to express her hopes and vent her frustrations about life on the island. Her blog gained significantly in notoriety after the addition of a reader comments function and was propelled to international fame by an article in *The Wall Street Journal* in late December 2007.[27] In 2008 and 2009 her blog received an average of 30,000 comments a month, with visits averaging out at ten million a month from May 2008 ('En busca de', pp. 217–218). Key posts were already being made available on a sister site in English by the end of 2007 and other translations of her work, both online and in book form, are also available. Given this amount of international visibility and the strength of her network of supporters, Sánchez does not feel the need to hide her real identity online and has become increasingly emboldened in her criticism of the Castro regime (that of Fidel and his brother Raúl). She has received a number of prestigious international awards such as the Spanish Ortega y Gasset prize for digital journalism in early 2008; was voted one of the top hundred most influential people in the world by *Time* magazine in the same year; and her blog even came to the attention of then US President Barack Obama in this period. In early 2008 the Cuban censors managed to limit access to Sánchez's blog on the island, which only served to further increase her fame internationally.

---

[26] Dagmar Monett, 'Estado de la blogosfera cubana: resultados de la primera encuesta realizada a sus bloggers', in *Buena Vista Social Blog: Internet y libertad de expresión en Cuba*, pp. 59–83 (p. 70).
[27] Ted Henken, 'En busca de la "Generación Y": Yoani Sánchez, la blogosfera emergente y el periodismo ciudadano de la Cuba de hoy', in *Buena Vista Social Blog: Internet y libertad de expresión en Cuba*, pp. 201–242 (pp. 219–220).

The 'Cuban blogosphere' is a virtual place where Cubans both on and off the island can meet and share experiences. Other concepts such as the possibility of the Internet offering those on the island 'una balsa virtual' ('a virtual raft') that they can use to escape their material confines, or a way of creating 'una isla virtual' ('a virtual island') that is an enhanced but not detached version of the real island also circulate. The important thing to note in all cases is that digital tools create virtual spaces for community relations, both domestic and transnational diasporic, which would be impossible 'on the ground' and that can have an impact on real lived experience and on place-based politics through the constant 'tacking back and forth' between the real and the virtual, as well as through creative responses to material limitations. Furthermore, given the Cuban government's antagonistic relationship to the US Cuban diaspora, the Cuban blogosphere offers the possibility of nourishing an extended concept of *cubanía*, very much more open to the transnational nature of what it means to be Cuban today than State-sanctioned *cubanidad*, and offers much in the way of healing for families separated by the on-island/off-island divide.

A more recent example of how digital media can be mobilised for activism related closely to a local place, while at the same time mobilising nationally and internationally, is the phenomenon of *#NiUnaMenos* in Argentina. Stemming initially from localised demonstrations in Rufino, Argentina, in May 2015, after the death of 14-year-old Chiara Pérez, *#NiUnaMenos* subsequently gained national and international reach, with the use of multiple social media platforms to mobilise rapidly and gain visibility. Organised around the slogan/hashtag '*#NiUnaMenos*', mobilisation took place on social media before spreading to mainstream media and has been highlighted as an example of how digital media platforms can be utilised to first circumvent, and then gain entry to mainstream media, so eventually reaching 'todo el arco mediático' ('the full media arc').[28]

Protesters were invited to the Plaza del Congreso de la Nación in Buenos Aires, and all the central squares around the country. María Belén Rosales, among others, has highlighted how *#NiUnaMenos* was able to mobilise within a short space of time, and provides a detailed analysis of the data, noting more than 130,000 likes on the Facebook page at the start of 3 June, and with the hashtag trending for several hours on Twitter in Argentina, and subsequently becoming a worldwide trend later that same day. In

---

[28] Rovetto, Florencia Laura Rovetto, 'Violencia contra las mujeres: comunicación visual y acción política en "Ni una menos" y "Vivas nos queremos"', *Contratexto*, 24 (2015), 13–34 (p. 18).

what Rosales has described as a 'temblor de datos' ('earthquake of data'),[29] 1.3 million web users participated in the debate, and the information was seen by an estimated 7.3 million people worldwide. The march brought together 500,000 people, and was rapidly duplicated in 240 other points in the country; 120 Facebook accounts were created using the name #NiUnaMenos in different locations, leading Rosales to declare that, rather than this simply being one, single march in a physical location, the event in fact became rhizomatic ('#NiUnamenos', p. 7). What is interesting here is the use of online platforms to rapidly create momentum for mobilising in offline place, and how these places themselves then re-appeared as new spaces created on these same online platforms. Indeed, Paz Cabral and Juan Antonio Acacio have stressed how *#NiUnaMenos* was particularly effective in bringing together online and offline practice, arguing that 'La movilización por "Ni Una Menos" es una clara muestra de que el mundo *on-line* y el mundo *off-line* se hallan en estrecha conexión' ('the mobilization by "Ni Una Menos" [Not one less] demonstrates clearly that the on-line and off-line words are in close connection'), in particular due to the visibilisation of the issue of femicide.[30]

Through this effective combination of online and offline protest, and the bringing together of local and global protest, *#NiUnaMenos* re-mobilises, in a tactical way, existing discourses of human rights in Argentina. As María Luengo has noted, '#NotOneLess journalists and activists associated the word "femicide" with human (women's) rights. By doing so, they channelled the human rights discourse that has been an essential part of Argentina's recent democratic history.'[31] In this sense, part of the success of *#NiUnaMenos* was its ability to connect with prior discourses and slogans, and, indeed, the title of the campaign itself doubtless speaks back to the widely recognised 'Nunca más' slogan that is immediately associated with the enquiry into human rights abuses at the end of the Argentine dictatorship of 1976–1983. Moreover, a detailed visual analysis of the tactics of *#NiUnaMenos* indicates how much it recalls and builds upon earlier pre-digital forms of protest, such as the earlier *silhuetazo* movement, both due to its continued use of previous images and also the material practice that 'pone[r] en escena el cuerpo de las mujeres asesinadas' ('puts on screen the bodies of murdered women') ('Violencia', pp. 18–19). In its circulation of images, its

[29] María Belén Rosales, '#NiUnaMenos y los debates fundantes en comunicación y género', *Con X*, 2, 1–39 (p. 6).

[30] Paz Cabral and Juan Antonio Acacio, 'La violencia de género como problema público: las movilizaciones por "Ni una menos" en la Argentina', *Questión: Revista Especializada en Periodismo y Comunicación*, 51 (2016), 170–187 (p. 181).

[31] María Luengo, 'Gender violence: The media, civil society, and the struggle for human rights in Argentina', *Media, Culture, and Society*, 40.3 (2018), 397–414 (p. 398).

visual style and in its foregrounding of the body, *#NiUnaMenos* achieves global reach, all the while mobilising pre-existing forms of protest that link closely to local place and localised protest.

In summary, these examples, both the artivist and the more fully activist, demonstrate the crucial transnational dimensions of Latin American digital products and practice while also connecting to, and reimaging, the local and the national. As Martha Zapata Galindo notes in her discussion of new forms of social organising and resistance facilitated by the Internet,

> Los nuevos movimientos de protesta en las Américas organizan sus intervenciones en los espacios públicos, incluyendo temas globales que superan los límites de las luchas particulares locales, abriendo paso a la configuración de nuevos espacios transnacionales, heterogéneos e interdependientes, así como a nuevos imaginarios colectivos transculturales.[32]

> (The new protest movements in the Americas organize their interventions in public spaces, including global issues that supersede the limits of specific local campaigns, resulting in the configuration of new transnational, heterogeneous and interdependent spaces, and new transcultural, collective imaginaries.)

The new forms of artivist and activist projects discussed in this chapter, involving mobilisation on the ground combined with the global reach of the Internet, the use of place-based tropes and practices in virtual space and mixed media according to the practical needs of the physical sites to be reached, allow us to re-think the local, national and regional.

Conclusion

We have explored in this chapter the rise of digital forms of communication and dissemination in the Spanish-speaking world, and the consequences for our understanding of Spanish studies. As we have argued, these new forms of creative practice and/or activism force a re-thinking of some of the assumptions underpinning Spanish studies. The advent of digital technologies is not the only driver in this re-thinking, but rather they come at a time

---

[32] Martha Zapata Galindo, 'Internet, actores sociales y nuevas formas de organización y resistencia en las Américas', in *Más allá de la nación: medios, espacios comunicativos y nuevas comunidades imaginadas*, ed. by Sabine Hofmann (Berlin: Tranvía, 2008), pp. 87–108 (p. 88).

of questioning of the (inter)discipline and are one of the factors that has contributed to rethinking disciplinary boundaries. These various examples of cultural and activist practice demonstrate that Latin American digital culture still has relevance to place, and hence to notions of Hispanism and Latin Americanism, but in different ways. Digital culture offers opportunities for place to be re-thought in a variety of ways, allowing new ways of approaching the nation-state or the region. These new and hybrid forms of communication raise important questions about the shape of the discipline; they contribute to the questioning of disciplinary norms and help us understand how the transnational is manifesting itself in Spanish studies today.

11

From 'Imagined' to 'Inoperative' Communities

The Un-working of National and Latin American Identities in Contemporary Fiction

Emily Baker

Over the last 20 years the Mexican writer Jorge Volpi has frequently questioned the existence of Hispanic/Latin American literature.[1] Sometimes this will be in the form of a diplomatic question: '¿De qué hablamos cuando hablamos de narrativa hispanoamericana?' ('What are we talking about when we talk of Hispanic American narrative?').[2] At other times it will be an explicit, controversial statement such as 'Latin American literature does not exist', the title of his article in the *Universidad de México* magazine.[3] His arguments usually unfold as follows: first, he acknowledges that a regional literature could be seen to have existed for almost two centuries following the Independence era (1810s) due to a common language and tradition. He suggests the 'Boom' writers of the second half of the twentieth century are the culmination of this history, because they saw themselves as 'parte del mismo tronco común' ('part of the same tree-trunk') ('La literatura latinoamericana', p. 91). But then he charts Latin American literature's demise and extinction leading up to the millennium.

---

[1] Volpi uses both terms. Here I am technically referring to Hispanic American literature, which excludes Portuguese-speaking Brazil. However, I shall predominantly use the term 'Latin American' since it is the broader frame within which the regional literature is usually discussed.

[2] Jorge Volpi, *El insomnio de Bolívar: cuatro consideraciones intempestivas sobre América Latina en el siglo XXI*. (Buenos Aires: Debate, 2009), p. 100. Unless otherwise indicated all translations from Spanish into English are my own.

[3] Jorge Volpi, 'La literatura latinoamericana ya no existe', *Revista de la Universidad de México*, 31 (2006), 90–92 (p. 90).

Taking into consideration Volpi's views, this chapter examines some of the challenges facing researchers in the study of contemporary Latin American literature, in particular in the decades before and after the turn of the millennium. In order to narrow the scope of the task, I examine a particular cluster of themes that has become popular among successful Latin American authors of recent times: Nazism, the Second World War and the Holocaust. Between 1996 and 2015 at least eight texts have taken one of these themes as their central concern, more than ten if Brazilian texts are included, and many others that mention the Nazis as part of a sub-plot.[4] This raises the question why are Latin American authors writing about Nazism, the Second World War and the Holocaust – and why now? What can this tell us about how Latin American authors understand the contemporary exercise of literary writing in the region? Can recourse to these themes be considered emblematic of a new phase of transnationalism in literature or is it part of a longer history in the process of literary globalisation? And if it is a new phase, what makes it 'new'? Answering these questions might offer clues as to how to go about designing research questions and critically approaching a diverse body of regional/transnational work.

Studying Latin American Literature

When designing research questions in Latin American literary studies it has been traditionally useful to use area-based delimitations. In influential cultural theory the region has been associated with strong historic ties between writing and nationhood. In his now-classic *Imagined Communities*, Benedict Anderson argued that print capitalism (novels and newspapers) were decisive in promoting 'national' sentiments. He noted that the need to promote such sentiments arose earlier in the Americas than in Europe: Latin American countries needed to differentiate themselves from their neighbouring countries, often with similar populations and comparably dense and diverse terrains.[5] Their peoples could not so easily be separated by the use of different languages and dialects as in Europe (*Imagined*, p. 49). To

---

[4] For example, Jorge Volpi, *En busca de Klingsor* (Barcelona: Seix Barral, 1999); *Oscuro bosque oscuro* (Madrid: Editorial Salto De Página S.L., 2010); Roberto Bolaño, Roberto, *La literatura nazi en América* (Barcelona: Seix Barral, 1996); Ignacio Padilla, *Amphitryon* (Madrid: Espasa-Calpe, 2000); Patricio Pron, *El comienzo de la primavera* (Barcelona: Literatura Random House, 2008); Juan Gabriel Vásquez, *Los informantes* (Bogotá: Alfaguara, 2004); Lucía Puenzo, *Wakolda* (Barcelona: Duomo, 2010).

[5] Benedict R. Anderson, *Imagined Communities: Reflections on the Origin and Spread of Nationalism*, rev. edn (London: Verso, 2006), p. 52.

make people feel connected within a given territorial unit, without them ever meeting most of their fellow citizens face-to-face, novels sought to undertake an imaginary mapping of a national community by enshrining in writing the identifiable features of the new nations such as their landscapes, military heroes, people and customs.

Even when formal independence from Spain had been proclaimed by most of the Latin American territories, there were ongoing (military) disagreements about the exact form the new states should take. During this time literature was frequently bound up with presenting a persuasive view of the preferred national project of the author, who would often be involved in military and political consolidation as well. Such was the case of Ignacio Manuel Altamirano, the Mexican novelist chosen by Doris Sommer to exemplify her argument in *Foundational Fictions: The National Romances of Latin America*. Sommer observes a trend in nineteenth-century Latin American novels to inspire patriotic sentiment through the resolution of class, racial or economic tensions within the new societies through love stories.[6]

The use of narrative fictions to create and strengthen communal identities had already been described by the French philosopher Jean-Luc Nancy as 'myth' or 'foundation-by-fiction'.[7] His example of myth-making is that of the storyteller in primitive communities who binds the members of a given people together by telling them a story about their origins. Myth-making is an integral part of creating a bond between people in a closed community, such as a nation-state. The interest in doing this is that the state can then make demands of its citizens to form a productive workforce contributing to the growth and development of the nation; or exclude people from its bordered territory if they do not possess the required characteristics of having been born there, or having family ties. If necessary, members of the community can be asked to sacrifice themselves to defend the territory in war. Myth-making is therefore naturally an arbitrary and contradictory process given that national borders may be arbitrary (and changeable) lines. Just because a person is born on one side of the line does not mean they necessarily share more characteristics with the people on the same side. Nancy argues that closed communities are necessarily violent and exclusionary and thus calls for us to work towards an 'inoperative' global

---

[6] Doris Sommer, *Foundational Fictions: The National Romances of Latin America* (Berkeley and Oxford: University of California Press, 1991). The influence of these novels when first written would have been limited to a small number of literate elites.

[7] Jean-Luc Nancy, *The Inoperative Community*, trans. by Peter Connor, ed. by Peter Connor, Lisa Garbus, Michael Holland and Simona Sawhney (Minneapolis: University of Minnesota Press, 1990 [1986]), p. 53.

community, a community that is inclusive of everyone, and does not 'make work out of death' (*The Inoperative Community*, p. 14). By this he means that lives should not be sacrificed for any community.

In the early twentieth century Latin American literature became more inclusive of voices that had previously been excluded, but nationhood and cultural nationalism in the arts strengthened. Through more universally accessible education, reading, writing and citizenship were increasingly democratised. The sectors of the population that needed to be fictionally 'incorporated' into the national project increased and conflicts such as the Mexican revolution, as well as the influx of European immigrants to countries such as Brazil and Argentina, catalysed the production of a more popular literature in the region.[8] This body of work reflected the plurality of voices and experiences within the nation-state. For Ángel Rama, the Mexican Revolution was a key turning point in weakening the close relationship between writing and power. Rama refers to novelist Mariano Azuela whose famous novel *Los de abajo* (Those below) is 'más crítico del intelectual que del jefe revolucionario' ('more critical of the intellectual than the revolutionary leader').[9]

These shifts further coincided with the rise in popularity of more accessible forms of culture, such as film, radio and television. In the early twentieth century global flows of migration from Europe to Latin America coincided with the increased circulation of forms of 'electronic mediation' of subjectivities, preceding the rupture in modern subject-formation that for Arjun Appadurai occurred after the 1970s. In *Modernity at Large* Appadurai takes 'media' and 'migration' as the defining factors in bringing about this rupture. The difference in relation to earlier moments, he argues, is that earlier narratives still formed subjectivities within 'national' imagined bounds. It is only since the 1970s that we have reached transnational or even post-national forms of subjectivity due to the now 'massive globalization' of the movement of people and images.[10] This timeline seems to coincide with Volpi's narrative of the decline of Latin American literature. However, there is another key factor more specific to the circulation of *literature* that Volpi seeks to highlight when accounting for the ultimate weakening of regional

---

[8] Gareth Williams, *The Other Side of the Popular: Neoliberalism and Subalternity in Latin America* (Durham, NC: Duke University Press, 2002). Examples include Nelly Campobello's *Cartucho* (1931), a chronicle of the Mexican Revolution told through the eyes of a child and Roberto Arlt's novel about the immigrant suburbs of Buenos Aires, *El juguete rabioso* (1926).

[9] Angel Rama, *La ciudad letrada* (Hanover, NH: Ediciones del Norte, 1984), p. 124.

[10] Arjun Appadurai, *Modernity at Large: Cultural Dimensions of Globalization* (Minneapolis, MN: University of Minnesota Press, 1996), p. 8.

literary bonds – a phenomenon he calls 'neocolonialismo editorial' ('neocolonial publishing').[11]

In *El insomnio de Bolívar* (Bolívar's insomnia) Volpi explains that during the Latin American economic crises of the 1970s, the large regional publishers were acquired by Spanish companies, which led to 'una distorsión en el campo literario en español donde un país con apenas una decimal parte de los hispanohablantes del mundo ejercía – y todavía ejerce – un control casi absoluta sobre la industria editorial de los demás países en conjunto' ('a distortion in the field of literature in Spanish where a country with barely one tenth of the world's Spanish-speakers exercised – and still exercise – almost absolute control over the editorial influence over the rest of the countries together') (*El insomnio de Bolívar*, p. 159).

In a more recent assessment of the Spanish publishing industry Bernat Ruiz confirms, 'The Spanish publishing bubble was accompanied by a lack of interest in publishing authors from the other side of the Atlantic.'[12] Ruiz's article highlights that even since 2008, when Volpi was writing, there have been further significant changes in publisher ownership, accentuating a trend towards control of the industry by a few extensive global media corporations. Global Planeta (ranked tenth largest in terms of revenue worldwide in 2016)[13] is the only remaining Spanish heavyweight after Grupo PRISA went bankrupt and sold literary brands such as Alfaguara to Penguin Random House ('The fall', p. 10). The so-called Big Five consist of Pearson (UK), Thomson Reuters (Canada), Reed Elsevier (UK/NL/US), Wolters Kluwer (NL) and Penguin Random House now owned by the German company Bertelsmann ('The fall', p. 10). Consumer markets by revenue are led by the United States, China, Germany, the United Kingdom and France.[14]

Clearly, Latin American authors are competing in a highly globalised market, with a deficit of Spanish-language stakeholders to champion their cultural production.[15] This shift in market share and orientation may be

---

[11] Jorge Volpi, *El insomnio de Bolívar: cuatro consideraciones intempestivas sobre América Latina en el siglo XXI* (Buenos Aires: Debate, 2009), p. 92.

[12] Bernat Ruiz, 'The fall of the Spanish publishing empire', *Logos: The Professional Journal for the Book World*, 26 (2015), 7–18 (p. 9). See Christina Banou, *Re-Inventing the Book: Challenges from the Past for the Publishing Industry* (Greece: Chandos Publishing, 2016).

[13] <https://www.publishersweekly.com/pw/by-topic/international/international-book-news/article/71268-the-world-s-52-largest-book-publishers-2016.html>, accessed 6 October 2018.

[14] 'International Publishers Association Annual Report 2015–2016', p. 15. International publishers.org.

[15] Jesús Montoya Juárez and Angel Esteban, *Entre lo local y lo global: la narrativa*

one reason for a topic such as Nazism (which appeals to a European and US market) becoming popular among Latin American writers who are targeting such markets. However, this is by no means the only or most significant hypothesis. Another key reason, I argue, is that the ideology of Nazism, and the particular horrors of the Second World War and the Holocaust exemplify some of the most extreme dangers of closed-communitarian or identity-based thinking. These dangers are not just relevant to states of exception, cases of authoritarian rule such as the Nazi government in Germany, but are also structurally inherent to territorial democracies as well, as is evident when modern states exclude access for refugees. Before moving on to examine the way in which Volpi and Ignacio Padilla seek to highlight the violence of identitarian thinking in their novels, I shall briefly chart the history of 'myth-making' in Mexico to further contextualise their 'postnational' gestures.

Mexican Myth-making

In Mexico, over the course of the twentieth century, a particularly strong myth-making apparatus was developed that tied writing to state power even more closely than in other parts of the region. This was due, in large part, to the cultural policy of the post-revolutionary government, the Partido Revolucionario Institucional (Institutionalized Revolutionary Party) (PRI) who were able to direct and shape Mexican myths during the 71 years they remained in power as a one-party state. Some of the most iconic examples of the state-led attempt to create an identification of the population with certain codes of 'Mexicanness' were the famous public murals by Diego Rivera, José Clemente Orozco and David Siqueiros. Among other written works, two influential texts set out to 'identify' the features of the Mexican national character: *El perfil del hombre y la cultura en México* (The Profile of Man and Culture in Mexico) by Samuel Ramos, and the deeply poetic-philosophical *El laberinto de la soledad* (The Labyrinth of Solitude) by Octavio Paz.[16] These texts identified certain archetypes that ostensibly characterised the Mexican national psyche: the 'pelado', the 'macho', 'la chingada' and the 'pachuco', and so presented a deeply essentialist understanding of the Mexican's so-called 'condition'.[17]

---

latinoamericana en el cambio de siglo, 1990–2006 (México D.F.: Iberoamericana Editorial, 2008).

[16] Octavio Paz, *El laberinto de la soledad. Posdata* (México D.F.: Fondo de Cultura Económica, 1981 [1950]); Samuel Ramos, *El perfil del hombre y la cultura en México* (México: Espasa-Calpe Mexicana, 1994 [1934]).

[17] 'Pelado' means a kind of vagrant, 'la chingada' means 'the raped one', referring

Mexico's representative of the 'Boom' generation, Carlos Fuentes, engaged at length with such archetypes to nuance and deconstruct them. A capable theorist and adaptable thinker, Fuentes' own ideas about the role of the writer and the intersection between nationhood and subjectivity shifted over the course of his career. The association of the writer's task with 'myth-making' was strong in Fuentes' own writing of the 1960s. In his *La nueva novela hispanoamericana* (The New Hispanic-American Novel), in many ways the 'manifesto' of the Boom generation, he describes the Latin American novel as consisting of myth, language and structure, explaining that he believed Latin American authors should engage in 'myth-making' to bring their national cultures into the position of the 'universal', a category claimed by Europeans for too long.[18] However, in novels such as *Cambio de piel* (Change of Skin) (1967) Fuentes radically highlighted the logical fallacy of national identity and the dangers of sovereignty.

In *La jaula de la melancholia* (The Cage of Melancholy) Mexican sociologist Roger Bartra examined the figures and myths used by Mexican intellectuals to construct a Mexican popular subject and is deeply critical of the works referred to above. He writes,

Me interesa [...] mostrar críticamente la forma que adopta el mito a fines del siglo xx, pues me parece que los mexicanos debemos deshacernos de esta imaginería que oprime nuestras conciencias y fortalece la dominación despótica del llamado Estado de la Revolución mexicana

(I am interested [...] in critically showing the way that myth is adopted at the end of the twentieth century, because it seems to be that we Mexicans should do away with this imaginary that oppresses our consciences and strengthens the despotic domination of the so-called State of the Mexican Revolution)[19]

Bartra, more forcefully than Fuentes, recognises myth-making as a mechanism of control, and shows how it operates at the heart of the interpellation of Mexicans by the post-Revolutionary state. He also argues that there is nothing

---

originally to the rape of indigenous women by the Spanish conquerors, and 'pachuco' is a member of a gang of young Mexican-Americans.

[18] Carlos Fuentes, *La nueva novela hispanoamericana* (México D.F.: Joaquín Mortiz, 1969), p. 20.

[19] Roger Bartra, *La jaula de la melancolía: identidad y metamorfosis del mexicano* (México: Grijalbo, 1996 [1987]), p. 17.

unique about Mexican myths since they are all based upon the same age-old Western archetypes used to interpellate citizens of modern capitalist states (*La jaula de la melancolía*, p. 191). For example, the dichotomy of the Virgin of Guadalupe, the Mexican patron saint and 'La Malinche', the indigenous woman attributed with facilitating the conquest of Mexico by translating for Hernán Cortés and becoming his lover, are compared by Bartra to the two biblical Marys: Mary the virgin mother of Christ and Mary Magdalene the prostitute (*La jaula*, p. 178).

Volpi and Padilla were by no means, therefore, the first Mexicans to question the role of the writer in articulating national imaginaries. Despite this, in 1996 they broke onto the scene with a literary manifesto called the 'Manifiesto Crack' (Crack Manifesto), co-written by five authors. In the Manifesto they each presented their vision of 'Crack' literature (that is, their own work) and how it was different from what came before. Padilla wrote:

> Ahí hay más bien una mera reacción contra el agotamiento; cansancio de que la gran literatura latinoamericana y el dudoso realismo mágico se hayan convertido, para nuestras letras, en magiquísimo trágico; cansancio de los discursos patrioteros que por tanto tiempo nos han hecho creer que Rivapalacios escribía mejor que su contemporáneo Poe.[20]

> (There is a kind of reaction against exhaustion; a weariness with great Latin American literature and its dubious magical realism that have become, in our literature, tragic magicmaking; weariness with patriotic discourse that, for so long, made us believe that Rivapalacios wrote better than his contemporary Poe.)

Padilla was forced to clarify that he was not criticising the grand masters of Latin American literature or the inventor of 'magical realism', Gabriel García Márquez, but rather, the market demand for magical realism that led to other Latin American authors producing magical realist works in the hope of producing bestsellers. The manifesto was met with hostility in Mexico. There was criticism of the audacity to break with the great Latin American literary tradition, and many pointed out that in every generation a rupture was attempted, so the authors were not as original as they seemed to think. Despite this shaky start, which pre-disposed critics to judge their works harshly, the authors eventually found success. Volpi and Padilla both won prestigious literary prizes in Spain and were acclaimed in Mexico.

---

[20] Jorge Volpi et al., 'Manifiesto Crack', *Lateral. Revista de Cultura*, 70 (2000), 1–6 (p. 5).

The two novels that won the prizes were those about Nazism and the aftermath of the Second World War. Published three years after the release of the manifesto these novels also caused a stir in Mexico due to the fact that they were not set in Mexico, had no Mexican characters and made no mention of Mexico whatsoever. The controversy proved the extent to which the expectations on Mexican/Latin American authors were still bound up with articulating national realities on the global stage. Time and time again Volpi and Padilla were forced to reiterate the same kind of statement that Jorge Luis Borges had made in mid-century Argentina, that 'Shakespeare se habría asombrado si hubieran pretendido limitarlo a temas ingleses' ('Shakespeare would have been shocked if they had tried to limit him to English themes').[21] Volpi's defence was as follows:

> Para mí era absolutamente natural escribir sobre un país que no fuera el mío -por un lado, continuando una vasta tradición latinoamericana que tiene su punto medular en Borges-, y no dejó de sorprenderme que la crítica señalara con tanta asiduidad esta aparente voluntad de distanciarme de lo latinoamericano. Ahora simplemente creo que un escritor latinoamericano puede escribir sobre cualquier tema posible con la misma naturalidad crítica.[22]
>
> (For me it was completely natural to write about a country that wasn't my own – on the one hand continuing a vast tradition with Borges at its centre – , and yet it surprised me that the critical establishment would signal so relentlessly this apparent desire to distance myself from the Latin American. I now believe quite simply that a Latin American author can write about any given topic with the same critical skill.)

Borges made his statement in the early 1950s at the peak of the influence of 'nationhood'. Postcolonial nationalist movements were breaking out all over the world and states such as Argentina and Mexico pursued economic self-reliance by means of Import Substitution Industries (ISIs). By the time Volpi was writing, on the other hand, the North American Free Trade Agreement (NAFTA) had been signed and globalised economic structures had

---

[21] Jorge Luis Borges, 'El escritor argentino y la tradición', in *Discusión* (Buenos Aires: Emecé, 1957), p. 156.

[22] Jorge.Volpi, 'Entrevista', in *En busca de Jorge Volpi: ensayos sobre su obra*, ed. by José Manuel López de Abiada, Félix Jiménez Ramírez and Augusta López Bernasocchi (Madrid: Editorial Verbum, 2004), pp. 372–373.

increasingly reduced the significance of national borders for the movement of trade and capital for a few decades. It is significant, however, that in both their respective periods, Borges and Volpi used the theme of Nazism in fiction to denounce closed identities and cultural nationalisms.[23]

Nazism in Contemporary Latin American Literature

Volpi and Padilla are not the first Latin American authors of recent times to take up the themes of Nazism and the Second World War. Nazi characters and themes feature in a number of Roberto Bolaño's texts including, most obviously, *La literatura nazi en América* (Nazi Literature in the Americas) published in 1996. A key difference with Volpi and Padilla's treatment of Nazism was that Bolaño's geographical scope was 'the Americas'. The book consisted of a fictional anthology of people from the region who were either Nazi 'precursors', connected to the Nazis, or Nazi/neo-Nazi sympathisers/ *aficionados*. This gesture worked to de-centre Nazism from geographically and temporally defined associations with Germany and the countries Hitler's army invaded. By suggesting there could be Latin American 'precursors' to Nazism Bolaño suggests that the ideology underpinning Nazism was, to a certain extent, global and timeless in its origins.

In literature from the Southern Cone, references to Nazism sometimes pick up on the fact that countries such as Argentina and Paraguay granted exile to a significant number of prominent Nazis following the Second World War. Lucía Puenzo's *Wakolda* (2011), for example, fictionally re-constructs the movements of the infamous Nazi doctor Josef Mengele at a time when he was known to be in Argentina, but when his activities and whereabouts were unclear as he fled the Israeli secret service following the capture of Adolf Eichmann in Buenos Aires. Likewise, Southern Cone narratives might be expected to trace parallels between the European fascist dictatorships and the Latin American military dictatorships of the 1970s and 1980s, or the subsequent transitions to democracy afterwards. By charting the journey of an Argentinian student through Germany, Patricio Pron's novel *El comienzo de la primavera* (2008) allows post-war questions of complicity within the German university system to speak to similar debates in Argentine society at about the time of the ongoing trials of unremorseful generals of the Dirty War (1974–1983). Finally, in the case of *Los informantes* (2004), Juan Gabriel Vásquez deals with the question of the integration of Second World War

---

[23] See Daniel Balderston's analysis of Borges' story 'El milagro secreto' in Daniel Balderston, *Out of Context: Historical Reference and the Representation of Reality in Borges* (Durham, NC: Duke University Press, 1993).

Jewish immigrants in Colombia, as well as the effects of Second World War foreign policies on German and Japanese populations already settled in the Americas.[24]

The novels of Volpi and Padilla stand out against these more recent works due to their lack of any reference to their own national (Mexican) realities. Instead both authors use their novels to explicitly thematise 'myth-making' and questions of identity, and to denounce the violence and suffering caused in the name of upholding or expanding national communities. Volpi's *En Busca de Klingsor* deals with the investigation by an American physicist (Francis Bacon) who has been employed by the United States army to identify 'Klingsor', the code name for Hitler's chief scientific advisor. The novel takes the form of three 'books' each formed of a series of 'Leyes' (Laws) (for example, 'Leyes del movimiento narrativo' (Laws of narrative movement)), 'Hipótesis' (Hypothesis) (for example, 'Sobre la infancia y la juventud de Bacon' (On Bacon's infancy and youth)), and 'Diálogos' (Dialogues), each interspersed with information about the lives of scientists working on the German Atomic Project, and narrated by the mathematician Gustav Links. The novel, therefore, makes explicit comparisons between literature and science: both legitimising discourses used in different ways. In doing so, it frames literature and science as discourses that can be used to the detriment of society if not monitored by careful ethical oversight. Science can be used to invent atomic bombs with the potential to kill millions of people, and fictions – in the form of 'myths' – can be used to underpin 'dominación despótica' (despotic domination) of populations (*La jaula*, p. 17).

Both *En busca de Klingsor* and Padilla's *Amphitryon* feature mythic figures in their titles and explicitly thematise myth: Amphitryon is the name of a figure from Ancient Greek myth, and Klingsor is the name of the evil magician in Richard Wagner's opera *Parsifal*. If myth is used, as described by Jean-Luc Nancy, as a mechanism of control and to bind people into closed communities, in *En busca de Klingsor* Volpi explicitly details the way in which Hitler's capacity to fabricate a myth of the future (the unification of German blood and soil) allowed him to dominate others:

> En medio de la confusión permanente, nunca falta quien aprovecha la ceguera ajena para aliviar sus propios temores. Alguien se eleva por

---

[24] For more on this novel and contemporary Latin American narratives dealing with Nazism and the Second World War see Emily Baker, '"Darse la mano es como desarmar una bomba": Division by language and reconcilliation by touch in *Los informantes* by Juan Gabriel Vásquez', *Revista de Estudios Hispánicos*. 51.2 (2017), 417–439.

encima de los otros y, como si se tratase del mayor acto de heroísmo, insiste en ser dueño de una verdad superior. Convencido de sus propósitos, se lanza a procurar el bien de su pueblo, de su raza, de sus amigos, de sus familias o de sus amantes, según el caso, imponiendo su propia fe a la incertidumbre ajena. Toda verdad proclamada es un acto de Violencia, una simulación, un engaño [...] Todo aquel que puede hacer creer a los demás – a los demás débiles – que *conoce* mejor el futuro es capaz de dominar a los otros [...]. Hitler era un *visionario*. (*En busca*, p. 440)

(In the midst of permanent confusion, someone is never lacking that will take advantage of the blindness of others to relieve their own fears. Someone raises themselves above the others and, as if it was the highest act of heroism, insists on being deliverer of a superior truth. Convinced of their proposition, they strive forth to seek the benefits for their race, their friends, their families or their lovers, according to the case, imposing their own beliefs onto others uncertainty. Every truth proclaimed is an act of violence, a simulation, a deceit [...] Whomsoever can make others believe – other weaklings – that they have a better sense of the future is capable of dominating others [...]. Hitler was a visionary.)

Volpi shows how this fabrication of a myth of the future is directed towards securing privileges for a closed community made up of the 'race, friends, family' of the speaker, and thereby predicated on the exclusion of others. Despite using the example of Hitler, the quotation is phrased in universal terms. By the narrator's logic anyone that presents a compelling vision of the future can impose themselves upon weaker people.

Padilla's *Amphitryon* deconstructs subjectivity at an even more radical and personal level than Volpi. The novel is divided into five parts each apparently corresponding to a different figure, location and date; for example, the first section is entitled: 'Una sombra sin nombre – Franz T. Kretzschmar: Buenos Aires 1957' ('A Shadow without a Name – Franz T. Kretzschmar: Buenos Aires, 1957'). However, as the novel progresses it proves almost impossible to match bodies to names since each of these men, who are going to fight in the First or Second World Wars, stake their fate on games of chess, swapping passports, ranks and destinies. The emphasis is on the anonymity and interchangeability of men at war, contrasted with the over-emphasis on national, ethnic or regional identities that nation-states play on to boost their fighting numbers. Referring to the First World War, the narrator says:

En esa guerra que parecía prolongarse hasta el infinito, tarde o temprano todos los hombres terminarían desangrándose en la misma trinchera. Y sus nombres, como sus vidas, se igualarían al fin en el más rotundo de los anonimatos. (*Amphitryon*, p. 23)

(In this war which seemed to go on ad infinitum, sooner or later all the men would end up bleeding to death in the same trench. And their names like their lives would all be equal at the end in the most decisive anonymity.)

In a postmodern fashion, the central enigma (never resolved) relates to the question: was the figure of Adolf Eichmann captured in Buenos Aires actually the 'real' Eichmann, particularly when the identical doubles of key members in the Nazi hierarchy were made for the purposes of a coup attempt. In neither of the novels is this question answered: we never know for sure who Klingsor was, or which Nazi officials managed to escape. This is a decisive break with, and subversion of, the myths that are incorporated into the narratives to lull readers into a sense of knowing how the stories will play out and significantly challenges the histories written by various nations in their narrativisation of perhaps the defining event of the twentieth century.

In addition to the thematisation of identarian violence, what Volpi and Padilla's novels achieve on another level is to *perform* the 'post-national'. In other words, by refusing to write about Mexico and Mexican themes they refuse to fulfil the function expected of Mexican/Latin American authors to carry on creating 'myths' to underpin the national/regional 'imagined communities'. Volpi's wish to re-shape the relationship between intellectuals and the Mexican state in the wake of the fall of the PRI government is explicitly set out in his article 'The end of the conspiracy'. He writes: 'if Mexican society has finally managed to complete its difficult divorce from the PRI party, then perhaps it is time for something similar to take place between Mexican intellectuals and political power'.[25]

This 'interruption of the myth' of communal identification is precisely the task set out for literature by Jean-Luc Nancy in *The Inoperative Community* (p. 63). The ultimate way in which this is done, according to Nancy, is by acknowledging that we are all singular human beings, with a matrix of differences in common with people from all over the world, of different backgrounds, ages, ethnicities and nations. It is appropriate, then, that both Volpi and Padilla end their novels by signing off with their proper names. They

---

[25] Jorge Volpi, 'The end of the conspiracy: Intellectuals and power in 20th-century Mexico', trans. by Carl Good, *Discourse*, 23.2 (2001), 144–154 (p. 145).

speak for themselves, and not on behalf of any community in particular; they refuse to conspire in the writing of national myths.

Conclusion

In this brief overview I have argued that, when studying contemporary Latin American literature, there is value in designing research questions by theme rather than sticking to area-based delimitations, particularly when authors such as Volpi and Padilla, following a long-standing tradition of cosmopolitan writing, seek to lay claim to the right to intervene in the narration of major events in 'world' history. The tracing of one particular set of themes, in this case Nazism, the Second World War and the Holocaust, illuminates a certain set of globalised flows of people and ideas that historically preceded the age of extreme interconnectedness in which we now live. It shows that authors may re-cast certain moments of history in order to critically intervene in present debates, and it also allows for the discussion of global editorial patterns of marketing and distribution. The theme itself is an entry-point into the condemnation of closed and violent formations that structurally underpin a territorial approach to community, and thus the implicit assumptions we make when we study literature in those terms. This approach should not prevent the novels from being adequately contextualised in terms of both the historical context from which they emerge, as well as the national and regional literary traditions they draw upon. With ongoing and greater integration of the Modern Language subdisciplines as a whole, a thematic approach can lead to more diverse connections between different cultures and academic disciplines in the future.

12

Post-Soviet (Re)collections

From Artefact to Artifice in the Wake of the 'Special Period' in Cuba

Elzbieta Sklodowska

The term 'Special Period in Time of Peace in Cuba' is commonly interpreted both as a profound socio-economic and ideological crisis, triggered in the early 1990s by the collapse of the Soviet Union (officially dismantled on 26 December 1991), and as a metaphorical construct that permeates everyday imaginary as much as it influences artistic and literary practices. As I will seek to demonstrate, the 'Special Period' is not merely a handy label for 1990s Cuba but a meaningful term of cross-disciplinary analysis. Since the scope of the present volume calls for a transnational perspective, I will further argue that analysing the crisis that enveloped Cuba in the throes of the demise of Eastern-European socialism can serve as a springboard from which to discern both the commonalities across the Cold War divides (East–West; First World–Third World–emerging Second World) as well as the differences that grew out of local soil once Soviet patronage came to an end.[1]

---

[1] The concepts of the post-Soviet/post-socialist might be seen as inherently comparative and transnational but I am also aware of the temptation to look for intriguing commonalities rather than differences among the many countries of the former Soviet bloc. A more finely nuanced approach to the plurality of (post) socialisms can be pieced together from a plethora of publications, including: Zuzsa Gille, 'Is there a global postsocialist condition?', *Global Society*, 24.1 (2010), 9–30; C. M. Hann, *Postsocialism: Ideals, Ideologies, and Practices in Eurasia* (London: Routledge, 2010); Tomas Kavaliauskas, *Transformations in Central Europe between 1989 and 2012: Geopolitical, Cultural, and Socioeconomic Shifts* (Lanham: Lexington Books, 2012); Michael Radu, *Collapse or Decay?: Cuba and the East European Transitions from Communism* (Miami, FL: Endowment for Cuban American Studies of the Cuban American National Foundation, 1997); Maria Todorova and Zsuzsa Gille, *Post-Communist Nostalgia* (New York: Berghahn Books, 2012).

Inspired by Björnar Olsen's manifesto 'in defense of things', while taking my cues from Igor Kopytoff's fundamental belief in 'cultural biography of things' and Hannah Arendt's words that 'remembrance and the gift of recollection, from which all desire for imperishability springs, need tangible things to remind them, lest they perish themselves',[2] I propose to focus more specifically on the materiality of everyday life in Cuba after the collapse of the Soviet system.[3] I will argue that after 1989 both Cuba and East Central Europe experienced a *material turn* of sorts, albeit on the opposite ends of the spectrum: whereas the extreme scarcity of the Special Period forced the Cuban population to retain the material remainders of the Soviet era as part of their daily lives, Eastern Europeans found themselves in a better position to embrace the glittering world of Western consumerism.[4]

There is, indeed, a world of difference between post-socialist nostalgia (*ostalgie*) commonly diagnosed across Eastern and Central Europe and Cuba's *estalgia* with its more utilitarian approach to 'what the Russians have left

---

[2] Björnar Olsen, 'Material culture after text: Re-membering things', *Norwegian Archaeological Review*, 36.2 (2003), 87–104; Hannah Arendt and Margaret Canovan, *The Human Condition* (Chicago, IL: University of Chicago Press, 1998), p. 170; Igor Kopytoff, 'The cultural biography of things: Commoditization as process', in *The Social Life of Things: Commodities in Cultural Perspective*, ed by Arjun Appadurai (Cambridge: Cambridge University Press, 1986), pp. 64–94.

[3] See the Russian Constructivists' reexamination of the relationship between humans and things, conceived in clear opposition to 'capitalism's commodity fetish' in Christina Kiaer, *Imagine No Possessions: The Socialist Objects of Russian Constructivism* (Cambridge, MA: MIT Press, 2005). Consider, in particular, Alexandr Rodchenko and his 1925 passionate appeal to build a radically new society premised on treating objects as comrades (*tovarishch*), Aleksandr Rodchenko and Varvara Stepanova, 'Letters to and from Paris (1925)', trans. by Galina Varese with Mike Weaver and Galin Tihanov, *History of Photography*, 24.4 (2000), 317–332, p. 325.

[4] Among the many useful and comprehensive studies on 'things' and materiality in general, see Judy Attfield, *Wild Things: The Material Culture of Everyday Life* (Oxford: Berg, 2000); Bill Brown, 'Thing theory', in *Things*, ed. by Bill Brown (Chicago, IL: University of Chicago Press, 2004), pp. 1–22; Webb Keane, Susanne Kuechler, Mike Rowlands, Patricia Spyer and Christopher Tilley, *Handbook of Material Culture* (Thousand Oaks, CA: Sage, 2006); *Evocative Objects: Things We Think With*, ed. by Sherry Turkle (Cambridge, MA: MIT Press, 2007); Raúl Rubio, 'Cosas cubanas: economía, ideología y estética de la cultura material cubana', *Espéculo*, 44 (2010), <https://dialnet.unirioja.es/ejemplar/240815>, accessed 3 April 2020. On Cuban material culture, María Cabrera Arús, 'Referencias y bibliografía relacionadas con la cultura material cubana', <http://cubamaterial.com/referencias-y-bibliografia/>, accessed 3 April 2020 and Elzbieta Sklodowska, *Invento, luego resisto: el Período Especial en Cuba como experiencia y metáfora (1990–2015)* (Santiago de Chile: Editorial Cuarto Propio, 2016).

behind'.[5] Throughout the European socialist bloc, Soviet-made products had been relentlessly derided as drab, shabby, crude, grey, dull, shoddy, out-of-date or outright primitive, perceived both as tangible symbols of an existence devoid of joy and colour and of the oppressive system exercising its 'dictatorship' over consumers' needs and tastes.[6] In post-Soviet Cuba, however, the proverbial ugliness of artefacts and appliances 'Made in the USSR' was superseded by their utilitarian value. To be sure, the sturdiness of these objects, paired with the legendary creativity of local mechanics, imbued them with more than just one afterlife, as they moved through multiple rounds of refurbishing, retrofitting, refunctioning and recycling. If we consider Russel Belk's stipulation that collecting hinges on 'things removed from ordinary use', it becomes clear that ordinary Cubans engaged in hoarding, rather than collecting.[7]

This is not to say that in the course of the past two decades Cubans have not participated in artistic and commercial exploitation of post-Soviet legacy and vintage aesthetics. As early as 1994 artists Ernesto Oroza, Diango Hernández and Francisco Acea went beyond their initial impulse to gather the 'folk' inventions generated by the crisis and began to handle them as if there were valuable

---

[5] *Las formas de la estalgia (cubana)*, Special issue, ed. by Carlos Muguiro Altuna, *Kamchatka: Revista de análisis cultural*, 5 (2015); Jacqueline Loss, *Dreaming in Russian: The Cuban Soviet Imaginary* (Austin: University of Texas Press, 2014); *Caviar with Rum: Cuba–USSR and the Post-Soviet Experience*, ed. by Jacqueline Loss and Manuel Prieto (New York: Palgrave Macmillan, 2012); Rafael Pedemonte, 'Birches too difficult to cut down: The rejection and assimilation of the Soviet reference in Cuban culture', *International Journal of Cuban Studies*, 9.1 (Spring 2017), 127–141; Damaris Puñales-Alpízar, *Escrito en cirílico: El ideal soviético en la cultura cubana posnoventa* (Santiago: Cuarto Propio, 2013).

[6] Ferenc Fehér, Agnes Heller and György Márkus, *Dictatorship over Needs: An Analysis of Soviet Societies* (Oxford: B. Blackwell, 1984); Krisztina Fehérváry, 'Goods and states: The political logic of state-socialist material culture', *Comparative Studies in Society and History*, 51.2 (2009), 426–459. The enormous scale of research on Eastern/Central European post-socialist material culture and various manifestations of (n)ostalgia can be gleaned from the following sample of publications: Paul Betts, 'The twilight of the idols: East German memory and material culture', *The Journal of Modern History*, 72 (2000), 731–765; Gwyneth Cliver, 'Ostalgie revisited: The musealization of Halle-Neustadt', *German Studies Review*, 37.3 (2014), 615–636; Martin Blum, 'Remaking the East German past: Ostalgie, identity, and material culture', *The Journal of Popular Culture*, 34.3 (2000), 229–253; Mitja Velikonja, 'Lost in transition: Nostalgia for Socialism in post-Socialist countries', *East European Politics and Societies*, 23.4 (2009), 535–551.

[7] Differences between collecting, curating, accumulating and hoarding are clearly delineated in Randy Frost and Gail Steketee, *The Oxford Handbook of Hoarding and Acquiring* (New York: Oxford University Press, 2014), p. 34.

archeological shards. In 1995, the trio founded an art collective *Cabinete Ordo Amoris* and honed their craftsmanship on refashioning these grassroots creations into museum-worthy ready-mades.[8] In 1996, at the Center for the Development of the Visual Arts in Havana, the group mounted an exhibition 'Agua con Azúcar y Muestra Provisional' ('Sugared Water and Provisional Show'), which showcased the original artefacts alongside the objects created by the artists themselves. Meanwhile, for an average Cuban the painstaking refurbishing of Soviet-made fans, clocks, washing machines or irons did not have any singular meaning beyond offering ersatz solutions to mundane problems.

From their position on the periphery of free-market economy, commonplace objects in revolutionary Cuba had always enjoyed an extended life span of ordinary use before being upcycled as antiquarian memorabilia, collectors' items and primary material for artful transformations or, in the least likely scenario, disposed of as 'garbage'. Even though many Cuban inventions would fall under the familiar rubric of the 'Three Rs' – 'Reduce, Reuse and Recycle' – by contrast to the so-called 'developing' countries Cuba's access to the detritus of the industrialised world continues to be limited. The Special Period intensified the need for hoarding, rather than discarding, and led to an onslaught of home-produced (re)inventions that, in the long run, solidified the reputation of Cuba as a DIY society (PBS, 'The bizarre, brilliant and useful inventions of Cuban DIY engineers').[9]

The makeshift creations of the Special Period available to scholars in today's Cuba are not particularly abundant, diverse or broad-ranging, because many of them have already found new homes in foreign collections while most are still leading their useful and private afterlives in Cuban kitchens, offices, shops and garages. In order to engage with these objects in ways that do not just crop them out of their context as exotic curiosities, I have chosen to follow Olsen's suggestion that social and humanist scholarship should overcome its own legacy of reducing things 'to subaltern members of the collective that have been silenced and "othered"' and, instead, to begin paying 'more attention to the other half of this story: how objects construct the subject' ('Material culture after text', p. 100). The circulation of ordinary objects – from

---

[8] Sarah Lightbody, 'Ordo Amoris Cabinet "The eternal object: Notes on a film"', *Theoretical Beach*, 26 January 2004: n.p., <http://www.diangohernandez.com/the-eternal-object-notes-on-a-film-by-sarah-lightbody/>, accessed 3 April 2020; Erica Segre, '"El convertible no convertible": Reconsidering refuse and disjecta aesthetics in contemporary Cuban art', in *Latin American Popular Culture: Politics, Media, Affect*, ed. by Geoffrey Kantaris and Rory O'Bryen (New York: Tamesis, 2013), pp. 109–138.

[9] *PBS*, 'The bizarre, brilliant and useful inventions of Cuban DIY engineers', 7 January 2015, <http://www.pbs.org/newshour/updates/bizarre-brilliant-useful-inventions-cuban-diy-engineers>, accessed 3 April 2020.

Figure 1. Photograph of Reina María Rodríguez.

production to consumption, whether in a society of scarcity or in a society of abundance – is not just a conduit for studying shallow consumerism or basic survival but, perhaps more interestingly, opens up a pathway into complex processes of identity (trans)formation and the constitution of self.

Let us pause for a moment to consider a monochromatic snapshot of Cuba's leading poet Reina María Rodríguez that accompanies the English translation of her poem in *MiPOesias Magazine* (Figure 1).[10] The photograph summons an

[10] J. Miralles, Photograph of Reina María Rodríguez, *MiPOesias Magazine*, 19.3 (2005), <http://www.mipoesias.com/Volume19Issue3Gudding/rodriguez.html%3EReina>, accessed 1 August 2016. Website no longer available.

immediate association with the threadbare materiality of the 'Special Period' and a sense of bewilderment amid the familiar slipping into the uncanny. Framed by the paraphernalia emblematic of the 'Special Period', a bicycle and a shopping bag, the poet's tired gaze and depleted body seem overwhelmed by her oversized clothing and an ostensibly empty shopping basket. And yet, both 'things' hint at the subject's defiant assertion of agency and her resolve to move on with *la lucha*. Gleaned only for 'sociological' information, the picture embodies the ineluctable assumptions about gender roles in the day-to-day provisioning and domesticity. Still, the material 'deficit' of the everyday is (over) compensated by the aesthetic aura of the photograph itself and the sense of wonder awakened by the immaterial 'surplus' of the accompanying verse.

The paradigms of 'the economy of scarcity' and 'the culture of shortage' (Fehérváry, 'Goods and states') have been commonly deployed in studies of the socialist system but in this case, too, applying them to Cuba comes with a few caveats. Prior to 1989, Cuba's relative isolation from the ebb and flow of transnational currents had hinged on a sui generis combination of various geo-political factors that appeared to load the dice against its people's well-being: the ever-growing pall cast on the island by the US embargo (imposed in 1962), the staggering economic dependency on the Soviet Union, along with the real and symbolic insularity, poignantly described by writer Virgilio Piñera as 'the cursed condition of water on all sides'.[11] Walter Benjamin's notion of 'state of exception', used metaphorically rather than literally, helps us to understand Cuba as an island-nation under siege, where the threat of the US-imposed embargo has been used by the revolutionary government to explain why the 'state of exception' has become de facto a chronic condition and a lifelong experience for several generations of its citizens.[12] Since the early 1960s, Cuba has been operating under such wartime provisions as the rationing system, always far from equilibrium and invariably at some critical juncture. Punctuated by occasional flare ups of fully fledged emergencies, of which the 'Special Period in Times of Peace' is the most poignant example, this entrenched 'state of exception' has altered the expectations as to what might be considered 'normal' by Cubans, in Cuba, and for Cuba.[13]

Cuba's Eastern-European counterparts faced their own barriers, the Berlin Wall and the Iron Curtain, erected in the name of 'states of exception'

---

[11] Virgilio Piñera, *La isla en peso* (Barcelona: Tusquets, 2000), p. 37.

[12] Walter Benjamin, *Illuminations* (New York: Schocken Books, 1969), pp. 248–249.

[13] I will leave for another occasion the intriguing possibility of connecting the concept of 'state of exception' with the widespread and frequently debated notion of Cuban exceptionalism. See Laurence Whitehead and Bert Hoffmann, *Debating Cuban Exceptionalism* (New York: Palgrave 2007).

of their own and designed to hinder, both physically and figuratively, free circulation of goods, people, information and culture while stifling any outward-looking attempts to connect across the socialist–capitalist divide. Its semi-peripheral and insular position notwithstanding, total isolation of the Soviet bloc from global interconnections was impossible even in the pre-Internet era, and the multilayered entanglements across the socialist sphere generated transnational currents of their own (including the Council for Mutual Economic Assistance of which Cuba became a member in 1972). Nonetheless, for Eastern Europe the 'plate tectonics' of the Berlin Wall represented a real opening beyond the antagonistic fault lines of Eastern Socialism versus Western Capitalism. For Cuban people, on the other hand, socialism was to remain coterminous with the Cuban Revolution or, to be more precise, with Fidel Castro's definition of socialism. As if echoing his own 'Words to the intellectuals' (June 1961) – 'from within the Revolution, everything goes; against the Revolution, nothing' – in 1989, amidst Gorbachev's *glasnost'* and *perestroika*, Castro banned the circulation of Soviet publications in Cuba alleging that they were disseminating 'ideas of imperialism, change and the counter-revolution' and undermining 'the policies of [...] socialism'.[14] Once again, Cuba was on its own, even though hardly on its own terms.

When Eastern Europe shook, rejoiced and accelerated on all fronts, Cuba was brought to a standstill, all but paralysed by extreme shortages of basic commodities. Along with the collapse of the USSR, the island lost the protective shield of sugar and oil subsidies, as well as the steady supply of goods, ranging from canned meat and appliances to tractors, fuel and fertilisers. As early as 1991, the centralised system that had provided each Cuban with an austere but equitable ration of food, together with cheap housing, electricity, transportation and clothing, disintegrated almost overnight. In the late 1990s, the grueling struggle for material sustenance eased somewhat, leaving in its wake an archive of works of art and literature, anecdotes, jokes, urban legends, shattered dreams and unhealed wounds. Sendhil Mullainathan and Eldar Shafir have demonstrated how the *feeling* of scarcity impoverishes the 'bandwidth' of emotions and decisions,[15] and Cuban art critic Gerardo Mosquera has described in vivid detail how the material deprivations suffered during the Special Period and its aftermath led to the breakdown of social bonds and undermined fundamental principles of civility, legality and decency: 'Systematic stealing, trickery and prostitution, in the broadest sense,

---

[14] Mervyn J. Bain, *Russian–Cuban Relations since 1992: Continuing Camaraderie in a Post-Soviet World* (Lanham: Lexington Books, 2008), p. 50.

[15] Sendhil Mullainathan and Eldar Shafir, *Scarcity: The New Science of Having Less and How It Defines Our Lives* (New York: Picador-Henry Holt Company, 2014).

have become habitual occupations and, therefore, mentally acceptable.'[16] The 'usual' survivalist modus operandi based on resourcefulness, ingenuity and ability to make do with little, or less, revealed its darker side of cunning deceit and pervasive illegalities.

Cuba survived, albeit not unscathed, the seismic repercussions of 1989 and is currently undergoing a major socio-economic metamorphosis into a hybrid of its own. Ever a *bricoleur*, the post-Fidel Cuba is mixing and matching disparate elements of socialism and capitalism in outright defiance to the engineering role of a 'gardening state', in search of an ending and a new beginning.[17] Meanwhile, the perceived erosion of old values predicated on communal solidarity, equity and revolutionary ethos continues to be bookended by the 'before' and 'after' of the Special Period. Unlike Eastern Europe, where the fall of the Berlin Wall in 1989 was perceived as a watershed moment, Cuba was not ushered into a new era by trading socialism for capitalism. The shockwaves that reverberated throughout the island did not dismantle any walls or topple any communist statues, nor did they carry the potentially liberating force of systemic political and economic changes.[18] Even in post-Raúl (2018–) and post-Fidel (2016–) Cuba, when 'trading with the enemy' has become part and parcel of the economic transition, the omnipresent adage of *después/antes del triunfo* reasserts the master narrative of Cuban exceptionalism and serves as an undisputable reminder that 1959 was the only real turning point in the nation's history since Independence.

---

[16] Gerardo Mosquera, 'New Cuban art Y2K', in *Art Cuba: The New Generation*, ed. by Holly Block (New York: Harry N. Abrams, 2001), p. 14.

[17] Zygmunt Bauman, *Intimations of Postmodernity* (London and New York: Routledge, 1992); Sam Binkley, 'Inventando: Between transnational consumption and the gardening state in Havana's urban spectacle', *Cultural Studies – Critical Methodologies*, 9.2 (2009), 321–344.

[18] For the most part, the extraordinary resilience of the Cuban regime and the 'Cuban way' of handling the Post-Soviet transition, as opposed to Eastern/Central European attempts at neoliberal restructuring, have met with bewilderment or vociferous criticism, which makes the occasional dissenting views stand out. In Kathy Powell's opinion, for example, 'Revolutionary Cuba's resistance to capitalism, and its neoliberal hegemonic form since the collapse of the Soviet bloc, has been important symbolically and materially to the Latin American left and beyond', see Kathy Powell, 'Neoliberalism, the Special Period and solidarity in Cuba', *Critique of Anthropology*, 28 (2), 177–197 (p. 171). According to Emily Morris, Cuba's 'stubborn refusal to embark on a course of liberalization and privatization' has not prevented its economy to perform 'in line with the other ex-Comecon countries, ranking thirteenth out of the 27 for which the World Bank has full data', see Emily Morris, 'Unexpected Cuba', *The New Left Review*, 88 (July–August 2014), 5–45 (p. 5).

It is not common knowledge that the Cuban military first devised a contingency plan for a 'Special Period in Time of War' in the early 1980s. Conceived as a set of survival strategies to weather a total blockade of the island in case of an open conflict between the Soviet Union and the United States, the basic blueprint put together in 1985 as *Guía para dar respuesta a las necesidades de la población en condiciones difíciles* (Guide to Responding to the Needs of the Population under Difficult Conditions) came in handy, ironically enough, in the wake of the demise of the Soviet Union.[19] The term itself underwent some semantic tweaking and on 28 January 1990 Fidel Castro announced that the country had to brace up for a 'Special Period in Time of Peace'.[20] *El Comandante* warned the population that surviving *El Período Especial en Tiempos de Paz* would require extreme austerity measures, similar to those called for in wartime. Even though the rhetoric of sacrifice and martyrdom had accompanied Cubans throughout their history – after all, according to the national anthem, 'to die for the country is to live' – this particular predicament was as unprecedented as it was momentous. While the grip of the US embargo tightened (Torricelli Act 1992; Helms-Burton Act 1996) and the world looked on, by 1993 the economic, logistical and psychological plight of the Cuban population reached catastrophic proportions, comparable only to a war or a massive natural disaster. After three decades of a lingering 'state of exception' the island was now immersed in a state of emergency.

In 1992, *The New York Times* journalist Lydia Chávez described Havana as a post-apocalyptic city where waste itself had become a rare commodity: 'No gasoline meant no traffic. No trading partners meant no food. No movement or trade meant no trash; the city looked as if it had been picked clean.'[21] Here, a somewhat overused metaphor of a shipwreck appears to be particularly well-suited for reinforcing Chávez's depiction of an island adrift, stripped to the bone of its most rudimentary staples, at a time when close to nothing was brought from the outside, as captured by a popular adage *poco, menos, nada* ('little, less, nothing') and where most of what was produced was hurriedly self-made.[22] It soon became evident that in order to be a consumer an average Cuban had to become a producer. Chávez's quote alone should suffice to

[19] *Guía para dar respuesta a las necesidades de la población en condiciones difíciles* (La Habana: Combinado Poligráfico Osvaldo Sánchez, 1985).

[20] Fidel Castro Ruz, 'Discurso pronunciado por Fidel Castro Ruz...en la clausura del XVI Congreso de la CTC el 28 de enero de 1990', *Discursos e intervenciones del Comandante en Jefe Fidel Castro Ruz*, <http://www.cuba.cu/gobierno/discursos/>, accessed 4 April 2020.

[21] Lydia Chávez and Mimi Chakarova, *Capitalism, God, and a Good Cigar: Cuba Enters the Twenty-First Century* (Durham, NC: Duke University Press, 2005), p. 2.

[22] Margarita Mateo Palmer, 'Signs after the last shipwreck', *boundary 2*, 29.3 (2002), 149–157.

suggest that a hypothetical curator of an exhibit on the Special Period would have to make do with a very limited material archive while, at the same time, having at his or her disposal myriad narratives to script such a display. There is no Museum of the Special Period in Cuba, and the two rooms on the ground floor of Havana's flagship Museum of the Revolution dedicated to the most recent history have a distinct feel of a temporary installation.[23] It is curious, but probably unintended, that the provisional character of this sparse exposition 'resonates', in Stephen Greenblatt's terms, with the spirit of transience, thrift, precarity and improvisation that defined daily existence during the 'Special Period'.[24]

As with any such designation, the precise definition of the 'Special Period' has generated its own debates and a massive bibliography (see Sklodowska, *Invento luego resisto*). However, the era itself is not neatly circumscribed by an agreed-upon closing date (1990–?), perhaps because the label 'Special Period' was introduced as an emergency measure but never officially revoked. Most commonly, scholars from across the disciplines acknowledge that the 'Special Period' marks a significant juncture in Cuba's recent history and they tend to agree that it denotes a closed chapter in a still unfinished book of the Cuban Revolution. A cataclysmic event, few would argue, but also one whose denomination as 'special' tends to dismiss it as a mere placeholder, as if it were just an aberration or a disruptive parenthesis within the 'state of exception' that has become a norm.

For Cuban people beset by widespread blackouts, massive shortages and breakdown of transportation, it was of little significance that the label 'Special

---

[23] In Eastern and Central European countries there is no shortage of private collections and state-run museums built around the vestiges of the Soviet era. In the former GDR in particular the commodification of nostalgia and the 'musealisation' of the past have reached industrial proportions. See Anne Winkler, '"Not everything was good, but many things were better": East German everyday life, material culture, and the museum', PhD thesis, University of Alberta, 2014, <https://era.library.ualberta.ca/files/76537218n/Winkler_Anne_201409_PhD.pdf>, accessed 4 April 2020. On a more personal note, my real and virtual visits to some of these sites, such as the permanent exhibition of Socialist Realism in Kozłówka in eastern Poland, Prague's Museum of Communism, Budapest's Statue Park, Moscow's Museum of Soviet Arcade Machines or the website of Soviet Lifestyle Museum in Kazan, have taught me not to expect a singular narrative of *ubi sunt* nostalgia but, instead, to be prepared for a patchwork of highly mediated and discordant (re)scriptings of the past, ranging from straightforward condemnation to oblique parody, and from retrospective reverence to introspective fantasy.

[24] Stephen Greenblatt, 'Resonance and wonder', *Bulletin of the American Academy of Arts and Sciences*, 43.4 (1990), 11–34.

Period' might have implied the finite and anomalous nature of their plight within the *longue durée* of the Revolution. Even today, more than a quarter of a century since the onset of the crisis, Cubans on the island and in the diaspora, those who lived through the predicament as well as those who inherited it in the guise of postmemory, seem to experience 'phantom pains' at the very mention of the 'Special Period'. For them, *El Período Especial* does not belong in a defamiliarising grip of parenthesis or quotation marks nor does it fit in the folkloric framework of a cabinet of curiosities (*Wunderkammer*). When the modest materiality of people's existence had turned into a pervasive lack, scarcity and deprivation began to define all dimensions of daily existence, a poignant illustration of Iurii Lotman's words that '[e]veryday life surrounds us like air, and like air, is noticeable only when there is a lack of it, or it is spoiled'.[25]

The day-to-day ordeal of grappling with drastic scarcity reveals two facets of the materiality of the 'Special Period': on one hand, the astonishing creativity inspired by the lack of resources (*el arte de inventar y resolver*) and, on the other, the despair and humiliation triggered by the abject misery and the all-consuming scheming involved in the struggle for survival (*la lucha*). In *No hay que llorar* (One Shouldn't Cry), a volume of heartbreaking testimonies compiled by Aristides Vega Chapú, the memories of the 1990s are poignantly captured through glimpses of familiar materiality tarnished by the overpowering instinct to survive: one witness recalls tearing up books to light a fire for cooking; others remember trading in precious family heirlooms for a chunk of meat.[26] In light of Olsen's observations about the two-way dynamic in human–thing relations, these examples depict the creative 're-functioning' of things (*el arte de inventar y resolver*), but they also reveal how objects 're-construct' the subject. For these witnesses, the act of having to use a durable or otherwise valuable artefact in order to satisfy a rudimentary biological need turns into a humiliating instance of regression of the revolutionary subject (Che Guevara's 'new man' or *hombre nuevo*) from the utopia of socialist modernity to the decidedly anti-modern backwardness. In the footsteps of Arendt, I would venture that during the early 1990s the work of *homo faber*, understood as 'fabrication' of a durable 'world of things', was for an average Cuban replaced by the lowly toil of *animal laborans*, whose labour left no lasting traces in the realm of 'wordliness' beyond the reproduction of his or her own biological existence (Arendt and Canovan, *The Human Condition*, p. 155, p. 173, p. 236).

---

[25] Iurii Lotman, *Besedy o russkoi kul'ture: Byt i traditsii russkogo dvorianstva (XVIII – nachalo XIX veka)* (St-Petersburg: Iskusstvo, 1994), p. 10.

[26] Arístides Vega Chapú, *No hay que llorar* (La Habana: Ediciones La Memoria, Centro Cultural Pablo de la Torriente Brau, 2011).

It is, indeed, in the sphere of such 'worldly' materiality that the experience of the 'Special Period' appears most tangibly incongruous with the modernising project of the Revolution. If modernity is, arguably, a transnational paradigm, its revolutionary Cuban version was conceived in open defiance to the capitalist model.[27] The dissolution of the Soviet Union put to the test Cuba's stubborn belief in attaining social welfare within the socialist framework by means of ever-increasing productivity, education for all and unwavering anti-imperialist ethos. In a startling twist, what (stereo)typically serves as a synecdoche for Post-Soviet Cuba is not what was made during the Revolution but rather what was destroyed: in a deluge of travelogues, photographs and films, the decaying buildings of Havana stand as ghostly – and nonetheless photogenic – sentinels to the wreckage of Soviet-enabled socialism. There is no denying that the ruins of Havana are, tragically, part and parcel of the history of Cuban Revolution but the ruination of Havana's cityscape is not equivalent to the material legacy of communism. The economic crisis of the 1990s certainly precipitated the deterioration of many structures already teetering on the brink of collapse, but systematic restoration also gained momentum in the mid-1990s in conjunction with the shift towards foreign tourism. Consequently, the 'body of evidence' of the 'Special Period' is hardly synonymous with the *corpus delicti* of Havana as a 'wounded city' and a victim of ideologically motivated negligence.[28]

It is far from obvious what awaits those willing to probe beyond and underneath the façade of Post-Soviet materiality in Cuba. The limits and limitations of the actual archive represent enough of a hurdle, but the pitfalls of folklorisation might be even more challenging. As I flip through the crumbling pages of *El libro de la familia* (Family Book) and *Con nuestros propios esfuerzos. Algunas experiencias para enfrentar el período especial en tiempo de paz* (With Our Own Effort. Some Experiences to Help Face the Special Period in Time of Peace), released, respectively, in 1991 and 1992 by Verde Olivo, the publishing house of Cuban Revolutionary Armed Forces, I appreciate both books not only for their documentary value but also, in light of Belk's definition, as collectible artefacts, 'removed from ordinary use and perceived as part of a set non-identical objects'.[29] But, sitting in my office on

---

[27] Anne E. Gorsuch and Diane Koenker, *The Socialist Sixties: Crossing Borders in the Second World* (Bloomington, IN: University of Indiana Press, 2013), p. 12.

[28] Esther K. Whitfield, *Cuban Currency: The Dollar and 'Special Period' Fiction* (Minneapolis, MN: University of Minnesota Press, 2008), p. 151.

[29] Russell W. Belk, *Collecting in a Consumer Society* (London and New York: Routledge, 2003), p. 65; Yi-Fu Tuan, 'The significance of the artifact', *Geographical Review*, 70.1 (October 1980), 462–472.

a university campus in the US, I am also acutely aware of everything that separates me from the actual experience invoked by these books. The tortuous and parallel paths that led to the acquisition of each of these publications, enabled by research funds and my ability to travel to Cuba, also remind me about the wisdom behind the ancient saying that books have their own fates while, at the same time, confirming my suspicion that recovering the material traces of the 'Special Period' is governed by the combined forces of randomness, serendipity and privilege.

Whereas *El libro de la familia* is a compendium of survivalist strategies devised by military experts, *Con nuestros propios esfuerzos* describes and illustrates in technical detail an array of artefacts, recipes and techniques actually invented or self-produced by the population and collected from all over the island by local authorities, regardless of the fact that some proposals, such as horse-drawn funeral vehicles converted into ambulances or windmills adapted to pump water, were never implemented.[30] It was up to the editors of Verde Olivo to make sure that these inventions were embedded in a nationalistic rather than socialist-inflected rhetoric. In a large section of the book dedicated to recipes, the most overused adjective appears to be 'criollo' (Creole), which underscores the symbolic connection between food and national tradition borne out of cultural and ethnic hybridity. The term *criollo* is meant to be reminiscent of the resourcefulness of the *mambises*, fighters for Cuban independence, and of the defiant ingenuity of *cimarrones*, runaway slaves. *Con nuestros propios esfuerzos* upholds the myth of Cuban exceptionality by embedding the grassroots inventions of the 'Special Period' within the longstanding tradition of a nation that claims to be unique at least on two counts: its ethno-cultural hybridity and its heroic, rebellious spirit. It is as if the revolutionary regime had to look back and inward in order to move forward.

Many of the artefacts of the 'Special Period' pictured in the pages of *Con nuestros propios esfuerzos* can be found in the physical and virtual archives assembled by Ernesto Oroza, who travelled across the island in the early 1990s gathering objects as diverse as lanterns made of glass containers and toothpaste tubes, shoes crafted from melted plastic bags or fans propelled by motors extracted from Soviet washing machines.[31] Some of these items are

---

[30] Various, *El libro de la familia* (La Habana: Editorial Verde Olivo, 1991); Various, *Con nuestros propios esfuerzos* (La Habana: Editorial Verde Olivo, 1992).

[31] Oroza, currently based in Florida, deserves special recognition for his perseverance in salvaging the relics of the 'Special Period' and for formulating the concept of 'technological disobedience', which helps approach Cuba's 'invented objects' and survival strategies through the dual lens of transgression and creativity. See Ernesto

idiosyncratic in terms of material and design, but they also respond to transnational, if not 'universal', human desires and needs generated by scarcity or inspired by thrift and frugality.[32] In the era of digital 'curating' Oroza's 'finds' can be easily juxtaposed with similarly ingenious inventions that in today's India fall under the rubric of *Jugaad, o Jugard* or are known in Brazil as *gambiarra*.[33] Pried from the precarious world of *animal laborans* by anthropologists, artists or casual collectors, crude and rudimentary objects borne out of desperate scarcity become 'artefacts' simply by virtue of having been collected, archived and (re)framed. The notion that things, like human beings, have their biographies – first suggested by Kopytoff (1986) and reminiscent of the ancient *Habent sua fata libelli* – helps perceive objects through the prism of their 'life stories', in intrinsic relation to social practices, historical processes and private and public spaces. Viewed from this perspective, the material remnants of the Soviet era have followed very different trajectories in various corners of the former 'bloc' as they migrated through myriad social spaces: 'exiled' to basements and attics, often discarded but, in some cases, eventually recovered as worthy of being collected, safeguarded, traded and displayed.

For a wistful observer from a country overflowing with mass-produced goods, it is tempting to view these artefacts (Cuban, Soviet, post-Soviet) through the lens of their rustic charm and minimalist artfulness or, conversely, as a future-oriented alternative to the 'fatal flow' of planned obsolescence inscribed in the logic of late capitalism. It will take time before ordinary Cubans appropriate or adapt myriad discourses of low-tech sustainability and begin perceiving the arguments about measured frugality of 'make do and mend' – not as an emergency measure or a whim generated by capitalist overabundance, but as a long-term mandate for their own communities. Meanwhile, those of us doing scholarly work on Cuba outside Cuba need to be

---

Oroza and Pénélope Bozzi, *Objets Réinventés: La Création Populaire à Cuba* (Paris: Ed. Alternatives, 2002).

[32] John Lastovicka and Lance Bettencourt, 'Lifestyle of the tight and frugal: Theory and measurement', *Journal of Consumer Research*, 26 (1999), 85–100.

[33] Even though attributing ecological motivation to people simply struggling to survive could be uncharitably condemned as yet another example of 'metropolitan' posturing, the accomplishments of grassroots 'fixers, remakers, refurbishers, customizers and hackers' should not be overlooked if the search for sustainable alternatives to the throwaway culture of planned obsolescence is to become viable. See Stefano Maffei and Massimo Bianchini, 'Microproduction everywhere. Social, local, open and connected manufacturing', <http://www.transitsocialinnovation.eu/content/original/Book%20covers/Local%20PDFs/93%20SF%20Bianchini,%20and%20Maffei%20Distributed%20economies%20paper%202013.pdf>, accessed 4 April 2020.

more aware of ways in which we are cropping and retouching these artefacts in order to make them fit the preconceived frames of our methodological, institutional or ideological allegiances. This self-awareness is not about raising some sense of guilt for us, the privileged, but rather about following Olsen's suggestion that these 'things' should not be treated as 'subaltern members' of a community. As we weave narratives such as this around competing discourses of commercialisation and nostalgia, uniqueness and globalisation, exoticism and 'alternative' modernities, let us paraphrase Benjamin one more time and perhaps find further inspiration in the idea that traces of the 'Special Period' will always cling to the objects left in its wake 'the way the handprints of the potter cling to a clay vessel' (*Illuminations*, p. 92).

13

Amphibious Visualities

Transnational Archipelagos of Recent Latin American Cinema

Francisco-J. Hernández Adrián

> Marginality as site of resistance. Enter that space. Let us meet there. Enter that space. We greet you as liberators.
>
> bell hooks[1]

Island Materials/Material Islands

In this essay, I argue that a series of recent Caribbean and Latin American films transcend national boundaries through their careful attention to the sensory qualities of island and littoral spaces (from the Latin *litus*, a beach or shore). I also argue that there is an ethical dimension to this audio-visual investment in the materiality of insular and littoral zones. By 'ethical' I mean an uncompromising attentiveness to another's place in the world, a generous openness to the conditions of her marginality and an awareness of my own limits as a spectator and as a place-bound subject.[2] The combined critical approaches of Atlantic and Caribbean studies can help us examine island and littoral spaces as fundamentally audio-visual and sensorial. This interdisciplinary lens encourages us to question how these spaces and their situated

---

[1] bell hooks, 'Choosing the margin as a space of radical openness', *Framework*, 36 (1989), p. 23.

[2] My understanding of ethics draws in part on Emmanuel Lévinas's ethical philosophy, and in particular on Glissant's notion of *relation*. See Édouard Glissant, *Poetics of Relation*, trans. by Betsy Wing (Ann Arbor, MI: The University of Michigan Press, 1997).

geopolitical histories, ethnocultural realities and environmental contexts appear in representation. What can these multiple critical perspectives teach us about a vision for 'transnational modern languages'? In what follows, I sketch an answer by engaging with scenes from four recent films.

My own disciplinary home, Caribbean and Latin American studies in dialogue with cinema and visual culture studies, is a kind of mobile observatory that travels short and long distances propelled by an ever-expanding understanding of the far-reaching historical and cultural phenomena that we call the Atlantic World. At every turn, this unruly discipline responds to the memories and legacies of generations of human beings who suffered and died at the hands of explorers and slave dealers, colonialists and empire-builders. It studies populations that were decimated and systematically exterminated, ecosystems and cultural worlds that were forever defaced, at best transformed and often destroyed. This interdisciplinary effort in remembrance and witnessing is also a project in ethical and intellectual acknowledgement: of the political, cultural and economic audacity of societies and nations in various sub-regions and periods of this Atlantic World.

Michel-Rolph Trouillot has underlined the urgency of this effort in a discussion of the Haitian Revolution as 'unthinkable history' and as 'a non-event': 'How many of us can think of any non-European population without the background of a global domination that now looks preordained? And how can Haiti, or slavery, or racism be more than distracting footnotes within that narrative order?'[3] This essay centres on the imaginative dimensions of such experiments in contesting and reimaging what Trouillot calls 'that narrative order'. I argue that concrete images produced within that order, representations of islands and littoral zones in Western imaginaries and their transformation over time, often fail to relate to the material objects they represent in an ethical manner, refusing to acknowledge and share in another's viewpoints and to listen to her attentively. I insist that the materiality of the living island should be an unavoidable reality beckoning us to look and listen otherwise, not only a propeller of fabulous, excessive and exorbitant images in literature and painting, photography and film.[4]

---

[3] Michel-Rolph Trouillot, *Silencing the Past: Power and the Production of History* (Boston, MA: Beacon, 1995), p. 107.

[4] See Sean Metzger, Francisco-J. Hernández Adrián and Michaeline Crichlow, 'Introduction: Islands, Images, Imaginaries', *Third Text*, 28, 4.5 (2014), 333–343; Michelle Stephens, 'What is an island? Caribbean studies and the contemporary visual artist', *Small Axe*, 41 (2013), 8–26; Francisco-J. Hernández Adrián, 'Tomás Sánchez on Exorbitance: Still Lifes of the Tropical Landfill', *The Global South*, 6.1 (2012), 15–37.

Before I discuss how littoral and insular spaces feature centrally in recent Latin American films, I will attempt a provisional definition of the material island. The Cuban poet Virgilio Piñera described the island as 'La maldita circunstancia del agua por todas partes' ('The curse of being completely surrounded by water').[5] My definition is more exploratory, less negative, relying on the visual and sensory aspects of island lives as they figure in film rather than on any universalist and overarching image of 'the island'.[6] Of course, an island is not only a body of land surrounded by water. But what we perceive as 'the island' is often dislocated and distant, displaced and fragmented. Relying on traditions of island representations in literature, travel writing and visual culture, we can imagine islands without exaggeration as *time machines*. As David Martin-Jones shows in his work on Deleuze and world cinema, Deleuzian machines can be relatively autonomous and have the capacity to set specific phenomena in motion.[7] Antonio Benítez Rojo displaces and tropicalises machines to refer to material, biopolitical and historical processes such as 'the sugar-making machine', 'the Caribbean machine' and 'the carnival's machine'.[8] Furthermore, islands can also be understood as limits, as liminal spaces, if we understand the liminal as 'situated at a sensory threshold: barely perceptible or capable of eliciting a response', and as 'in-between, transitional'.[9] In cinema and visual culture, islands are often used as background scenarios for liminal or 'in-between', extreme or 'transitional' experiences. We can thus also conceive of islands as transitional or

---

[5] Virgilio Piñera, *La isla en peso. The Whole Island*, trans. by Mark Weiss (Exeter: Shearsman Books, 2010), pp. 6–7.

[6] Deleuze maintains that there are two main types of islands: continental or accidental, and oceanic or originary. See Gilles Deleuze, *L'île déserte et autres textes: Textes et entretiens, 1953–1974*, ed. by David Lapoujade (Paris: Minuit, 2002), p. 11. For Bongie, 'the island can be viewed in either a negative or a positive light [...] As a negative figure, the island becomes the site of a debilitating or dangerous isolation'; and 'the figure of the island also beckons in another more positive direction, offering the prospect of defining boundaries and a desirable self-sufficiency', Chris Bongie, *Islands and Exiles: The Creole Identities of Post/Colonial Literature* (Stanford: Stanford University Press, 1998), p. 18, p. 20. There are elements of both 'figures' in the films I consider here. The islands of cinematic visuality often exceed and complicate the literary traditions on which they are based.

[7] David Martin-Jones, *Deleuze and World Cinemas* (London and New York: Continuum, 2011).

[8] Antonio Benítez Rojo, *The Repeating Island: The Caribbean and the Postmodern Perspective*, 2nd edn, trans. by James Maraniss (Durham, NC and London: Duke University Press, 1996), pp. 5–10, p. 18, p. 311.

[9] *William Webster Dictionary*, <https://www.merriam-webster.com/dictionary/liminal>, accessed 21 January 2018.

in-between *space machines*: specific enclaves that generate spatiotemporal distortions, altering and transforming perceived notions of space and place.[10]

Even a fleeting sense of liminality can extend into what we may call border zones, in cinematic terms, a beach, cliff-edge or sailing scene.[11] Border zones can be articulated audio-visually as littoral and fluvial systems that incite us to engage with sensory and erotic memories, experiences or desires that we associate with 'the coast', 'the beach', 'the South' and 'the tropics' in the popular, literary or visual imagination. The *shorescapes* and *islandscapes* I explore in the following sections are aspects of a broader category that we might call transnational *island visualities*. As shorthand for the range of audio-visual approaches to island spaces and how they figure in Latin American and Caribbean cinemas, island visualities can be conceptualised in turn as an aspect of the broader domains of littoral, coastal and other *amphibious visualities*. In the next sections I consider specific scenes from four littoral and island films to help us test and nuance these initial ideas on the transnational archipelagos of recent Latin American cinema. In each of these scenes, I carefully examine a range of relational and ethical situations that resist reassuring assumptions about national boundaries, cultural stereotypes and exoticist displacements.

El vuelco del cangrejo (*Crab Trap*)

In *El vuelco del cangrejo* (2009) by Colombian director Óscar Ruiz Navia, a young *paisa* (from *paisano*, a generic term that refers to Colombians from the north-western interior) named Daniel arrives in the remote subregion of La Barra in the Valle del Cauca Department of Colombia's Pacific coast looking to earn some money while awaiting a boat to an unknown destination. This is a film about waiting, patience and frustration. It is also a film about listening, empathy and solidarity that responds to Juana Suárez's admonishment to Colombian filmmakers to broaden the focus beyond the requirement that

---

[10] This is often the case in travel and adventure narratives from different periods of European conquest and colonial expansion. See *Islands in History and Representation*, ed. by Rod Edmond and Vanessa Smith (London and New York: Routledge, 2003), pp. 1–18; Chris Bongie, *Islands and Exiles*, pp. 3–24; and Diana Loxley, *Problematic Shores: The Literature of Islands* (New York: Palgrave Macmillan, 1990), pp. 1–12.

[11] The borders, boundaries and liminal zones we experience through audio-visual technologies fit the domain of Nail's definition of the border as relational regime: 'A border is not simply an empirical technology to be resisted or not; it is also a regime or set of relations that organize empirical border technologies. What I call a border regime does not transcend the material technologies that constitute it', Thomas Nail, *Theory of the Border* (Oxford: Oxford University Press, 2016), p. 13.

'en países como Colombia, parte de la producción fílmica aún aspira a alentar discusiones sobre contextos y momentos políticos' ('in countries like Colombia, part of the film production still seeks to fuel discussions about political contexts and moments').[12] In *El vuelco*, the broader focus addresses specifically political processes and junctures, while simultaneously locating the cinematic fable in an intriguing liminal space.

Daniel meets Cerebro, a local Afro-Colombian patriarch who puts him up for a few days. As the boat has not returned from its fishing trip, Daniel must wait and spend time with the villagers. He develops a friendship with Lucía, an inquisitive school girl who keeps him company and helps him integrate with the local fishing community. Daniel not only befriends other young Afro-Colombians, but also becomes entangled in a sexual relationship with Jazmín, who is both Cerebro's niece and lover. The gender dynamics around Jazmín suggest that prostitution is an aspect of the community's difficult economic situation. Meanwhile, Jazmín has sex with another character simply called *el Paisa* in exchange for food. He smuggles fish into the village, starts developing a tourist area and polluting the local soundscape with loud music, brings industrial brick architecture into the wooden environment and trespasses the communal beach area.

In a decisive sequence Daniel accompanies Cerebro on a fishing trip. The cinematography captures the strange beauty of the inner mangroves of La Barra, a territory that is coastal and continental, littoral and fluvial. The soundscape is multi-layered and vibrates with the sounds of water, insects and birdsong against a persistent ambient silence. As the two men move on a wooden canoe (an indigenous artefact), we witness their incursion into an ever more complex region of rhizomatic undergrowth and towering trees. We hear the song of local birds, we see Cerebro opening a large coconut with his machete and both men carrying heavy pieces of wood (wood is an important leitmotiv throughout the film). But we also notice how their efforts at casting a small net are almost entirely fruitless, due to overfishing by people from other areas, as well as by the locals who rely on fishing for their subsistence.

During the excursion, Cerebro educates Daniel: he explains that many different species of fish were still available when he first arrived in La Barra as a boy, that his people had to abandon their homes between Barradentro and Boca de San Juan when the sea claimed the beach of Boca de San Juan and that the fish are now almost extinct (Figure 1). But there is an intertwined narrative thread that adds complexity to the sequence. In this thread, Daniel expresses curiosity about various aspects of life in La Barra, and Cerebro both

---

[12] Juana Suárez, *Sitios de contienda: Producción cultural colombiana y el discurso de la violencia* (Madrid and Frankfurt am Main: Iberoamericana/Vervuert, 2010), p. 99.

Figure 1. Cerebro educates Daniel, *El vuelco del cangrejo*.

guides and expands on Daniel's questions by recalling the history, ethnic realities and current difficulties of the place. When Daniel asks Cerebro where they are going, the latter replies enigmatically: 'quede tranquilo, hermano, que esto a penas es el comienzo' ('calm down brother, this is only the beginning'). Daniel also asks whether other people had lived in La Barra when black folks started to settle, a possible reference to the historical dynamics of shared cultural and political lives involving indigenous and Afro-descended communities multiply displaced across the Pacific coast, elsewhere in Colombia and in neighbouring countries.[13]

There is a *third* voice, an implied outsider to this scene of inter-ethnic bonding that remains elusive and therefore important as a central aspect of the film's denunciation of lived precarity in La Barra. This *voice* is perhaps best described as an absent presence, an uncannily perceived yet not easily apprehended dimension to Cerebro and Daniel's fraternal exchanges. As the two men smoke quietly and seemingly absent-mindedly, Cerebro says: 'Escuche, socio, si se queda más de cinco minutos en silencio, se enloquece'

[13] Arturo Escobar, 'Settlement, habitats, and peoples of the Colombian Pacific', and 'Place making and localization strategies in the 1990s: The Pacific as region-territory of ethnic groups', in *Territories of Difference: Place, Movements, Life, Redes* (Durham, NC and London: Duke University Press, 2008), pp. 43–52, pp. 52–62.

('Listen man, if you stay quiet for more than five minutes, you go crazy'). The scene is carefully crafted, constructed as a series of slow close-ups of both protagonists, whose intense gaze and listening attitude invite our own attention to the soundscape of birdsong. Cerebro continues:

'Mire ese pájaro, se llama *chicao*'	(Look at that bird. It's called *chicao*.)
'¿Dónde?'	(Where?)
'Mírelo, ahí'	(There, don't you see it?)
'No, no lo veo'	(No, I don't.)
'Ay, hermano, usted está ciego'	(Brother, you must be blind!)

Throughout this dialogue, as the camera circles around the characters, we see Cerebro's face and can measure his engagement with the environment. Daniel, however, is filmed both frontally and from the back, thus prompting a more questioning attitude in our potential identification as viewers. In this intense fable (a fable is a story, especially an orally transmitted tale or anecdote) there is a vast world of understanding and misunderstanding, opacity and perception that can guide our metaphorical articulation of the entire film. The littoral and liminal dimensions of *El vuelco* intersect in this sequence, inciting us to reflect on the materiality of environmental erosion, human intervention and sensory attentiveness. The *third voice* or absence-presence mentioned earlier can be perceived in the *chicao*, the elusive bird whose song we hear and, like Daniel, cannot see, as the camera refuses to show it (*chicao* is an indigenous word that means golden bird).

Perhaps a more elusive dimension to this ethical outsider (referred to in the conversation, yet absent), is the figure, or the vague memory, of these lands' indigenous dwellers. Approached from this fragile perspective, La Barra can be seen to harbour a residual liminality. The mangrove scene suggests through its absences and coded silences other latent liminalities that traverse Colombian and Latin American cultures and film histories.[14] Cerebro's perceptiveness prompts us, for example, to enquire about the indigenous dweller's singular sensory experiences, her cultural narratives and the materiality of her own lived experiences within this environment. Transcending national cinema in provocative ways, the mangrove sequence is therefore a littoral and liminal space in more ways than meet the spectator's senses.

---

[14] Juana Suárez, 'Agarrando el margen: cine y espacios liminales en Colombia', in *Cinembargo Colombia: Ensayos críticos sobre cine y cultura* (Bogotá: Editorial Universidad del Valle, 2009), pp. 89–114.

Post Tenebras Lux

Post Tenebras Lux (2012) by Mexican director Carlos Reygadas is also a film about seeing and sensing, audio-visual and sensory exploration, that nonetheless departs in many ways from *El vuelco*. Reygadas has argued that in this film dreams are an aspect of reality and not external to it. Allan Sullivan describes the film as '[e]ntrancingly beautiful and calculated to confound', and 'as beguiling a cinematic object as one is likely to encounter this year'. He adds, perceptively: 'Far more invested in the audio-visual rendering of physicality than in narrative, Reygadas aims to evoke pure sensation.'[15] The film includes a series of outdoor and indoor scenes in which locations, characters and situations 'rhyme' internally while also prompting viewers to try out sensory connections and resonances, narrative repetitions and audio-visual insights. As white well-off Mexicans, Juan and Natalia are immersed in the contradictions and fears that make Mexico less unique and more recognisably global than one might expect.

In a scene that the DVD version calls 'The surf at dusk', there are elements that link it narratively with the rest of the film, such as the two small children who appear in the previous scene, as well as quite centrally throughout. But there is also a staggering change in atmosphere. Indeed, abrupt transformations or perhaps even metamorphoses constitute an important rhetorical device in *Post Tenebras Lux*. These swift shifts between atmospheres and environments place powerful aesthetic, ethical and ultimately political demands on spectators. We 'enter' a luxuriously sensual beachscape and overwhelming soundscape through the rapid advance of the camera towards a group of children playing in the surf (Figure 2). The generous, almost square screen format and characteristic refracted edges, an effect made possible by Reygadas's use of a special lens, intensify our sensorial awareness of foreground and background, sand, sea and sky ('Review of *Post Tenebras Lux*', p. 67). Vicky Lebeau's questioning remark seems intensely appropriate here: 'Who can say whom, or where, the child is in this scene?'[16] We must ask no less about this shorescape. This must be one of the most unsettling waterscapes in twenty-first century Latin American cinema.

---

[15] Allan Sullivan, 'Review of *Post Tenebras Lux*', *Film Comment*, 49.2 (2013), p. 67. On the stylistic and conceptual stakes in Reygadas, see Cynthia Tompkins, *Experimental Latin American Cinema: History and Aesthetics* (Austin, TX: University of Texas Press, 2013), pp. 159–185. Also, Robert Koehler and Carlos Reygadas, 'The impossible becomes reality: An interview with Carlos Reygadas', *Cinéaste*, 38.3 (2013), 10–15.

[16] Vicky Lebeau, *Childhood and Cinema* (London: Reaktion Books, 2008), p. 190.

Figure 2. A luxuriously sensual beachscape, *Post Tenebras Lux*.

Sliding towards the group of three young people, the camera projects a realistic, vertiginous perspective into this playful composition. But it also helps distort our initial understanding of the foam-chasers. Indeed, the two smaller children (their names are Rut and Eleazar and they are played by the director's own children), who are playing almost inside the edge of the breaking waves, are in fact considerably older and taller than the boy in the foreground. The opening sequence then cuts to an 'inner' or continental view of the coast, where a group of adults and a baby are enjoying a picnic as a closely knit assemblage against the mild shorescape of a large, pale sandy beach, a receding green hillside and a low, overcast yet bright skyline. As the youngest of the foam-chasers joins the group from the breaking waves to the left, we notice ever more intensely to what extent this tiny human community has been framed in a precise, picturesque manner. The young character is followed by the two taller teenagers who looked much smaller some distance away from the boy in the opening sequence. But we remain removed from the group's interactions. What language are they speaking? Are they 'Latin Americans'? They could pass as clichéd, white North Americans or Europeans, whatever those categories might mean beyond the screen. We are then given access to the intimacy of the gathering through a medium, almost full-body shot of the boy playing on the sand and we hear that they are chatting in Spanish.

Robert Koehler notes in Reygadas's films 'a detectable tension between a harshly composed realism and a cosmic transcendentalism' ('The impossible', p. 10). If by 'cosmic transcendentalism' we understand those aspects of the material, elemental or 'natural' world we call the cosmos, then the littoral scene in *Post Tenebras Lux* is not only cosmic but also political, since it points in the direction of social and communal intimacies, transcending the predictable dimensions of national and hemispheric cinemas and locating the cosmic, the material domains of sensory exploration and sense-making, defiantly across their discursive limits. Embedded in a film that challenges our conventional understanding of narrative and spacetime categories, this scene represents a sensory reckoning with the visualities of littoral spaces, and with the concrete material demands of place in cinema. As Reygadas himself comments: 'We're animals, but we're also rational, we play, and we have human communication. I'm suggesting at the end, okay, let's not be devastated, let's carry on' ('The impossible', p. 15). By 'carrying on', Reygadas, and the characters on the beachspace in *Post Tenebras Lux*, place a burdensome ethical demand on us as spectators and witnesses: to transcend received notions of indoors and outdoors, darkness and brightness, body and mind, and to dwell in a more fluid and amphibious perspective on the littoral and insular spaces of transnational cinema. The next section takes yet another playful and unconventional turn in the direction of the island, and focuses on a different set of sensory and material speculations.

Jeffrey

Perhaps the most memorable aspect of *Jeffrey* (2016), by Dominican director Yanillys Pérez, is this documentary film's persistent focus on music as cultural practice, as a transnational language, and as an expression of communal dreams and individual hope. Jeffrey, the young protagonist, wants to become a reggaeton performer one day. But his current predicament as a working child makes us wonder how he might ever attain his dreams. In *Jeffrey*, somehow, music keeps the narrative carrying on.

The film does not reduce Jeffrey to an example of global precarity. Nor does it obscure the material pressures that endemic poverty, failed national and developmental projects and insidious neoliberal forces objectively place on his material circumstances and on millions of other lives across the Caribbean. At the heart of the film, a gigantic ceiba tree stands as a powerful symbol whose meaning is wildly complex, given its rich material and metaphorical connotations across Caribbean cultures and historical experiences (Figure 3). But there are other symbols, spaces and places that project the Dominican Republic as an amphibious islandscape in *Jeffrey*. Perhaps the most salient

Figure 3. At the heart of the film, a gigantic ceiba tree, *Jeffrey*.

of these is the urbanscape. The film narrates Jeffrey's life as an urban boy, a citizen (however precariously) of Santo Domingo, the Caribbean's largest port city and one of the largest metropolitan areas in the Americas.

One of the most unexpected and stylistically effective scenes in the film is an aerial view of a bridge crossing the vast Ozama River that borders Santo Domingo in the east. From this wide aerial viewpoint we gain a grand panoramic view of the river extending beyond our sight. The magnificence and sheer scale of its meandering advance across the urbanscape short-circuits our preconceived notions of the Dominican Republic as tourist paradise and quaint tropical island. Instead, this un-exotic, metropolitan view of the river conjures a different imaginary, activating a kind of visual catalogue of the vast fluvial routes, cultural and trade passages of the Americas: the Magdalena, Río de la Plata and Mississippi, for example.[17] Signalling global and hemispheric trade, economic modernity and urban complexity, the traffic on the high steel bridge above the river invokes yet another imaginary: of the histories of immigration and cultural diasporas connecting Santo Domingo with New York City, another archipelagic, fluvial metropolis, where Dominicans are currently the largest Hispanic group.[18]

---

[17] See Rory O'Bryen, 'Affect, politics and the production of the people: Meditations on the Río Magdalena', in *Latin American Popular Culture: Politics, Media, Affect*, ed. by Geoffrey Kantaris and Rory O'Bryen (Woodbridge: Boydell and Brewer, 2013), pp. 227–248.

[18] See Lorgia García-Peña, *The Borders of Dominicanidad: Race, Nation, and the*

In choosing to approach the island and the urbanscape from this perspective, Pérez's film dialogues with a rare set of Caribbean films where cityscapes are important vantage points to meditate on issues of globalising modernity and development; economic colonialism and cosmopolitan sophistication; and elitist identifications with Western centres of power and cultural subservience. Such films include Tomás Gutiérrez Alea's *Memorias del subdesarrollo* (1968); and Raoul Peck's *Moloch Tropical* (2009), *Assistance mortelle* (2013) and *Meurtre à Pacot* (2014). What stands out in *Jeffrey* in thought-provoking ways is the measured contrast between congested urbanscapes and unexpected water scenes. Jeffrey and his friends play symbolically charged games with mock weapons on a small boat against picturesque tropical urbanscapes. Or the camera films them underwater and we witness their joyous, carefree swimming, in yet another iteration of the amphibious in recent Latin American cinemas. The relative ease with which these children move across different aspects of the city starts to unlock the complex temporalities of life in a metropolitan space, on a Caribbean island, in areas that are poor and often subjected to appalling levels of abjection and abandonment, yet are not hopeless.

Laura Podalsky's arguments in 'Migrant feelings: Global networks and transnational affective communities' illustrate an emphasis in Latin American film studies on affect, trauma and the movement/emotion dimensions of the cinematic experience.[19] From this perspective, *Jeffrey* might be approached as a 'child predicament' film, the kind that explores childhood trauma in conflicted economic and geopolitical border zones. We might read affect and trauma into the film by locating it in dialogue with discussions of other recent 'amphibious' films, such as Deborah Martin's extended analyses of the child, authenticity and spectatorship in Pedro González-Rubio's *Alamar* (2009).[20]

Archives of Contradiction (Durham, NC and London: Duke University Press, 2016) on the 'in-between' dynamics of Dominican subjectivities, and Jesse Hoffnung-Garskof, 'Yankee, go home ... and take me with you!', in *A Tale of Two Cities: Santo Domingo and New York after 1950* (Princeton and Oxford: Princeton University Press, 2008), pp. 68–96, on the historical background and socioeconomic underpinnings of Dominican migrations to New York City.

[19] Laura Podalsky, *The Politics of Affect and Emotion in Contemporary Latin American Cinema: Argentina, Brazil, Cuba, and Mexico* (New York: Palgrave Macmillan, 2011), pp. 125–160.

[20] Deborah Martin, 'What is the Child for Latin American Cinema? Spectatorship, Mobility and Authenticity in Pedro González Rubio's *Alamar* (2009)', in *A Companion to Latin American Cinema*, ed. by María M. Delgado, Stephen M. Hart and Randal Johnson (Malden, MA: Wiley Blackwell, 2017), pp. 187–200.

Although such fiction and documentary films do not constitute a genre, existing in very different registers, they often project a sense of urgency and precariousness, commenting on local and global crises as they unravel. In other words, they are apt, localised illustrations of Wendy Brown's observation that '[w]hat we have come to call a globalized world harbours fundamental tensions between opening and barricading, erasure and reinscription'.[21] Jeffrey's chances at a better material future do seem foreclosed by the overwhelming realities he must inhabit, endure and outgrow. Undoubtedly, the Caribbean city's neighbourhoods resonate with other transnational imaginaries of the precarious Global South: from the favelas of Brazilian cinema to the coastal zones in Moroccan and other Maghrebian cinemas, to the shantytowns of South African films.[22] As Michaeline Crichlow and Patricia Northover insist:

> No longer is the world interested in its most vulnerable citizens, those occupying such economically inconsequential places as the Caribbean, despite the fact that in the eighteenth and nineteenth centuries the region's free and unfree peoples fueled the Atlantic world economy and that, from the twentieth century to the present, large numbers of free Caribbeans have migrated to rebuild Europe's shattered infrastructure and to take part in U.S. imperial, private, and corporate ventures in Cuba, Costa Rica, Panama, and the United States itself.[23]

Island soundscapes are a precarious beginning, yet their very precariousness signals an openness from the margins that not only resonates with other locales, but also amplifies the specificities of local sound, challenging us to read precarity and liminality across multiple transnational soundscapes. Jeffrey is not only a figure of the child in cinema or the child in *these* times. Beyond the specific material contexts and temporalities he traverses, he is also a young Dominican living in Santo Domingo who might perhaps one day become a reggaeton performer. He embodies potentially and aurally what Lorgia García-Peña calls 'Dominican subjectivities across national spaces'

---

[21] Wendy Brown, *Walled States, Waning Sovereignty* (New York: Zone Books, 2010), p. 7.

[22] See Lúcia Nagib's explorations of 'landscapes of tourist appeal', 'the promise of wealth on a paradisiacal seashore' and 'the utopian sea', among other dimensions of Salles and Thomas's *O primeiro dia* (Midnight) (1999), in *The New Brazilian Cinema*, ed. by Lúcia Nagib (London: I.B. Tauris, 2003), pp. 157–172 (p. 159, p. 168).

[23] Michaeline Chrichlow with Patricia Northover, *Globalization and the Post-Creole Imagination: Notes on Fleeing the Plantation* (Durham, NC and London: Duke University Press, 2009), pp. 43–44.

(*The Borders of Dominicanidad*, p. 3). In his performances as the protagonist of *Jeffrey*, he transcends his own place and travels far through musical and cinematic mobility. As for the objective mobility that his material constraints may afford, we know that the island does not end on screen, but imposes its solid weight on the character, the Caribbean child and the future of their relationship with the world.

The scenes I discuss below transpose some of these concerns onto another mode of Caribbean cinema, on a different islandscape.

Keyla

An intimate story about island lives, *Keyla* (2017) is also a revealing reflection on unstable transnational presents and uncertain geopolitical futures that could apply to other Caribbean island regions and locales across the Global South. Island intimacies and lives are therefore starting points from which to approach this first fiction feature by Colombian director Viviana Gómez Echeverry. As in *El vuelco*, there is an emphasis on background sound that enhances our perception of a search for the island as a space of sensory attentiveness, immediacy and intimacy. And as in *Jeffrey*, a sensory exploration of islandscapes both connects and transcends locales across transnational and diasporic routes. But there are other contexts for this intensely multi-layered film. Gómez Echeverry 'discovered' the island of Providencia during a work assignment. For her, and for Ruiz Navia, Colombia can be understood, but also escaped, by working through some of its peripheral, ethnic, economic and political entanglements. The relative remoteness and isolation of littoral and insular spaces provide an invitation to image new stories about national, regional and hemispheric contexts: in the Colombian Pacific, the Caribbean and across Latin America.

It is Keyla's 18th birthday and, although her boyfriend tries to cheer her up, she is gloomy and distant. Her father Breggie has gone missing during a fishing trip. She and her uncle Richard fear him dead, but they alert contacts and acquaintances across the islands, and from Tampa in Florida to the neighbouring Central American countries of Nicaragua and Costa Rica. The family drama unfolds against the background of a slow-burning crisis with neoliberal undertones: there are political tensions between Colombia and Nicaragua around fishing rights and territorial borders, as the warship that appears ominously on the horizon suggests. Soon after Keyla's birthday, Breggie's Spanish ex-partner Elena comes to stay with Richard and Keyla from Madrid. She brings Keyla's half-brother Cisco (Francisco). Keyla and Cisco have never met before. They get to know each other as older sister and younger brother, Colombian and Spaniard, island girl and European boy.

Figure 4. She shows him the island, *Keyla*.

Their accents and experiences of the world differ, but they share a painful awareness of being disjointed members of a fragmented family. As Keyla investigates Breggie's mysterious disappearance, she helps Cisco gain an understanding of who he was as a father. She shows him the island and they share a series of intimate moments (Figure 4). But Keyla is angry at Elena. She resents her for leaving Breggie and keeping Cisco from visiting until now. Just as Elena left after tiring of Breggie's infidelities, so, it seems, has Breggie now disappeared. But while Elena's empowered choice stands as a denunciation of island masculinity, Breggie's disappearance is linked symbolically to the historical experiences of the *desaparecidos* in Colombia's slow-burning civil and narco-trafficking wars.

Elena reminds us of Luisa in Alfonso Cuarón's *Y tu mamá también* (2001) in that both characters act as strong female counterpoints to culturally defined male roles, and as honest critical outsiders. Indeed, both Luisa and Elena embody the leitmotiv of the *perceptive* Spanish traveller and tourist in Latin America, a familiar type in the transnational Hispanic cinema of the last two decades that appears, for example, in *Lista de espera* (2000) by Juan Carlos Tabío, *También la lluvia* (2010) by Icíar Bollaín and *El faro de las orcas* (2016) by Gerardo Olivares. Andrea Noble writes that 'in their failure to see Luisa's predicament, the male travellers are presented to us as crassly insensitive, an insensitivity that parallels their blindness to the anonymous figures they encounter along the journey'.[24] By contrast, both female characters come

---

[24] Andrea Noble, *Mexican National Cinema* (London and New York: Routledge, 2005), p. 146. Deborah Shaw nuances Noble's reading in a thought-provoking section

across not only as sensitive and insightful, but also as profoundly invested in an ethical denunciation of sexist and patriarchal roles. In a flirtatious scene on the beach, Richard tells Elena: 'Acá en principio todo el mundo es feliz' ('Everyone is happy here in principle'). Yet, she brings him face to face with the bitter realities of the not-so-idyllic island culture. Recalling the kinds of toxic masculinity that she herself encountered in the past, she observes that 'los hombres isleños son unos cabrones' ('island men are swine'). She also confronts Richard about Breggie's involvement in drug trafficking, insisting ironically: 'Ya, y ahora viene el discurso de todo depende de cómo lo mires' ('Indeed, and here comes the speech on it all depends on how you look at it').

In a scene at the house, after hearing the bad news that the extensive search for Breggie remains fruitless, Keyla and Cisco sit on a wooden terrace overlooking the Caribbean. Cisco observes: 'Aquí el mar es muy claro. No sabía que podía ser así de bonito' ('The sea is so clear here. I didn't know it could be so pretty'). 'Sea of seven colours', replies Keyla, 'el mar de los siete colores'. Cisco offers Keyla some shark-shaped gummies and the gloomy mood dispels as they tease each other in this scene of fraternal intimacy, in which Keyla also tells Cisco about Carnival. The scene is carefully framed in terms of scale and depth. It starts with a view of an empty blue boat swaying in the breezy sea (its name is *Little Skip*), a painful reminder of Breggie's unknown whereabouts. Before the shot/countershot of the brief conversation, the camera frames the siblings from the inside of the house: a medium shot of their backs and heads against the skyline, surrounded by wood as if they were inside a boat. As Cisco comments on the beauty of the sea, the screen fills with a stunning view of towering cumulonimbus clouds across the entire horizon, the vast undulating surface of blue, green and turquoise sea shades extending in all directions. At the scene's closure the mood has changed; we see another medium shot, this time of their feet dangling against the sea line.

Pedro Adrián Zuluaga writes that '[u]n cambio de enfoque en la mirada a las obras del cine colombiano implica también el acercamiento desde una posición de extrañeza, no de exotismo' ('A change of focus in the way we look at works of Colombian cinema also implies an approach from a position of wonder, not exoticism').[25] *Keyla* contains a series of exoticist clichés, but alters them in provocative ways, clearing a space for our intrigued awareness, if not wonder (*extrañeza*). There is carnival and dance, exotic food and

---

on *Y tu mamá también*, 'Here's to the clitoris', in Shaw, *The Three Amigos: The Transnational Filmmaking of Guillermo del Toro, Alejandro González Iñárritu and Alfonso Cuarón* (Manchester: Manchester University Press, 2013), pp. 195–197.

[25] Pedro Adrián Zuluaga, *Cine colombiano: Cánones y discursos dominantes* (Bogotá: Cinemateca Distrital, 2011), p. 95.

flirtatious sexual innuendo, but the film does not indulge in facile sexual fantasies. Against the male islanders' presumed promiscuity, *Keyla* juxtaposes other layers of cultural wonder and transnational excess: a mix of historical, linguistic and sexual entanglements (notice the film's aural and linguistic complexities).[26] The stunningly beautiful, sunbathed images in which *Keyla* ends punctuate the film's darker second half, marking the light-heartedness and strength that Keyla shares with Cisco. After all, Keyla only just turned 18 and has her life before her to live.

Dwelling in the Material: Amphibious Visions of Precarity and Hope

Keyla's stories about marooned slaves in the age of piracy might seem unnecessarily clichéd, but they are not from a local and regional history viewpoint. They must be distinguished from the fantasy-driven stereotypes of such mainstream fantasy films as *Pirates of the Caribbean* (a five-part franchise that ran from 2003 to 2017). Instead, they are a persistent element of what Benítez Rojo sees as '[t]he theme of piracy and buried treasure which, in competition with historiographic discourse, runs through Caribbean tradition and literature going back four centuries' (*The Repeating Island*, p. 214). For Benítez Rojo, it all starts on *the repeating island*: 'Which one, then, would be the repeating island, Jamaica, Aruba, Puerto Rico, Miami, Haiti, Recife? […] That original, that island at the center, is as impossible to reach as the hypothetical Antillas that reappeared time and again, always fleetingly, in the cosmographers' charts' (pp. 3–4). The shorescapes and islandscapes I have been discussing refer indexically to material enclaves in continental Latin America and the insular Caribbean. But islands, as Benítez Rojo suggests, are simultaneously material enclaves and spaces of the imagination. Here, as in

---

[26] There is song in Spanish and English, calypso and background sound; San Andrés-Providencia English creole and different dialects of Spanish spoken by local Colombians and by Elena and Cisco. *Keyla* extends and alters a tradition of films about Caribbean sex tourism and colonial entitlement, such as Robert Rossen's *Island in the Sun* (1957) and Laurent Cantet's *Vers le sud* (*Heading South*) (2005). See Leah Rosenberg's analysis of *Island in the Sun* and the novel on which the film is based in Rosenberg, 'It's Enough to Make Any Woman Catch the Next Plane to Barbados: Constructing the Postwar West Indies as Paradise', *Third Text*, 28, 4.5 (2014), 361–376. For Brazil, see Lúcia Nagib on 'The black paradise' in Lúcia Nagib, *Brazil on Screen: Cinema Novo, New Cinema, Utopia* (London and New York: I.B. Tauris, 2007), pp. 83–97, and the discussion on the Raizals (Afro-descended islanders from the San Andrés, Providencia and Santa Catalina archipelago) in Wilhelm Londoño and Pablo Alonso González, 'From plantation to proletariat: Raizals in San Andrés, Providencia and Santa Catalina', *Race & Class*, 59.1 (2017), 84–92.

other recent Latin American island and littoral films, the stories and contexts are far from definitive. These places are transitional and experimental, suggesting starting points rather than fixed destinations, sensorial approaches not definite knowledge.

The paradoxes of connectivity and openness (of hospitality and generosity) in these shorescapes and islandscapes transcend location and invite our far-reaching reflections on possible futures for those who will grow up, dream and move on across Latin American, Caribbean and other transnational environments. In *El vuelco* and *Post Tenebras Lux*, *Jeffrey* and *Keyla*, anxieties and lived experiences around connecting, communicating and escaping present predicaments translate on screen as motorboats and delayed fishing boats, awkwardly picturesque communal gatherings, transnational telecommunications and narco-trafficking networks, engineered bridges and global seaports in an archipelagic region of devastating hurricanes and earthquakes, mass tourism and irreversible environmental degradation. In these four films, dreaming and aesthetic escapism also translate as forms of sensory relation and amphibious visuality, and as means to reflect on present, future and past perceptions of material spaces across countless Latin American liminal enclaves. These transitional audio-visual spaces stand in excess of our exoticist expectations and of the limits imposed by their particular national locations. But the sensory excess, the wonder or *extrañeza* they project is neither self-involved nor self-explained. Instead, it contains a material and aesthetic opacity, an unknowability, that opens excessively and generously onto other locations, cultural contexts and filmic spaces. We must catch up with their amphibious auralities and visualities, and take on their invitation to think ethically and politically, challenging and transgressing our own aesthetic boundaries. There has never been a more urgent task than to think and act attentively and responsibly from these littoral, archipelagic, amphibious visualities.

Section 4

Subjectivities

The theme of the final section is subjectivity, that paradoxically de-centred 'centre' of modern life that, while commonly used as a by-word for individual self-consciousness, identity and agency (that is, autonomy) in thought and feeling, remains haunted by its legal and political sense of *subjection to* (that is, capture and captivity by) hidden structures and pervasive forms of power. The chapters included here all presuppose the *contingent* (that is, uncertain, impermanent) nature of subjectivity in exploring the formation of subject-narratives at points of contact and convergence in the margins, and at the intersection, of traditionally nation-centred histories. In this sense, albeit without recourse to so much theoretical baggage, they tease out the implicitly spatial dimension of Jacques Lacan's play on the Cartesian 'cogito' (the 'I think'). While Lacan's 'I think where I am not, therefore I am where I do not think' situated the thinking 'I' *elsewhere* insofar as it located thought in the *unconscious*,[1] the narratives of sexual, racial and class forms of identity explored in these chapters give that *elsewhere* a broader geographical sense by locating their distinct ways of seeing and feeling in wide-reaching transnational processes. They also remind us that subjectivity is always *embodied*, which is to say impossible to understand independently of the real, material effects of forms of bodily discrimination.

Building on studies of women's exclusion from literary culture, Henriette Partzsch, whose chapter opens this section, explores how nineteenth-century women writers in Spain turned to international magazines not only to

---

[1] Jacques Lacan, 'The agency of the letter in the unconscious, or reason since Freud', in *Écrits: A Selection*, trans. by Alan Sheridan with an introduction by Malcolm Bowie (London and New York: Routledge, 1977), p. 183.

compensate for their marginalisation from national institutions, but also to established commercial and literary forms of collaboration and support. Her examination of these collaborations offers important insights into the explicitly transnational genesis of Spanish literary nationalism. Thus, as she shows, it is in no small part thanks to the serialised publication of works by a certain Cecilia Böhl De Faber Larrea – the daughter of a German merchant, bibliophile, and promoter of English, French and German Romanticism, Johann Nikolaus Böhl de Faber – that an appetite for authentically 'Spanish' works depicting folk customs and popular practices grew internationally. If ever one needed confirmation of Jorge Luis Borges's view that there is no greater an artifice than nationalism – which for the Argentinian author always implied the perspective of a foreign, 'cosmopolitan' or 'touristic', outsider – one need not look much further than the works of 'Fernán Caballero': a German woman, writing in the guise of a Spanish man, 'Fernán Caballero', for whom Spanish was not her first, nor her second, but her third language. At the risk of scandalising some colleagues: isn't there a sense here that (Spanish) literary nationalism is always written in drag, and in borrowed tongues?

While Partzsch's chapter situates the emergence of Romantic narratives of 'Spanishness' within a sphere of 'world literature' that was tied to the traffic in goods and ideas among a cadre of particularly well-heeled 'worldly' subjects, Helen Melling's study of black confraternities in the closely related genre of *costumbrista* painting reminds us that cosmopolitan cultural circuits (and subjects) have also obscured (while nonetheless relying on) the labour of Africans who were radically de-subjectified or dehumanised as they were shuttled around the same Atlantic circuits by the slave trade. Paintings by the Afro-Peruvian Francisco Fierro and by the French Léonce Angrand, for example, provide visual testimony of the reach of these trafficking routes, and of the endurance of slavery in early Republican Peru. They also offer specific insights into the ways the Catholic Church instrumentalised multi-ethnic black sodalities (religious brotherhoods) as ways to ensure the acculturation (or conversion) and policing of former slaves longer after their release from bondage. But they indicate too how the confraternities opened up avenues for preserving memory, allowing Afro-descendants to inscribe the story of their struggle for recognition into the fabric of 'white' *criollo* religious and cultural practices, to assert their agency as producers of Peruvian culture and to build solidarity in the face of a long history of dehumanisation.

If Hispanophone discourses on the Caribbean have, for a long time, explored the region's criss-crossing by diasporic histories, its significance as the site of the 'birthing' of trans-Atlantic capitalism and its erosive effects on hermetic inward-looking national histories, Conrad James's focus on recent

Dominican writing 'fleshes out' how these discourses are lived and embodied in ways that vary according to the interlocking constraints of racial and sexual difference. Here, as is the case in Benjamin Quarshie's chapter, subjectivity is notably unthinkable without reference to the body, as a source of pleasure and of punishment. Indeed, James's study of the poetry of Frank Báez and others provides a platform from which to interrogate the all too routine exclusion of gay, intersex and other *'trans-'* subjects in Caribbean cultures. These exclusions have been widely studied in works on Revolutionary Cuba, where the would-be 'decadent' homosexual artist became the site of projection for deep-seated anxieties about the all-male institution of the 'New Revolutionary Man'. Less has been said about the difficulties experienced by the more indeterminate subjects, such as those who populate Báez's world, for whom the 'passing lines' of racial difference, sexual dissidence and immigration control can, in addition to ideological dissident, soon become hellish spaces of detention.[2]

In the final chapter, Quarshie further elaborates on the ways in which drag, of the sort touched on by James, 'drags into' its signifying processes a host of entangled social, racial, ideological, geopolitical and bodily forms of difference. Thus, he explores the multiple constraints placed on the articulation of dissident forms of subjectivity in the *crónicas* of the 'queer' Chilean writer and performance artist Pedro Lemebel. Situating Lemebel's *crónicas* in such a way as to bring them into dialogue with key discourses in 'queer' and 'crip' (disability) theory, Quarshie shows how Lemebel's racialised *locas* – queer working-class inhabitants of Santiago's impoverished *poblas* – performatively *dis-able* the mobilisation of such discourses in post-dictatorial Chile, and in ways that align the *crónica* with the articulation of 'chronically' entrenched forms of structural-economic violence. Material dimensions related as much to geography as to forms of embodiment are once again brought to bear as constraints on subject-formation, and Quarshie's chapter is an exemplary account of how to 'read' both theoretical and literary texts with an eye to what is lost and gained as texts travel (or indeed fail to travel) from one national context to another, from north to south and back.

---

[2] For more on the intersections between immigration and sexuality see *Passing Lines: Sexuality and Immigration*, ed. by Brad Epps, Katja Valens and Bill Johnson González (Harvard: Harvard University Press, 2005).

14

The Transnational Space of Women's Writing in Nineteenth-century Spain

Henriette Partzsch

Feminist scholars have long pointed out that national belonging does not sit easily with women. As far as representations and rhetoric are concerned, Woman certainly plays a prominent place in national imaginaries. Female allegorical figures such as Britannia (Great Britain) or Marianne (France) often embody a nation symbolically, while the collective imperative of protecting one's women and children from a hostile other is frequently invoked to create group cohesion in situations of perceived conflict.[1] In contrast, the situation of actual women is more ambivalent, a problem that the Spanish writer Carolina Coronado (Almendralejo, 1820–Lisbon, 1911) addressed in her often-quoted poem 'Libertad' (Freedom) in 1846.[2] Culminating in the line 'No hay nación para este sexo' ('There is no nation for the female sex'), the poem provides a lucid comment on the gendered nature of nation building in nineteenth-century Spain.

During Coronado's lifetime Spain underwent a radical transformation from an absolute monarchy to a modern European nation state. People fought passionately over the direction of those changes, often with weapons rather than words. The question of whether a woman could ascend the Spanish throne triggered a series of civil wars. Coups and counter-coups punctuated constitutional debate and the Glorious Revolution of 1868 led to the short-lived First Spanish Republic (1868–1874) before monarchy was restored again. Coronado's text questioned women's investment in these struggles

---

[1] Nira Yuval-Davis, *Gender and Nation* (London, Thousand Oaks and New Delhi: SAGE Publications, 1997), p. 45.

[2] Carolina Coronado, *Treinta y nueve poemas y una prosa*, ed. by Gregorio Torres Nebrija (Mérida: Editora Regional de Extremadura, 1986), p. 140.

over the Spanish nation. She argued that liberal victories did not really matter to women because they continued to be legislated for and thus ruled by men, regardless of how political differences were settled between feuding parties. The Spanish legislation that emerged over the century as the result of a continuous modernisation process illustrates her point. In this body of laws, women were partly envisaged as the domestic angel of the house, in accordance with liberal ideology, partly as devoid of the capacity to have legal rights and responsibilities, in line with older misogynistic traditions. Only in a limited number of areas did they enjoy a legal status similar to men.[3] The election law of 1890 finally cemented the gap that had opened between male and female Spaniards by establishing universal male suffrage, for the first time explicitly restricting the right to vote to men ('La mujer en el discurso', pp. 245–246).

If citizenship was clearly gendered, so was nationality. Similar to legislation in other countries, the Spanish Civil Code of 1889 (article 22) stipulated that a woman who married a foreigner lost her nationality; it was assumed that she would acquire that of her husband, a consistent measure in a society with a hierarchical two-gender system that understood women through their relationships with men.[4] Thus, women inhabited a national space with porous borders at a time that converted national belonging into an essential and defining characteristic, an ideology that also underpinned the formation and consolidation of literary history as a discipline that operated within national frameworks. This perspective curtailed the understanding of past literature by at best reducing complex transnational dynamics to a question of literary influences. In the Spanish-language context, this limited outlook proved particularly damaging to the study of women's writing. Given that women only had restricted access to the national institutions that legitimised literary prestige, many of them tried to carve out a position as a writer on the transnational market of Spanish-language publishing, especially through the medium of magazines.[5] Arguably, the need to find subscribers not only in Spain but

---

[3] Cristina Enríquez de Salamanca, 'La mujer en el discurso legal del liberalismo español', in *La mujer en los discursos de género: Textos y contextos en el siglo XIX*, ed. by Catherine Jagoe, Alda Blanco and Cristina Enríquez de Salamanca (Barcelona: Icaria, 1998), pp. 219–252 (p. 241).

[4] *La mujer en los discursos de género: Textos y contextos en el siglo XIX*, ed by Catherine Jagoe, Alda Blanco and Cristina Enríquez de Salamanca (Barcelona: Icaria, 1998), p. 262.

[5] Henriette Partzsch, 'How to be a cultural entrepreneur', in *Spain in the Nineteenth Century: New Essays on Experiences of Culture and Society*, ed. by Andrew Ginger and Geraldine Lawless (Manchester: Manchester University Press, 2018), pp. 191–215.

also in the Americas and probably the Philippines situates these writers in a space that does not easily fit national narratives.

This chapter explores how perception changes if we approach women's writing in nineteenth-century Spain with a focus on its transnational dimensions rather than its alleged national uniqueness, taking into account the impact of national boundaries without severing the connections that crossed and permeated the literary system. The first part discusses Cecilia Böhl de Faber Larrea (Morges, 1796–Seville, 1877) who, under the male pen name 'Fernán Caballero', came to embody the supposedly authentic spirit of Spain for nineteenth-century readers in Europe and the US. A brief study of the circulation and reception of her acclaimed first novel *La Gaviota* ('The Sea-gull') (1849) shows that this reading of her work was produced by the dynamic interplay of narrative technique, translation decisions, reader expectations and the constraints and opportunities of the expanding international print market. The second part of this chapter studies how this transnational market was negotiated by the press. A short analysis of the serialisation of novels in newspapers is followed by a discussion of the role played by magazines targeting a female readership. After outlining the connectedness across borders that characterised these periodical publications, it examines the ways in which this setup shaped the literary texts that the magazines brought to their readers, suggesting that women's writing in this context was an intrinsic part of entrepreneurial practice.

Becoming Spanish: Fernán Caballero, the True Spirit of Spain and the International Book Market

If asked to name a contemporary Spanish writer, many nineteenth-century European and US readers would have mentioned Fernán Caballero. Versions of her narrative fiction circulated in languages such as German, English (from both sides of the Atlantic), French, Dutch, Danish, Hungarian, Polish and Portuguese. In 1864, her novel *La familia de Alvareda* ('The Alvareda Family') (1856) was even directly translated from Spanish into Slovenian.[6] Her works were also taken up by publishing houses that targeted the international book market, such as Brockhaus in Leipzig (Germany). Brockhaus produced a commercially successful collection of Spanish-language texts from 1860 to 1887, about 40 per cent of which consisted of works by Caballero, including

---

[6] Tania Badalič, *Reception of European Women Writers in Slovenian Multicultural Territory of the 19th Century until the End of the First World War*, PhD dissertation (University of Nova Gorica, 2014), p. 139, <http://repozitorij.ung.si/IzpisGradiva.php?id=1632&lang=eng>, accessed 6 April 2020.

re-editions.[7] Using the absence of an international copyright agreement between Spain and several German states, these well-made but inexpensive books were mostly destined for exportation, often via French booksellers.[8] Printing Spanish-language texts outwith Spain could also be linked to learning and teaching, as several examples from the US illustrate.[9] These editions included, for instance, bilingual vocabulary lists (1901) or used parallel text (1910).[10] The handwritten annotations in a copy of *La familia de Alvareda* from Boston show how intensive some readers worked with the text.[11] Fernán Caballero thus came to represent the quintessence of Spanishness to an international reading public, an appreciation shared by many contemporaneous literary critics and historians.

The exemplary status achieved by Caballero's writing is all the more remarkable if we consider that Spanish was only the author's third language of written expression. Although her early manuscripts have not survived, the evidence suggests that the first version of *La familia de Alvareda* was drafted in German, and that of *La Gaviota* in French.[12] This is a reflection of Cecilia Böhl de Faber Larrea's cosmopolitan background. Her parents met in Cádiz, in the late eighteenth century one of the most vibrant cities in Spain, a gateway to the Americas and a hub of the international trade in Spanish wines. Cecilia's mother, Frasquita Larrea y Aherán (Cádiz, 1775–1838), was of Irish-Basque descent, while her father Johann Nikolaus Böhl/Juan Nicolás Bohl de Faber (1770–1836) belonged to an important merchant house that had its main seat

[7] Álvaro Ceballos Viro, 'Die "Colección de autores españoles" von F. A. Brockhaus (1860–1887): rentabler Konservatismus', in *Beiträge zur Nationalisierung der Kultur im Spanien des aufgeklärten Absolutismus*, ed. by Jan-Henrik Witthaus (Frankfurt: Peter Lang, 2010), pp. 159–172.

[8] Álvaro Ceballos Viro, *Ediciones alemanas en español (1850–1900)* (Madrid and Frankfurt: Iberoamericana; Vervuert, 2009), pp. 91–96.

[9] Pura Fernández, 'La editorial Garnier de París y la difusión del patrimonio bibliográfico en castellano en el siglo XIX', in *Tes philies tade dora: Miscelánea léxica en memoria de Conchita Serrano* (Madrid: CSIC, 1999), pp. 603–612.

[10] Fernán Caballero, *La familia de Alvareda: novela original de costumbres populares*, ed. with notes by Percy B. Burnet (New York: Henry Holt and Company, 1901), <https://hdl.handle.net/2027/ucl.b5202646>, accessed 6 April 2020 (HATHI Trust); Fernán Caballero, *Narraciones en español y en inglés, traducido y aumentado*, ed. by Raphael Diez de la Cortina, 4th edn. (New York: R. D. Cortina Company, 1910), <https://hdl.handle.net/2027/nyp.33433075920912>, accessed 6 April 2020 (HATHI Trust).

[11] Fernán Caballero, *La familia de Alvareda: novela original de costumbres populares* (Boston: De Vries, Ibarra y Company, 1865?), <https://hdl.handle.net/2027/coo.31924027710254>, accessed 6 April 2020 (HATHI Trust).

[12] Demetrio Estébanez Calderón, in Fernán Caballero, *La Gaviota*, ed. by Demetrio Estébanez Calderón (Madrid: Cátedra, 1998), p. 52, p. 73.

in Hamburg, Germany.[13] Cecilia spent important formative years with the German part of her family and attended a French finishing school in Hamburg before returning to Spain at the age of 17; her letters show that as late as in the 1820s she struggled with written Spanish (Herrero, pp. 152–153). According to Estébanez Calderón, her insecurities in this area shaped her publications, notably her first published novel, *La Gaviota*.[14] Serialised in the newspaper *El Heraldo* in 1849, the Spanish version of the French manuscript was signed by the publication's editor in chief, the writer José Joaquín de Mora (1783–1864), a former friend of the Böhls but with rather different aesthetic and political convictions. Cecilia was disappointed by the translation. She produced a new version in collaboration with a fellow of the Real Academia de la Lengua (Royal Academy of Language), Mexican-born Fermín de la Puente y Apezechea (1812–1875), only to revise it again for the definitive edition of 1861.

International readers were fascinated by Caballero's depiction of Andalusian customs and people that seemed to capture the true spirit of Spain, as reviews and comments attest. An influential article in the *Edinburgh Review*, cited in the prefaces of at least two English translations of *La Gaviota*, by J. Leander Starr (1864) and Augusta Bethell (1867), sees her as 'a really original writer of fictions offering vivid delineations of the manners and characters of the living populations of the most poetic province of the Peninsula', thus showing 'genuine national inspiration', unlike her Spanish fellow authors.[15] If anything, 'these tales are perhaps too essentially Spanish ever to attain a great popularity in foreign countries', although 'they are well calculated to revive the interest of cultivated minds in that noble language and that romantic people' ('Obras completas', p. 129). Characteristically, the review thus ends with a generalisation of Caballero as 'essentially Spanish' after a more nuanced discussion of her as an idiosyncratic writer who set her stories in specific locations rather than a generic Spain. It was all too easy to transform that individual author into the embodiment of Spanishness, a fact also illustrated in a contemporaneous German novel, *Zwei Schwestern: Eine Erzählung aus der Gegenwart* ('Two Sisters: A Contemporary Tale') (1863) by the successful author Ida von Hahn-Hahn (1805–1880). In this novel, a character reads aloud from the German translation of *La Gaviota*, 'worin das spanische Volksleben so frisch und charactervoll dargestellt ist'

[13] Javier Herrero, *Fernán Caballero: Un nuevo plantamiento* (Madrid: Gredos, 1963), p. 150.

[14] Demetrio Estébanez Calderón, in Fernán Caballero, *La Gaviota*, ed. by Demetrio Estébanez Calderón (Madrid: Cátedra, 1998), pp. 71–79.

[15] Anonymous, 'Obras completas de Fernan Caballero. 13 vols. Madrid: 1856–1859', *Edinburgh Review* 114 (July 1861), pp. 99–129, p. 100.

(in which the life of the Spanish people has been depicted so refreshingly and full of character').[16] Rather stereotypically, the scene Hahn-Hahn's characters are enjoying together is the fatal bullfight that prepares the ending of *La Gaviota*.

This transformation worked so smoothly because Caballero 'wrote primarily not for a Spanish but for a foreign public', a claim illustrated by the narrative techniques deployed in *La Gaviota*, starting with its frame.[17] Most accounts of the novel overlook that the story begins in a truly transnational location: a steamship leaving Falmouth on its way to the Mediterranean in 1836. This situates the readers at the heights of colonial, globalising modernity. Ocean-going steam ships were a new and still controversial technology.[18] From 1830 onwards, they were used to transport mail and passengers from Falmouth to Gibraltar, stopping in Vigo, Oporto, Lisbon and Cádiz. From Gibraltar, the journey could continue to Malta and Alexandria, the next leg on the way from England to India.[19] Accordingly, the passengers on the ship in *La Gaviota* include many nationalities and come from different stations in life, from the governor of an unspecified British colony to a French artist, officers' wives and sea-sick children. Among them, the reader is introduced to the two positive male protagonists of the novel, the German doctor Fritz Stein and the Spanish Duke of Almansa, who recognise each other as kindred spirits in the midst of a chaotic departure and strike up a conversation in Latin. Latin was Europe's vanishing cosmopolitan language that allowed an intellectual elite 'to make one's claims about the political world on a notionally universal stage' that 'seemed unsuited to the modern era of competition among nations'.[20]

The complex, modern space represented by the ocean steamer is the necessary foil to the celebrated depiction of supposedly typical Spanish life that starts in the second chapter. Set two years later, it transports us to rural Spain. Stein, broken by his experience of the civil war in the north of the country, finds refuge in the fictional Andalusian village of Villamar. His

---

[16] Ida von Hahn-Hahn, *Zwei Schwestern: Eine Erzählung aus der Gegenwart* (Mainz: Franz Kirchheim, 1863), p. 340.

[17] Catherine Davies, *Spanish Women's Writing 1849–1996* (London and Atlantic Highlands, NJ: The Athlone Press, 1998), p. 45.

[18] Ben Marsden and Crosbie Smith, *Engineering Empires: A Cultural History of Technology in Nineteenth-century Britain* (Basingstoke and New York: Palgrave Macmillan, 2005), pp. 88–128.

[19] W. S. Lindsay (1876), *History of Merchant Shipping and Ancient Commerce*, vol. 4 (Cambridge: Cambridge University Press, 2013), p. 284.

[20] Alexander Beecroft, *An Ecology of World Literature: From Antiquity to the Present Day* (London and New York: Verso, 2015), p. 144.

learning process as an outsider who is interested in the way of life and stories of a community mirrors that of the non-Spanish reader, eager to immerse themselves in a delightfully alien, exotic world. It is for their benefit that the narrator introduces explanatory descriptions of everyday cultural practices, such as the singing of *romances* (ballads) (*La Gaviota*, 1998, pp. 236–237). As the novel advances, Stein loses protagonism while the Spanish characters come to the fore. Both the German doctor and the readers have found their place in Caballero's Spain.

La Gaviota thus caters to the readers' desire to encounter a 'window on the world', one of the functions of reading often discussed today in the context of world literature.[21] This supposed window into Spain provided, however, a rather particular view. Caballero repeatedly claimed to offer 'una idea exacta, verdadera y genuina de España' ('an exact, true and genuine idea of Spain') (*La Gaviota*, 1998, p. 123), but many contemporaneous Spaniards would reject her vision of the country, shaped by Caballero's militant Catholicism and hostility towards change. In *La Gaviota*, the nostalgic yearning for the supposedly good old days does not only manifest itself in the narrator's explicit value judgements; it is also embedded in the very setting of Villamar. Dominated by two ruined buildings, a former monastery dissolved after the Spanish liberal government expropriated Church assets and a fortress only manned by one commander and a 'guarnición de lagartos' ('garrison of lizards') (*La Gaviota*, 1998, p. 191), Villamar's community is depicted as a last bastion of rural culture and traditions, condemned to oblivion by an emerging new order.

Caballero's novel illustrates the close relationship between a nationalist agenda and the transnational dimension of nineteenth-century literature in Europe. The advance of capitalism during the nineteenth century, in conjunction with the introduction of new technologies in book production and transport, incentivised publishing houses like Brockhaus to grow new markets beyond regional and national boundaries. As Ceballos Viro underlines, the increasing internationalisation of the book market was intertwined with the agenda of ethnic nationalisms, inasmuch as the latter provided 'una diversidad de culturas específicas susceptibles de ser explotadas comercialmente por separado' ('a diverse range of specific cultures that are susceptible to being commercially exploited one by one') (*Ediciones alemanas*, p. 124). The resulting opportunities were two-fold. In addition to selling books in Spanish to a Spanish-language readership worldwide, translations of some Spanish texts could be marketed to readers who wanted to experience life in Spain from the comfort of their homes.

---

[21] David Damrosch, *What is World Literature?* (Princeton and Oxford: Princeton University Press, 2003), p. 15.

Reviews and prefaces to foreign-language versions show that a difficult balancing act between the familiar and the outlandish was considered necessary in order to sell Caballero's books to a non-Spanish audience. Translators and publishers tried to second-guess their readers' preferences, a practice that affected many translation decisions. Both the American translator J. Leandro Starr and his British peer Augusta Bethell explain that their versions corrected the prolixity of the original, leaving out passages judged 'without attraction to those who were not born under the bright sun of Iberia' or segments 'which it was thought might prove tedious or distasteful to the English reader'.[22] The German translator Ludwig Gustav Lemcke gives the discussion a specific twist by explaining that he supressed, as far as possible, anything of a religious nature that could be considered polemical, in addition to passages that in his eyes were only relevant to readers in Spain.[23] Lemcke was clearly worried about the effects that Caballero's famous pro-Catholic interventions could have on his German readership at a time when conflict was rife between the Catholic Church and Protestant German states. Interestingly, he uses Caballero for his own nationalist agenda, as an example of the workings of the German spirit beyond national boundaries (*Ausgewählte Werke*, x–xi).

The supposedly authentic Spain that readers were eager to encounter in *La Gaviota* was hence the result of complex negotiations between different cultural, commercial and political agendas; its otherness was designed to validate rather than to challenge readers' views. Caballero's works were different enough to rouse interest but could be marketed as sufficiently familiar to be easily enjoyed. Branding her as the Spanish Walter Scott hit that mark exactly. The comparison with the arguably most famous novelist of the time was first used by Spanish critic Eugenio de Ochoa in 1849 to underline the quality and importance of Caballero's Spanish debut.[24] In the long run, the reiteration of the sobriquet, especially in the English-language context, had the same function as the suggestion 'Readers who enjoyed X also enjoyed Y' in online marketing today: a promise of more of the same, but with pleasing variations. Thus, Fernán Caballero's work points towards the ambiguous fascination exercised

[22] J. Leandro Starr in Fernán Caballero, *La Gaviota: A Spanish Novel*, trans. by J. Leander Starr (New York: John Bradburn, 1864), p. 6 (HATHI Trust); Augusta Bethell in Fernán Caballero, *The Sea-Gull (La Gaviota)*, trans. by Augusta Bethell (London: Richard Bentley, 1867), p. iv, https://archive.org/details/seagulllagaviot00ay-algoog/page/n5/mode/2up>, last accessed 6 April 2020. (Internet Archive).

[23] Ludwig Gustav Lemcke in Fernán Caballero, *Ausgewählte Werke; 1: Die Möve*, trans. by Ludwig Gustav Lemcke (Braunschweig: Westermann, 1859), pp. xxiii–xxvii.

[24] Eugenio de Ochoa in Fernán Caballero, *La Gaviota*, 1998, p. 144.

by the idea of world literature, still fiercely debated today.[25] Its problematic nature was already highlighted by her contemporaries Karl Marx and Friedrich Engels in an often-quoted passage from *The Communist Manifesto*. As world literature arises 'from the numerous national and local literatures', it promises a victory over 'national one-sidedness and narrow-mindedness', but it is also inextricably linked to the emergence of new 'industries that no longer work up indigenous raw material, but raw material drawn from the remotest zones; industries whose products are consumed, not only at home, but in every corner of the globe'.[26] As capitalism's survival depends on the continuous creation of 'new wants, requiring for their satisfaction the products of distant lands and climes', literature and its study become entangled with commodification and unequal power relations, too.

Playing the Transnational Market: The Press, Fashion Magazines and Enterprising Women

Caballero's career as the Spanish Walter Scott exemplifies the impact of the international print market on nineteenth-century literature. In the case of *La Gaviota*, the inspiration, writing process, publication, circulation and reception of the novel contributed to creating a transnational product that paradoxically relied on the promise of national authenticity as its unique selling point. From today's perspective, this complex process of negotiating meaning is probably best traceable in translations published as books. However, the most vibrant medium for exchanges of this kind was arguably the less prestigious periodical press, thanks to exponential growth fuelled by technological innovation in conjunction with social changes that broadened its accessibility during the nineteenth century. Often neglected in literary studies, newspapers and magazines are the very embodiment of a transnational cultural space. On the one hand, they played an important role in creating the 'imagined community' of the nation, according to Benedict Anderson's now famous analysis, and as a matter of course, they had to comply with national legislation and rules, ranging from forms of censorship to business rates.[27] On the other hand, these publications were shaped by

---

[25] See *Re-mapping World Literature: Writing, Book Markets and Epistemologies Between Latin America and the Global South*, ed. by Gesine Müller, Jorge J. Locane and Benjamin Loy (Berlin: Der Gruyter, 2018).

[26] Karl Marx and Friedrich Engels, *The Communist Manifesto* (London: Penguin, 2004 [1848]).

[27] Benedict Anderson, *Invented Communities: Reflections on the Origin and Spread of Nationalism*, rev. edn (London and New York: Verso, 2006 [1983]).

connections that crossed borders, both in terms of format and content. It was, for instance, standard practice to insert material from other papers, often without acknowledging the provenance of information or the fact that pieces had been adapted from a different language and cultural context.[28]

The way in which newspapers engaged most obviously with literature was through the serialisation of novels and other texts, usually printed at the bottom of the first and second page; this was also how the first version of *La Gaviota* had been published in 1849. This so-called *folletín* could have considerable traction with readers, and newspapers competed by trying to publish as quickly as possible the latest offerings by the stars of the (mostly) European literary scene. Sometimes, translations were serialised before the original text had been completed. In Spain, texts originally written in French dominated this specific market, to the great chagrin of those who wanted to restore Spain's literature to its former glory.[29] A quick count of authors serialised in six ideological diverse and widely read Spanish newspapers from the period of 1850 to 1870, made possible thanks to the digital newspaper archive (*Hemeroteca Digital*) of Spain's National Library, confirms this perception, even though the numbers are only approximate – not all newspapers appeared throughout the whole period and the numbers depend on what we consider to be a literary, serialised contribution. Taking into account this caveat, results are as follows: out of a total of 61 identified writers who appear in the *folletín* of *La Esperanza*, only four wrote in Spanish, less than 7 per cent; seven writers, just over 11 per cent, were women, with Fernán Caballero being the only Spanish writer. In *La Época*, the relation was ten out of 36, roughly 28 per cent (with five women writers, including brief pieces by Fernán Caballero, Gertrudis Gómez de Avellaneda and Ángela Grassi); in *La España*, 15 out of 46, about a third of the total (with two Spanish writers, Fernán Caballero and María Mendoza de Vives, out of a total seven women writers); in *La Correspondencia*, ten out of 66, about 15 per cent (with eight women writers, but none of them writing in Spanish); in *El Clamor Público*, four out of 39, approximately 10 per cent (with four women writers, only one of them, Carolina Coronado, writing in Spanish), and in *La Discusión*, arguably the most progressive title, eight out of 18, almost 48 per cent (with no woman writer; however, the paper closely followed Carolina Coronado's career).

---

[28] Elizabeth Amann, 'Plotlifting: The transposition of French stories in the nineteenth-century Spanish press', *Forum for Modern Language Studies*, 52.3 (2016), 293–310.

[29] Elisa Martí-López, *Borrowed Words: Translation, Imitation, and the Making of the Nineteenth-century Novel in Spain* (Lewisburg: Bucknell University Press, 2002).

The predominance of translations from French in the *folletín* also applies to women writers. The most visible author in our sample, serialised in four titles, wrote in French, under the pen name of George Sand (Aurore Dupin, 1804–1876). Sand's position points towards the alignment of Spain's literary market with the rest of Europe and the Americas; she was the most widely read Western woman writer of the time.[30] However, establishing rankings of names can only be a starting point for further enquiry into the place of women writers and their texts in the complex world of literary culture as it manifested itself in the press. We also have to ask which texts were selected, when and in which context, how they were adapted, how writers were discussed in other sections of the press and what the agency of women in the process was.

A brief look at *La Esperanza* illustrates this point. The paper was notorious for its right-wing, ultramontane defence of the absolutist pretender to the Spanish throne and many of the texts selected for the *folletín* fit this worldview, such as the annual lent sermons delivered at Notre-Dame de Paris by the Jesuit Father Felix, the autobiography of René de Chateaubriand (1768–1848), a writer famous for his poetical defence of the Catholic faith, and papal documents in Latin condemning the unification of Italy. Nevertheless, at times pragmatism seems to have trumped ideology. Thus, the newspaper collaborated with the French fashion journal *La Mode* and followed their lead serialising several novels by society writer Countess Dash (Anne-Gabrielle de Cisternes de Coutiras, vicomtesse de Poilloüe de Saint-Mars, 1804–1872), but always insisting in the merit of the chosen works (see *La Esperanza*, 24 September 1853).

At first sight, *La Esperanza* is therefore a surprising vehicle for the (probably) first Spanish serialisation of narratives by one of Europe's most celebrated authors, the Swedish writer Fredrika Bremer (1801–1865).[31] Bremer was a convinced Protestant who denounced slavery in the United States and Spanish Cuba in her American travelogue (1853) and tried to build a women's peace alliance during the Crimean War (1854); her novel *Hertha* (1856) would provoke a parliamentary debate and subsequent changes to women's legal status in Sweden. *La Esperanza* ignored all aspects of her writing and activism that contradicted their editorial line. Instead, they presented Bremer as a Christian writer of domesticity, comparable to Fernán Caballero and like

---

[30] *George Sand. La réception hors de France au XIXe siècle*, Oeuvres & Critiques XXVIII.1 (2003, special issue), ed. by Suzan Van Dijk and Kerstin Wiedemann.

[31] For a full account see Henriette Partzsch, 'The complex routes of travelling texts: Fredrika Bremer's reception in Spain and the transnational dimension of literary history', *Comparative Critical Studies*, 11.2–3 (2014), 281–293.

her an example of 'ese movimiento consolador hácia la moral cristiana que se advierte en Europa, del uno al otro cabo, y en el que toman tanta parte las mujeres' ('this consolatory movement towards Christian morality that has appeared all over Europe, and in which women participate so much') (*La Esperanza*, 15 September 1854). Thus, *La Esperanza* tried to co-opt Bremer's name for a transnational movement supposedly built on Christian values that opposed the secular modernisation of nation states.[32] Presenting women as an essential part of this movement had strategic advantages. It appropriated the discourse of women's liberation and tried to capitalise on women's perceived closeness to the Catholic Church, arguments that would reappear in the debate about votes for women that accompanied the beginning of the second Spanish Republic in 1931. In a typical move, *La Esperanza* played off 'their' women writers against more liberal and progressive authors, especially George Sand, to mark their ideological position.

However, women writers did not necessarily allow themselves to be instrumentalised in that way. In an open letter to *La Esperanza* (29 September 1859), Fernán Caballero demonstrated that it was not necessary to denigrate George Sand's talent and lifestyle or downplay the genius of poets Gertrudis Gómez de Avellaneda and Carolina Coronado in order to appreciate her own literary and ideological contribution. The letter warrants further analysis; in the context of this chapter, it is a timely reminder of women writers' agency in nineteenth-century literary culture. Although the hegemonic discourse about women's role in society did shape their opportunities for expression and the forms it took, it did not predetermine how they would use, change or challenge their allocated place. This insight is particularly relevant when studying the medium in which most of nineteenth-century literature written by women can be found, Spanish-language *revistas de modas y salones* (fashion and society magazines). A closer look at the constraints under which these magazines operated, starting with their commercial setup and the readership they tried to capture, will allow us to develop a better understanding of women writers' room for manoeuvre, beyond the limited number of cases who have become part of the literary canon.

Following a well-established French model, these periodical publications typically targeted female readers and families with information about the latest sartorial developments, society news and literature. The most successful titles were *El Correo de la Moda* ('The Fashion Post') (Madrid, 1851–1886) and *La Moda Elegante* ('Elegant Fashion') (Cádiz/Madrid,

---

[32] *Culture Wars: Secular–Catholic Conflict in Nineteenth-century Europe*, ed. by Christopher Clark and Wolfram Kaiser (Cambridge: Cambridge University Press, 2003).

1861–1923). Even though it seems impossible to reconstruct the exact number and geographical distribution of subscribers to titles like *El Correo de la Moda*, recent work on the circulation of the shorter-lived fashion magazine *La Violeta* ('The Violet') (first series Madrid, 1862–1866) suggests that this kind of publication penetrated the whole national market and had a strong presence in Spanish-speaking America; they may even have circulated as far as the Philippines (Partzsch, 'How to be a cultural entrepreneur'). In addition, fashion magazines relied on strong connections with the fashion industry in Paris to access information and high-quality fashion plates, which were extremely popular with subscribers. Some titles joined forces across borders in this endeavour. Thus, *La Moda Elegante* was part of the syndicated publications inspired by *Der Bazar* in Berlin.[33] In these collaborations, engravings and fashion descriptions would be typically shared (or pirated), while society news and literary content reflected more the specific cultural context of each title. A strong presence in Paris also facilitated contacts with Latin America thanks to its community of American expats and visitors. Essentially, this transnational setup with (post)colonial inflections responded to the same imperative as Brockhaus's expansion into new markets. Selling magazines in Spain could be difficult because of low literacy rates, especially among women, and problems with transport infrastructure. This situation limited the pool of potential subscribers, the main source of income. It was therefore vital to exploit the opportunities arising from the use of Spanish in the newly independent Latin American states and the remaining Spanish colonies, especially Cuba.

Consequently, editors had to find the smallest common denominator of a very diverse audience.[34] Subscribers were often more interested in detailed information about the latest developments in Parisian fashion than in literature. Furthermore, in many cases the paterfamilias would have paid the subscription. It is therefore not surprising that the literary texts published in or distributed with fashion and society magazines did not stray much from accepted conventions, in terms of form as well as content. Written in the so-called idealist or sentimental style, they emphatically did not follow the emerging realist mode of narration. Given that the realist novel was increasingly perceived as a national literary form,[35] publishing the approximate

---

[33] Marianne Van Remoortel, 'Women editors and the rise of the illustrated fashion press in the nineteenth century', *Nineteenth-Century Contexts*, 39.4 (2017), 269–295.

[34] Henriette Partzsch, 'Mujeres de letras y de negocios: Faustina Sáez de Melgar y el mercado de las revistas de moda isabelinas', *Ínsula*, 841–842 (2017), 8–12, p. 10.

[35] Jo Labanyi, *Gender and Modernization in the Spanish Realist Novel* (Oxford and New York: Oxford University Press, 2000), pp. 6–11.

equivalent of what we would call today genre fiction, that is, literature that clearly fits established commercial categories like fantasy or crime, may well have been a safer choice for transnational magazines and the writers that depended on them. The texts drew on the combination of well-known elements, sometimes with surprising results, especially regarding the agency of female characters. Although situated in a stylised world of conventional fiction, they nevertheless could address problems that writers and readers would encounter on a daily basis, such as the difficulty to reconcile family life with a professional vocation.

An ambitious example of this literature is the novel *Los miserables de España o Secretos de la Corte* ('Spain's Villains or the Secrets of the Capital') (1862–1863) by the director of *La Violeta*, Faustina Sáez de Melgar (Villamanrique de Tajo, 1834–Madrid, 1895), as already discussed on an earlier occasion (Partzsch, 'Mujeres de letras', p. 11). The novel was available at the editorial office of *La Violeta*, with a special discount for the subscribers to the magazine. This type of commercial arrangement complemented the delivery of literary texts in instalments together with the magazine, and the inclusion of (sometimes serialised) pieces in the issues themselves. The narrative of *Los miserables de España* follows the model of the very successful mystery and adventure literature popularised by the French writer Eugène Sue and his followers, although Sáez freely admits in her opening remarks that the title itself was inspired by Victor Hugo's newly published novel *Les misérables* (1862). The plot abounds in surprising twists, with frequent melodramatic scenes appealing to the reader's emotions. The novel thus frames reading as pleasure, but a pleasure that the explicit narrative voice tries to channel towards a moralising, Christian interpretation of the world, in a conscious attempt to provide entertaining reading material that could be reconciled with widespread notions of decorum.[36]

One of the most striking features of *Los miserables de España* is its reliance on global connectedness, despite being mostly set in Madrid. Its protagonist, Sao Paulo-born Alejandrina, countess of the Brazilian region of Paraná, hides behind the name of Blanca *la Extranjera* ('Blanca the Stranger/ Foreigner') to fight against evil and right past wrongs. Together with her title, she has inherited riches in Rio de Janeiro and Minas Gerais from her mother, who may have been of black African origin. The topic of race haunts the whole novel, although it only surfaces occasionally. It is presented as an unstable and disquieting phenomenon to a readership that is implicitly imagined as white. While on rare occasions the novel seems to defend the dignity of all human

---

[36] Faustina Sáez de Melgar, *Los miserables de España o Secretos de la Corte* (Barcelona: Vicente Castaños, 1862–1863), 2 vols, vol. I, p. 5.

beings, the reaction to the unmasking of a white character who had blackened up to pursue his obsession for Alejandrina clearly echoes a racist worldview. Alejandrina herself can pass at will as black or white but at the end she is fully reinstated in the hegemonic canon of Caucasian beauty.

Throughout the novel Alejandrina is the puppet master who draws the strings, albeit without openly challenging received opinions about women's role in society. Rather, her intelligence and immense wealth allow her to take behaviours and activities considered to be worthy in a woman to unforeseen levels and consequences. This is most obvious in her use of charitable work. According to the ideology that positioned women as domestic angels, exercising charity was an important part of a woman's life; however, charity is also an area that straddles the assumed divide between a female-connoted private and a male-connoted public sphere. The scale of Alejandrina's initiatives transforms the imperative of assisting others into social engineering on a par with the big projects of nineteenth-century urban planning in Madrid, as she builds a new neighbourhood that houses a utopian community of workers and their families left stranded by evildoers as well as economic and social injustice.

The way in which Alejandrina develops charity into an entrepreneurial activity must have chimed with women who, like Faustina Sáez, worked on establishing themselves as authors. Often this included more than writing and submitting manuscripts for publication. Ángela Grassi (Cremá, Italy, 1823–Madrid, 1883), Rogelia León (Granada, 1828–1870), Pilar Sinués de Marco (Zaragoza, 1835–Madrid, 1893), Joaquina García Balmaseda (Madrid, 1837–1893), Emilia Serrano Baroness Wilson (Granada, 1843?–Barcelona, 1922) and Concepción Gimeno de Flaquer (Alcañiz, 1850–Buenos Aires, 1919), to name just a few, also worked for, co-directed or founded commercial periodical publications, although the scarcity of sources can make it difficult to establish the exact scale and nature of their contributions. This situation is exacerbated because of the informal nature of many practical arrangements that helped circumvent the legal restrictions women faced when they wanted to act on the market. Nevertheless, these writers used the global nature of the Spanish-language print market to create business opportunities, drawing on their personal networks that spanned the Atlantic.[37] Adopting a commercially proactive attitude helped them compensate – up to a point – for their exclusion from or marginalisation by the institutions of literary culture.[38]

---

[37] *No hay nación para este sexo: Redes culturales de mujeres de letras españolas y latinoamericanas (1824–1936)*, ed. by Pura Fernández (Madrid: CSIC, 2015).

[38] Famous cases are Gertrudis Gómez de Avellaneda's (Puerto Príncipe, 1814–Sevilla, 1873) and Emilia Pardo Bazán's (A Coruña, 1851–Madrid, 1921) failed

Although it seems to have been their love of literature that attracted them to the print market rather than the other way round, their writing cannot be separated from their economic activity. Therefore, analysing how their texts intersected with the practice of cultural entrepreneurship allows us to gain a more nuanced understanding of the complex cultural dynamics that shaped nineteenth-century literature in Spanish.

Conclusion

Studying nineteenth-century women's writing from a transnational perspective changes our understanding of the history of literary culture inasmuch as it draws attention to an intrinsic dynamic connectedness that does not stop at national borders. The case of Fernán Caballero's *La Gaviota* shows how the interplay between an individual author, the globalising market of publishing and contemporaneous readers outwith Spain created a transnational product that was hailed as the embodiment of Spanishness. Examining the circulation and reception of texts can therefore help us find the 'présence de l'Autre' ('presence of the Other') in national literatures, as Jacques Beyrie put it.[39] Focusing on the circulation of texts and ideas also means that we have to take a careful look at the ways in which ideas, texts and print products spread across the market. This perspective leads to a reassessment of less-prestigious formats, such as newspapers, but especially the *revistas de modas y salones*. The data known so far suggest that the latter reached more readers than book publications and also gave a considerable number of women the opportunity to see their work in print.[40] Consequently, following transnational connections leads into the realm of the 'great unread', in the phrase popularised by Franco Moretti as a reminder of the fact that literary history tends to consider only a negligible percentage of texts that circulated in the literary system.[41] Reading texts linked to the world of magazines, such as Sáez de Melgar's *Los miserables de España*, opens new windows not only onto the

---

attempts to be elected as fellows of the Real Academia Española (Royal Spanish Academy). See Joyce Tolliver, '"My distinguished friend and colleague Tula": Emilia Pardo Bazán and literary-feminist politics', in *Recovering Spain's Feminist Tradition*, ed. by Lisa Vollendorf (New York: MLA, 2001), pp. 217–237.

[39] Jacques Beyrie, *Qu'est-ce qu'une histoire nationale? Écriture, identité, pouvoir en Espagne* (Toulouse: Le Mirail, 1994), p. 180.

[40] Judith Rideout, *Women's Writing Networks in Spanish Magazines around 1900*, PhD thesis, University of Glasgow, 2017, <http://theses.gla.ac.uk/7859/>, accessed 6 April 2020.

[41] Franco Moretti, 'The slaughterhouse of literature', in *Distant Reading* (London: Verso, 2013), 63–89, pp. 66–67.

cultural imaginary of nineteenth-century women writers and readers. If we understand these publications as one aspect of women's cultural entrepreneurship in the transnational market of nineteenth-century Spanish-language publishing, they also invite us to develop forms of cultural analysis that treat texts as practices and explore how they 'intersect with broader cultural processes in a particular historical moment and place'.[42]

---

[42] Jo Labanyi, 'Doing things: Emotion, affect, and materiality', *Journal of Spanish Cultural Studies*, 11.3–4 (2010), 223–233, p. 230.

15

Envisioning African-descent Confraternities in Early Nineteenth-century Lima, Peru

Helen Melling

This chapter considers the transnational transplantation of religious and cultural traditions of African origin to the New World as a result of the slave trade, and how these forms were maintained, adapted to and in turn shaped Creole religious and civic culture through Catholic lay confraternities. Black confraternities were transnational institutions that emerged in Latin America from the sixteenth century and persisted into the nineteenth century, in which members actively preserved and fostered prior ritual practices and traditions in syncretism with Catholic and secular practices; this can be conceived as an example of transculturation. By the nineteenth century, Black confraternities in Lima, Peru had evolved as semi-autonomous sites of religious and cultural expression, fulfilling a broad social role and civic function and demonstrating Black cultural agency. This chapter examines the public and private activities of these sodalities, and how aspects of their broader cultural legacy were visually encoded in pictorial narratives of early Republican Lima.

Present in the Viceroyalty of Peru from the moment of conquest in the sixteenth century, enslaved Africans fulfilled a number of indispensable roles within the colonial enterprise. They served as military auxiliaries alongside the Spanish conquistadors and as the builders of cities, and went on to supplement indigenous labour in the mines of the highlands. Peruvian slavery was a markedly urban and coastal phenomenon, however, with the largest demographic of enslaved and free Afrodescendants residing in the plantations, haciendas and private households of the coast and the capital, the primary sites settled by Spanish colonialists. As essential participants in colonial life, they ran much of Lima's daily business in occupations that traversed the private and public spheres – from domestic servants, to artisans, street vendors, water carriers and small business owners. This enforced geographical and cultural proximity meant that Peru's African-descent population played a crucial role in shaping the coastal culture that would later become the predominant, creole 'model' of integration and national identity after independence. As late as 1790, 46 per cent of Lima's inhabitants were of African descent,[1] and this population had long been formed into Catholic lay confraternities or religious sodalities by the time of Peruvian independence in 1826.

Confraternities were established institutions in the Iberian Peninsula[2] that subsequently made their way to colonial Latin America to facilitate the conversion of African and indigenous peoples to Roman Catholicism, as well as attend to the religious needs of Spanish immigrants. Each confraternity was dedicated to a specific patron saint or Marian devotion, and was typically based in and around local churches, hospitals and parishes. One of the primary activities of a confraternity was to celebrate their saint's day; this often involved dressing and decorating the image of their advocation, which would then be taken out for a procession or celebrated with masses and sermons. Beyond their religious functions, they also assumed a social role that was of crucial significance for enslaved and free Africans and their descendants in the New World. As mutual aid societies, they extended credit and advanced money for manumission, allowed members to care for the sick and bury their dead and they were fundamental to the building of new kinship networks, communities and collective identities. These organisations were at once Atlantic and local, with Black brotherhoods dating to as early as the 1400s in Iberian cities that received the largest number of enslaved Africans, such as Seville and Lisbon. In Latin America they emerged from

---

[1] Tanya Golash-Boza, *Yo Soy Negro: Blackness in Peru* (Gainesville, FL: University Press of Florida, 2011), p. 65. This chapter is based on a paper presented at the 'Border Subjects/Global Hispanisms Conference' organised by Birkbeck, University of London (Iberian and Latin American Studies) and the University of Pittsburgh (Department of Hispanic Studies), November 2017.

[2] For a historical context of the confraternity and its origins in the Iberian world, see Christopher F. Black & Pamela Gravestock, eds, *Early Modern Confraternities in Europe and the Americas: International and Interdisciplinary Perspectives* (Aldershot: Ashgate, 2006). On African-descent confraternities in colonial Lima, see Karen B. Graubart, '"So color de una cofradía": Catholic confraternities and the development of Afro-Peruvian ethnicities in early colonial Peru', *Slavery & Abolition*, 33.1 (2012); Tamara J. Walker, 'Queen of los Congos. Slavery, gender, and confraternity life in late colonial Lima, Peru', *Journal of Family History*, 40.3 (2015), 305–322; Ciro Corilla Melchor, 'Cofradias en la ciudad de Lima, siglos XVI y XVII: Racismo y conflictos etnicos', in *Etnicidad y discriminacion racial en la historia del Peru*, ed. by Elisa Dasso et al. (2002), pp. 11–34.

the sixteenth century onwards.[3] The first Black confraternities in Lima were founded within a decade of the conquest of Peru.[4]

While Black confraternities were conceived by the Roman Catholic Church and Spanish Crown as vehicles of social control and assimilation into the dominant culture, they became foundational spaces of Black socialisation and practices of subjectivity through the agency of their members.[5] More broadly, recent scholarship has productively examined transnational connections in how Africans[6] and their descendants in the Americas used Christianity and Christian-derived celebrations as spaces for autonomous cultural expression and social organisation,[7] alongside their fundamental contributions to Catholicism and its practices across the region. Confraternities provided Africans and their descendants with linguistic and cultural commonalities, promoted social prestige and mobility through leadership positions and were spaces in which they created their own expressions of Afro-Catholic devotion by adapting previously established ritual practices and religious beliefs to the New World context of enslavement. In the case of Brazil and Cuba in particular, confraternities were some of the most efficient incubators of Afro-Latin American ritual traditions.[8]

By the eighteenth century and early nineteenth, Black confraternities

---

[3] Patricia Mulvey and Barry Crouch provide a brief survey of these brotherhoods in 'Black solidarity: A comparative perspective on slave sodalities in Latin America', in *Manipulating the Saints: Religious Brotherhoods and Social Integration in Postconquest Latin America*, ed. by Albert Meyers and Diane Elizabeth Hopkins (Hamburg: Wayasbah, 1988), pp. 51–65.

[4] Corresponding with larger patterns of legal and social segregation in colonial society, confraternities in Latin America tended to be divided and organised according to ethnicity. Most African and indigenous members worshipped in ethnically specific confraternities in colonial Peru, as formerly flexible and multi-ethnic sodalities soon excluded their participation (Graubart, pp. 1–2).

[5] On Black confraternities in colonial Mexico as sites of social and cultural agency, see Miguel A. Valerio, 'Black confraternity members performing Afro-Christian identity in a Renaissance festival in Mexico City in 1539', *Confraternitas*, 29.1 (2018), 31–54; Nicole Von Germeten, *Black Blood Brothers: Confraternities and Social Mobility for Afro-Mexicans* (Gainesville, FL: University Press of Florida, 2006).

[6] For a discussion of the regional and ethnic origins of enslaved Africans in colonial Peru, please see pp. 286–287 (below).

[7] Cécile Fromont, ed., *Afro-Catholic Festivals in the Americas: Performance, Representation, and the Making of Black Atlantic Tradition* (University Park, Pennsylvania: Penn State University Press, 2019).

[8] Paul Christopher Johnson and Stephan Palmié, 'Afro-Latin American religions', in *Afro-Latin American Studies: An Introduction*, ed. by Alejandro de la Fuente and George Reid Andrews (Cambridge: Cambridge University Press, 2018), p. 443.

in Lima had evolved as semi-autonomous sites of religious and cultural expression, fulfilling a broad social role and civic function, and providing an environment in which members preserved and fostered their own traditions in syncretism with Catholic and secular practices. Alongside these activities, Afro-Peruvians and their confraternities had long been essential participants in Lima's public processions and occupied an institutionalised position in official, ceremonial performances of a creole religious identity. We can encounter glimpses of some of the public and private activities of these sodalities, and how aspects of their broader cultural legacy were visually encoded, in pictorial narratives of early Republican Lima, through the watercolours of the Afro-Peruvian artist Francisco 'Pancho' Fierro (1807–1879) and those of the French Vice-Consul and draftsman Léonce Angrand (1808–1866).[9]

This chapter forms part of a broader project that examines representations of Black subjects in Peruvian visual culture, from colonial travel accounts and classificatory projects of the Enlightenment, to *costumbrista* iconography, print culture and photographic portraiture of the nineteenth century. This vast and thematically expansive corpus constitutes a visual tradition in the portrayal of Afro-Peruvians, the heart of which is identified in the works of Fierro, Angrand and the German romantic painter Johann Moritz Rugendas (1802–1858).[10]

Costumbrismo was arguably the most significant literary and pictorial genre to emerge in nineteenth-century Peru. The depiction of local manners, types and customs played a foundational role throughout Latin America, in shaping regional and national identities in the aftermath of the wars of Independence. A self-taught watercolourist,[11] Fierro was the foremost

---

[9] For scholarship on representations of Afro-Catholic performance and festivals in the visual culture of the Portuguese-speaking Atlantic World see Cécile Fromont, 'Dancing for the king of Congo, from early modern central Africa to slavery-era Brazil', *Colonial Latin American Review*, 22.2 (2013), 184–208; 'Envisioning Brazil's Afro-Christian Congados: The black king and queen festival lithograph of Johann Moritz Rugendas', in *Afro-Catholic Festivals in the Americas: Performance, Representation, and the Making of Black Atlantic Tradition* (University Park, Pennsylvania: Penn State University Press, 2019), pp. 138–161.

[10] This research was funded by the Arts and Humanities Research Council, a Kluge fellowship at the Library of Congress and a post-doctoral stipendiary fellowship at the Institute of Latin American Studies, School of Advanced Study, London.

[11] Although much of Fierro's early life and education remains a mystery to researchers, he was born to an enslaved mother named María del Carmen in 1807. León y León suggests that his father was most likely Nicolás Mariano Rodríguez del Fierro y Robina, a creole vicar of noble ancestry and the brother of María del Carmen's enslaver. Fierro was manumitted on the day of his baptism in 1809, and León y León

illustrator of nineteenth-century Lima and the greatest exponent of Peruvian *costumbrismo*.[12] His vivid scenes of daily life capture the diversity of nineteenth-century Lima's multi-ethnic society, where Afro-descendants were key economic and cultural protagonists of the urban landscape.[13] Beyond his official duties as a diplomat, Angrand was an avid collector of archeological and ethnographic materials, in addition to being an artist in his own right. During his time in Lima in the 1830s, he produced a number of watercolours and sketches depicting composite street scenes and urban types that populated the city, in which Black subjects feature prominently.[14] A contemporary and collector of Fierro's watercolours, Angrand returned to France with an album of his works that currently resides in the Bibliotheque Nacionale in Paris; a hand-written note by Angrand that accompanies the album identifies and describes Fierro in terms that suggest they met during his time in Lima.[15] These *costumbrista* works invoke a transnational understanding of Lima's cultural identity, forged from interactions between local and foreign artists, and embedded in global networks of production, circulation and consumption.[16]

asserts that while he was never officially acknowledged or recognised by the del Fierro family, he was raised in their household. See Gustavo León y León, *Apuntes histórico-genealógicos de Francisco Fierro: Pancho Fierro* (Lima: Biblioteca Nacional del Perú, Fondo Editorial, 2004).

[12] Fierro's images have long enjoyed an iconic, patrimonial status in Peru. His prolific artistic production originated in the 1830s, resulting in a career that spanned almost five decades. For the most comprehensive scholarship of his work and of Peruvian *costumbrismo* as a whole, see Natalia Majluf, 'Convención y descripción: Francisco Pancho Fierro (1807–1879) y la formación del costumbrismo peruano', *Hueso húmero*, 39 (2001), 3–44; *Reproducing Nations: Types and Costumes in Asia and Latin America, ca. 1800–1860* (New York: Americas Society, 2006); Natalia Majluf Natalia and Marcus B. Burke, *Tipos del Perú: la Lima criolla de Pancho Fierro* (New York: Hispanic Society of America, 2008); Natalia Majluf, *La creación del costumbrismo: las acuarelas de la donación Juan Carlos Verme* (Lima: Museo de Arte de Lima, IFEA: Instituto Frances de Estudios Andinos, 2016).

[13] See Arrelucea and Cosamalón for an overview of the history and economic and cultural contributions of Afro-descendants in Peru. For the classic study of Peruvian slavery, see Frederick Browser, *The African Slave in Colonial Peru, 1524–1650* (Stanford: Stanford University Press, 1974).

[14] Carlos Milla Batres, *Imagen del Perú en el siglo XIX* (Lima: Milla Batres, 1972) remains the most comprehensive examination of Angrand's Peruvian oeuvre to date.

[15] Pascal Riviale, 'Entre lo pintoresco, el costumbrismo y la etnografía: relaciones e influencias recíprocas en las artes gráficas peruanas y francesas en el siglo XIX', *HISTOIRE(S) de l'Amérique latine*, 6 (2011), 1–53 (p. 15).

[16] For more on the relationship between local *costumbrismo* and traveller-artists in Peru, see Majluf (2008) and Riviale (2011).

Angrand depicts the ceremonial role of Afro-Peruvians and confraternity members as musicians and pallbearers alongside members of the religious orders and the clergy, featuring as key participants and Black emblems of the identity of the Creole Church. The appropriation and possession of public religious activities by African-descent confraternities reached its zenith in the dance *el son de los diablos* ('dance of the devils'), represented in a unique series of images by Fierro. Originating in the Corpus Christi processions of colonial Lima, its trajectory and eventual secularisation in Republican Peru is illustrative of the ways in which imposed religious and cultural norms were transformed by Afro-Peruvian confraternities, contested by the colonial authorities and went on to infiltrate collective expressions of a popular creole identity. Fierro's singular propensity to visualise the Black presence and experience extends to an exceptional and unacknowledged representation of some of the private rituals of Lima's Black sodalities in the context of indoor funeral practices. An examination of this imagery alongside travel accounts and historical analysis of the period reveals how African-descent confraternities and their legacy are envisioned through the iconography of early Republican Peru.

African-descent confraternities in colonial Lima were organised according to the different 'nations' or ethnic groups to which the enslaved were thought to belong. The eighteenth-century Creole enlightenment newspaper the *Mercurio Peruano* dedicates two essays to Lima's *bozal* confraternities (*bozal* was the term used to identify African-born, non-Hispanicised slaves) and in the first the author lists a number of these African 'nations', making reference to 'Terranovos', 'Mandingas' and 'Congos' among others.[17] It should be noted that such ethnicities were New World constructions that were frequently imposed by slave traders and administrators for the purpose of commercial and bureaucratic efficiency; the enslaved could therefore be grouped and identified according to a port of origin, or a region near their site of capture, for example (Graubart, pp. 2–3). However, Africans and their

---

[17] 'Idea de las congregaciones públicas de los negros bozales', 16 June 1791; 'Conclusión del rasgo sobre las congregaciones públicas de los negros bozales', 19 June 1791 in *Mercurio Peruano 1791–95* (12 vols), Facsimile edition (Lima: Biblioteca Nacional del Perú, 1964), II, no. 48 pp. 112–117; II, no. 49 pp. 120–125. Its creole contributors envisaged the newspaper as a means of promoting reforms from an enlightenment and proto-nationalist perspective; the cultural practices of Lima's African-descent population, and their proximity to elite creole society (most notably in the domestic sphere) are scrutinised and critiqued at length. For an examination of this discourse, see Mariselle Meléndez, 'Patria, Criollos and Blacks: Imagining the nation in the *Mercurio Peruano*, 1791–1795', *Colonial Latin American Review*, 15.2 (2006), 207–227.

descendants, both enslaved and free, adopted, reclaimed and redefined these markers of identity and belonging in the New World.[18] While the earliest enslaved populations arrived in Peru primarily from Guinea and Angola, and to a lesser extent, Biafra and Congo, by the eighteenth century they were also arriving from Mauritania, Sierra Leone, Senegal, Cabo Verde and Cameroon.[19] In contrast to the Cuban[20] and Brazilian contexts, the dilution of African ancestral practices alongside processes of cultural syncretism[21] impeded the preservation of any clearly identifiable religious practices derived from specific African regions and ethnicities, as argued by Peruvian historians Arrelucea and Cosamalón:

> Oshun, Yemaya, Elegua, Shango, Obatala son nombres extraños en el Perú. En cambio, son cotidianos en países como Cuba y Brasil que recibieron cientos de miles de africanos de las mismas etnias hasta bien avanzado el siglo XIX. En Perú, las religiones africanas fueron diluyéndose. (Oshun, Yemaya, Elegua, Shango, Obatala are uncommon names in Peru. In contrast, they are quotidian in Brazil and Cuba, countries that received hundreds of thousands of Africans of the same ethnicities until well into the 19th century. In Peru, however, African religious practices were diluted over time.) (Arrelucea and Cosamalón, p. 60)

---

[18] For an example of how historians of the African diaspora in Peru have productively examined these resignifications, see Rachel O'Toole, 'From the rivers of Guinea to the valleys of Peru: Becoming a Bran diaspora within Spanish slavery', *Social Text*, 92.3 (2007), 19–36.

[19] Maribel Arrelucea and Jesús Cosamalón, *La Presencia Afrodescendiente en el Perú, Siglos XVI – XX* (Lima: Ministerio de Cultura, 2015), pp. 36–38.

[20] The Cuban *naciones* or *cabildos* have been the subject of some of the most in-depth scholarship on African-descent confraternities in colonial and nineteenth-century Spanish America. See Elvira Antón-Carrillo, 'Los cabildos de nación', in *Un cambio de siglo 1898: España, Cuba, Puerto Rico, Filipinas y Estado Unidos*, ed. by José Girón Garrote (Oviedo: Universidad de Oviedo, 2008), pp. 267–272, and Philip Howard, *Changing History: Afro-Cuban Cabildos and Societies of Color in the Nineteenth Century* (Baton Rouge: Louisiana State University Press, 1998).

[21] For more on the related concept of *Transculturación* (transculturation), coined by the Cuban anthropologist Fernando Ortiz, see his *Contrapunteo cubano del tabaco y el azúcar* (Madrid: Cátedra, 2002 [1940]). Transculturation addresses the complex processes of linguistic, economic, racial and cultural exchange involved in the colonial and post-colonial encounter in the Americas. In contrast to acculturation, defined by one or more cultures being assimilating into a more powerful one, Ortiz instead conceives of this as a multi-directional process of exchange, resulting in the loss, transformation and production of new cultural forms.

The survival of African-descent sodalities in early Republican Lima can be primarily attributed to the endurance of slavery following Peru's independence, although their numbers by this stage represented a fraction of those that had existed in in the colonial period, heralding their decline and eventual disappearance by the late nineteenth century.[22] In spite of this, they continued to serve as a significant locus of socialisation and solidarity among the Afro-Peruvian population, and to play a role in the emancipation of slaves during the early years of the Republic. They operated as highly stratified bodies that incorporated positions of leadership and the possibility of social mobility for members, and this was most powerfully expressed through the practice of electing kings and queens.[23] Some members acquired such positions of status within these sodalities through their claims of royal African ancestry or lineage. The traveller W. B. Stevenson describes this tradition in 1825:

> I was well acquainted with a family in Lima, in which there was an old female slave, who had lived with them for upwards of fifty years, and who was the acknowledged Queen of the Mandingos, she being, according to their statement, a princess. On particular days she was conducted from the house of her master, by a number of black people, to the cofradía, dressed as gaudily as possible; for this purpose her young mistresses would lend her jewels to a considerable amount, besides which the poor old woman was bedizened with a profusion of artificial flowers, feathers and other ornaments. Her master had presented her with a silver sceptre, and this necessary appendage of royalty was on such occasions always carried by her.[24]

This public, ceremonial custom conveyed the social prestige of the queen and therefore of the confraternity as a whole through the display of elite attributes. Stevenson's account also reveals that in some cases these ranks were recognised and supported by slaveholders; the historian Christine Hunefeldt corroborates this, stating that 'this support often led owners to loan

---

[22] According to Forment, by the early 1840s Lima had about 20 confraternities remaining. Carlos A. Forment, *Democracy in Latin America, 1760–1900*, 2 vols (Chicago: University of Chicago Press, 2003), vol. I, p. 136.

[23] See Walker, 'Queen of los Congos', for a detailed examination of slavery, gender and African-descent confraternities in late colonial Lima.

[24] William Bennet Stevenson, *A Historical and Descriptive Narrative of Twenty Years' Residence in South America: Containing Travels in Arauco, Chile, Peru and Colombia*, 3 vols (London: Hurst, Robinson, 1825), vol. I, pp. 304–305.

clothes and jewels and to attend the ceremonies as spectators'.[25] Numerous contemporaneous accounts attest to the importance of exhibitions of prestige and status in both public and private expressions of religious devotion.[26] Differentiations of rank within these sodalities were visibly communicated through a range of material objects and attributes, and musical practices were significant markers of spiritual values, as well as individual and collective cultural identities.

Religious processions in colonial Lima counted with the significant presence and participation of Afro-Peruvians and confraternity members as worshippers, pallbearers, musicians and dancers. Their frequent location at the forefront of processions made them a highly visible component of these spectacles, which tended to follow a rigid hierarchical order and often began with those of the lowest rank in society.[27] This continued to be the case in the early Republican period, and their participation in processions such as Corpus Christi and Holy Week was prominent, as noted by both Peruvian writers and foreign observers.[28] Angrand provides glimpses of this presence in which Black subjects can, on the one hand, be seen to operate as a form of symbolic capital in the service of the Church. However, they are also indicative of the institutionalised role of Black participants in these events and consequently in shaping Lima's distinct religious and cultural identity. Figure 1 depicts a group of clergymen accompanied by four elegantly attired confraternity members engaged in preparations prior to the procession.

---

[25] Christine Hünefeldt, *Paying the Price of Freedom: Family and Labor among Lima's Slaves, 1800 – 1854* (Berkeley, CA: University of California Press, 1994), p. 101.

[26] For examples, see Stevenson, vol. I, pp. 304–305; J. J. Von Tschudi, *Travels in Peru*. Translated from the German by Thomasina Ross (New York: A.S. Barnes and Co, 1854), p. 78; William Ruschenberger, *Three Years in the Pacific; Including notices of Brazil, Chile, Bolivia, and Peru*, 2 vols (London: Richard Bentley, 1835), vol. II, pp. 38–39.

[27] Roberto Rivas Aliaga, 'Danzantes negros en el Corpus Christi de Lima, 1756 "Vos Estis Corpus Christi" (1 Cor. XII, 27)', in *Etnicidad y discriminación racial en la historia del Perú*, Tomo I, ed. by Ana Carrillo et al. (Lima: PUCP-IRA, Banco Mundial, 2003), pp. 35–64 (p. 48).

[28] As one of the most significant Black contributions to Peru's religious, and even national, identity, it is striking that the procession of *El Señor de los Milagros* does not feature in the iconography of the nineteenth century. However, this African-descent devotion, dedicated to a miraculous image of Christ painted by an Angolan slave in seventeenth-century Lima, only came to be appropriated and nationalised by Limeño elites at the end of the nineteenth century and beginning of the twentieth. See Julia Costilla, 'Una práctica negra que ha ganado a los blancos: símbolo, historia y devotos en el culto al Señor de los Milagros de Lima (siglos XIX-XXI)', *Anthropológica*, 34.36 (2016), 150–176.

Figure 1. *Hermandad de una cofradía portando la cera de la procesión.* Léonce Angrand, 1837. Courtesy of the Bibliothèque Nationale de France.

Dressed in matching uniforms, two of the members transport a large chest balanced on their heads, containing candles. The other two figures wear long black cloaks and can be seen collecting large, thin, tapered candles for use in the procession or within the Church itself.

Black subjects are fully integrated into the pageantry of such events in Figure 2, in which they transport a statue or painting of the Virgin, festooned with flowers, which is led or 'announced' by two musicians at the head of the group. The more informal and rudimentary attire of the figures here is notable – three of the figures wear headscarves,[29] while some of them appear to be barefoot; their long coats with gold trim, however, are reminiscent of those in Figure 1. Afro-Peruvian pallbearers are also portrayed in Figure 3, a work recently acquired as part of a *costumbrista* collection by the Museo de Arte de Lima, and that has been attributed to the Ecuadorean artist Francisco

---

[29] Headscarves feature as a recurring attribute in the visual depiction of Afro-descendants, especially of women of African-descent in Peru, from the late colonial period onwards. This is most notable in the representation of street and market vendors in nineteenth-century *costumbrista* iconography.

Figure 2. *Negros y frailes llevando las andas de Nuestra Señora de los Incurables*. Léonce Angrand, 1837. Courtesy of the Bibliothèque Nationale de France.

Javier Cortés (1775–1839). Based in Lima, Cortés was an important predecessor of both Fierro and of Peruvian *costumbrismo* as a whole.[30] Here, the long coats with gold trim are highly redolent of those featured in Angrand's scenes; two of the figures at the front appear to be bearing a box or chest of sorts, perhaps also containing candles for the procession or Church ceremony as in Figure 1. They are accompanied by an elegantly attired *sahumadora* or incense-burner, a role overwhelmingly associated with Afro-descended women in nineteenth-century Lima, and a motif that features prominently in the *costumbrista* iconographic production of the period.[31] Alongside his depiction

---

[30] Cortés was chair in botanical drawing at the Medical College of San Fernando in Lima, and a painter and illustrator who participated in some of the most important scientific expeditions of the late colonial period. For more on Cortés, see Majluf (2001, 2006, 2016). Afro-Peruvians also feature in the procession depicted in Fierro's expansive Holy Week Scroll, housed at the Hispanic Society of America, and reproduced in Majluf (2008, 2016).

[31] They accompanied religious processions while burning incense as a means of purification prior to entering the Church and were another staple presence of these religious spectacles.

of three African-descent *sahumadoras*, Angrand notes that many of these women were known to be slaves or servants of wealthy, aristocratic families, and were dressed in clothing and jewelry belonging to their 'mistresses' for such occasions.[32] In this way, they functioned as Black symbolic capital not only for their enslavers and for the Church itself, but also as signifiers of Lima's religious and cultural identity in the public realm.[33]

What is not readily apparent in these scenes, however, is the potentially subversive role of Black festive practices in a public, religious context. Their potential to effectively hijack public expressions of devotion of the Catholic Creole church is epitomised by the Afro-Peruvian dance *el son de los diablos*.[34] Believed to originate from the Corpus Christi processions and morality dramas of colonial Lima, the most significant representation of this tradition in the Republican period is provided in a unique series of images by Fierro. Religious processions such as Corpus Christi were organised according to a rigid hierarchical order that began with the lowest ranking sectors of society. In colonial Lima, African-descent confraternities largely fulfilled this role as they outnumbered the indigenous population in the city and therefore represented the key subaltern presence in these celebrations. Afro-Peruvian dancers and musicians led the procession, dressed as devils and grotesque figures known as *mojigangas* or *invenciones*, representing the evil that had been triumphantly conquered by Christ and the Church (Rivas, pp. 43–44). Conversely, however, these practices also provided a public platform of

---

[32] 'Mujeres negras o mulatas en atavío de fiesta, criadas o antiguas esclavas de señoras de la ciudad, adornadas por sus amas con sus propias joyas y sus más bellos chales, acompañando las grandes procesiones, caminando delante del palio y quemando perfumes o llevando bandejas de mistura enviadas como ofrenda a la iglesia. Se han visto a veces, de esas mujeres, hasta cincuenta reunidas', Milla Batres, p. 144.

[33] The visual approximation of the enslaved with slaveholder was a symbolic activity that to some observers established an alarming similarity between women of diametrically opposed social conditions. In effect, both parties had interests in perpetuating these opulent displays, and, as Walker reveals, some slaves in colonial Lima gained access to luxury goods as signifiers of their own status, identity and self-fashioning. See Tamara Walker, *Exquisite Slaves: Race, Status and Clothing in Colonial Lima* (Cambridge: Cambridge University Press, 2017).

[34] See Heidi Carolyn Feldman, *Black Rhythms of Peru: Reviving African Musical Heritage in the Black Pacific* (Middletown, CT: Wesleyan University Press, 2006), pp. 32–47 for a discussion of the role of *el son de los diablos* and Fierro's representations of the dance, as part of the Afro-Peruvian revival of the 1940s and 1950s, led by creole intellectuals such as José Durand and motivated by a creole nostalgia for 'una Lima que se fue'.

Figure 3. *Procesión*. Francisco Javier Cortés, ca. 1827–1838. Acuarela y témpera sobre papel 24 x 19.10 cm. Courtesy of the Museo de Arte de Lima Donación Juan Carlos Verme. Fotografía: Daniel Giannoni. Archi, Archivo Digital de Arte Peruano.

cultural expression for Afro-Peruvians – an opportunity to foreground and exhibit the stratification, status and prestige of their sodalities.

The colonial authorities displayed a fraught and highly paradoxical attitude towards the incorporation of Black confraternities within public religious festivities; while these exhibitions of 'difference' were an essential symbolic component of these events, the extent of this alterity was regarded as deeply unsettling. As Raúl Romero affirms, the seventeenth and eighteenth centuries were characterised by 'numerous attempts to repress the black slaves' cultural expressions in the fiestas of Lima, through explicit prohibitions from the municipality and the Church'.[35] The persecution and repression of Black music in colonial Spanish America was an expression of the fundamental hierarchies that operated within processes of cultural syncretism. The ambivalent fascination of the creole elite with Black musical traditions, however, compounded these repeated efforts to limit transgressive public displays of Black musical expression, subjectivity and identity. Paradoxically, not only were Afro-Peruvians the preferred dance teachers of high society,[36] but the creole elite were also known to participate in their music and dance practices as spectators, as per Robert Proctor's testimony in 1825:

> I have seen what were considered respectable women looking on and enjoying these gross exhibitions. I was informed that even the haughty viceroys, in the times of their prosperity in Lima, had been known to attend them in disguise.[37]

El son de los diablos was eventually banned altogether from being performed in conjunction with religious celebrations by the Church in 1817, however the dance continued to enjoy a broad public platform in the unregulated sphere of carnival celebrations.[38] In the largest portrayal of the dance (Figure 4), the scene is dominated by three figures wearing large evil masks and elaborate costumes.[39] They are accompanied by a group of musicians playing percussive instruments that are hallmarks of the genre and of Afro-Peruvian origin. A trio of musicians is depicted playing the *quijada* – the jawbone of a donkey, horse or mule that is struck and rattled with a mallet or stick, while on the

---

[35] Raúl R. Romero, 'Black music and identity in Peru: Reconstruction and revival of Afro-Peruvian musical traditions', in *Music and Black Ethnicity: The Caribbean and South America*, ed. by Gerard H Béhague (University of Miami: North-South Center, 1992), pp. 307–327 (p. 312).

[36] Juan Carlos Estenssoro Fuchs, 'Música y comportamiento festivo de la población negra en Lima Colonial', *Cuadernos Hispanoamericanos*, 451–452 (1988), 161–168 (p. 165).

[37] Robert Proctor, *Narrative of a Journey Across the Cordillera of Andes, and of a Residence in Lima, and Other Parts of Peru, in the Years 1823 and 1824* (London: Hurst, Robinson and Co, 1825), p. 238.

[38] William Tompkins, 'Afro-Peruvian traditions', in *Handbook of Latin American Music*, ed. by Dale Olsen and Daniel Sheehy, 2nd edn (New York: Routledge, 2008), p. 478.

[39] This large scene would appear to be two separate images joined together. My thanks to Natalia Majluf for bringing this to my attention. It is featured in Manuel Cisneros Sánchez, *Pancho Fierro y la Lima del 800* (Lima: Importadora, Exportadora y Librería García Ribeyro, 1975) but its current whereabouts is unknown.

Figure 4. *Danzando al son de los diablos*. Francisco 'Pancho' Fierro, undated (Cisneros Sánchez: 1975: 5).

left a figure plays the *cajita*, a small wooden box with a hinged lid, often suspended from the player's neck by a rope, that is struck and rattled with a stick (Feldman, p. 32). Two additional musicians can also be seen playing the harp and the guitar. This combination of instruments illustrates the effects of cultural syncretism or what Romero describes as the 'creolization' of coastal musical traditions in Peru, which intensified in the nineteenth century (Romero, p. 313). A selection of smaller images depicting the dance provides further examples of this; the inclusion of a harp (Figures 4 and 6) points to the possible influence of Andean music, and both scenes also feature multi-ethnic groups of musicians. The outline of a sizeable group of spectators can be made out in Figure 4, suggesting the popular appeal the performance wielded in Lima and the recognition accorded to these performers by Limeño society, and this is reinforced in Figure 5, which also includes a member of the clergy among the crowd.

While *el son de los diablos* was eventually limited to secular events and the context of carnival, contemporaneous travel accounts suggest that this ban was perhaps not wholly successful in its implementation. African-descent confraternities continued to participate in religious festivities in the early nineteenth century, and, in doing so, the vibrant costumes, dances and distinctive instruments typically associated with *el son de los diablos* remained a feature of their processions. William Ruschenberger's description of their displays in the Corpus Christi celebrations of 1835 sheds further light:

> All the tribes assemble and form a procession... they are accompanied by noisy and disagreeably toned instruments.... there is scarcely a procession in Lima, whether civic, religious or military, in which

Figure 5. *Sigue el son de los diablos* (1830). Francisco 'Pancho' Fierro, undated. Courtesy of the Pinacoteca Municipal 'Ignacio Merino' de la Municipalidad de Lima.

> some of these instruments are not seen, and... heard...The Negroes... dress and decorate themselves in a most grotesque manner; some paint their faces with various colours, and others resemble so many fiends from another world. (Ruschenberger, vol. II, pp. 38–39)

His observation regarding the ubiquity of Afro-Peruvian instruments and musicians in public events is particularly noteworthy. Described as a staple feature of all of the city's public processions 'whether civic, religious or military', this is a striking indication of the widespread prominence and penetration of Black musical practices within official, institutionalised public

Figure 6. *El son de los diablos*. Francisco 'Pancho' Fierro, undated. Courtesy of the Pinacoteca Municipal 'Ignacio Merino' de la Municipalidad de Lima.

events in the city. This testimony attests to the popularity, influence and dissemination of African-descent traditions as a key element of nineteenth-century Limeño religious and civic culture.

Figure 7 provides a compelling, private counterpoint to depictions of the public participation and pageantry of Afro-Peruvians and confraternity members in Lima's religious and civic processions. This large watercolour forms part of a collection of Peruvian *costumbrista* works housed at the Yale Art Gallery.[40]

[40] It is believed that Hiram Bingham bought the collection in Paris in 1913. For more information see Riviale and Majluf (2016).

Figure 7. *The Interior of an Inn*. Francisco 'Pancho' Fierro, ca. 1832–1841. Courtesy of the Yale University Art Gallery, Donation of the Bingham Family.

While the itinerary identifies this scene as 'The interior of an inn', the pictorial evidence coupled with textual accounts of the period suggest that this may in fact be a representation of a wake held by an Afro-Peruvian confraternity. A closer examination of the central altarpiece and surrounding figures reveals striking similarities with a later image by Fierro (Figure 8). All confraternity members, irrespective of their own means, wealth and legal status, were guaranteed a dignified funeral upon their death, including a mass, music and candles. The costs for this were assumed by the sodality via a fund set aside for this purpose, and that was accumulated from the quotas or contributions paid by members. While Figure 8 does not include any signs of music, a number of instruments are prominently located on the floor of Figure 7.[41] On the left, a seated man holds a bottle and offers a glass to his neighbour, while the male figure on the far left can be seen smoking a pipe, elements that may account for the image's title as the 'Interior of an Inn' within the Yale art gallery inventory.[42] Signs of alcohol consumption are also identifiable in Figure 8, in which several empty bottles litter the floor. The role of music, dancing and alcohol within these sodalities was prominent, and these were an important feature in both religious and social contexts. They were central markers of a confraternity's prestige and status as an institution and a collective, and for individual members as demonstrated by their role in recognising and commemorating the deceased.[43]

The centrality and prominence of the two women dressed in black and seated at the front in both scenes is striking; they may be relatives or indeed

---

[41] According to the ethnomusicologist William Tompkins (p. 475), sodalities played a major role in the preservation of African-descent musical traditions in Peru. The instruments here are highly reminiscent of those included in the Black civic processions depicted by Fierro. See *Acuarelas de Pancho Fierro y Seguidores: Colección Ricardo Palma* (Lima: Municipalidad Metropolitana de Lima, 2007).

[42] Fierro did not date, sign or give titles to any of his works; these were typically added by traders, or by those who purchased and collected them, producing a diverse interweaving of visual and textual discourses that at times are unclear, puzzling or even contradictory. Foundational literary figures of the *criollo* tradition were among the earliest admirers and commentators of Fierro's work; Ricardo Palma, Peru's literary giant of the nineteenth century, annotated the most well-known portion of Fierro's repertoire, providing titles, dates and in some cases brief comments and descriptions. See *Acuarelas de Pancho Fierro y Seguidores: Colección Ricardo Palma* (Lima: Municipalidad Metropolitana de Lima, 2007).

[43] In his study of medicine in colonial Peru, Warren cites several accounts, including the *Mercurio Peruano*, that describe the sharing of aguardiente as part of their burial and wake rituals, in which a cup would be offered to the deceased, before being passed around to other confraternity members in a specific order. See Adam Warren, *Medicine and Politics in Colonial Peru: Population Growth and the Bourbon Reforms* (Pittsburgh: University of Pittsburgh Press, 2010), pp. 171–172.

widows of the deceased. Warren observes that African-descent sodalities in Lima included extended periods of ritualised grief for widows under the brotherhood's supervision, thereby pointing to the significance of mourning as an external, performative ritual that reinforced kinship ties. The gathering appears to be somewhat spatially divided according to gender; women entirely occupy the right-hand side of the room, with men confined to the left, with the exception of a seated female figure, contributing to the impression of an organised, ceremonial event. The range of clothing and attributes on display denotes gradations of socio-economic status and possibly of rank among members of this organisation. The men in particular show a range of sartorial habits, from ponchos to the formal, full-length coat of the central male figure by the altar.

The presence of two large paintings on the walls corresponds with several accounts that highlight secular murals and frescos as a significant feature of African-descent confraternities in Lima. This is first identified in the late colonial period, in an article from the *Mercurio Peruano*, in which the writer states that 'todas las paredes de sus quartos, especialmente las interiores, están pintadas con unos figurones que representan sus Reyes originarios, sus batallas y sus regocijos' ('the walls of their confraternities, especially the interiors, are painted with figures that represent their original Kings, their battles and their triumphs').[44] Several travel accounts from the early Republican period also describe the walls decorated with images of African Kings, animals and scenes of battles, and provide tantalising glimpses of Black confraternities as sites of collective ancestral memory. W. B. Stevenson refers to their walls as 'ornamented with likeness in fresco of the different royal personages who have belonged to them' (vol. I, p. 306). Jacob Von Tschudi concurs with his observation, stating that 'the walls of the rooms are painted with grotesque figures of negro kings, elephants, camels, palm trees' (Von Tschudi, p. 78). These paintings portray dark-hued figures of evident wealth and status, but they are a far cry from Von Tschudi's exoticised visions of African royalty. Instead, they appear to be dressed in military uniforms and clothing typical of the early Republican period. The inclusion of small numbers and letters alongside the instruments and several of the figures suggests that a key was produced to identify different pictorial elements, a key that has sadly been lost. The size and unique subject matter of this piece make it all the more intriguing in terms of its deviation from the norms and typical characteristics of *Panchofierrista* images.[45]

---

[44] *Mercurio Peruano 1791–95* (12 vols.), Facsimile edition (Lima: Biblioteca Nacional del Perú, 1964), vol. II, no. 49, pp. 120–125.

[45] The repetition of models via a standardised format is a key hallmark of the subgenre of 'types and customs' within the *costumbrista* tradition. This format

Figure 8. *Duelo por el difunto.* Francisco 'Pancho' Fierro. Courtesy of the Pinacoteca Municipal 'Ignacio Merino' de la Municipalidad de Lima.

Confraternities were a fading institution in Peru, a remnant of the colonial past surviving in the early Republican present and, in this respect, Fierro's depiction is perhaps not so atypical as it may seem; it ties in to some of the broader aims of the *costumbrista* genre, not only to portray local types and customs, but

typically consists of a single figure portrayed on a white background in a decontextualised setting, and makes up the largest portion of Fierro's repertoire, although he also produced a lesser number of composite scenes, such as those depicting *el son de los diablos*.

in particular those that were disappearing with the onset of modernisation. Its significance is heightened by the fact that it is one of very few nineteenth-century images that represent some of the autonomous, private cultural and religious practices of Afro-Peruvians, outside of and beyond the shared public spaces and environments of Lima. Many questions remain, however, not least as to the origin of this image; might it have been specifically commissioned and if so by whom?[46] And is Figure 8 inspired in part by this earlier watercolour? The musical instruments on display in Figure 7 are very reminiscent of those featured in Fierro's renderings of Black civic processions, which Ricardo Palma attributes to their confraternities in his textual commentary.[47] As a whole, the ambivalences embedded in this imagery are indicative of the ways in which foundational *costumbrismos* were critically unstable sites of signification – in this case, suggesting how a hegemonic creole religious and cultural identity in nineteenth-century Lima was shaped by and contingent on Afro-Peruvian spaces and practices of subjectivity as enshrined in their confraternities.

[46] Figure 7 is dated 1832–1841 and was therefore produced during the earlier part of Fierro's career. Majluf highlights the larger narrative scenes and vistas of the city from the same collection acquired by the French diplomat Chaumette des Fossés, noting that these pictorial themes do not resurface in other early collections, suggesting that they may have been specifically commissioned. See Majluf, *La creación del costumbrismo*, p. 12.

[47] Figure 8 and Fierro's scenes of Black civic processions are part of a large collection originally commissioned by the Peruvian historian Agustín de la Rosa Toro and that dates from the later portion of Fierro's career. This collection was bequeathed to Ricardo Palma and is housed at the Pinacoteca Municipal Ignacio Merino in Lima.

16

Dominican *Trans*

Frank Báez's Global Poetics

Conrad James

Compared to that of its counterparts in the Spanish Caribbean, Dominican literary production languished in relative obscurity until very late into the twentieth century. Although the reasons for this lack of global visibility were complicated and multi-faceted, the Trujillo dictatorship and its stringent policing of both creative conception and output are often cited as principally significant in this respect. As a result, prevailing critical discourse on Dominican literature continues to engage its putative parochialism. Another obsessive focal point of criticism has been the dictatorship and its perpetrated atrocities (political, social, epistemological, psychological and sexual). This critical approach has, of course, yielded and continues to yield highly fruitful understandings of Dominican society and its cultural output. And, in fact, there remains a great deal of the textualities of Dominican isolation and domination that have not yet even begun to be addressed. However, Dominican literature has also always been nourished by and contributed to wider regional, hemispheric and global imperatives. This was the case even during the *Trujillato*.[1] Today, the literature produced by several young Dominican writers constitutes crucial participation in a number of important global conversations that place contemporary Dominican literature in a central position within highly interconnected transnational geographies. This literature showcases Santo Domingo as a global city that is engaged in a variety of North–South and South–South conversations.[2] The work of Frank

---

[1] The *Trujillato* is the hard-line dictatorship of Rafael Trujillo that lasted from 1930 until his assassination in 1961.

[2] Writers such as Rita Indiana Hernández, Rey Andújar and Juan Dicent are also key players in the production of a global Dominican discourse.

Báez typifies this trend. For Báez, the poetic text is necessarily a transnational product that is engendered in and continues to remake itself through dialogue with spaces, feelings, motivations and politics from around the world. This essay explores some of the suggestions inherent in his trans-migratory poetic practice. In the process it engages with scholarship on Dominican transnationalism and concludes with brief reflections on related arguments concerning the discourse on transgender migrations. The term *trans*, in my title, therefore, is activated for its potential to indicate crossings and disruptions of geographical and national boundaries. But it is also deployed to point to the productive traversing of the corporeal and psycho-social territories that constitute gender.

In 1949 Pedro Mir, the most celebrated Dominican poet of the twentieth century, famously (un)veiled his country to the world in a piercing lament.[3] 'Hay un país en el mundo' ('There is a country in the world') served as an occasion for Mir to expose and explore the multiply exploitative dynamics of Dominican history in a diachronic context.[4] In this landmark poem, histories of numerous invasions, inversions, enforced silencing, dictatorship and fraud render the country 'improbable' – 'país inverosímil' ('unlikely, improbable country'). The horrors of the past, as well as the immediate temporal referent in 1949, the Trujillo dictatorship, led Mir to make the ultimate denunciation. Not only is the country improbable but it does not even deserve to be called a country: 'Éste es un país que no merece el nombre de país' ('This is a country that is not worthy of being called a country'). It is instead better conceived of as 'tumba', 'féretro', 'hueco o sepultura' ('tomb', 'coffin', 'hole', 'grave'). In his reading of 'Hay un país en el mundo' Silvio Torres-Saillant comments on the 'sociohistorical weight that the poem places on the geography of the country connecting it with colonialist histories of oppression' (*Caribbean Poetics*, p. 234). What is even more significant about the construction of the national terrain are the incongruities that are thrown up between a felicitous geography and a spiteful, destructive political history that condemns the average citizen to the status of hapless victim. The country is located 'en el mismo trayecto del sol' ('right in the sun's path'). It is fruitful, fluvial and material. But it is also synonymous with the violation of the defenceless. Even though the country has vast expanses of arable land, its farmers die penniless and de-territorialised. Mir's poem calls up questions of tropical desire and of death in the tropics. It mourns the destruction of primordial,

---

[3] In 1982 the Dominican Congress conferred on him the title of National Poet. Silvio Torres-Saillant, *Caribbean Poetics: Towards an Aesthetics of West Indian Literature* (Cambridge: Cambridge University Press, 1997), p. 213.

[4] Pedro Mir, *Hay un país en el mundo y otros poemas* (Santo Domingo: Taller, 1982).

pre-Columbian and pre-capitalist glories but also constructs a future of egalitarianism and respect for the worker, the poor, the violated and the abused. Mir's poem, with its emphasis on the imperialist capitalist effects on Dominican society serves as an ideal laboratory to test all the premises out of which the country's current (twenty-first century) economic crisis has emerged.

As a literary occasion that opens up some of the horrors of the Dominican Republic to the world, 'Hay un país en el mundo', Mir's mid-twentieth-century poetic condemnation of national history, curiously anticipates some of the transnational dialogues that will feature as key motifs in Dominican narratives of this century. While it is correct, as Maja Horn has noted, that Frank Báez and others of his generation, such as Homero Pumarol, Rita Indiana Hernández and Juan Dicent, abandon the exploration of an oppressive political past in favour of the travails of the immediate present, it is also correct that the politics of representation of the past weigh heavily on the interpretative lenses that we bring to the work produced by this generation.[5] It is also possible to read the focus on the immediate present as a revisiting of older crises but with new narrative solutions. In the case of Frank Báez, direct dialogues with the key texts and textual preoccupations of Pedro Mir show twentieth-century Dominican poetic texts as routes through which the twenty-first century transnational poetic imagination is fostered. A quintessential transnational exilic product, 'Hay un país en el mundo' like Mir's other major work 'Contracanto a Walt Whitman' ('Countersong to Walt Whitman'), is written, published and circulated while he is living in exile in Cuba. While focusing on specifically national concerns it brings together many of the social and political histories that are core catalysts for transnational and trans-media movement and creativity.

Dominican Transnationalism

If we accept Lorgia García Peña's idea of *Dominicanidad* as 'a category that emerges out of historical events that placed the Dominican Republic in a geographical and symbolic border between the United States and Haiti since 1844' then transnational conflicts, contests and 'contra*dictions*', in the words of García Peña, are at the core of the nation's conception.[6] Dominican Transnationalism has developed as a significant field of study since the

---

[5] Maja Horn, *Masculinity after Trujillo: The Politics of Gender in Dominican Literature* (Gainesville, FL: University Press of Florida, 2014), p. 126.
[6] Lorgia García Peña *The Borders of Dominicanidad: Race, Nation and Archives of Contradiction* (Durham, NC: Duke University Press, 2016), p. 3.

1990s. Developing mainly in response to the mass migration of Dominicans to the USA (in particular New York) scholarship on Dominican transnationalism engages questions of exile, diaspora, migration, citizenship, belonging and the politics of naming. Jorge Duany observes that, unlike Cuba, the Dominican Republic has been seen as the 'prototype' of transnationalism and he affirms that it is now a 'full-fledged transnational nation-state' incorporating its diaspora far more than any other Spanish Caribbean territory.[7] Dominican transnationalism is also a highly contested field. There is no consensus as to whether Dominican migrants are transnational or diasporic subjects. Diaspora, migration and exile are accorded competing claims as to their validity to name the specific circumstances of Dominicans who find themselves off the island. Similarly, a proliferation of terms, loaded with varying degrees of disparagement and reclaimed to varying degrees manifest, in linguistic terms, the tensions surrounding the place that the Dominican abroad occupies in the national imaginary.[8]

In this regard, literary production and literary criticism have been indispensable in redrafting what Danny Méndez refers to as 'the normative coordinates of the Dominican national space'.[9] Since the 1990s Dominican voices in English emanating from the US have not only raised the profile of the nation's history on a global scale but have also productively interrogated its official ideologies of belonging along lines of race, space, class, gender and sexuality. Josefina Báez's performance piece *Dominicanish* is a case in point.[10] A playful and provocative text, it also engages with identity politics in highly combative terms. Josefina, the voice in the performance piece, rejects all fixed doctrines of cultural identity. Being Dominican does not respond to any precise formula. And while the text implicitly claims the deprecated affiliation of Dominican Yorkness, that identifying marker is also articulated as a mutable, unstable and shifting concept. And the text further disrupts the discourse on Dominican cultural ethnicity through its historical and stylistic engagement with India. All boundaries are destabilised in *Dominicanish*. Language is both fluid and deceptively recalcitrant.

---

[7] Jorge Duany, *Blurred Borders: Transnational Migration between the Hispanic Caribbean and the United States* (Charlottesville, NC: University of North Carolina Press, 2011), p. 170.

[8] García Peña prefers to use the term *Dominicano ausente*, 'absent Dominican', to refer to Dominicans in the diaspora. This designation, for her, neutralises the race and class prejudices that inhere in the term Dominican York, pp. 170–202.

[9] Danny Méndez, *Narratives of Migration and Displacement in Dominican Literature* (London: Routledge, 2012), p. 146.

[10] Josefina Báez, *Dominicanish: A Performance Text* (New York: Josefina Báez, 2000). Josefina Báez is not related to Frank Báez.

Race simultaneously includes and excludes. Home is both present and absent. Belonging constitutes both private and public performances that are at once quotidian and transcendental acts. Hence, from the space of diaspora the poetic voice declares 'Aquí también los pantis se tienden en el baño' ('Here too your knickers are hung out to dry in the bathroom', p. 7) and 'Home is where theatre is' (p. 42).

Frank Báez: Poetic Border Crossings

As Duany correctly observes, despite the criticism of its detractors, transnationalism has proved a 'resilient paradigm to understand Dominican migration' (*Blurred Borders*, p. 172). With the consolidation of scholarship on the Dominican diaspora in the USA developing well apace more and more opportunities are presenting themselves for Dominican transnationalism to be explored from other sites such as through the expanding communities of Dominicans in Europe.[11] But we can also learn a great deal about how ideas and cultural goods circulate in the Dominican diaspora through examining texts that activate the transnational imagination from the vantage point not of diaspora but from the contested site of 'home'. I turn to Frank Báez's work to tease out elements of a transnational literary practice articulated from a non-immigrant perspective. A transnational imagination does not require physical displacement to flourish. The transnational, after all, 'can occur in national, local or global spaces across different spatialities and temporalities'.[12] Reading Frank Báez throws light on the location of the Dominican Republic, and the Caribbean in general, as a global nexus in which multiple cultural and political influences cohere in ways that produce various forms of exchange and facilitate a multi-focality of experience and creativity. Approaching Báez from this perspective also draws attention to the far-reaching effect that transnationalism has had on collective identities in the Spanish Caribbean (*Blurred Borders*, p. 33).

Like Mir before him, Frank Báez constructs transnationalism by focusing on the direct vicissitudes of life in the Dominican Republic that force Dominicans into exile. His texts highlight the politics of yearning, yearning to escape, the impossibility of escape and the harrowing consequences whether

---

[11] The growing presence of Dominicans in major European cities such as Madrid, Berlin and London is being accompanied by highly visible community organisation and cultural production. In order for twenty-first century Dominican transnationalism to be fully understood these sites of movement must be studied more rigorously.

[12] François Lionnet, *Minor Transnationalism* (Durham, NC: Duke University Press, 2005), p. 6.

one succeeds or fails in the quest to escape. Many of his poems narrate a fractured society, broken human beings and a social structure that punishes the weak and reinforces their marginalisation. This is very similar to what is accomplished in the oeuvre of his contemporary, Rita India Hernández, from her debut novel, *La estrategia de Chochueca* to *La mucama de Omincunlé*.[13] What might be called Báez's social poetry excoriates local and national prejudices as expressed by society's economic and cultural elites.[14] Báez also employs a wide range of poetic strategies to challenge hypocrisy at all levels of society. Humour, irony and sarcasm are all marshalled to assuage the social cruelty that is the subject and meaning of many of his poems. Much of his poetry is hilarious and the comedic value is inflated significantly in performance.

However, the hilarity is almost always just a vehicle to communicate painful and embarrassing truths about the nation. This is humour in all seriousness that at various points censures the North American inspired consumerist ethos of Dominican society that is inextricably linked with criminality and various forms of anti-social behaviour. For example, 'Devuélvanle la mackbook a mi hermana' ('Give back my sister's MacBook') expresses humour that also challenges the capitalist models of cultural development in the Dominican Republic. In 'La industria cinematográfica cubana' ('The Cuban film industry') the speaker is tasked with writing a script for the booming film industry but fails repeatedly, only managing to produce poems. There is no space for his 'non-commercial creativity' and he declares that, but not before pointing to a different possibility of creativity and a different ethics of cinema making through evoking the Cuban film industry.

Báez's poetry extends outwards beyond the geographical, historical, political and cultural borders of the Dominican Republic in order to explore and better understand that society as home. This poetic practice is particularly well-placed to engage the questions of marginality and displacement that serve as its focus. Like several of his contemporaries, Báez's cultivation of a spoken word tradition places him outside of the official *ciudad letrada* ('city of letters') that was associated with the Dominican national project both during the *Trujillato* and its aftermath.[15] Looking beyond the national

---

[13] Rita Indiana Hernández, *La estrategia de Chochueca* (San Juan: Editoriales Isla Negra, 2003); *La mucama de Omicunlé* (Madrid: Editorial Periférica, 2015).

[14] Báez's poetry also has a deeply introspective strand that focuses on self, the poet and the nature of poetry.

[15] It is possible to see the various spoken word collectives and video art groups, among others, operating within the Dominican Republic as constituting a kind of 'cultural diaspora' within the home nation.

borders facilitates the process of looking within and of making diagnoses of the country's problems even if the texts themselves refuse to be prescriptive in offering modes of curing those ills. Dialogues with Walt Whitman, the invocation of Pedro Mir, showcasing the desire for New York and engaging the politics of transgender tribulations are some of the many avenues through which Báez's poetry participates in a series of global conversations about art, race, class, sexuality and displacement.

The poem 'Nocturno'[16] ('Nocturne') imagines the entire city of Santo Domingo as an unmoored vessel set sail at night. There is no indication of the ship's destination. What the poem wants to foreground is the romance of departure. The speaker observes freighters and cruise ships leaving the city's harbour and is captivated by the allure of the glowing lights and, by inference, what lies ahead on the shores to which these vessels are headed. There is, of course, a robust tradition of maritime literature within the Caribbean in which the sea comes to represent, among other issues, many of the unresolved traumas of history as well as the contemporary dilemmas of defining nationhood and belonging. The nautical symbols in 'Nocturno' call up the history of the Caribbean as a site of maritime traffic. More specifically, through the image of the 'crucero' ('cruise ship'), the poem registers the Dominican Republic as a destination for tourism and with that evokes the complicated politics of discovery, desire, fantasy and control that inevitably accompany the 'pleasure tours' on which the nation's economy depends. But if the nation attracts tourists for pleasure it also forces its own citizens out, effectively expelling them from their own homeland. Silvio Torres-Saillant's evaluation of the New York Dominican diaspora stridently rejects desire and enticement as credible motives for Dominican migration. Coercion rather than enthusiasm, for him, explains the putative desire to emigrate: 'Emigra quien no puede quedarse. Se van aquellos a quienes la economía nacional les ha cerrado las puertas' ('Those who emigrate can't stay. They leave because the doors of the national economy are closed to them').[17] This consideration ironises the romance with which the prospect of the navigatory city is imbued in 'Nocturno': 'Entonces uno imagina que las luces parpadeantes/de la costa también se transforman en barcos/y que las casas y los edificios se desplazan por el mar/y que Santo Domingo entero se echa a navegar' ('And then you imagine those flickering/coastal lights also transforming into ships/ and the houses and buildings begin to unmoor/and all of Santo Domingo sets sail').

[16] Frank Báez, *Anoche soñé que era un dj* (Miami: Libros Jai-Alai, 2014), p. 34.
[17] Silvio Torres-Saillant, *El retorno de las yolas: ensayos sobre diáspora, democracia y dominicanidad* (Santo Domingo: Trinitaria, 1999), p. 18.

The fantasy of the city setting sail announces a subconscious desire for social transformation that in turn draws attention to the materiality beyond the harbour, Santo Domingo's position (social, economic, cultural, political) vis-à-vis that of the countries to which it might sail and the reasons for the difference. In other words, the text masks a vexation with the increasing disparities between rich and poor nations and the exploitation of the resources of the global South to fortify the economies of the North. As Françoise Lionnet (*Minor Transnationalism*) reminds us, such dystopic views on globalisation generate sites of resistance that ultimately constitutes a 'transnationalism from below' as opposed to the 'transnationalism from above' that sustains the interests of multinational corporations, global financial institutions and the global media.

Artistic hubris that expresses itself in a disengagement with the local Dominican cultural landscape is evoked and chastised in Báez's poetry. Accordingly, 'Memorias de un vanguardista'[18] ('Memoirs of a vanguardist') reveals and repudiates the idea that culture is somehow always created elsewhere. The entitled young speaker/poet (we learn that he has just turned 20) is used to mock the image of the 'artista de vanguardia' for whom the sine qua non of creativity is abandonment of the Dominican Republic. He wants his parents to give him money to go abroad in order that he may heed his artistic vocation. Like the unmoored ship in 'Nocturno' a specific destination is not the priority. What matters is that he does not want to spend his youth stranded on the island ('varado en la isla'). Any major city will do. He just requires an allowance to be able to survive and produce his art 'en cualquiera de / las capitales de la/ vanguardia, o sea, / Nueva York, Paris, / Tokio, aunque/ también podría/ ser Berlín, Londres/ o Barcelona' ('In whatever/ of the capitals of the / avant-garde, it could be/ New York, Paris,/ Tokyo, although/ it could also /be Berlin, London/or Barcelona').

The poem satirises the 'twenty-something year old' poet who invests all his energies in trying to escape Santo Domingo. His attempts are frustrated at every turn. None of the authorities to whom he appeals collaborates with his project or shares his vision of becoming 'el gran artista vanguardista dominicano' ('the great vanguard Dominican artist'). His parents deny his request for financial support and the embassies refuse him visas suspecting that his is really an attempt to flee the country and reside permanently in the 'developed' West. The contemplative walks around the great capital cities of the Western world, the 'camisas de florecitas tropicales', 'el extraño bigote' ('flowery tropical shirts', 'strange moustache'), stereotypes of the self-important artist,

---

[18] Frank Báez *Este es el futuro que estabas esperando* (Bogotá: Editorial Planeta Colombiana, 2017), pp. 19–23.

whose greatest qualification is his sojourn in Europe, abound in 'Memorias de un vanguardista'.[19]

Satire becomes the vehicle through which the deferral and ultimate demise of the young artist's ostensible capacity for productivity is communicated. Having reached 30, he has not succeeded in honing his skills in the great cultural capitals of the West. His future as cultural trend-setter lies in ruins. Unsurprisingly, he produces nothing in the Dominican Republic. His twenties are a lost decade yearning for Europe and the USA. Fittingly, the poem draws on German fiction, to communicate the tragedy of the 'writer's block' of the young Dominican and his failure to achieve artistic goals. Belated realisations and horizons not reached link the 'would be' Caribbean avante-garde artist to the protagonist of Thomas Mann's *Death in Venice*: 'no tuve más remedio /que olvidarme de la vanguardia/tan pronto cumplí los treinta/y confiar en lo que podría hacer/cuando tuviera la edad/del protagonista de *Muerte en Venecia* ,/es decir, ya muy tarde' ('I had no other option/ but to forget the avant-garde/ as soon as I turned 30/ and focus on what was really possible/ when I arrived at the age of the protagonist of *Death in Venice*/ that is to say, too late'). 'Memorias de un vanguardista' is clearly a reflection of premature masculine panic about the passing of youth.[20] But it also pillories the yearning for Europe and the US as a mechanism for cultural production. The yearnings of the artist in this poem express a condition of severe underdevelopment. It is this idea, the notion that the Caribbean is anathema to inventive cultural production, that Báez ironises and rejects. Indeed, the text itself stands as the strongest refutation of that idea.[21]

With Santo Domingo as the assumed locus of creation, numerous foreign cities (Paris, Mexico City, Venice, Tokyo, London and Chicago among others) appear in the poetry of Báez. But New York is the city that is most recurrent

---

[19] The Dominican avant-garde was trained in Europe, mostly France, and artists learned to think about being in Europe as being 'home', or rather as bringing Europe home as a way of claiming a natural sense of belonging to a social elite. The Dominican avant-garde was a sort of naturalised principle of a class trained abroad but always keeping the national referent in mind.

[20] The decline of youth and masculine anxiety about production, value and belonging are also major concerns in Junot Díaz's *This is How You Lose Her* (London: Faber and Faber, 2013).

[21] This invites comparison with Derek Walcott's satirising of the idea of the Caribbean as a zone with 'no visible history' in 'The Almond Trees', *The Castaway* (London: Jonathan Cape, 1965), p. 36. Andrés L. Mateo's discussion of the arrival and reception of European avante-garde literary figures in the Dominican Republic is also instructive as another context within which to read Báez's poem. See Andrés L. Mateo, *Al filo de la dominicanidad* (Santo Domingo: Trinitaria, 1996).

and through which some of the most powerful aspects of transnational negotiations are articulated. This recurrence of New York as both theme and symbol is consistent with the demographic significance of the city in Dominican transnational migration. After Santo Domingo New York has the second-largest number of Dominican residents in the world. And for many Dominicans, Jorge Duany reminds us, '*irse a los países* ('going abroad') is almost synonymous with moving to New York (*Blurred Borders*, p. 174). But far more significant, I would argue, is the weight that the idea of New York has on the Dominican cultural imaginary.

Images of New York are invariably imbricated within many of the metaphors of both failure and success that are encoded in official as well as popular culture. It is not unusual for institutional rhetoric to use New York as a marker for social and infrastructural development or regression,[22] and both Dominican and US Dominican literature have narrated the pivotal role that the city has had in the destiny and identity politics of the Caribbean nation. The inscription of New York in Báez's poetry is complex, multi-layered and nuanced. The city is at times synonymous with the death of artistic creativity as in 'Mi amigo camina hacia el silencio' ('My friend walks towards silence') (*Este es el futuro*, pp. 13–14). It can also function as a sign of the rejection of the local in favour of the foreign. In 'Milky Way' (*Este es el futuro*, pp. 27–28), for example, a father's first visit to New York results in the son's spurning all local chocolate products ('Crachi, chocolate embajador, más más')[23] in favour of the all inviting Milky Way. Later, both New York and Milky Way chocolates will become associated with infantile obsessions, disappointments and friendships strained by time and distance. Through the intense and sustained engagement with Walt Whitman in several poems New York resounds as both muse and source of discouragement. If Pedro Mir's address to Whitman in the poem 'Contracanto a Walt Whitman' in the mid-twentieth century pronounced the way US imperialist egoism commodified Latin America and deprived its nations of their autonomy,[24] then Báez's' invocation of the US poet points out the many dangers that infringe the lives of 'brown' bearded men who are constantly at risk in a post-9/11 world that is obsessed with racialising

[22] See, for example, ex-president Leonel Fernández's statement to the Dominican Congress in 2012, 'La República Dominicana ha experimentado una extraordinaria transformación y desde el aire se observa un verdadero Nueva York chiquito' [*sic*], *El Día*, 12 febrero 2012, p. 5.

[23] These are all names of local brands of chocolate sold in the Dominican Republic.

[24] Jean Franco, 'Foreword to the countersong', *Countersong to Walt Whitman and other Poems*, trans. by Jonathan Cohen and Donald D. Walsh (Washington, DC: Azul Editions, 1993), pp. xiii–xv, p. xv.

the idea and fact of terror. Thus, in 'Una espístola para Walt Whitman' ('A letter to Walt Whitman') a long beard denotes the authority and dignity of the white North American poet. Similarly, the Brooklyn bridge points to his status as poetic icon and literary prophet. But the poem's troubling thesis is that both beard and bridge reinforce the precarity of life for brown masculinity in the twenty-first century in New York and beyond.

But it is with the resonance of New York as a site used to articulate transgender tribulations that I wish to conclude my discussion of transnational concerns in the poetry of Frank Báez. The city is used to stage major dilemmas concerning citizenship and belonging that impact gendered and racialised immigrant bodies. It also becomes the location that illuminates crises of marginalisation in the Dominican Republic, proffers potential solutions and, tragically, confirms the circularity of depravation that hounds the marginalised both at home and in the diaspora. Ultimately, New York signals the inevitability of exile and return and the transnational continuity of discourses of prejudice that ironically link the Global South to many of the ideologies and practices of the developed North.

Arguably Báez's signature poem, 'La Marilyn Monroe de Santo Domingo', follows the travails of a black transgender woman both at home in Santo Domingo and as an undocumented migrant in New York.[25] A study of the spectre of multiple marginalisation and the brutal violence against difference, the poem announces and simultaneously denounces the notion of *trans* as grotesque. The transgender woman introduces herself as 'monstruo que menstrua' ('monster who menstruates') but the poem immediately undercuts that idea by its detailed exposé of her psyche and her humanity. What the poem shows as monstrous are the homophobic and transphobic attitudes that are ingrained in all levels of established society. In this regard Pedro Mir serves Báez very well in his attempt to censure social prejudices. In this poem Báez engages frenetically with Pedro Mir's 'Hay un país en el mundo'. The engagement with Mir in this poem magnifies the sense of Dominican society as 'improbable' and at the same time shows that, as a country in the world, the Dominican Republic also holds the world within it. The anguish of the Dominican Marilyn Monroe is therefore borne of both local and global forces: 'Hay un país en el mundo colocado en el mismo trayecto del sol / hay en el mundo un mismo país colocado en el trayecto del sol / Hay el mismo trayecto del sol colocado en un país en el mundo' ('There is a country in the world positioned in the very path of the sun/ There is in the world a very

---

[25] A spoken word artist and musician, Báez's work functions largely, although not solely, in performance. 'La Marilyn Monroe de Santo Domingo' is one of the most popular poems he performs with his band, El Hombrecito.

country positioned in the sun's path / There is the sun's very path positioned in a country in the world') (*Anoche soñé*, p. 31).

The country is shocking and improbable for many reasons. The social hypocrisy is phenomenal, for example. Victimised by machista heteronormativity in public, the *trans* woman has sex with men from all levels of society in private: 'Salgo con poetas de los ochenta. / salgo con chiriperos, guachimanes, modelos, ingenieros, artistas plásticos, levantadores de pesas, abogados, rubios, / funcionarios, toleteros, parqueadores de carros' (*Anoche soñé*, p.28) ('I go with poets from the eighties / I go with handymen, security guards/ models, engineers, artists/ weight-lifters, lawyers, white lads/ bureaucrats, sluggers, car valets'). Anti-black racism and Europhile pretensions also feature in the poem as pressing questions that deform Dominican society. As a black transgender woman, the Marilyn Monroe of Santo Domingo also internalises these prejudices and hence she yearns for escape into whiteness. Her role models, whether Dominican (Charytín Goyco) or US (Marilyn Monroe), are not just white but also blonde.[26]

The tragic craving of both place and race are communicated most poignantly, through acerbic humour, when – trying to hitchhike to her destination – the *trans* woman is flirtatiously offered a lift by a man on a motorbike: 'Hola rubia mi amol pa dónde tu va /y yo respond go LA /all the way down to LA /o sea, Los Alcarrizos' ('Hey my blonde where are you goin' honey/ and I answer headin' to LA/ all the way down to LA/ you know what I mean, Los Alcarrizos'). The temporary flight of fantasy to the USA (Los Angeles) is, of course, underlain with sexual tension and desire. The brutal return to the reality of place, Los Alcarrizos,[27] Santo Domingo, disrupts spatial, cultural and sexual make-believe. But the society, here in the form of men flirting with the trans woman also collude with her desire for a different racial identification through referring to her, albeit mockingly, as 'rubia' ('blonde'). Sadly, her yearning for the USA is not just a yearning for escape from the transphobic abuse and poverty of the Caribbean; it is also a yearning for whiteness. Arriving in New York with a false passport, she enjoys a full range of coveted experiences (breakfast at Tiffany's, champagne in limousines, reading her poetry at the Nuyorican café). But the cycle of violent abuse repeats itself in diaspora. Abused by local citizens as well as official institutions she is eventually deported. But facing her fate with equanimity she

---

[26] For a discussion of the career of the blonde TV star, Charytín Goyco, within the context of race in the Dominican Republic see Danny Méndez 'Charytín Goyco, la rubia de América: A case study of Dominican stardom in the Dominican Republic in the 1970s', *Studies in Latin American Popular Culture*, 33 (2015), 27–40.

[27] Los Alcarrizos is an economically challenged municipality in Santo Domingo.

resumes her mask in all its glory in Santo Domingo and reaffirms her mantra '¿Qué se va a hacer?' ('What's a girl to do?').

'La Marilyn Monroe de Santo Domingo' invites reflection on key questions concerning transgender diaspora. Both her temporary success (real or imagined) and subsequent failure terminating in deportation point to the particularities of marginalisation that transgender bodies experience in movement across national and international borders. The poem thereby participates in current debates that seek to interpret the different dynamics of *trans* diasporas. Comprising movements of desire and agency without unitary subjects or foundations transgender migrations may be highly useful in unlocking a great deal of meaning for cross-border Caribbean movements more generally.[28] The language of the poem points to the experiences of the *trans* woman as holding the keys to unravelling meanings in Dominican society both nationally and transnationally. The lessons gleaned from her experiences both in Santo Domingo and New York are vital for addressing questions of identity politics but also of justice in terms of race, class, gender and sexuality.

Caribbean discourses of transnationalism routinely exclude gay, intersex and *trans* subjects. Transgender theory continues to marginalise, if not exclude, questions of racial and ethnic difference. Transgender studies, interestingly, have articulated for some time now ideas of transit, journeys of national and sexual transition that find resonance nonetheless within the literary work of many Caribbean writers. Frank Báez, like many of his contemporaries, produces a Dominican literature that is fully engaged with a wide range of subjects of global concerns. His poetry engages productively with key literary icons of the past (national and international) but it also lays claim to a clear and unequivocal stake in the construction of a Global Dominican literary future in which numerous forms of *trans*fer have a place.

---

[28] Trystan Cotten, *Transgender Migrations: The Bodies, Borders and Politics of Transition* (London: Routledge, 2012), p. 2.

17

'Signos y cicatrices comunes'

Queerness, Disability and Pedro Lemebel's Poetics and Politics of Embodiment

Benjamin Quarshie

Pedro Lemebel was a Chilean writer, artist and sexual liberation activist. He first gained recognition in the late 1980s, still under the military dictatorship of Augusto Pinochet, when he and his friend Francisco Casas exploded on to the streets and cultural spaces of Santiago with a series of irreverent artistic interventions, calling themselves Las Yeguas del Apocalipsis ('The Mares of the Apocalypse'). Throughout the 1990s, their performance art, *la performance* in Spanish, mobilised the homosexual body in an array of feathers, high heels and stockings, barbed wire, glass and fire, for an incendiary critique of the cultural and political narratives of Chile's so-called 'transition' to democracy. By testifying to the AIDS crisis and the marginalisation of Chile's sexual minorities, in tandem with the memory of political violence and the marginalisation of Chile's poor, Las Yeguas laid bare the continued exclusions and oppressions underlying a *Transición* that safeguarded the free-market agenda violently inaugurated by Pinochet.

Lemebel is perhaps best known for his *crónicas*, short texts first published in magazines, broadcast on the feminist AM station Radio Tierra, and collected in numerous book publications, including *La esquina es mi corazón* (1995), *Loco afán* (1996), *Zanjón de la Aguada* (2003) and *Háblame de amores* (2012). These hybrid chronicles departed from the urban itineraries of Santiago's sexually and socially marginalised, commenting on Chilean popular culture, politics, history and memory. Lemebel also published the novel *Tengo miedo torero* (2001) and, right up to his death in 2015 from cancer of the larynx, he continued to stage artistic interventions in an intertextual, self-referential and embodied language, a poetics and politics of denunciation, but also of desire.

Lemebel might be described as a 'queer' writer and artist for his non-conformity to binary understandings of gender, sex and sexuality, and his creation of a political language concerning bodies and behaviours that refuse normative paradigms. However, his corpus points to problems with the designation 'queer' outside the US and British contexts in which it originated. Speaking from the particularities of other bodies, languages and cultural histories, his work includes a sustained critique of an identity politics scripted from the Global North, to the exclusion of Southern minorities who inhabit geographies marked by colonial violence and state terror. I employ the terms 'North' and 'South' here as Lemebel used them, namely to delineate the asymmetry of transnational capitalism and the material conditions of 'Southern' difference it produces, which engender different ways of inhabiting and theorising the body.

This chapter explores Lemebel's poetics and politics of embodiment, across both his writing and performance art. By highlighting the ways in which he *locates* bodies within profoundly uneven geographies of cultural and political representation, I question the universalisation of queer theory, and bring Lemebel's ideas to bear on disability studies and 'crip theory'. I focus in particular on the potential for dialogue with 'crip' critiques of queerness's exclusions, and of the calculated distribution of neoliberalism's disabling impacts, drawing largely on the work of Robert McRuer. I do so, however, in order to insert Lemebel, as well as his main theoretical influence Néstor Perlongher, into a more expansive genealogy of theories of embodiment.

Queer Contingencies

So, what's in a name? The reappropriation of 'queer', and its proliferation of political and identitarian possibilities, have developed in tandem with a critical interrogation of its limits, from the earliest and most cited forays into what became Queer Theory. In 'Critically Queer' (1993), Judith Butler warned against the solidifying of exclusive identity categories, arguing that the difficult task of queer politics is to remain open to the 'democratizing' possibilities of 'a more enabling future'.[1] Although it runs the risk of misappropriations, this 'openness' of categories, she argued in another essay, 'ought to be safeguarded for political reasons'.[2]

Brad Epps, however, has problematised the 'mobility' of Anglophone terms such as 'queer' from the dominant sites of supposedly universal knowledge production, and the corresponding 'immobility' of languages and expressions

---

[1] 'Critically queer', *GLQ: A Journal of Lesbian and Gay Studies*, 1 (1993), 17–32 (pp. 19–20).

[2] 'Imitation and gender insubordination', in *Inside/Out: Lesbian Theories, Gay Theories*, ed. by Diana Fuss (New York: Routledge, 1991), pp. 13–31 (p. 19).

supposedly specific to distant elsewheres.[3] More recently, 'queer' has spread through Spanish-language contexts in the increasingly transliterated form *cuir*, an 'epistemic and visual reconfiguration', which, for the editors of one recent volume, re-orients queerness towards the Global South as 'un locus de enunciación con inflexión decolonial, anti-heteropatriarcal y anti-racista' ('a locus of enunciation with decolonial, anti-heteropatriarchal and anti-racist inflections').[4] While this uptake of 'queer', *cuir*, and its Brazilian transmutations[5] in Latin America has certainly emphasised intersections with anti-capitalism and anti-colonialism, it remains, for many, a translated and abstracted term that disavows local embodiments and modes of being.[6]

In his *crónica* 'Loco afán' ('Mad Desire'), which he read during an intervention into an appearance by Félix Guattari in 1991, Lemebel addressed the question of how to take part in a globalised sexual identity politics from a 'Third-World' body on the margins of neoliberal globalisation:

> Cómo levantar una causa ajena transformándonos en satélites exóticos de esas agrupaciones formadas por mayorías blancas a las que les dan alergia nuestras plumas; que hacen sus macrocongresos en inglés y por lo tanto nuestra lengua indoamericana no tiene opinión influyente en el diseño de sus políticas.
>
> (How to take up someone else's cause, transforming ourselves into exotic satellites of those associations formed of white majorities, who react allergically to our feathers; who conduct their mega-conferences in English and, therefore, our Amerindian tongue has no opinion and no influence over the design of their politics.)[7]

---

[3] 'Retos y riesgos, pautas y promesas de la teoría queer', *Debate Feminista*, 18 (2007), 217–270 (pp. 246–247).

[4] Virginia Villaplana Ruiz and others, 'Memoria queer/cuir: usos materiales del pasado, narrativas postglobales e imaginarios del sur global', *Arte y Políticas de Identidad*, 16 (2017), 9–14 (p. 10). My translation.

[5] These include *cuir*, *kuir*, *tropiqueer* and *cu-ir* (a call to 'go for the anus'). The Brazilian sociologist Berenice Bento is responsible for the cultural translation of *Queer Studies* into *Estudos transviados*. See Paola María Marugán Ricart, 'Algunas reflexiones sobre las prácticas queer en Pindorama', *Arte y Políticas de Identidad*, 16 (2017), 75–96 (pp. 85–87).

[6] See, for example, yos (erchxs) piña narváez, 'No soy queer, soy negrx, mis orishas no leyeron a J. Butler', *Zineditorial*, 2018, <https://zineditorial.files.wordpress.com/2018/04/no-soy-queer-soy-negrx-lectura.pdf>, accessed 23 December 2018.

[7] 'Loco afán', in *Loco afán. Crónicas de sidario* (Santiago: Seix Barral, 2015), henceforth *Loco*, pp. 163–168 (p. 166). This and all subsequent translations are mine.

Sexual, racial and gender difference converge in a history of colonisation that relegates Latin America's sexual minorities to a stigmatised time and place of anachronism and 'doble marginación' ('double marginalisation') (p. 165). Lemebel's vindication of local geographies of difference, while engaged with similar questions to a more globalising Queer Theory, is inscribed within its own cultural and critical genealogy of violence, pathologisation and desire. Thus, in his poem 'Manifiesto' ('Manifesto'), recited at a 1986 demonstration, he condemns the Chilean left for excluding sexual minorities from a militant liberation cause they shared. Speaking from a voice and body doubly marginalised, he declares: 'Hablo por mi diferencia' ('I speak through and for my difference') (*Loco*, pp. 121–126, p. 121).

In his first two collections of *crónicas*, *La esquina es mi corazón* (1995) and *Loco afán* (1996), the local figure who embodies this differential history of pathologisation, persecution and radical non-conformity is the *loca*. I will hedge an inadequate translation of *loca*, literally, 'crazy woman', as somewhere between the derogatory *faggot* and the reclaimed feminine defiance of *queen*. In incongruous terms, *loca* designates an 'effeminate' or otherwise 'gender-non-conforming' 'male-born' 'homosexual', while a self-identifying *loca* may defy any or all of these categories. While its meaning varies across the lexicons of vernacular sexuality in different Spanish-speaking locations, the epithet invariably bears a history of stigma and pathologisation attached to homosexuality, feminine non-conformity, sexual 'deviance' and madness.[8] It is culturally and linguistically contingent, unstable and divergent. And, like 'queer', it has been proudly reappropriated by the stigmatised.

Lemebel's own *loca* embodiment spoke to an open notion of 'becoming' ('devenir') rather than a delimited identity. He variably wore heels, shawls and headscarves, dressed in full drag, or painted his face with the hammer and sickle; his *mariconaje* manifested in gesture and vocal intonation, and he inflected the first-person 'yo' with both masculine and feminine forms.[9] In his

---

My translations of Lemebel are mere approximations of the rhythmic syntax, dense play-on-words, neologisms and colloquialisms of his *loca* poetics. For one critical transgender approach to translating Lemebel, see Arielle A. Concilio, 'Pedro Lemebel and the Translatxrsation: On a Genderqueer Translation Praxis', *TSQ*, 3 (2016), 462–484.

[8] See Melissa M. González, 'La loca', *TSQ*, 1 (2014), 123–125.

[9] For this sensibility of 'becoming' in his writing, see, for example, 'Homoeróticas urbanas', *Loco*, pp.115–118: 'La maricada gitanea la vereda y deviene gesto, deviene beso, deviene ave, aletear de pestaña, ojeada nerviosa por el causeo de cuerpos masculinos' ('The faggotry teases the sidewalk and becomes gesture, becomes kiss, becomes bird, flutter of eyelashes, nervous glance occasioned by masculine bodies') (p. 115).

crónicas, la loca is associated with *la fuga, el vagabundeo, la deriva*: a flight or escape, a wandering or drifting, a counter-current of bodies and behaviours scripting the trajectories of desire. These terms come from Lemebel's primary theoretical influence, the Argentine neo-baroque poet, anthropologist and militant sexual liberation activist Néstor Perlongher.

Perlongher, with Lemebel, belongs to a Latin American theoretical corpus that I hesitate to call 'queer'. In 'La noche de los visones' ('The Night of the Mink Coats'), which I explore in depth below, Lemebel recalls this 'otro corpus tribal' ('other tribal corpus'), a sexual-political moment in Latin America, before HIV/AIDS and before the imported LGBT politics of the 1990s: 'Otros delirios enriquecían barrocamente el discurso de las homosexualidades latinoamericanas. Todavía la maricada chilena tejía futuro, soñaba despierta con su emancipación junto a otras causas sociales' ('A different delirium adorned the baroque discourse of Latin America's homosexualities. When the Chilean faggotry still spun its future, daydreaming of emancipation alongside other social causes').[10] This 'baroque' discourse on plural homosexualities within an expansive project of social emancipation speaks directly to Perlongher, who, in his 1984 *crónica* 'El sexo de las locas' ('The Sex of *Locas*'), described the marginalisation of Latin America's 'popular' sexualities via a normalising 'modelo gay' ('gay model').[11]

Against this normalisation of homosexuality into a model of conduct, Perlongher proposes letting sexuality spring from everyday life: 'Hacer saltar a la sexualidad ahí donde está' (literally, 'to make sexuality jump out wherever it is') (p. 34). Sexualities become nodal points in a fleeting passage, micro-intensities of desire on the move. For Perlongher, moreover, the street-level names for every inflection of 'masculine' and 'feminine' homosexuality carry a 'fleshly' materiality, a stigma of socio-sexual pathology that is inseparable from the bodies denoted.[12] While their reappropriation bears similarities with 'queer', their specificity navigates markedly different bodies, histories, transactions and desires, which evade totalising categories. By attesting to their singularities, we inevitably, and desirably, run into their messiness.

I do not wish, therefore, to substitute 'loca' for 'queer', but rather to read both as 'señas de pasaje' ('signs of passage') (Perlongher, p. 47), and to think

---

[10] *Loco*, pp. 15–34 (p. 33).

[11] *Prosa plebeya: ensayos 1980–1992*, ed. by Christian Ferrer and Osvaldo Baigorria (Buenos Aires: Colihue, 1997), pp. 29–34 (p. 33).

[12] See 'Avatares de los muchachos de la noche' (1989), a condensed version of Perlongher's anthropological thesis on male prostitution in São Paulo (Perlongher, 1997, pp. 47–48).

about the different trajectories each entails. To this end, we might bring Butler's call for queer 'openness' into dialogue with her Southern contemporaries Perlongher and Lemebel. We might, for instance, consider the implications of queer's 'democratisation', in the light of Lemebel's suspicion of the 'cueca democrática' of early 1990s Chile ('Manifiesto', *Loco*, p. 121), a token 'folk-dance democracy' that merely expedites the consolidation of neoliberalism. Furthermore, I wish to hold up Butler's desire for 'a more enabling future', to Lemebel's perspectives on pathologisation and the embodiment of material differences, via some critical perspectives from disability scholarship.

Geografía local/loca geografía

For Lemebel, *la loca* becomes the hypostasis of the *local*, the sign of difference and particularity in a geography scarred by inequality. She embodies a sensibility and a way of being that metaphorises a whole constellation of cultural symbols and signs, under threat of effacement by the aggressive importation of commoditised lifestyles. Thus, in 'Loco afán', Lemebel configures the sexual margins of Chile into 'nuestra loca geografía' ('our *loca* geography'), inscribing Chile's minority sexualities into a historical continuum of colonisation, manifested in that 'gay' model of normalised homosexuality decried by Perlongher:

> Aterrados por el escándalo, sin entender mucho la sigla gay con nuestra cabeza indígena [...] Acaso estuvimos locas siempre; locas como estigmatizan a las mujeres.
> Acaso nunca nos dejamos precolonizar por ese discurso importado. *Demasiado lineal para nuestra loca geografía.*
>
> (Terrified by the commotion, struggling to get our indigenous head around the acronym "gay" [...] Maybe we were always locas; crazy locas like they stigmatise women.
> Maybe we never allowed ourselves to be pre-colonised by that imported discourse. *Too linear for our loca geography.*) (*Loco*, pp. 165–166, my italics)

The imported discourses of globalising identity politics represent a 'pre-colonisation' of this '*loca* geography'. Their 'linearity' disavows local counter-histories of stigmatisation, and the genealogies of survival and resistance in which those stigmatised bodies are constellated.

This *loca*-lising of history is exemplified by 'La noche de los visones' ('The Night of the Mink Coats') (1996), in which Lemebel re-writes Chilean history, the Allende years, Pinochet's coup and, particularly, the narrative of *la Transición*, from the vantage point of Santiago's *locas*. The *crónica* recalls a *loca* New Year's Eve party in 1972, which becomes a Last Supper in drag for Allende's Unidad Popular, and the centrepiece of loca-lised historical memory. In Lemebel's allegory, the coup of 1973, which inaugurates seventeen years of state violence, is also an augury of neoliberalism's most violent assault on Latin America's sexual minorities, namely the importation of *lo gay*, which follows the transition to nominal democracy. The decimation of Santiago's *locas*, who once dreamed of emancipation under Allende, is accelerated by the arrival of AIDS, packaged up in the muscled bodies of this free-market-friendly homosexuality (*Loco*, pp. 32–33).

Redeploying what Susan Sontag famously called the 'metaphorizing' of AIDS,[13] Lemebel inverts the spatial-temporal trajectory of the virus, so that it becomes a 'nueva conquista de la imagen rubia' ('new conquest by the blond image'), a First-World invasion of the 'Third World'. In a metaphorical twist both harrowing and subversive, the devastation of AIDS becomes inseparable from the 'capitalist curse' of *lo gay*:

> Y junto al molde de Superman, precisamente en la aséptica envoltura de esa piel blanca, tan higiénica, tan perfumada por el embrujo capitalista. *Tan diferente al cuero opaco de la geografía local* [...] venía cobijado el síndrome de inmunodeficiencia, como si fuera un viajante, un turista que llegó a Chile de paso, y el vino dulce de nuestra sangre lo hizo quedarse.
>
> (And along with the Superman mould, right inside that aseptic packaging of white skin, so hygienic, so perfumed with the capitalist curse, so *different from the dark hide of the local geography* [...] there came concealed the immune deficiency syndrome, like a traveller, a tourist who was passing through Chile, and the sweet wine of our blood made him stick around.) (*Loco*, p. 33, my italics)

In the slippage between 'geografía local' and 'loca geografía', 'local geography' and '*loca* geography', Lemebel reproduces a well-rehearsed notion of the 'local' as the site and cipher for various cultural erasures under the flow of global capital, but he critically transvestises it through the insubordinate sign of *loca* particularism. In this landscape, the global exportation of queer politics, with its particular Anglophone cultural history, necessarily comes up against bodies marked by different languages and signs.

---

[13] Susan Sontag, *AIDS and its Metaphors* (Harmondsworth: Penguin, 1989).

Thus, in the same *crónica*, the funeral procession of working-class *loca* la Chumilou, who has died of AIDS-related illness, momentarily blurs with a street party celebrating the arrival of Chilean democracy, turning the funeral car into 'un carro alegórico' ('an allegorical carriage'). This moment of confused transition, of mourning blurred with joy, produces a confusion of cultural signs, out of which Lemebel configures his *loca* temporality. The dream of sexual liberation is crushed by the arrival of 'el neoliberalismo en democracia' ('neoliberalism in democracy'), which brings 'la desfunción de la loca sarcomida por el sida, pero principalmente diezmada por el modelo importado del estatus gay' ('the last agony of the loca sarconsumed by AIDS, but decimated, above all, by the imported model of gay status') (*Loco*, pp. 31–32). By verbalising 'sarcoma', Lemebel reappropriates the figurative potency of AIDS as pathology and tragedy, displacing it to express the decimation of local expressions under neoliberalism.

La Chumilou is symbolically buried with 'una bandera con el arco iris vencedor' ('a flag with the triumphant rainbow'), the logo of the campaign against Pinochet's rule. Ambivalent in its gesture towards a democracy that might include Chile's sexual minorities, or else herald their death, the rainbow flag takes on another meaning in 'Crónicas de Nueva York' ('Chronicles of New York'), where it emblematises, discordantly, the whitening and gentrification of Manhattan's gay culture.[14] By playing with the contingencies of cultural–political symbols, Lemebel denounces the way that neoliberal 'democracy' tolerates, even celebrates, certain subjects only by disenfranchising or, as has been the case in Latin America, disappearing others. In a Chilean version of the AIDS Memorial Quilt, the tribute 'Víctor por siempre' ('Víctor forever') cannot help but evoke the singer Víctor Jara, assassinated in the days following the 1973 coup. Thus, in a kind of 'cross-current' of symbolization, the viral epidemic converges with state violence in 'un cruce político inevitable' ('an inevitable political intersection'), producing 'una marea de nombres sidados o desaparecidos' ('a tidal swell of names disappeared by AIDS or by the dictatorship').[15] Such 'expresiones locales' ('local expressions') (p. 133) point to the ways in which Lemebel's 'loca geografía' disrupts the neoliberal arrangement of space and time around bodies – think of those euphemistically named 'structural adjustments' accompanying Chile's brutal neoliberal experiment – and makes visible those modes of being denied passage in the 'free' market.

Part of what might be translated as the 'queerness' of Lemebel's work is precisely this locating and historicising of embodiment, which, in fact, *disables* any attempt at translation, particularly by gesturing to local variants

---

[14] *Loco*, pp. 93–95 (p. 95).
[15] 'El Proyecto Nombres', *Loco*, pp. 127–133 (pp. 132–133).

of pathologisation and disability itself. Indeed, 'loca geografía' also plays on the image of Chile's *geografía accidentada*, or 'accidented geography', a Spanish descriptor for a landscape broken up by dramatic geological formations. By transforming Chile's 'crazy' cross-section of terrains and natural resources into a colonised territory of pathologised subjects, Lemebel critically focalises the local and global 'accidents' to which Southern bodies are, in fact, disproportionately vulnerable.

Various disability theorists have highlighted these disabling impacts of global capitalism. Robert McRuer recalls the insight, often cited in disability studies, that 'everyone will become disabled if they live long enough'.[16] He does so, however, in order to problematise the universalising truism, pointing to those subjects who simply don't live long enough under the conditions created for and by neoliberal capitalism. Michael Davidson, citing the same refrain, similarly argues that 'many aspects of what we call international modernity are founded upon the unequal valuation of some bodies over others'.[17] Lemebel's 'accidented' geography, as I go on to show, highlights precisely those subjects deemed disposable for the steady flow of capital under neoliberal 'structural adjustment'.

Un futuro crónico

In 'La esquina es mi corazón' ('The Street Corner is My Heart') (1995), the 'bloques' ('blocks') that house Santiago's poorer residents are spaces of precarious bodies in contact, neglected by the state and supported by popular modes of being-in-common. The very fabric of the neighbourhood, the cheap 'plaster-board wall', is a porous membrane of intimacies on the margins: 'utilería divisoria que inventó la arquitectura popular como soporte precario de intimidad, donde los resuellos conyugales y las flatulencias del cuerpo se permean de lo privado a lo público' ('a prop of partition, an invention of popular architecture that serves as the precarious support for intimacy, where the creaking of the conjugal bed and the flatulencies of the body cross-permeate from the private to the public').[18] 'Precarity', 'intimacy' and 'support' are thus bound in a poetics of vital prosthetics.

---

[16] Robert McRuer, *Crip Theory: Cultural Signs of Queerness and Disability* (New York: New York University Press, 2006), p. 200. Henceforth *Crip Theory*.

[17] 'Universal design: The work of disability in an age of globalization', in *The Disability Studies Reader*, ed. by Lennard J. Davis, 3rd edn (New York: Routledge, 2010), pp. 133–146 (pp. 134–135).

[18] Pedro Lemebel, *La esquina es mi corazón* (Santiago: Seix Barral, 2014), henceforth *Esquina*, pp. 29–36 (p. 31).

Indeed, if the 'street corner of the "pobla"' – the colloquial name that marks these urban neighbourhoods as poor, peripheral and stigmatised – is 'un corazón donde apoyar la oreja' ('a heart on which to lay your ear'), then the 'personal estéreo amarrado con elástico' ('Walkman held together with elastic') becomes '[u]n marcapasos para no escuchar la bulla, para no deprimirse con la risa del teclado presidencial hablando de los jóvenes y su futuro' ('a pacemaker to drown out the noise and not get depressed by the cackling of the typed-out presidential script about the future of our young') (*Esquina*, pp. 30–31). The pathologisation, both rhetorical and real, of these sites of neoliberal abandonment is channelled into an image of social precarity-as-vitality. Lemebel's *pobla* resonates with McRuer's recent intent 'to imagine a *disabled* sociality that [...] refuse[s] the very distinction between the social and bodies engaged in *a range of intimate practices* that can certainly include sex' – as, I might add, Lemebel's *crónicas* make clear – 'but that can also include other embodied ways of being-in-common'.[19]

For Lemebel, the street corner is the pounding heart of social life, and the battered Walkman a pacemaker that drowns out political appeals to a future that the 'chicos del bloque' ('kids on the block') may not live to see. Condemned to pile up in 'cemetery niches' at the bottom of the social pyramid, they are simply 'South American waste', 'cannon fodder in the traffic' of political discourse (*Esquina*, pp. 34–36). The *crónica* opens with an irreverent dedication to these kids, who drink, smoke marihuana and are literally disabled by the glue they inhale to make a precarious existence bearable, 'expuestos y dispuestos a las acrobacias de su trapecio proletario. Un pasar trashumante de suelas mal pegadas por el neoprén que gotea mortífero las membranas cerebrales' ('exposed and disposed to the acrobatic ups-and-downs of proletarian life. An itinerant existence of worn-out shoes stuck together badly by glue that drips death on cerebral membranes'). Lemebel turns this normality of vulnerable bodies into a vital and intoxicating 'brindis de yodo por su imaginario corroído por la droga' ('iodine toast to their drug-addled universe') (pp. 29–30).

Lemebel's poetics of embodiment is a 'Southern' precursor of those more recent cultural vocabularies concerning disability identity politics. Disabilities are woven into gender-evading rites of *loca* nicknaming, with 'limps', 'hemiplegias' and 'la carga sidosa' ('the burden of AIDS') incorporated into an inventive 'poética [que] desfigura el nombre' ('poetics [that] disfigures the name') ('Los mil nombres de María Camaleón', *Loco*, pp. 83–88, pp. 84–87). Or else, in the 'gueto homosexual' ('homosexual ghetto') where AIDS is the norm,

---

[19] Robert McRuer, *Crip Times* (New York: New York University Press, 2018), p. 93. Italics in original.

'el estigma sidático pasa por una cotidianeidad de club' ('the stigma of AIDS becomes an everyday part of the club'), in a performative *loca* vernacular: '¡Te queda regio el sarcoma linda!' ('That sarcoma looks fierce on you, sweetie!') ('Los diamantes son eternos', *Loco*, pp. 101–106, p. 101). These corporeal marks, the flesh made word, disrupt the ableist metaphors on which the 'health' of the neoliberal nation depends. Thus, in 'Censo y conquista' ('Census and Conquest'), Lemebel again re-imagines Chile's *geografía accidentada* in a 'disabling' of the government census and its normalising taxonomies of social control: 'Una radiografía al intestino flaco chileno expuesta en su mejor perfil neoliberal, como ortopedia de desarrollo' ('An X-ray of the skinny Chilean intestine put on show, in its best neoliberal profile, like an orthopaedics of development') (*Esquina*, pp. 107–113, p. 112).

His 'loca geografía' can, therefore, be read as an enquiry into the local contingencies that critically disable a certain kind of North–South theoretical travel, by making legible the disproportionate pathologisation, violence and vulnerability to which certain Southern bodies are subject. Lemebel, who witnessed the effects of AIDS on Santiago's *locas* and homosexuals, inscribes the epidemic into the intertwined histories of social marginalisation and state terror that frame Latin America's social and sexual liberation movements, as well as the decimation of the welfare state. This is what McRuer, in a coinage akin to the reappropriation of queer, might call 'crip' politics, and what I, in order to stress the South–North theoretical travel that motivates this chapter, will call *una política crónica*.

Indeed, Lemebel's 'loca geografía' might displace McRuer's crip theory, which, in anticipation of its 'desirable futures', marks 'crip' as a 'permanently and desirably contingent' term 'that in various times and places must be displaced by others' (*Crip Theory*, pp. 40–41). If affirming the contingency of 'queer' was both 'necessary' and 'impossible' for Butler, due to the political need for stable identities (*Critically Queer*, p. 21), crip politics makes way more readily for the precarious, unruly bodies that populate Lemebel's textuality. We might, furthermore, consider 'crónica' as an alternative to Butler's 'critically queer' and McRuer's crip version, 'severely disabled' (*Crip Theory*, p. 31). With its double meaning of 'chronicle' and 'chronic', the term focalises Lemebel's attention to intersecting forms of pathologisation and marginalisation, expanding on what 'disability' might mean when it is located in specific cultural–historical landscapes.

By subverting the ways in which 'desirable' and 'undesirable' bodies figure in political temporalities, Lemebel pre-empted later debates surrounding the temporalities of queer and crip embodiment, which routinely stake out the very future. A number of cultural disability theorists, motivated by queer theory's disavowals of disabled experiences, have radically affirmed that a *disabled* future is not only possible but also desirable. McRuer argues that 'most left movements, including most queer movements, cannot conceptualize such an idea because in general they are tied to liberationist models that need disability as the raw material against which the imagined future world is formed' (*Crip Theory*, pp. 71–72). While images of disability abound in queer theory, disabled experiences are implicitly disavowed in the service of an increasingly legible queerness, and the metaphorised disabled body obstructs utopian queer temporalities.[20]

In *No Future*, Lee Edelman famously expounds the thesis of queer antifuturity. Claiming that queerness 'names the side of those not "fighting for the children"', he positions it outside a regime of 'reproductive futurism' that circumscribes political consensus.[21] In Lemebel's tribute to the children of the *pobla*, by contrast, it is neoliberalism that produces no-futurity in the urban distribution of structural inequalities, which cut short children's lives in the name of a 'futuro inalcanzable' ('unreachable future') (*Esquina*, pp. 34–35). While Edelman categorically positions queer time against futurity, reproduction and, at times, disability, Lemebel projects a desire for the future through vitally 'over-populated' living spaces figured as desirably disabled, in his toast to the prosthetics sustaining *pobla* life.

In his recent *Crip Times* (2018), McRuer explores 'crip' resistance to the current intensification of neoliberalism known as austerity politics, in various locations including Chile. While disability may or may not be explicitly centred in these protest movements, McRuer observes 'the ways in which subjects in those locations collectively linger over scars, woundedness, and disability' (p. 101). By way of widening the historical scope of McRuer's incisive political analyses, Lemebel's work might mischievously 'pre-colonise' McRuer's. More than two decades before McRuer's observation, Lemebel salvaged a 'militant' language of embodiment from the margins of political representation in strikingly similar terms:

Una militancia corpórea que enfatiza desde el borde de la voz un discurso propio y fragmentado [...]

Tal vez lo único que decir como pretensión escritural desde un cuerpo políticamente no inaugurado en nuestro continente sea el balbuceo de signos y cicatrices comunes.

---

[20] See Alison Kafer, *Feminist, Queer, Crip* (Bloomington, IN: Indiana University Press, 2013).

[21] *No Future: Queer Theory and the Death Drive* (Durham, NC: Duke University Press, 2004), p. 4.

(A corporeal militancy that, from the edge of the voice, defines a fragmented discourse of its own [...]

Perhaps the only thing to say, by way of written petition from a body not yet inaugurated in the politics of our continent, is the stuttering of shared signs and scars.) ('Loco afán', *Loco*, p. 167)

This 'stuttering' exemplifies the way in which Lemebel's *crónicas* speak through a critically 'chronic' voice. And these are the 'shared signs and scars' over which I linger.

Signos y cicatrices comunes

In 1990, Lemebel and his friend Francisco Casas, performing as Las Yeguas del Apocalipsis, staged an intervention at an art exhibition titled 'Cuerpos contingentes', arriving in wheelchairs, naked, covered in plastic and their frequent motif of barbed wire and stuffed birds.[22] Attempting to reroute the meaning of 'contingent bodies' through an embodied vision of AIDS, they mobilised the supposed 'obstruction' of wheelchairs to normative space, and AIDS to normative timeframes and bodies. Their performative embodiment of conspicuously pathologised homosexuality rendered momentarily visible those existences sidelined by the politics of *la Transición*.

While Las Yeguas's use of wheelchairs made disability particularly legible in 'Cuerpos contingentes', throughout his work Lemebel found ways to articulate intersections between social stigmatisation and disability that may not be immediately legible. By affirming and embodying what I am calling here 'chronic' modes of being-in-common, or 'signos y cicatrices comunes', Lemebel was less concerned with delineating a politics of 'identity' than with an expansive political geography of pathologisation and stigmatisation. In a 1989 interview, he stated this intent clearly, regarding a series of photographs of transvestites, which Las Yeguas exhibited under a bridge. Here, the 'sickness' of a disdained homosexual body, figured in the material degradation of the photographs, stands with an array of social pathologies:

[La muestra] [e]nfatiza todo lo que implica la homosexualidad como material de desecho y connotación de delincuentes, a quienes se nos coloca junto a las prostitutas, los *neopreneros*, los drogadictos. Es

---

[22] Yeguas del Apocalipsis, FONDART, Gobierno de Chile, <http://www.yeguasdelapocalipsis.cl/1990-cuerpos-contingentes/>, accessed 14 December 2018. Henceforth Yeguas.

decir, en un margen en el cual la homosexualidad no es una opción, sino es una enfermedad. Y ponle doble enfermedad si es araucano; homosexual y mapuche, y además pobre, significa doble o triple marginalización.

([The exhibition] highlights everything that homosexuality implies as a waste material with connotations of criminality, along with prostitutes, glue-sniffers, drug addicts. That is, on a margin where homosexuality isn't an option but a sickness. And make that a double sickness if you're Mapuche; to be homosexual, Mapuche, and poor on top of that, means double or triple marginalisation.)[23]

If the *crónicas* I have examined here weave their poetics from the discursive 'waste material' of stigmatisation on the global peripheries, they are also in constant play with materials that Lemebel ritually brought into contact with his stigmatised body. Pedro Montes, who has compiled and curated audiovisual records of his post-Yeguas artwork, recognises the continuum between Lemebel's written corpus, visual art, interventions and mode of being: 'Lo que no expresa con palabras lo hace con actitud, con movimiento, con luz, con fuego, es lo mismo, no hay distinción alguna' ('What he doesn't express in words he expresses with attitude, with movement, with light, with fire, it's all the same, there is no distinction').[24] Lemebel's multimedia poetics emerges from a grammar of strange materials and transient materialities, through which he constructs his 'chronic' temporality. This embodied grammar became a means of reengaging a dissident politics and a painfully unfinished process of political memory and mourning in Chile, disavowed by the smooth linearity of *la Transición*.

Chilean performance artist and academic María José Contreras provides a crucial account of Lemebel's use of *neoprén*, a highly flammable industrial glue, as the 'intertextual materiality' that weaves together some of his earliest art interventions with his last, across space and time.[25] The flammability of

[23] Lemebel quoted in Maura Brescia, '"Las Yeguas del Apocalipsis" en una acción de arte', *La Época*, 17 October 1989, p. 27, Yeguas, < http://www.yeguasdelapocalipsis.cl/la-epoca-17-de-octubre-de-1989-pagina-27/>, accessed 2 February 2019.

[24] Quoted in Javier García, 'Arder, el libro que reúne la obra visual de Pedro Lemebel', *La Tercera*, 29 December 2016, <https://www.latercera.com/noticia/arder-libro-reune-la-obra-visual-pedro-lemebel/>, accessed 13 December 2018.

[25] 'El neoprén como materialidad intertextual en las dos últimas performances de Pedro Lemebel: *Desnudo bajando la escalera* y *Abecedario*', *Revista Estudios Avanzados*, 25 (2016), 92–110.

the substance, and the psychoactive effects of toluene, the volatile solvent found within it, lend *neoprén* to multiple uses by those living in Santiago's peripheries, most notably as an inhalant by teenagers and children, like those kids in 'La esquina es mi corazón'. In Lemebel's own words:

> Siempre he usado fuego y neoprén, por toda la carga simbólica que tiene ese pegamento inflamable desde la dictadura; la droga del tolueno para el hambre, los jóvenes cesantes, la barricada, el corazón molotov, hasta ahora que se vuelve a potenciar en la calle incendiada de la marcha estudiantil.
>
> (I have always used fire and neoprén, for all the symbolic charge that this flammable glue has had since the dictatorship; toluene as a drug against hunger, the unemployed youth, the barricade, the Molotov heart, and now it is being reignited once again in the burning streets of the student protests.) (Quoted in Contreras, p. 97)

The volatility of *neoprén*, literal and figurative, produces a poetic ignition that fleetingly illuminates its prior usages.

As Contreras argues, *neoprén* carries the double symbolic charge of 'lo marginal' ('marginality') and 'la potencia de la resistencia' ('the power of resistance') (p. 98). I wish to bring this symbolic charge into play with the *prosthetic* function of *neoprén*, in the ways described above by Lemebel. Notwithstanding the lethal damage it can cause to the central nervous system, the inhalation of this volatile solvent is a means of surviving hunger, cold, pain, joblessness and the violence to which bodies are left vulnerable by the abandonment of the neoliberal state. Its flammability, meanwhile, has lent it to political protest since the dictatorship. Lemebel thus enlists the metonymic potential of *neoprén* to make such connections legible politically, across a violently fractured social history.

In his performative grammar, *neoprén* and fire produce flashes of radical alliance, cut through with painful memory. Thus, at a book fair under democratic neoliberalism, the face of Carmen Quintana, severely scarred after being set on fire by the military during a protest in 1987, is a legible page that defies historical amnesia. From the vantage point of neoliberal Chile, like Walter Benjamin's revered angel of history, Lemebel evokes the burning bodies of Quintana and her murdered companion Rodrigo Rojas: 'iluminados como antorchas en el apagón de la noche protesta [...] Sus cuerpos al rojo vivo, metaforizados al límite como estrellas de una izquierda flagrante' ('lit up like torches in the blacked-out protest night [...] Their bodies red-hot embers, metaphorised to the limit like stars caught red-handed in the heat of the leftist night').²⁶ This is the 'metaphorising limit' at which Lemebel locates his work, between the ineffable materiality of bodies in pain, and the symbolic charge of their resistance.

In 1989, Lemebel staged a *performance* called *Hospital del Trabajador*, in the abandoned shell of what would have become the largest public hospital in South America under Allende, before construction was violently interrupted by the coup. In a *crónica* of the same name, Lemebel recounts how the building was repurposed for detentions and torture, and later became home to a host of social outcasts ('El Hospital del Trabajador', *Perlas*, pp. 275–279, pp. 276–277). For his intervention, he recycled materials found in the building to outline an uncanny stage on one of its abandoned floors: a ring of barbed wire, a cypher for AIDS throughout Las Yeguas's *performances*; and a circle of discarded shoes, evoking an absent audience of the *desaparecidos* and *neopreneros* haunting the building.²⁷ Video artist Gloria Camiruaga documented the strange event: Lemebel buries himself in bricks, covers them in *neoprén* and sets them on fire. A single brick, placed above his heart, is the last to remain burning in the darkness.²⁸

One might recall, condensed in this image, 'La esquina es mi corazón', which wove *neoprén* into the poetics and prosthetics ('marcapasos') of everyday life, or Lemebel's reference to 'el corazón molotov'. In another flash of political memory, recounted in the *crónica*, Lemebel recalls how a woman with Parkinson's disease once torched a fence, erected around the hospital by the military, in a militant demand for public healthcare, social visibility and an end to the dictatorship (*Perlas*, p. 277). By resituating the discarded materials of the hospital, and bringing them into contact with his *marica* body, Lemebel excavates the absent materiality of these other bodies, *neopreneros*, protestors and *desaparecidos*, in the neoliberal landscape.

Hospital del Trabajador was also a tribute to Sebastián Acevedo, the worker who, in 1983, set himself on fire on the steps of the Cathedral in Concepción, in protest at the detention of his children by the secret police. In 1991, Las Yeguas del Apocalipsis created a corporeal installation titled *Homenaje a Sebastián Acevedo* (Tribute to Sebastián Acevedo), to mark

---

[26] 'Carmen Gloria Quintana', *De perlas y cicatrices* (Santiago: Seix Barral, 2010), henceforth *Perlas*, pp. 111–113 (p. 112).

[27] Carolina Robino. 'Las últimas locas del fin del mundo', *Hoy*, no. 736, 26 August to 1 September 1991, 42–45, Archivo de Referencias Críticas, Biblioteca Nacional Digital de Chile, <http://www.bibliotecanacionaldigital.cl/bnd/628/w3-article-288064.html>, accessed 13 December 2018 (p. 44).

[28] Gloria Camiruaga, *Yeguas del Apocalipsis; Casa particular*, 1990, video, Heure Exquise, <http://www.exquise.org/video.php?id=651&l=uk>, accessed 14 December 2018.

the International Day of Action Against AIDS. Covered in lime, a natural resource mined in the area, and used to decay bodies thrown into mass graves during the dictatorship, Lemebel and Francisco Casas arranged their bodies in a vertical line to form the Chilean land mass, an 'N' and 'S' marking the poles. While five monitors played the video of Lemebel's earlier intervention in the hospital, an assistant drew a horizontal line of coal, dissecting this body-map North from South, and set it alight with the aid of *neoprén*.[29] Their *loca* bodies merge with Chile's geological matter, mapping out an arresting corporeal cartography of the 'loca geografía', in alliance with those other 'waste materials' of the proverbial 'social body'. This is the *geografía accidentada* I have theorised throughout this chapter, a landscape of 'contingent bodies' bound in a cultural–political constellation of local signs.

Conclusion: cuerpos contin(g)entes

Las Yeguas later projected a video of *Homenaje a Sebastián Acevedo* during a series of 'homoperformances' inaugurating a 1996 conference at the City University of New York (CUNY), 'Crossing National & Sexual Borders: Queer Sexualities in Latin/o America'.[30] My intention in this chapter has not been to abandon the word 'queer', but to think about its cultural contingency: which narratives, which bodies, are occluded by a wholesale globalisation of the term? To this end, we might ask what travelled in that 'border crossing' at the City University of New York, and what did not. Applied to Lemebel's work, 'queerness' comes up against particular interfaces between minority sexualities, marginalisation and embodiment in locations under specific cultural, political and material conditions. This is not just a problem of translation; it is a question of how certain ideas travel, and others do not, in the asymmetrical traffic of neoliberal globalisation.

Lemebel felt these inequalities on his pulse, radically engaging the discursive and material implications of embodiment in 'peripheries' that were the stage for neoliberalism's violent consolidation, and the sites of abandonment by the neoliberal state. His irreverent naturalisation of difference into a unique geology of marginalisation and non-conformity underscored the unequal interplay between 'Northern' models, like 'queer', and 'Southern' experiences. Against the unencumbered flow of capital, naturalised into a national narrative of 'transition' and a global narrative of neoliberal

---

[29] Yeguas, <http://www.yeguasdelapocalipsis.cl/1991-homenaje-a-sebastian-acevedo/>, accessed 14 December 2018.

[30] The intervention, *Cadáveres*, was dedicated to Néstor Perlongher. See Yeguas. <http://www.yeguasdelapocalipsis.cl/1996-cadaveres/>, accessed 14 December 2018.

'development', Lemebel brings living and dead bodies into discourse. These are the HIV-positive *locas*, the *neoprenero* kids from the *pobla*, the protestor with Parkinson's disease, the scarred face of Carmen Quintana, the body of Sebastián Acevedo.

In 2011 Lemebel was diagnosed with throat cancer. In 2013 he underwent a total laryngectomy and was fitted with a voice prosthesis. Although he described the difficulty of finding his new voice, he spoke of it with unrelenting humour: 'La voz es importante para los homosexuales, porque siempre se reconocen por la voz [...] Y aunque tengo voz de muerta, estoy enferma de vida' ('The voice is important for homosexuals, because they are always recognised by their voice [...] And while I may have the voice of a dead old woman, I'm infected with life').[31] His irreverent idiom attests to the fact that signs of disability were always inseparable from his poetics of *loca* embodiment. As he underwent treatment, Lemebel was uncertain whether he would write about his cancer.[32] It should not surprise the reader, however, that he had already written about the metaphorical and material assault of cancer on women's bodies,[33] just as he wrote about AIDS, or the different mode of communication of a child with Down's syndrome ('la minoría entre todos mis lectores homosexuales, mujeres, proletarios con rasgos indígenas y militantes de izquierda' ['the minority among all my readers– homosexuals, women, proletarian readers with indigenous features, and leftist militants']) who, incidentally, listens religiously to his voice on the radio.[34] Lemebel's was always a prosthetic voice, which made visible an embodied socio-political geography of 'shared signs and scars'.

A 'disability reading' helped to foreground Lemebel's mapping of bodies in relation to material and political geographies, but his work equally helps to displace terms like 'disability' and 'crip', for a more variegated, less prescriptive politics, one that involves 'more people than can be identified' (*Crip Times*, p. 93), and that 'offer[s] up disability loosened from a certain kind of identity politics more legible [...] in places like the United States' (p. 110). Lemebel's poetics expands, trans-historically, on what disability can mean. His sensibilities attuned to the locality of Chile's peripheries, he pre-empted

[31] Carolina Rojas, 'Pedro Lemebel: "Esta lengua tiene sus costos"', *Clarín*, 17 December 2012, section Ñ, <https://www.clarin.com/literatura/entrevista-pedro-lemebel-hablame-de-amores_0_B1f4Rinjvmg.html>, accessed 2 February 2019.

[32] Pedro Bahamondes, 'Lemebel y la vida después del cáncer', *La Tercera*, 30 June 2013, section El Semanal, pp. 10–12 (p. 12), <https://cronicasperiodisticas.wordpress.com/2014/05/02/lemebel-y-la-vida-despues-del-cancer/>, accessed 2 February 2019.

[33] See 'Pabellón de la oncología femenina', in *Zanjón de la Aguada* (Santiago: Seix Barral, 2008), pp. 104–107.

[34] 'Los ojos achinados de la ternura mongólica', *Zanjón*, pp. 40–43 (p. 42).

more globalising debates on embodiment with irreverence, theoretical clarity and searing poetic beauty.

Reading Lemebel's multimedia, multi-sited 'corpus' in its dense intertextuality, I have traced the ways in which his work testifies to multiple and intersecting forms of violence that converge on different bodies, and generate very different forms of resistance. By holding up the tenets of McRuer's 'crip' sensibility to the particularities of more 'peripheral' embodiments marshalled by Lemebel's work, I took Lemebel's *crónicas*, and the entirety of his work, as a critically 'chronic' mode of expression, attentive to the common assaults against victims of state persecution as well as sexual pathologisation, and those literally disabled or disposable under neoliberal capitalism. By drawing these living, dead and disappeared bodies into radical political alliance, Lemebel found ways of keeping alive a desire for emancipation and the emancipation of desires.

Postscript

On 29 June 2014, Lemebel carried out his last recorded intervention, *Abecedario*, on the Pasarela Italia, a footbridge located opposite the Cementerio Metropolitano, where he would be buried just seven months later beside his mother. Visibly frail from cancer treatment, he walked down the *pasarela* in black heels, writing the alphabet in *neoprén* and setting it, letter by letter, on fire. By igniting the alphabet, leaving behind a burnt-out trace on the concrete, Lemebel momentarily relinquished the word, giving way to all those prior flashes of *neoprén* and fire, a final act of language destruction, and corporeal connection, towards a liberatory, transcendent poetics and politics of embodiment.

Index

1492 11, 15, 45, 55, 156, 157, 161–162, 171
1898 23, 108, 148, 151, 168–169

ACIN (Asociación de Cabildos Indígenas del Norte del Cauca) 204–205
Africa 10–11, 18, 19, 34, 51, 59–60, 67, 148, 149, 161–162, 169, 171, 191, 255
Afro-descent subjects
    in Latin America 20, 33–34, 51, 95, 247–248, 259n26, 262, 283–304
    in Spain 122, 125, 148–149, 161–163, 169–171
    see also Al-Andalus
Al-Andalus 10–14, 40, 43, 59–72, 73–88, 161–164, 169, 171
Alfonso X *El sabio* 14, 45, 48, 110
aljamiado texts 12, 40, 71–72
Allende, Isabel 191–193
Allende, Salvador 325, 334
Alvarus of Cordoba 60–63
Amazonia 112, 191
    see also Andean-Amazonian languages
Andalusia 9–14, 19, 24, 40, 161–162, 167–174, 269–270
    see also Al-Andalus
Andean-Amazonian languages 94–101
Anderson, Benedict 25–29, 142, 214–215, 273
Andes 112, 149
Angola 289, 291n28
Angrand, Léonce 262, 286–288, 291–294
Anzaldúa, Gloria 7, 35
Appadurai, Arjun 28, 37, 200, 216
Arabia 10, 14, 59, 161
Arabic
    and Andalusi music 161–163, 169–173
    and Hispanophone literature 22–23, 19n46, 41, 59–72, 73–88
    and the Spanish language 10–16, 49, 59–72, 73–88
Arendt, Hannah 228, 237
Argentina 17, 18, 20, 23, 56, 148, 208–209, 216, 221–222
Artivism 195, 200–203, 210

Index

Atlantic history 18–19, 29–30, 32–35, 111, 119, 150, 152, 155, 217, 243–244, 255, 262, 267, 279–280, 284–285
  see also 'Black Atlantic'; 'conquest'; modernism; Portugese-speaking world; slavery
Averroes 14, 83
Aymara 2, 16–17, 21, 94, 95, 112
Aztecs 16–17
  and Aztec calendar 137–141

Bacardi 183–184
Báez, Frank 305–317
Barcelona 15n37, 111, 192, 312
Basque/basques 9–10, 14, 17, 19, 23–24, 52, 95, 111, 121, 168, 208, 268
Bello, Andrés 46
Benítez Rojo, Antonio 35, 245, 259
Benjamin, Walter 27, 154, 232, 241, 333
Berbers 10–11, 60, 65, 67, 84, 161
Berlin Wall 233–234
Bestsellers 220
bilingualism 7, 12, 16n39, 22, 40–41, 52–56, 92, 99, 268
'Black Atlantic' 33–34, 286n9
Bolaño, Roberto 35, 214n14, 222
Bolivia 2, 17, 23, 31, 33, 89–101
Boom in Latin American literature 31, 36–37, 189–190, 213, 219
borders 5–6, 8, 23–24, 28–30, 34–35, 84n35, 147, 150, 154–155, 157–159, 177–179, 181, 187, 189, 192, 195–196, 198, 200–203, 215, 222, 246, 254–256, 266–267, 273–274, 277, 280, 307–317, 335
  and/as metaphorical border crossings 30–35, 119, 198–203, 306–317, 335
Borges, Jorge Luis 29, 147, 153, 221–222, 262

Bourbon dynasty 16, 20–22, 107, 111–112
branding 29, 109, 177–178, 182–184, 171, 314n23
Braudel, Fernand 144
Brazil 2, 16, 18, 19, 20, 119, 177, 182, 184, 186, 187, 216, 240, 278, 285, 289, 321
Buenos Aires 17, 56–57, 149, 208–209, 216n8, 222, 224–225, 279
bullshit 189
Buñuel, Luis 150
Butler, Judith 320–321, 324, 329

Caballero, Fernán 262, 267–282
Cabeza de Vaca, Alvar Núñez 19, 30, 33–35
Cádiz 110, 111, 270
  see also Constitution of Cádiz 1812
Caliphate of Cordoba 10–11, 61–72, 73–88
Caribbean
  identity 35, 186, 245–246, 262–263
  geographical region 2, 16, 19, 24, 243–246, 252–260, 262–263
  lexical contributions to Spanish 17
  literature 31–32, 35, 105, 148–149, 153, 190, 306–317
  tourism 181
Carpentier, Alejo 190
castas 20, 104, 111–112, 125
castellano 4, 13, 14–17, 19, 20, 21, 27, 45, 97, 112
Castells, Manuel 28n66, 205
Castile 11, 14–16, 18, 19, 23, 39, 43, 47–48, 57, 71, 109–111, 119, 125, 167–168
Castro, Fidel 184, 189, 207, 233, 235
Catalan/Catalans 10, 14, 16, 18, 19, 60, 149–150, 168, 184
Catalonia 23–24, 52, 60, 111
  see also bilingualism

Catholic monarchs
Catholicism 4, 12, 15, 18–19, 41,
    50, 107, 110–111, 113, 116, 125,
    156–157, 163–164, 169, 272–272,
    275, 283–304
  and colonial power 12, 14, 18, 41,
    107–108, 110, 111, 285
  and modernism 156–157
  and race 262, 283–304
  and readings of Spanish history
    163–164, 167–172
  and syncretism 50, 283–304
  and women 271–272, 276
Central America 2, 7, 17, 24, 32, 52,
    112, 256
  see also Mesoamerica
Cervantes Institute 109, 112
Cervantes, Miguel de 18, 112, 119, 154
  see also Don Quijote
chabacano 51
Charles I 17, 110
Charles III 21, 171
Charles V, Emperor 17–18, 107, 109n2,
    110, 115, 120, 130
Chateaubriand, René de 26, 171, 275
Chicanos 7, 28, 31, 35, 53, 186
Chile 263, 319–337
chronicles 91, 113–125, 319–327
cinema
  as transnational medium 30, 35,
    181, 189–192, 216, 243–260
  see also Hollywood
  Latin American cinema 181, 186,
    243–260
  national readings of 37, 93, 178,
    186, 252, 255, 258, 259, 310
class 12, 31, 33, 35, 63, 92, 215,
    261
  and bilingualism in the Andes
    92
  and booze 29
  and borders 35
  and food 182

  as intersectional category 185, 215,
    308, 311, 313n19, 317, 319–337
cocoliche 56–57
code-switching 7, 52–57, 112
Cold War 29, 178, 184, 227
  see also post-Cold War
Colombia 17, 23, 24, 34, 51, 95, 98,
    149, 155, 179, 204, 223, 246–249,
    256–259
colonialism/coloniality 31–37, 45,
    90–95, 101, 103–105, 107–125,
    136–143, 149–159, 162–172,
    169, 181–193, 196, 244, 254, 277,
    283–303, 306, 320
Columbus, Christopher 15, 16, 19, 33,
    120, 128
commerce 19, 116, 156, 162, 178, 229,
    241, 262, 267–268, 272, 276–279,
    288, 310
'conquest' and colonisation of the
    Americas 26, 33, 91, 110, 112–125,
    137–138, 152, 156, 220, 246n10,
    283, 285, 329
Constitution of Cádiz 1812 108–111,
    124–125, 148
Copernicus 127, 132
Cortés, Hernán 16, 139, 155, 182, 220
cosmopolitanism 29, 153, 226, 262,
    268, 270
  and capitalism 26, 190, 254,
    283–286, 306
costumbrismo 262, 286–304
Crack generation 29, 178, 191,
    220–222, 223–226
creoles (linguistic) 41, 51, 57, 259n26
  see also criollos
'Crip theory' 320, 329–331, 336–337
Cuba 7, 19, 23, 30–31, 34, 35, 37, 108,
    149, 151, 178, 245, 271, 275, 277,
    285, 289, 307, 308, 310
  and exceptionalism 232n13, 234,
    239
  and the blogosphere 206–208

and the Cuban Revolution 30–31, 188–189, 206, 227–241, 263
and the 'Latin' imaginary 182–184, 188–189
and the 'Special Period' 227–241
as DIY society 230, 234
'cultural insiderism' 34
cyber-culture 199–211

dance 83, 90, 105, 162, 168, 185, 258, 288, 291, 294, 296–297, 324
Darío, Rubén 151, 157
decoloniality 3n1, 4, 31–32, 321
dialects 7, 9, 12, 14, 23, 40, 47–48, 60, 68, 77, 84n33, 214, 259n26
diaspora
    and Latinos in the USA 7, 253, 317
    and slavery 34–35, 289–304
    and the Cuban Revolution 206–208, 237
    and trans-imperial history 24, 36, 108, 161, 177–178, 205–206
digital culture 27, 28, 103, 178, 195–211
    and activism 200–210
    and Hispanism 195, 211–212
    and the nation-state 197–200
'discoveries' 16–17, 21, 45, 104, 117–121, 128, 257, 311
dislocation 34, 138, 245
Dominican Republic 7, 15, 179, 252–256
    and Dominican literature 305–317
Don Quijote 18, 54, 113, 119, 156, 181
    see also Cervantes, Miguel de
drug use 186, 328, 331–333

Eastern Europe 18n43, 109, 227–236
Ecuador 17, 23, 55, 89, 93–95, 117, 183, 292
Eichman, Adolf (in Buenos Aires) 222, 225

Empire 1–2, 4, 8n18, 18, 23, 30, 37, 40, 45, 57, 96, 107, 244
    British Empire 37, 149, 169, 270
    Byzantine Empire 15
    First French Empire 20, 22
        see also Napoleon Bonaparte
    Hapsburg Empire 16, 18–20, 122
    Holy Roman Empire 22, 110
    Inca Empire 104, 114–117, 122
    Ottoman Empire 15, 18n43
    Portuguese Empire 2, 16, 18–19, 34, 187
    Roman Empire 9–10, 87, 207, 110
    Spanish Empire 23, 30, 34, 107–112, 120, 123, 127–143, 168
    Umayyad Caliphate 10–11, 59
Epps, Brad 25n55, 34, 150, 263n2, 320–321
Equatorial Guinea 19, 23, 34, 148, 289
estalgia 178, 228–229
    see also ostalgia
exclusion 29, 35–36, 98, 127, 164–166, 174–175, 196, 215, 224, 261, 263, 279, 319–320
exile 11, 34, 55, 71–72, 113, 116–118, 150, 222, 307–309, 315
exploration/explorers 17n40, 30, 95, 183, 191, 244, 246

Facebook *see* social media
fashion 183–186, 273–277, 294n33
festivities 138–139, 200–201, 286n9, 294–302
Fierro, Francisco 262, 286–288, 293–304
flamenco 105, 161–175
flows 28–29, 31, 39, 104, 179, 198, 216, 226, 327–337
    see also globalisation
Foucault, Michel 26, 136

France
  French culture 87, 154, 171–172, 190, 193, 215, 262, 267–268, 274–276
  French imperialism 122–123, 167
  French language 20–23
  French Revolution 45, 145–146
Franco, Francisco/Franquismo 11n26, 105, 163, 168–169, 171–174
Franco, Jean 25n55, 187–188
Fronteiriço 56
Fuentes, Carlos 219

Galicia 11, 14, 50, 60, 87, 111
Galician 10, 15n36, 16, 19, 23, 24, 44, 52
García Canclini, Néstor 29n71, 128n6, 150, 165
García Lorca, Federico 73n1, 166–167, 170, 172
García Márquez, Gabriel 190–191, 220
Garcilaso de la Vega, 'El Inca' 112–124
  see also Incas
gender 35, 53, 154, 199, 232, 247, 265–266, 302, 306, 307, 308, 311, 315, 319–320, 322, 329
Generación de 1898 167–168
genre 63–68, 73–88, 165, 172, 195, 255, 262, 277–278, 286, 302n45, 303
Gibraltar 270
Gipsy Kings 193
globalisation 214, 216, 226, 241, 254–255, 270, 312
  and capitalism 26, 32, 199, 221, 228, 321
  and identity models 322, 334–337
  and Latin Americanism 183–184, 197, 199, 214–217
  and modernity 24, 103
  and social networks 181–182, 195
  and standardisation 103, 177–178

and the Spanish language 24, 28, 32, 40, 42, 103, 178
  as 'imagined' 29–30
Granada 11, 14, 15, 60, 72, 162, 166, 174
Greenwich Time 133
Guaman Poma de Ayala, Felipe 41, 91
Guaraní 2
Guevara, Ernesto 'Che'/Guevarismo 31, 237
gypsies 161–172

Haiti 2, 15n38, 21n49, 206, 244, 259, 307
  Haitian Revolution 244
Hapsburg Empire see Hapsburgs, Empire
Havana 181, 188–189, 234, 235–236, 238
Hebrew 13, 14, 15, 16, 40, 68–69, 70, 77, 83, 141
hegemony 15, 32, 48, 96, 98, 163, 195, 205, 234n18, 276, 279, 304
heresy 111, 141, 157
Hispania 1, 9–11, 15–16, 22, 23, 59, 110, 114
  see also Iberian Peninsula
'Hispanic Studies' 1–2, 3, 24–25, 26
HIV/AIDS 319–326
Hollywood 29, 181, 182, 185, 188–189
homophobia 315, 319, 322–335
homosexuality 35, 66, 263, 319–337
hybridity 4, 7, 12, 22, 32–33, 41, 55–57, 59–60, 71, 112, 121, 123, 150, 161–175, 195–211, 234, 239, 319

Iberian Peninsula 9–16, 22, 40, 43–49, 59–72, 73–88, 107–112, 161–162, 164, 284
Ibn Hazm 40, 64–66, 67, 75–76
Ibn Quzman 40, 67–69, 73n1, 77–81, 85, 87

Ibn Tufail 69–70
imperialism 36, 39, 46, 145, 233
    see also Empire
Incas 16–17, 21, 32, 92, 104
    see also Garcilaso de la Vega, 'El Inca'
'Indies' (las Indias) 17, 18, 20, 21, 22, 23, 107–109, 110–112, 123, 125
indigenous
    conceptions of time 137–142, 149–150
    conversion 41, 45
    histories 32, 113–122
        see also Garcilaso de la Vega, 'El Inca'
    languages and literacies 2, 16–17, 19–20, 23, 32, 40–41, 52, 89–101, 125
        see also bilingualism
    peoples 2, 15, 16–17, 19–20, 30, 125, 150, 155, 187–188, 220, 294
    resistance to power 16, 21, 30, 203–206
interculturality 32, 141
    see also hybridity
interdisciplinarity 27, 243–244
internationalism 5–6, 8n18, 18, 33, 49–50, 98, 133, 135–136, 190, 197, 261–262, 267–273, 317, 327, 334–335
    cyber-internationalism 199n8, 203–208
Internet 6, 11n6, 195–211, 233
Iran 59, 71
Iraq 163
Isabel I 15, 45, 110
Islam 4, 10–15, 18, 22, 24, 40, 59–71, 73–88, 105, 110, 149, 163–164, 169–171

Jamaica 259
Jara, Víctor 326

Jeffry (film) 252–256, 260
Jesuits 19, 20, 117, 118, 141, 187–188, 275
Jews 11, 12, 13, 14, 40, 55, 64, 69, 73n1, 161–162, 223
journalism 93, 207, 209, 235
Judaism 12, 18

Keyla (film) 256–259
kharjas 68–69, 73–88

Las Casas, Bartolomé de 19
Las Iguanas 181–183, 193
Latin (language) 1, 9–10, 13, 14, 20, 43, 49, 50, 59–61, 73–74, 84n33, 87, 121
Latin American Subaltern Studies Group 30–31, 33
Latinity 29, 108, 148, 177–178, 181–193
Lemebel, Pedro 319–337
Lopez, Jennifer 178, 182, 186–187

magical realism 29, 178, 189–190, 220
Maimonides 15, 68, 83, 90, 135–136, 273
Manco Capac 123–124
Manifiesto Crack 29, 178, 191, 220
Martí, José 31–32, 105, 148, 153, 158–159
Marx, Karl 26–27, 90, 135–136, 273
Mayans 14, 16–17
media lengua 55–56
Menéndez Pidal, Ramón 3, 46–48
Mesoamerica 137–142
Mestizos and *mestizaje* 20, 21, 23, 26, 32–33, 37, 40–41, 92, 108, 112–117, 122–123, 125, 149–150, 152, 192
Mexico 7, 16–17, 23, 31, 33, 41, 91, 98, 108, 110, 112, 119, 137–141,

147, 149, 150, 178, 179, 191, 195, 200–203, 218–225, 250–252, 285n5
Mignolo, Walter 31–32, 37, 156, 196–197
migrants/migration 5–9, 13, 16, 19–20, 23, 28, 35, 57, 93, 111, 140, 149–150, 185, 201–203, 216, 223, 240, 253, 254, 255, 263, 284, 305–317
mobility 33–36, 98, 177–179, 256, 285, 320–321
    and disability 263, 320, 324, 327–336
        see also border-crossings
    and public mobilisations 209–210
    and social mobility 98, 254–256
Moctezuma II 139
modernism 151–152, 155–157
modernity 145–159
    and coloniality 34, 36–37, 103–105, 107–126, 127–143
    and narrative of Spain's 'exclusion' from modernity 36, 127, 152, 153–154, 247
    as transnational process 142–159
    singular or plural? 154–155, 156–159
Morocco 11, 23, 148, 171
multiculturalism 18, 23, 40, 98–99, 163–164, 188, 199, 267–273
    see also cosmopolitanism; hybridity
multilingualism 7, 18, 23, 28, 37, 41, 95, 98, 149
Muslims/*Moriscos* 10–14, 30, 40, 59–71, 73–88, 164, 169, 171
    expulsion from Spain 13, 60, 71
    see also Islam
muwashshahs 40, 68–69

Nahuatl 17, 19
Nancy, Jean-Luc 215–216, 223, 225
Napoleon Bonaparte 20, 22

narco-trafficking 30, 181, 257, 258, 260
Narcos (TV show) 181
nationalism 22–23, 25–26, 28–29, 37, 46
    cultural nationalism 216, 222
    literary nationalism 25–26, 271–273
        see also post-nationalism; transnationalism
nation-state 1–9, 16, 22–24, 28–29, 31–33, 39, 41, 90, 98, 146–150, 178, 195–211, 215–216, 224
Nazis/Nazism 29, 178, 191, 218, 221–226
Nebrija, Antonio de 15, 45, 96
neoliberalism 31, 32, 33, 199, 202–204, 234n18, 252, 256, 321–337
neoprén 328, 332–335, 327
Netflix 29
New Spain 17, 19, 136
New York 178, 185, 191, 253, 307–317
Nicaragua 31, 151, 157, 256
#*NiUnaMenos* 208–209

Olsen, Björnar 228, 230, 237, 241
Oroza, Ernesto 229, 239–240
Ortega, Julio 32–33
Ortiz, Fernando 30, 289n21
ostalgie 228–229, 236n23
    see also estalgia

Padilla, Ignacio 29, 178, 191, 220–226
Palenquero 51
Palma, Ricardo 301n42, 304
Paz, Octavio 218
Peralta Barnuevo, Pedro 104, 120–123
Período Especial / Special Period (Cuba) 227–241
Peru 17, 21, 32, 41, 89–101, 107–125, 262, 283–304
Philip II, 'Sun King' 17, 45, 107, 111
Philip IV 18, 107, 111

Philippines 17, 46, 148, 149, 151, 267, 277
  see also chabacano
picaresque genre 33, 136
Pizarro, Francisco 113, 115, 118, 123
Portuguese language 2, 9, 10, 14–15, 16, 49, 51, 56, 87, 267
  Lusophone world 1–2, 16, 18–19, 33–34, 187, 213, 286n9
Post Tenebras Lux (film) 250–252, 260
postnational/postnationalism 28–29, 216, 225
precarity 236–241, 248, 252–253, 255, 259–260, 315, 319–337
printing 25, 126, 128, 215, 267, 267–280, 286
Providencia (island) 256–259

Quechua 2, 16–17, 21, 23, 41, 55–56, 91–100, 104, 112, 117–118, 125, 149
queerness 263, 319–337
  see also homosexuality
Quijano, Aníbal 31, 94

racism 20, 33–34, 35, 97–98, 149, 152, 158–159, 165–172, 174–175, 215, 244, 262–263, 284n2, 307–317
railways 133–134, 142
Raizals 259n26
Rama, Ángel 153, 216
Reconquista 11, 14, 110
recycling 229–230, 334
Rodríguez, Reina María 231–232
romance (ballad) 22, 271
Romance (language) 9–14, 39–40, 43–44, 47–50, 57, 59–60, 63, 68–69, 73–88
Romanticism 22–23, 26–27, 31–32, 262, 286
Rugendas, Johann Moritz 286

Sáez de Melgar, Faustina 278–280
Santana, Mario 36–37
Sarlo, Beatriz 153–154
Sarmiento, Faustino Domingo 148, 150
scarcity 228–241
  and creativity 229–230, 237
  and depersonalisation 231–234, 237, 238–240
    see also Cuba and the 'Special Period'
Shakespeare, William 22, 112, 143, 174, 221
slavery 18–19, 30, 33–35, 36–37, 51, 149, 187, 239, 244, 259, 262, 275, 283–295
  runaway slaves/marronage 51, 239, 259
social media 6, 181–182, 204–205, 208
Socialism 32, 156, 227–241
  see also Eastern-European socialism 227–230, 232–234
son de los diablos 288–304
Soviet Union 29, 228–241
Spain 1–2, 9–16, 19–20, 33, 34, 36–37, 44–45, 48, 57, 92, 104–105, 107–126, 127, 129–132, 139, 142, 149, 151, 152, 154, 161–175, 181–182, 206, 215, 261–262, 265–281
  Spanish nation-state 4, 9–10, 22, 23–24, 142
    see also Empire; Hispania; Iberian Peninsula
Spanglish/espanglish 7, 40, 52–54
Spanish Civil War 171, 172, 175
Spanish Netherlands 17, 104, 127
Spivak, Gayatri Chakravorty 90, 94
standardisation (language) 21, 23, 39, 43–46, 48, 49, 52, 55

subalternity 28, 30, 90, 191, 195, 294
  and Latin American Subaltern Studies Group 31–33
  of things 230, 241
sugar 19, 49, 60, 181–182, 230, 233, 245
Surwillo, Lisa 37

Tawantinsuyu 104, 118–119, 121
television 27, 192, 216
Tenochtitlán 16, 139
The Mission (film) 187–189
Tijuana 201
time
  and labour 133–134, 135–136
  and sacred calendars 132–133, 134, 136–143
  and space 128–129, 135
  and standardisation 103, 133
  and the obstacles to standardisation under Empire 133, 135–143
Tordesillas, Treaty of 16, 134
tourism 168, 172, 174, 181, 189, 201, 238, 247, 253, 255n22, 257, 259n26, 260, 262, 311, 235
Traffic (film) 30
trans-Atlantic capitalism 18–19, 30, 33–36, 262–263, 267–280, 284

transculturation 4, 7, 20, 24, 30, 33, 35, 36n90, 136, 153, 164–175, 210, 283, 289n21
transgendered identities 311, 315–317, 322–327
transnationalism 5, 8, 103, 177, 214, 306, 307, 308, 309, 312, 317

Uruguay 17, 56, 153

Vasconcelos, José 33, 152
  see also *mestizos* and *mestizaje*
Venezuela 17, 23
vernaculars 9, 14–15, 25, 39–40, 43–44, 50, 51, 60, 68–71, 90, 110, 112, 322, 329
Vespucci, Amerigo 128
video games 191, 202
Volpi, Jorge 29, 178, 191, 213–214, 216–218, 220–226
Vuelco del cangrejo (film) 246–249

Wiracochas 112
'world literature' 26, 152, 262, 270–273

Yeguas del Apocalipsis 319, 331–332, 334, 335

Zajal/zejel 67–68, 78–88
Zapatismo 178, 185, 195, 203, 204, 207
Zorro (film) 178, 192–193